MICROCOMPUTER KEYBOARDING

AND DOCUMENT PROCESSING

Authors

Jack E. Johnson, Ph.D.
Director of Business Education
West Georgia College
Carrollton, Georgia

Carole G. Stanley
Keyboarding and Computer Literacy Teacher
Rains Junior High School
Emory, Texas

Reviewers

Susan George
Johnson City High School
Johnson City, New York

Dolores Joyce
Boyd H. Anderson High School
Lauderdale Lakes, Florida

Donna Murray
Business and Management Center
Dallas, Texas

Phyllis Skidmore
Rio Americano High School
Sacramento, California

Kathy White
J. Everett Light Career Center
Indianapolis, Indiana

GLENCOE

McGraw-Hill

New York, New York   Columbus, Ohio   Woodland Hills, California   Peoria, Illinois

Photography Credits

Cover: ©Aaron Haupt. Level One: ©Mark Fronk 1989, ©Chris Rogers, General Motors.
Level Two: ©Stevie Grand/Science Photo Library, ©Mehau Kulyk/Science Photo Library.
Level Three: ©Red Huber/Orlando Sentinel, NASA. Level Four: ©David O. Stillings,
©Lawrence Migdale. Level Five: ©Ocean Images/Al Giddings
Bahamas 1990, ©Ocean Images, Chuck Niklin 1990, ©Ocean Images, Al Giddings
1990. Level Six: Maria Paraskevas Photography, ©Photo Dassault-Breguet/Science
Photo Library, ©Check O'Rear "High Tech".

Microcomputer Keyboarding and Document Processing

Imprint 1997

Copyright © 1996 by The McGraw-Hill Companies, Inc. All rights reserved. Originally
copyrighted in 1993 as Gregg Microcomputer Keyboarding and Document Processing and
in 1987, 1982, 1977, 1973, 1972, 1967, 1962 by McGraw-Hill, Inc. as Gregg Typing. Except
as permitted under the United States Copyright Act, no part of this publication may be
reproduced or distributed in any form or by any means, or stored in a database or retrieval
system, without the prior written permission of the publisher.

Send all inquiries to:
Glencoe/McGraw-Hill
936 Eastwind Drive
Westerville, OH 43081

ISBN 0-02-814096-6 (Student's Edition)

5 6 7 8 9 10 027 04 03 02 01 00 99 98

Preface

Microcomputer Keyboarding and Document Processing, formerly *Gregg Typing,* has been designed specifically for use with the microcomputer. The information presented in this program can also be applied if typewriters are used, but the microcomputer shortcuts cannot be used.

Information processing skills are developed through a carefully planned, step-by-step process that progresses from simple to complex. It starts with learning to operate the computer itself, especially the keyboard, and then continues until the computer can be used as a tool in creating a variety of documents for personal and business use.

COMPONENTS OF THE PROGRAM

The Student Text. The one-year text offers 150 lessons. The first 75 lessons (one semester) concentrate on learning the keyboard and preparing documents for personal use. The next 75 lessons focus on preparing business documents and learning advanced word processing concepts. The text also contains a comprehensive Reference Section and Glossary.

Advanced Word Processing: How-To's and Applications. This supplementary project is designed to be completed in three weeks. Activities in the project progress from simple to complex and exceed the complexity of the activities in the textbook. Specific formatting directions are included for *WordPerfect, Microsoft Works,* and *AppleWorks.*

Desktop Publishing: How-To's and Applications. This supplementary project is designed to be completed in three weeks. Activities in the project progress from simple to complex. Specific formatting directions are included for *Pagemaker, Ventura Publishing,* and *PFS First Publisher.*

Software Instruction Guides. Screen prints of all special instructions not found in the textbook (software commands and special formatting instructions) appear in these Guides. Guides are available for WordPerfect 6.0 and WordPerfect 5.1 (DOS) and for the internal word processor (DOS and Macintosh).

The Teacher's Annotated Edition. The Teacher's Annotated Edition includes all the pages in the student text plus annotations intended only for the teacher. The teacher's edition also includes a separate section of teaching methodology, and lesson-by-lesson teaching notes for all the lessons in the text.

The Teacher's Classroom Resource. Included in the Resource are the following:

Lesson Plans. Full-size formal lesson plans for each lesson in the textbook.

Testing and Evaluation. This segment of the Resource contains masters for the timings as well as the objective, production, and LAB (Language Arts for Business) tests that should be assigned at the end of every 25 lessons. Also included are solutions to the tests and suggestions for grading and evaluation.

Solutions. Complete solutions to all the textbook production activities.

Keyboard Charts. Six large, full-color keyboard charts illustrate the most commonly-used keyboards today.

Transparency Masters. These masters cover every major new learning activity.

Cross-Curricular Applications. A variety of timings, letters, memos, reports, and tables that cover such topics as geography, history, foreign language, health, home economics, accounting, driver education, ethics, and economics.

Tech Prep. Strategies for implementing Tech Prep in Keyboarding.

Multicultural Timings. The long timings pertain to people, language, and attitudes of different ethnic groups.

Extending the Text. Included are additional production exercises, LAB worksheets, and learning guides. The LAB worksheets and learning guides can be used in the classroom or assigned for homework. Solutions to the production exercises and the LAB worksheets are also included.

Computer Courseware. Every activity in the text is guided by the software. All timings are scored for speed and accuracy. Most documents are also scored. For preparing documents, teachers can select the use of the internal word processor or WordPerfect 5.1 or WordPerfect 6.0 for DOS.

Reports are maintained for all scored activities. Entire lessons, individual activities, and/or the reports can be printed.

FEATURES OF THE PROGRAM

Microcomputer Keyboarding and Document Processing incorporates many time-tested features from past editions of *Gregg Typing.* It also introduces some new features, for example:

Diagnostic Exercises. Many timings utilize the Pretest/Practice/Posttest routine, which allows each student to diagnose areas in which skill development is needed.

Short Skillbuilding Routines. A variety of other skillbuilding routines are provided in the program to help maintain student interest while developing basic keyboarding skill.

Language Arts for Business (LABs). Concise, easy-to-understand LABs help students to review the basic uses of punctuation, capitalization, and number usage. Students reinforce and apply the LAB rules as they key sentences and production assignments.

Cyclical Approach. In *Microcomputer Keyboarding,* concepts are taught once and recycled several times, with each cycle building on the previous one and becoming progressively more complex. Each cycle is a "level" that lasts five weeks.

Five-Week Tests. At the conclusion of each level of work, a test provides both the student and the teacher with an opportunity to check the student's level of performance.

Information Processing. Word processing and data processing terminology and applications are integrated into the text. Software notes throughout the text point out features of software programs that facilitate formatting. Also included is a glossary of information processing terms that are referenced to the text page on which they are introduced.

Various Input Modes. Students will format documents from various input modes—for example, unarranged copy, handwritten copy, rough drafts, and incomplete information.

The *Microcomputer Keyboarding* program greatly reflects input from teachers across the country. We sincerely appreciate their contributions.

The Authors

Contents

INTRODUCTION The Textbook x; The Microcomputer, Hardware xi; Parts of the Computer xii; Software xiii; Getting Ready to Keyboard xv

Goal: 35/3'/5e   Level 3

UNIT 9 Tables

UNIT 10 Correspondence

UNIT 11 Reports

Goal: 37/5'/5e   Level 4

UNIT 12 Correspondence

UNIT 13 Business Reports

UNIT 14 Tables

Index

Introduction

The Textbook

Microcomputer Keyboarding and Document Processing has been specially designed to help you develop your keyboarding skills through a carefully planned, step-by-step process. To be sure that you understand the terms, the procedures, and the directions used throughout this book, as well as the operation of the equipment you are using, be sure to read this introduction and refer to it whenever you have any question or problem.

SKILLBUILDING ROUTINES

Keyboarding is a skill, and a skill is best developed through directed practice. *Microcomputer Keyboarding* provides a variety of effective skillbuilding routines to improve the speed and the accuracy of your keyboarding, including the following:

A variety of **Pretest/Practice/Posttest** routines is offered—all designed to improve either speed or accuracy through proven, step-by-step procedures. First, the **Pretest** (a 1-, 2-, 3-, or 5-minute timing) helps you identify your speed or accuracy needs. Having identified your needs, you then do the **Practice** exercises, a variety of intensive improvement drills. After you have completed the Practice exercises, you take a **Posttest**. Because the Posttest is identical to the Pretest, the Posttest measures your improvement.

12-Second timings are routines in which you take a series of short timings to boost speed.

30-Second timings are slightly longer routines in which you take a series of short timings to boost speed. You try to maintain your 12-second speed.

"OK" Timings are 30-second timings that help you build accuracy on alphabetic copy (that is, copy that includes all 26 letters of the alphabet). You take a series of 30-second timings to see how many error-free copies you can key.

SCALES AND INDEXES

Microcomputer Keyboarding uses a variety of scales and indexes designed to help you (1) measure quickly—with little counting—how many words you have keyed, (2) analyze whether you should practice speed drills or accuracy drills, and (3) identify the relative difficulty of the copy you are keying.

Word Count Scales. You get credit for keying a "word" whenever you advance 5 spaces. Thus when you have keyed a 60-space line, you have keyed 12 words.

To save you time, word counts that appear at the right of a timing tell you the cumulative number of words you have keyed at the end of each completed line. The scale shown at the right, for example, is used with timings that have 12 words in a line.

```
12
24
36
48
60
72
```

To quickly determine the words keyed for **in**complete lines, use the scale that appears below each timing:

```
|1  |2  |3  |4  |5  |6  |7  |8  |9  |10 |11 |12
```

This scale quickly indicates the number of words keyed. Just align the last word keyed with the number on the scale.

When you take a 3- or 5-minute timing, use the **speed markers** (the small numbers above the copy) to quickly find your words-a-minute speed.

This special scale appears with 12-second timings:

```
    5    10    15    20    25    30    35    40    45    50    55    60
```

It converts your keyboarding speed during a 12-second timing into words a minute.

Practice Guide. In certain skillbuilding routines, you will use the following chart to find the drill lines you should practice:

Pretest errors	0-1	2-3	4-5	6+
Drill lines	25-29	24-28	23-27	22-26

For example, if you made only 1 error in the Pretest, then the guide directs you to complete "Drill lines 25-29"; if you made 3 errors, you should complete "Drill lines 24-28"; and so on.

Syllabic Intensity (SI) Index. To indicate the relative difficulty of timed writing copy, syllabic intensity (SI) is often listed. The SI number is computed by dividing the number of actual words in the copy into the total number of syllables of all words. Thus 1.00 indicates copy that has one syllable per word; 1.50 indicates copy that has an average of one-and-a-half syllables per word; and so on. The higher the number, the more difficult the copy.

LABs

Effective keyboarding requires a knowledge of at least the basics of grammar, punctuation, and style. The *Microcomputer Keyboarding* program provides Language Arts for Business (LABs) that offer concise, practical reviews and application exercises on punctuation, capitalization, and number use, for example. Thus you review the most common language arts principles *as you key* sentences, timings, and production exercises.

SOFTWARE NOTES

This symbol is used to point out a special feature in word processing software that makes formatting easier. For example, when you learn how to center horizontally, the software note will describe the automatic center feature available in most software programs.

Our society is being driven by information technology rather than industrial technology, and the Information Age has changed the way we process all types of data. The computer is now central to the efficient operation of any business. Because information may now need to be sent to Europe, Asia, the Middle East, or South America as frequently as it was once sent across the United States, both business people and private individuals are using computers to help them function more easily. This section will help you understand the components required in a microcomputer system.

HARDWARE

All of the computer *equipment* is called hardware. The main components of any computer are its input devices, processing-storing devices, and output devices.

Input Devices. The variety of input devices is growing daily. The most common devices are the keyboard and the mouse. The mouse enables you to move a pointer around the screen without pressing keys on the keyboard. Other devices now in use are the trackball, touch screen, voice-activated devices, optical scanners, light pens, joysticks, and graphics tablets.

Processing-Storing Devices. The processing and storing of data takes place in the central processing unit (CPU). The CPU is where the computer interprets and processes information. The computer also has a memory which is active during your work session. This memory is measured in **kilobytes** (1,024 bytes) or **megabytes** (1 million bytes). A byte is the amount of memory required to hold a single piece of information—each letter of a word is a byte.

The speed of processing and the capacity of storage are continually increasing. Early computers had only 64 kilobytes (64K) of memory. Now most computers need at least 1 megabyte (1 meg) and up to 4 megabytes of memory to operate efficiently.

The memory in the computer is only active while the computer is turned on; it is not a permanent place to store information. Data can be stored on a hard disk located inside the computer, or on diskettes which are inserted into disk drives. The most popular diskette sizes are the 3 1/2-inch microdisk and the 5 1/4-inch floppy disk. Diskettes may be single sided or double sided and may be single density, double density, or high den-

sity. The type of diskette used will determine the amount of data that can be stored on it. Hard disks may contain 20, 40, 80, or even more than 100 megabytes of memory capacity. Computers are also using laser disks (CD ROM) to store data.

Output Devices. Common output devices are the monitor, the printer, the plotter, and the modem.

Monitors. The most popular monitors today come with color screens, but they are also available in a variety of monochrome (single-color) screens. Monitors are also called screens, video display terminals (VDTs), and cathode ray tubes (CRTs).

Diskette (Floppy disk, Microdisk) Used to store data created on a computer. Comes in a variety of sizes and densities. Type of diskette determines the amount of data that can be saved. See also *Hard Disk*.

Disk Drive Reads from and writes information to a diskette.

Del (Delete) Key Deletes (erases) characters positioned above the cursor. Used in conjunction with other keys to delete words, lines, and the remainder of the page.

Cursor Movement Keys Enables the user to move the cursor up, down, left, or right. Each key is marked with arrows pointing in the direction the cursor will move.

Cursor Shows the position on the screen where the next function will take place. Either a blinking line or a blinking square; sometimes changes shape between insert and typeover mode.

Ctrl (Control) Key Changes another key's function when pressed with the other key.

Caps Lock Key Makes all letters of the alphabet uppercase (capitals).

Backspace Key (→) Moves the cursor backwards (to the left) a space at a time. On most computers, deletes characters to the left of the cursor position.

Alt (Alternate) Key Changes another key's function when pressed with the other key.

Monitor Displays the data that has been entered in memory; may be the color or monochrome (one color). Also called *CRT* (*cathode ray tube*) or *VDT* (*video display terminal*).

Keyboard Contains alphabetic, numeric, symbol, and special function keys. An input device.

Ins (Insert) Key Changes the function from insert (adds to previously keyed text) to typeover (erases previously keyed text).

Hard Disk Used instead of diskettes to save data. Can save more data at a faster rate than diskettes. Part of the computer. Usually identified as drive C:.

Function Keys Used to send special instructions to the computer. Some keyboards have 10; others have 12. Keys are labeled F1 to F12.

Esc (Escape) Key Erases a line just keyed in DOS; function differs depending on the software program being used.

Enter/Return Key (⏎) Enters information into a computer and causes the cursor to move down a line and return to the left margin.

Tab Key Moves the cursor to a preset tab stop.

Space Bar Moves the cursor forward one space at a time and fills the line with blank spaces; used to leave a blank space between words.

Shift Key (↑) Changes another key's function when pressed with the other key. Most common use is to make capital letters or to access the upper portion of a number/symbol or punctuation key.

Prompt Asks the user to enter information that allows the computer to start an application.

Print Screen Key Prints the information that is visible on the screen without having to access the print function of a software program.

Numeric/Movement Keypad Used to enter numbers, similar to a calculator, or for other functions marked on the keys (cursor movement, insert, delete, and so on).

Num (Numeric) Lock Changes the function of the keys on the numeric/movement keypad from entering numbers to cursor movement and other functions.

Mouse Used to move the cursor around the screen without using the keyboard.

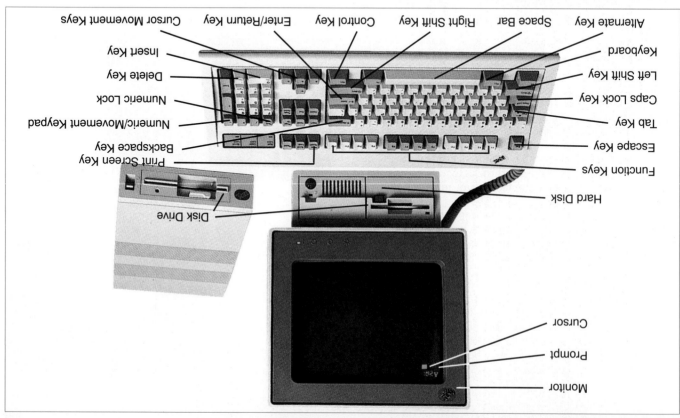

Printers. Printers are manufactured in hundreds of varieties, capabilities, and prices. The two most common types of printers are the dot matrix and the laser. Dot-matrix printers are impact printers; images are formed by pins (which create a series of dots) striking an inked ribbon and pressing it against a piece of paper. Laser printers project images through tiny beams of light which form the characters to be printed. Laser printers are becoming very popular because they operate quietly. Other types of printers are the daisy wheel (a metal disk on which the letters have been molded) and the ink jet (ink is sprayed on the paper to form the characters).

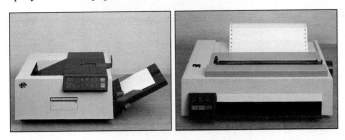

Plotters. A plotter, which is a different type of printer, *draws* output using one or more pens that are controlled by instructions from the computer. Plotters are generally used to print graphic displays such as maps, architectural drawings, and engineering drawings. Plotters are a common tool in Computer Aided Drafting (CAD).

Modems. Data can be sent from one computer to another over telephone lines by using a modem. Many libraries, research centers, and publishing centers use modems to access information and transmit it from one location to another. Other uses of the modem include banking, travel reservations, bulletin boards, and discount purchasing services.

SOFTWARE

The computer hardware cannot function without a set of instructions to drive its operation. Computer software is what makes the hardware operate. Software is classified as either operating systems software or applications software and is composed of a set of programs, procedures, and related documentation. Computer operators issue directions to the computer in the form of commands which activate the programs.

Software is developed by skilled programmers/authors, just as printed materials are written by authors. Software is protected by a copyright just as printed materials are protected. Therefore, it is illegal to copy software just as it is illegal to copy printed materials.

Operating Systems Software. One type of software is the operating system. This software is manufacturer-developed, allows the user to interact with the hardware, and provides a link to the applications software. The operating system software must be in place and functioning before the application software can be accessed and used. The operating system is also used for a variety of other functions. Some of these functions are formatting disks; creating, renaming, or erasing files; listing files; copying files; and checking disk status and space. You will need to use your computer's operating manual to identify specific commands for your operating system.

Applications Software. The software used to complete the exercises for this program is called applications software. There are many kinds of applications software: tutorial, word processing, spreadsheet, database, desktop publishing, and presentation graphics. Computer operators select different software to perform different tasks when they use the computer. Some of the new applications software is integrated—the operator can perform word processing, spreadsheet, graphics, and database functions all within the same software.

Tutorial software. Although much of the knowledge necessary to learn to operate a computer and to learn to use the computer as a tool of communication can be found in printed documents, many tutorial programs either accompany the printed material or stand alone as elements of instruction for the user. *Microcomputer Keyboarding* offers a tutorial for the complete program. Most of the commercial applications software programs include excellent tutorials on the disks along with the rest of the software.

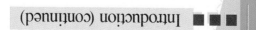

Word processing software. Word processing applications allow you to enter text which appears on the screen. Once displayed on the screen, you can edit (change) it, save it, and print it. Word processing programs allow you to insert, delete, move, copy, reformat, merge, and print the text in any configuration you choose. Word processing software is used to create letters, memos, and reports.

Spreadsheet software. Paper and pencil spreadsheets have been used by accountants for many years, but electronic spreadsheet application programs have greatly simplified the process. A spreadsheet has rows, which run across the sheet, and columns, which run down the sheet. The intersection of a row and a column is called a cell. Three types of data can be entered into a spreadsheet—text, numbers, and formulas. Once the data is entered, it can be copied, moved, changed, reformatted, calculated, and recalculated. The data can also be converted to line, bar, and pie graphs.

Some common uses for spreadsheets are teacher's grade-books, monthly financial reports, and business forecasting.

Database software. For years individuals and businesses have spent hours setting up filing systems to store all types of data. Modern database management systems that run on the computer allow these tasks to be completed more efficiently. Four categories of information are involved when databases are created. A *field* is one small piece of information entered separately (such as your last name). A *record* includes all the fields created about one person or item (such as your last name, your first name, your address, and your telephone number). A *file* includes several records (such as all of the students in your keyboarding class). A *database*, then, can include many files which are all related (such as all of the students who are enrolled in your school).

When you create a database, you must first set up a plan called a *structure* into which you can then enter the data. The way you set up your structure will determine how you can retrieve data and use your database later.

Some common uses of databases are student records for a school, patient records for a hospital, client records for a law office or an insurance office, and membership records for a church or a civic organization. Databases can also be used for inventorying personal property.

Desktop publishing and presentation graphics software. Once only professional printing companies could prepare eye-appealing documents. With desktop publishing and presentation graphics software, it is possible to prepare attractive documents using your own computer. Combining text and graphics produces a variety of unique designs depending upon the printer used and the software capabilities.

Desktop publishing and presentation graphics programs allow you to change margins and tabs; change the size, density, and style of type; and add clip art in many ways. Computer operators can create a variety of graphs, charts, brochures, programs, and reports in a professional manner.

CARE AND HANDLING OF HARDWARE AND SOFTWARE

Computer hardware is becoming more and more "people-proof," but care still needs to be taken when using it. Some items to remember include:

1. Keep food and drink away from the computer.
2. Protect the computer from sudden electrical surges by using surge protectors.
3. Turn the computer on and off properly to prevent damage to the disk drives or any data that may be stored on them.
4. Protect hardware when moving it by following manufacturer directions very carefully.
5. Turn off the computer when connecting or disconnecting component parts.

Diskettes also need special care:

1. Do not touch exposed parts of the disk if you are working with 5 1/4-inch disks.
2. Store 5 1/4-inch disks in their sleeves when the disks are not in use.
3. Store disks in a disk file away from extreme temperatures.
4. Store disks away from magnets which may cause all the data to be erased.
5. Do not bend or fold floppy disks.
6. Do not write on 5 1/4-inch floppy disks with a pencil or ballpoint pen. Use a felt-tipped pen.
7. Insert and eject disks from the drive carefully.
8. Never remove a disk from a drive while the drive is running.
9. Make backup (second) copies of disks containing information that cannot be replaced.
10. Set up a systematic way to keep track of what is stored on your disks.

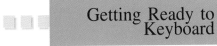

Getting Ready to Keyboard

YOUR POSTURE

Your keyboarding accuracy and speed are affected by the way you sit while you are using the computer. Follow these guidelines:

1. Head erect and back straight, with the body leaning forward slightly; shoulders level.
2. Body a handspan from the keyboard, centered opposite the J key.
3. Eyes looking at the copy if you are working from *hard copy* (printed or handwritten input) or looking at the screen if you are composing an original document.
4. Feet apart, flat on the floor, one foot slightly ahead of the other.
5. Fingers curved so that only the tips touch the keys.
6. Wrists up slightly, off the front of the keyboard so that the fingers are free to move as you key.
7. Arms hanging loosely at your sides, with the forearm at the same angle as the keyboard; elbows close to the body.

YOUR WORKSTATION

Your workstation is your desk, chair, computer, printer (or printer access), and any supplies and reference materials you may use to do your work. It is important to arrange your workstation so that you will be able to complete your work in the most efficient way possible. Follow these guidelines:

1. Place the materials to be keyed (the hard copy) on one side of the computer, usually the right side.
2. Place supplies to the other side, usually the left side.
3. Store away all other items that are not being used.
4. Position the monitor so that you do not have to tilt your head either up or down in order to read the copy on the screen.

Consult your operating manual for the correct way to turn on the computer and/or to boot your computer. Once your computer is booted, you will need to access the appropriate software program. Your teacher will give you specific instructions for doing this. The following information is common to most computers and applications programs.

DOS prompt. When your computer is booted, the DOS prompt will appear on the screen. If you have a hard drive, the DOS prompt will look like this: C:\. If you do not have a hard drive, the DOS prompt will look like this: A:\. The letter C or A is an indication of what drive is to receive the command.

Cursor. The cursor is the blinking light on the screen—it may be in the form of a line or a square. The cursor is the point at which text or a command is entered. The cursor will be in the space following the DOS prompt.

Cursor movement. The cursor will move to the right as you key characters or spaces. It can also be moved to the left or up and down the screen with the arrow (cursor control) keys.

Menus, help screens, and tutorials. All applications software programs have directions which either automatically appear on the screen or can be accessed by command. Reading the directions from the screen will help you learn the software.

Default settings. Software programs have preset formats which can be used or changed to suit the information you are entering. Most word processing programs use the following default settings: single spacing, 10 characters per inch, 5-space tab indention, and 1-inch margins (left, right, top, and bottom). Database and spreadsheet software also have defaults for fields and columns.

In this course, your defaults should be set for single spacing, 10 characters per inch, 5-space tab indention, 1-inch margins, left justification (or justification off), and hyphenation off. You will learn about changing these defaults and others throughout this course.

Word wrap. As you key data, you will notice that if you keep on keying, the data will eventually wrap around to the next line automatically. This is known as word wrap or a *soft return.* If you strike the enter/return key at the end of a line, it is known as a *hard return.* If you reformat a document, soft returns will change automatically, but you will have to delete hard returns to change the line endings.

Scrolling. The screen that you see when you are entering data is only a window—you can actually enter data wider than the screen, and, of course, longer than the screen. As you enter data wider or longer than the screen, the data scrolls either left to right or up and down.

Editing. One of the best features of word processing is the ability to change data with relative ease. If you want to insert a character, you simply make sure that the insert function is on and insert the character at the point where you want it placed. If you want to delete a character, simply place the cursor under the character you want to delete and depress the delete key.

Items can be moved, copied, and reformatted just as easily. You can also insert, delete, move, or copy columns and rows of data. Consult your operating manual for specific directions.

Screen codes. When you want to enhance the print of a document, you can use bold or underlining, or you can change the font. When you want to vary the format, you can indent, double space, or center. Codes that show on the screen let you know whether you have activated the functions before you print a hard copy of your document. In addition, many software packages include a preview feature which allows you to see how your document will print before you actually print it.

File names. Each document produced and saved on the computer must have its own file name. Some software programs require you to name a file before you can open (start) a document. Other programs only require a file name when you save the document. Most software programs allow you to select up to 8 characters for a file name. The file name may be followed by a period and a 3-letter extension. With integrated software packages, the extensions are sometimes automatically assigned by the software to denote whether a file was created as a spreadsheet, a database, or a word processing file. You can always change file names to fit the individual situation.

The file name allows the computer to save a document under that name very much like filing a document in a file folder. The document can then be retrieved later by using that same file name. The file name should include the type of document and the sequence if it is part of a series of documents. For this course, the type of document is denoted with a letter, and the sequence in a series with a number. The extension is the number of the lesson in which the document appears.

Examples: D4   (Drill lesson 4)
C3.28   (Centering job 3, lesson 28)
R4.35   (Report job 4, lesson 35)
L3.43   (Letter job 3, lesson 43)
T7.53   (Table job 7, lesson 53)
M5.104 (Memo job 5, lesson 104)
F6.110 (Form job 6, lesson 110)

Directory. Once a file is saved on a disk, it is listed on the directory of the disk. You can access the directory with a command so that you can see the names of all the files on the disk, find out how much disk space has been used by existing files, and find out how much space is left for future use.

Document Codes. A document code is different from a file name because it is keyed on the document. Many companies use document codes, particularly if the documents are prepared in word processing centers. The document code enables someone other than the person who keyed the document to find it on a disk. It may include the disk number, the file name, and/or an identification of the person who keyed the document.

In this course, use the file name (see examples above) as the first part of the document code followed by your initials, or your initials and last name. Separate the two parts by a space.

Examples: D16 BNOakley (Drill lesson 16)
D16 BNO   (Drill lesson 16)
R4.35 BNO   (Report 4, lesson 35)

Level 1

Computer-controlled robots on the assembly line are just one of the ways computers are used in the automobile industry. The computer is also used in auto body design, in acoustics—to decrease interior noise levels, in testing wind resistance—to make automobiles more fuel efficient, and in testing fuel economy.

Goals

1. Demonstrate which fingers control each key on the keyboard.
2. Use home key anchors to assist in developing location security.
3. Control the keyboard at a useful level of operation with a goal of 27 words a minute for 2 minutes with 4 or fewer errors.
4. Use proper spacing after common marks of punctuation.
5. Compose phrases and simple sentences at the keyboard.

Orphans: The first line of a paragraph that has been left alone at the bottom of a page. [p. 95]

Outline Style: A feature that automatically formats the levels and division headings needed to generate an outline. [p. 84]

Page Numbering: A feature that automatically counts and prints each page number of a document. [p. 95]

Parenthetical Reference: A reference that credits a source by placing it in parentheses in the text immediately after quote has been completed. [p. 157]

Password: A word that is used to limit access to a file or a computer system.

Plotter: An output device used to create hardcopy drawings on paper, usually in a variety of colors. [p. xiii]

Primary File: A file, such as a letter, that contains text as well as merge commands. This file works with the secondary file to produce a document.

Print Enhancement: A method of emphasizing print, such as bold, underline, or all caps. [p. 71]

Prompt: A question or other indication that the computer is waiting for user input. [p. xii]

Random Access Memory (RAM): Temporary storage of data and program instructions in a computer. When computer power is turned off, these instructions are eliminated. Typical RAM capabilities of microcomputers is 2 megabytes or greater.

Read-Only Memory (ROM): Permanent, nonchangeable storage of program instructions in a computer. When computer power is turned off, these instructions remain in ROM.

Reference I.D.: The initials or initials and last name of the person who keys a document. [p. 36]

Relative Tab: A tab that adjusts when the left margin is moved. [p. 37]

Repeat Value: A feature that allows the user to repeat a character through a single keystroke. [p. 133]

Reveal Codes: A feature that allows a user to display on the screen any formatting codes that are hidden in the document. [p. 72]

Right Alignment: A feature that positions copy at the right margin. [p. 239] (See *Flush Right*)

Right Justification: A feature that automatically aligns copy at the right margin and produces a ragged left margin. [p. 281]

Right Tab: Causes the cursor to indent to the tab stop. As text is keyed, it moves to the left from the tab position. [p. 37]

Routing List for Memos: A list that appears at the bottom of a memo to require all addressees to read the memo, initial it, and send it on to the next person on the routing list. [p. 297]

Ruler Line: A line that can be displayed on the screen to show where the margins and tabs are set. [p. 37] (See *Tab Ruler*)

Scrolling: Activity of moving text up or down, or left and right, on a computer screen. [p. xvi]

Search: A feature that allows the user to look for a character, word, or phrase used throughout a document. [p. 113]

Search and Replace: A feature that allows the user to look for a word or phrase used throughout a document and replace it with another word or phrase. [p. 113]

Secondary File: A file that contains variable data that is merged with a form document to produce letters, forms, lists, and so on.

Slash: A diagonal. [p. 20]

Soft Page Break: A page break that is created automatically by the software. [p. 95]

Sort: A feature that allows the user to rearrange data that has been prepared as a table. Also, a database feature that rearranges data within the database. [p. 259]

Spell Checker: A feature that "proofreads" a document and highlights misspelled words. Some spell checkers suggest possible correct spellings. [p. 61]

Spread Center: A print enhancement technique in which the user leaves 1 space between letters and 3 spaces between words. [p. 71]

Spreadsheet: A software format that enables the user to create tables of numbers on a screen. If the numbers are changed, then the answers are recalculated automatically. [p. 218, 220]

Stored Format: A format that can be saved as a file and recalled at a later time. [p. 106]

Subscript: A feature that lowers a character a half line below the writing line. [p. 74]

Superscript: A feature that raises a character a half line above the writing line. [p. 74, 266]

Tab Ruler: A line that can be displayed on the screen to show where margins and tabs are set. [p. 37] (See *Ruler Line*)

Tab Stop: Used to make the cursor move to a preselected point. [p. 37]

Top Margin Command: A feature that instructs the printer to advance the paper a specified number of lines or inches before printing the text. [p. 64]

Turnover Line: A line that extends beyond the first line of print after a soft return has been enabled. [p. 81]

Tutorial Software: Software designed to assist a user in learning how to run a particular software package. [p. xiii]

Typeover Mode: A keyboard option that allows one letter or word to be replaced by another. [p. 62]

View Document: A feature that allows the user to view an image of the full page, in reduced form, on the screen. [p. 95]

Widow: The last line of a paragraph that has been carried to the top of another page. [p. 95]

Wild Card Characters: Asterisks used in DOS to indicate that the action specified is to be performed on all files.

Windows: A feature that partitions the screen into two separate areas or "windows." Each window can contain a separate document or a different section of the document that is currently active.

Word Delete: The action of deleting a word at a time through a command in the software. [p. 62]

Word Wrap: A feature that automatically drops the cursor down to the next line without the user having to press Enter/Return. [p. 3, 78]

Works Cited: An alphabetic listing of all the books and articles used in writing a report, including all parenthetical references cited in the report. [p. 161]

UNIT 1

Keyboarding— The Alphabet

Unit Goal 16 Words a Minute

Lesson 1

Objective Strike the home keys, holding anchors.
Operate the space bar.
Return to a new line.

Format Spacing: single
Margins: default

A. Home Key Position

In keying by touch, each finger controls a limited number of keys. To make sure that the correct fingers are used, all reaches will be made from the middle row of alphabet keys. The dark keys shown with white letters in the keyboard chart below are the **home keys.**
Left Hand. Place your fingertips on the **A S D** and **F** keys.
Right Hand. Place your fingertips on the **J K L** and **;** keys.

Curve your fingers so that only their tips lightly touch the keys. (Drop your arms to your sides; shake your hands to relax. Without moving your fingers, raise your hands up and place them over the keyboard. Your fingers will be in the correctly curved position.)
Your fingers are named for the home keys on which they rest: A finger, S finger, D finger, and so on, ending with Sem finger on the **;** key.

Top Row
Third Row
Middle (Home) Row
Bottom Row

B. Using Anchors

An anchor is a home key position that will help you bring each finger back to its home key position. When you learn new keys, the fingers to be anchored will be shown next to the keyboard along with the message "Hold Those Anchors." If more than one anchor is

given for a key, the first one shown is the most important. Try to hold all the anchors listed, but be sure to hold the number one anchor.
Note: Touch the anchor keys lightly; pressure on them will result in creating those characters.

C. Space Bar

Tap the space bar with the thumb of your writing hand—the right thumb if you are right-handed, the left thumb if you are left-handed. Whichever thumb you use should be poised above the middle of the space bar. The other thumb is not used; hold it close to its adjacent forefinger.

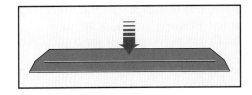

Tap center of the space bar with thumb.

Distribution List: An extensive list of addressees that is placed at the bottom of a memo to identify all individuals who are to receive the memo. [p. 297]

Document Code: A code that is keyed on a document to indicate the file name and/or the name or initials of the person who keyed the document. [p. xvi, 36]

Document Number: A number used in this text to identify the work being completed, such as T16.56 (Table 16, Lesson 56). [p. 36]

Dot Leaders: A feature that will automatically print leaders from one column to another. [p. 261] (See *Leaders*)

Electronic Mail: Messages that are sent electronically from one terminal to another; often called E-mail.

Endnotes: Used instead of footnotes and placed at the end of a report to identify the sources used in preparing a document. [p. 267]

Facsimile Copy: Text and graphics copy that is sent over telephone lines from one "fax" machine to another "fax" machine.

Field: An area in which information is filled in on a preprinted form. [p. 249]

Field Identifier: A character (such as an asterisk) that is inserted into a document to identify a field that requires information from a merge file. [p. 287]

File Name: The name given to a document so that it can be saved on a computer disk. [p. xvi, 35]

File Name Extension: An extension of up to three characters that can be used after the period of a file name to add further length to the name or to designate a specific type of file. [p. xvi]

Flush Right: A feature that positions copy at the right margin. [p. 239] (See *Right Alignment*)

Font: A style of print such as courier, bookman, or letter gothic. Sometimes referred to as typeface. [p. 71]

Footers: Items of text that are repeated at the bottom of a page. [p. 36]

Footnote Feature: A feature that automatically places footnotes at the bottom of the page on which they are referenced. [p. 268]

Format: The design of a page that includes such settings as margins, line spacing, tabs, type size, fonts, and so on. [p. 78]

Forms Software: Programs that allow the user to create forms and to fill them in. [p. 249]

Full Justification: Aligns lines of text at both the left and right margins.

Function Keys: Special keys on the keyboard (such as F1, F2, F3, and so on) that are used in combination with **Ctrl, Alt,** and **Shift** keys to execute word processing software commands. [p. xii]

Graphics: Information that is displayed in a graph, chart, or similar drawing. [p. 260]

Hanging Indent: A temporary left margin that indents all lines but the first line of text. [p. 81]

Hard Copy: Images that are output by a printer or plotter to paper.

Hard Formats: Formats that are designed so that they cannot be altered, even in insert mode or when an Enter/Return key is depressed. [p. 249]

Hard Page Break: A command that forces pages to end before the software's calculation—often executed with a Ctrl-Enter Key combination. [p. 95]

Hard Return: Depressing the Enter Key to move the cursor back to the left margin and down to the next line. [p. 3]

Hardware: Computer equipment that includes the computer itself, a monitor, a keyboard, a printer, and other devices. [p. xi]

Headers: Items of text that are repeated at the top of a page. [p. 95]

Indent: A temporary left margin that is used to indent text to the next tab setting on the ruler line. [p. 81]

Insert Mode: A mode that allows the operator to add new text and move the old text to the right one space for every new character that is added. [p. 62]

Inserts: Variable information that can be added to a document. [p. 290]

Kilobyte (K): 1,024 bytes of computer storage. This unit of measure is usually rounded off to an even thousand bytes of computer memory; thus, 5K is typically thought of as 5,000 bytes. [p. xi]

Leaders: Rows of periods used to lead the eye across a page, usually from one column to another. [p. 261] (See *Dot Leaders*)

Left Justification: Aligns text at the left margin; produces a ragged right margin.

Left Tab: Usually the default tab that causes the cursor to indent to the tab stop. As text is keyed, it moves to the right from the tab position. [p. 37]

Letterhead: Information (such as the company name, address, and telephone number) that is printed at the top of official company stationery. [p. 110]

Line Delete: A feature that allows deleting one line at a time or deleting from the cursor to the end of the line. [p. 62]

Line Draw: A feature that enables a user to draw a variety of lines in a document. [p. 298]

Line-Spacing Command: A command that allows the user to set various line spacing options (such as single, double, and triple) in a document. [p. 64]

Macro: A single instruction that takes the place of several words or functions. [p. 159]

Megabyte (MB): Approximately 1 million bytes of computer storage, equal to 1,000 K. [p. xi]

Merge: A feature that allows one file (such as a letter) to join with another (such as a list of addresses). [p. 287]

Military Style Date: A date keyed in the following sequence: day of the month, month, year. [p. 89]

Mixed Punctuation: The most common punctuation style in letters; a colon follows the salutation and a comma follows the complimentary closing. [p. 101]

Modem: A device that will translate digital signals from a computer into analog signals for a telephone and then back into digital signals again for computer processing. [p. xiii, 271]

Monitor: A device for viewing computer output. Also known as a cathode-ray tube (CRT), screen, or video display terminal (VDT). [p. xi]

OCR Format: A format for addressing an envelope in which all lines of the address are keyed in all caps with no punctuation. [p. 106]

Operating System Software: Software that starts up a computer and perform various computer commands. [p. xiii]

Now practice using the space bar with the right or left thumb.

Space once [*tap the space bar once*] . . . twice [*tap the space bar twice*] . . . once . . . once . . . twice . . . once . . . twice . . . once . . . twice . . . twice . . . once . . . once . . . .

Repeat.

 Enter/Return Key

The cursor will automatically move down one line and return to the left margin when it reaches the right margin setting. This is called **word wrap**.

As you press a key, the cursor on a computer moves from left to right. Depressing the enter key will move the cursor back to the left margin and down to the next line. This is called a **hard return**.

Extend the Sem finger to the adjacent enter/return key. Lightly press the key, causing the cursor to move back to the left margin and down to the next line, and return the Sem finger to home key position.

Now practice using the enter/return key.

Space once . . . twice . . . once . . . twice . . . . Ready to return [*move finger to enter/return key*]. Return! [*Return the cursor.*] . . . Home! [*Place fingers on home keys.*] . . .

Repeat.

Hold Those Anchors
For **A** anchor F
For **S** anchor F or A
For **D** anchor A S
For **F** anchor A S D

Hold Those Anchors
For **;** anchor J
For **L** anchor ; or J
For **K** anchor ; L
For **J** anchor ; L K

Stroking Practice

Practice the F and J and space strokes shown in the drill below. Key each line once. After completing a set of lines, return twice.

Left forefinger, spacing thumb. fff fff ff ff f f ff ff f f   Return.

Right forefinger, spacing thumb. jjj jjj jj jj j j jj jj j j   Return twice.

F. **F** **J** Keys

Use forefingers.

Key each line once.

1 fff jjj fff jjj fff jjj ff jj ff jj f j   Return.

2 fff jjj fff jjj fff jjj ff jj ff jj f j   Return twice.

Glossary

Absolute Tab: A tab that remains in the same place when a margin is changed. [p. 37]

All Caps: A method of enhancement in which all characters are keyed in "All Capital Letters." [p. 30]

Anchor: A home key position that will help the user bring each finger back to its home key position. [p. 2]

Applications Software: Software designed to carry out a specific task such as word processing, payroll calculation, spreadsheet analysis, and so on. [p. xiii]

Ascending Sort: A feature that sorts data in ascending alphabetical (A–Z) or numerical (0–9) order.

Automatic Addressing: A feature that will automatically address envelopes from information in a database. [pp. 106, 287]

Automatic Centering: A feature that automatically centers text on a given tab setting or between margins. [pp. 1, 37, 64]

Automatic Page Break: A feature that automatically calculates the end of each page of a document. [p. 95]

Block Center: A method of centering a group of lines so that the longest line in the group is used to determine the left margin or tab stop at which the lines are keyed. [p. 74]

Block Command: A feature that is used to highlight a section of text for the purpose of executing a command that will affect the entire block.

Block Copy: A method of copying text by first highlighting the text and then copying it as a block to another area in the document. [p. 103]

Block Delete: A method of deleting text by first highlighting the text and then depressing the delete key to remove it. [p. 62]

Block Move: A method of moving text by first highlighting the text and then moving it as a block to another area in the document. [p. 103]

Block Protect: A feature that allows the user to keep a block of text together so that it will not break between pages. [p. 167]

Block Style: A letter style in which all parts of a letter begin at the left margin. [p. 101]

Boilerplate: A file that can be created and then saved on a disk to be used repeatedly from one application to another. [p. 237]

Bold: A type of print enhancement that makes the text appear darker and broader for emphasis.

Cartridge Font: A cartridge that plugs into the printer to provide additional fonts.

Case Conversion Command: A feature that converts a block of text keyed in lowercase letters to all caps, or vice versa. [p. 106]

Cell: The intersection of a row and a column, usually found in a spreadsheet and in the table edit feature of word processing software. [p. 220]

Center Justification: A feature that centers text between the margins.

Center Page: A feature that automatically centers copy vertically on the page. [p. 69]

Center Tab: A tab that forces text to be centered from a tab stop. [pp. 37, 211]

Coupon Letter: A form letter that allows the addressee to tear off a coupon at the bottom of the letter and return it to the sender. [p. 243]

Courseware: All of the software capabilities correlated with the textbook.

Cursor: A pointer on the screen, usually in the shape of a rectangle, that indicates the place where keyed text or codes will appear. [p. xii]

Database: An organized collection of data that is stored in a file. [pp. 256, 259]

Date Insert: A feature that automatically inserts the current date into a document. [p. 101]

Decimal Tab: A tab that moves text to the left until a decimal point is keyed. [pp. 37, 82]

Default: A standard setup that is used for margins, line spacing, tabs, justification, and so on.

Default Margins: The standard preset margins in a software package. Most default margins are set at 1 inch. [p. 78]

Default Tabs: The standard preset tabs in a software package. Many word processing default tabs are set 5 spaces apart. [p. 37]

Delivery Notation: A notation on a letter that designates a delivery method other than by standard first-class mail, such as overnight mail or fax. [p. 242]

Descending Sort: A feature that sorts data in descending alphabetical (Z–A) or numerical (9–0) order.

Desktop: A temporary holding area in word processing software that allows a file to be copied into a "desktop" and then transferred to a document that is currently active. [p. 223]

Desktop Publishing: A concept that allows the operator to combine word processing and graphics in designing a page. [p. 308]

Directory: The location on a fixed disk or diskette where files are located. A directory tells the user the file names, file extensions, file sizes, and the dates and times when the files were created or last changed.

Disk Drive: The part of the computer hardware that either (1) reads the data on a disk or (2) writes data on a disk.

Disk Operating System (DOS): An internal operating system for a microcomputer. It consists of a series of instructions that are necessary for performing essential operating tasks of the microcomputer.

Hold Those Anchors
For **A** anchor F
For **S** anchor F or A
For **D** anchor A S
For **F** anchor A S D

Hold Those Anchors
For **;** anchor J
For **L** anchor ; or J
For **K** anchor ; L
For **J** anchor ; L K

G.  **Keys**

Use second fingers.

Key each line once.

3 ddd kkk ddd kkk ddd kkk dd kk dd kk d k

4 ddd kkk ddd kkk ddd kkk dd kk dd kk d k

H.  **Keys**

Use third fingers.

Key each line once.

5 sss lll sss lll sss lll ss ll ss ll s l

6 sss lll sss lll sss lll ss ll ss ll s l

I. [A] [;] **Keys**

Use fourth fingers.

Key each line once.

7 aaa ;;; aaa ;;; aaa ;;; aa ;; aa ;; a ;

8 aaa ;;; aaa ;;; aaa ;;; aa ;; aa ;; a ;

J. Technique Checkpoint

Keep eyes on copy, fingers on home keys.

A Technique Checkpoint is a drill designed to give you a chance to practice the keys you just learned. It is an opportunity for your teacher to check your development of proper technique in using the correct fingering and anchoring; using the enter/return key without looking; maintaining correct posture and correct arm, hand, and elbow positions; and keeping eyes on copy. Marginal notes accompany the checkpoints to assist you in improving your skill as you key.

Key lines 9–10 once. Then repeat lines 1 (page 3), 3, 5, and 7.

9 ff jj dd kk ss ll aa ;; f j d k s l a ;

10 ff jj dd kk ss ll aa ;; f j d k s l a ;

K.  PRETEST

Key lines 11–12 for 1 minute. Repeat if time permits. Keep your eyes on the copy.

11 sad sad fad fad ask ask lad lad dad dad

12 as; as; fall fall alas alas flask flask

Bibliography. A bibliography identifies all the sources that were used in preparing the report and all the sources cited in the footnotes. It is the last major section of a report. To format a bibliography page:

1. Center *BIBLIOGRAPHY* on line 13 in all capitals; triple-space after this heading.

2. Use margins identical with those used in the body of the report.

3. Alphabetize all entries by authors' last names.

4. Single-space all entries, but use a double space between individual entries.

5. Begin the first line of each entry at the left margin; indent turnover lines 5 spaces.

6. List the name of the first author in each entry in inverted order (last name first).

7. Follow the report style for page numbers.

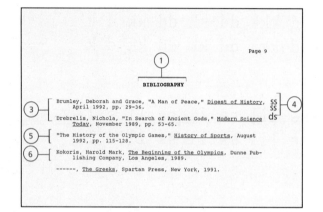

Endnotes. Footnotes placed in a special section at the end of a report are called *endnotes*. To format endnotes:

1. Center *NOTES* on line 13 in all capitals; triple-space after this heading.

2. Use the same margins that were used to key the body of the report.

3. Single-space each note, and leave 1 blank line between individual notes.

4. Indent the first line of each note 5 spaces. Turnover lines within the same note should begin at the left margin.

5. Number the endnote page(s) in the same way you numbered the report.

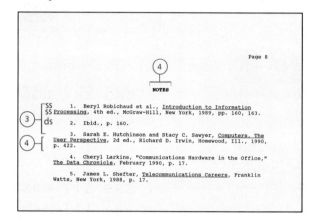

SPECIAL REPORT FORMATS

Variations of the report format are used for minutes of a meeting and magazine articles.

Minutes of a Meeting. The minutes of a meeting usually consist of three parts—*ATTENDANCE, UNFINISHED BUSINESS,* and *NEW BUSINESS*—which are keyed as side headings in all caps at the left margin. Key the title on line 7, and single-space the minutes. Use the margins for a bound report.

Magazine Article. Use a 50-space line (1.75 inch side margins). Follow the standard report format for the article title and the byline. On all pages except the first, key the author's last name and the page number at the right margin.

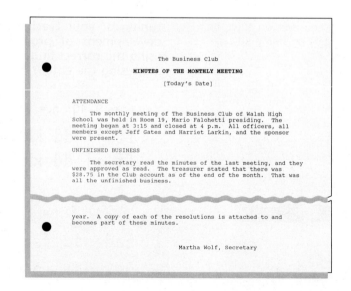

Hold Those Anchors
For **A** anchor F
For **S** anchor F or A
For **D** anchor A S
For **F** anchor A S D

Hold Those Anchors
For **;** anchor J
For **L** anchor ; or J
For **K** anchor ; L
For **J** anchor ; L K

L. PRACTICE

Leave a blank line after each set of drills (13–14, 15–16, and so on) by returning twice. (See example below.)

Key lines 13–24 once.

```
13  aaa lll lll all all sss aaa ddd sad sad
14  aaa lll lll all all sss aaa ddd sad sad

15  fff aaa ddd fad fad aaa sss kkk ask ask
16  fff aaa ddd fad fad aaa sss kkk ask ask

17  lll aaa ddd lad lad aaa ddd ddd add add
18  lll aaa ddd lad lad aaa ddd ddd add add

19  ddd aaa ddd dad dad aaa sss ;;; as; as;
20  ddd aaa ddd dad dad aaa sss ;;; as; as;

21  l la las lass lass; f fl fla flas flask
22  l la las lass lass; f fl fla flas flask

23  a al ala alas alas; f fa fal fall falls
24  a al ala alas alas; f fa fal fall falls
```

M. POSTTEST

Key lines 25–26 for 1 minute. Repeat if time permits. Keep your eyes on the copy. Compare the number of words you keyed with those you keyed in the Pretest.

```
25  sad sad fad fad ask ask lad lad dad dad
26  as; as; fall fall alas alas flask flask
```

N. End-of-Class Procedure

To keep the hardware and software in good working order, you will need to treat them carefully. Your teacher will tell you exactly what should be done at the end of every class period and at the end of the day. You will need to do at least the following:

1. Save your work on a disk.

2. Exit the program.

3. Remove the disks from the computer and store them properly.

Other things you may have to do include exiting the system, dimming the monitor or turning off the equipment, and covering the equipment at the end of the day.

SPECIAL REPORT PAGES

A long report contains the following special pages: (1) cover page, (2) contents, and (3) bibliography. A report may also include (4) an Endnotes page if footnotes are not placed at the bottom of the pages.

Cover Page.   Cover page information may vary greatly, depending on the purpose of the report. Formal reports, for example, often require additional information. Note the following guidelines:

For Academic Reports and Most Business Reports

1. In the top half of the page, center the title of the report and the name of the person who prepared the report.

2. In the lower half of the page, center the name of the person

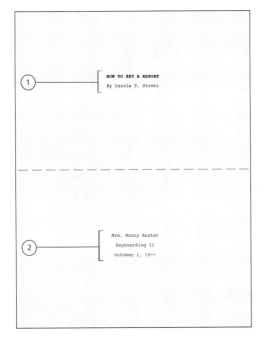

or company for whom the report was prepared (teacher), the person's title or company (the course name), and the date.

For More Formal Reports

1. Center the report title in all caps 2 inches from the top (line 13).

2. Center the subtitle or the first line of a multiline subtitle on line 15 in capital and lowercase letters. Single-space additional lines in the subtitle.

3. Center vertically on the page, in capital and lowercase letters, the author's name and title, department name, and company name.

4. Center the date 2 inches from the bottom of the page.

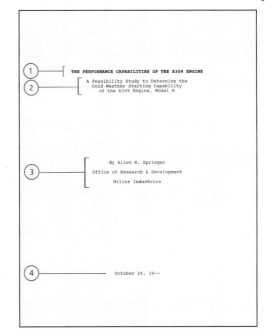

Contents.   The contents page follows the cover page of the report.

1. Center *CONTENTS* or *TABLE OF CONTENTS* on line 13 in all capitals; triple-space after the heading.

2. Key each entry in the contents (a chapter, a major section, and so on) in capital and lowercase letters.

3. Precede each entry with a Roman numeral (I, II, and so on). Use leaders between each entry and its page number. Use a right justified leader tab, if available.

4. Number the contents page or pages with lower-case Roman numerals (ii, iii, and so on), and center each number at the bottom default margin (1 inch).

5. Use the same side margins as you used for the report.

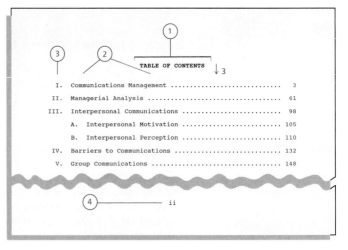

Lesson 2

Objective Control H, E, and O keys by touch.
Format Spacing: single
Margins: default

A. Keyboard Review

Leave 1 blank line after each set of lines.

Hold Those Anchors
For **H** anchor ; L K
For **E** anchor A
For **O** anchor J or ;

Key each line twice. Repeat if time permits.

1 ff jj dd kk ss ll aa ;; f j d k s l a ;
2 adds adds fads fads asks asks lads lads

B. H Key

Use J finger.

Key each line twice. Repeat if time permits.

3 jjj jhj jhj hjh jhj jjj jhj jhj hjh jhj
4 jhj had had jhj has has jhj ash ash jhj
5 jhj a lass had; adds a half; a lad has;
6 half a sash has a slash; dad shall dash

C. E Key

Use D finger.

Key each line twice. Repeat if time permits.

7 ddd ded ded ede ded ddd ded ded ede ded
8 ded he; he; ded she she ded led led ded
9 ded he led; she fell; he slashes sales;
10 she sealed a lease; he sees sheds ahead

D. O Key

Use L finger.

Key each line twice. Repeat if time permits.

11 lll lol lol olo lol lll lol lol olo lol
12 lol foe foe lol hoe hoe lol odd odd lol
13 lol old oak hoes; hold a foe; load sod;
14 he folded old hoses; she sold odd hooks

BUSINESS REPORTS

The parts of a business report and the format for a business report appear below.

PARTS OF A BUSINESS REPORT

1. *Report Title*: Centered, keyed in all-capital letters, and bold on line 13 (2 inches from the top).

2. *Subtitle*: Centered in capital and lowercase-letters a double space below the title.

3. *Byline*: Centered in capital and lowercase letters a double space below the subtitle.

4. *Side Heading*: Keyed in capital and lowercase letters, bold, flush with the left margin.

5. *Paragraph Heading*: Indented, in capital and lower-case letters, underscored, and followed by a period.

6. *Short Quotation* (not longer than three keyed lines): Keyed in quotation marks as part of the text of the report.

7. *Long Quotation* (longer than three keyed lines): Single-spaced, preceded and followed by a blank line, and indented 5 spaces from both margins.

8. *Page Numbers*: Keyed at the right margin on line 7. A double space is placed below the page number.

9. *Footnote Separation Line* (if the automatic footnote feature is not used): Key a 2-inch line, beginning at the left margin. Single-space before the separation line, and double-space after it.

10. *Footnote* (if the automatic footnote feature is not used): Keyed at the bottom of the page from margin to margin; single-spaced, with a double space between footnotes. Indent the first line of the footnote 5 spaces. **Note:** Footnotes may also be placed in their entirety on a separate page at the end of the report. See "Endnotes" on page 266.

11. *Displays and Tables in Business Reports*:

   (a) Separate the table from the text with a quadruple space before and after the table. **Note:** If the table does not have a title, double-space before and after the table.

   (b) Center the table horizontally between the set margins.

   (c) Single-space the body of the table.

Format.   Observe the following rules when keying business reports:

1. *Spacing*: Double is used. Single may be used to save space.

2. *Side Margins*:
   (a) For unbound reports: Default—1 inch (6 1/2-inch line).
   (b) For bound reports: Change the left margin to 1 1/2 inches, right margin stays at 1 inch (6-inch line).

3. *Paragraph Indention*: 5 spaces.

4. *Top Margin*: 2 inches (line 13) on the first page; 1 inch (line 7) on other pages.

5. Bottom Margin: Default (1 inch).

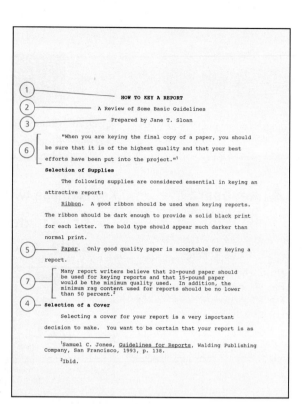

E. Technique Checkpoint

Key each character with a quick, sharp stroke. Hold anchor key positions.

Key lines 15–16 once. Then repeat lines 3, 7, and 11 (page 6).

15 he has half a salad; she has old jokes;
16 she sold jade flakes; he sold old hoses

F. PRETEST

Key lines 17–18 for 1 minute. Repeat if time permits. Keep your eyes on the copy.

17 hole head folk hash elf; hoof jade heed
18 half dead hold sash jell look lake seed

G. PRACTICE

When You Repeat a Line:
Speed up on the second attempt.

Make second attempt smoother.

Leave a blank line after second attempt (return twice).

Key each line twice. Repeat if time permits.

19 hole hole hale hale hall hall half half
20 head head heal heal deal deal dead dead
21 folk folk fold fold sold sold hold hold
22 hash hash lash lash dash dash sash sash
23 elf; elf; self self sell sell jell jell
24 hoof hoof hood hood hook hook look look
25 jade jade fade fade fake fake lake lake
26 heed heed feed feed deed deed seed seed

H. POSTTEST

Key lines 17–18 for 1 minute. Repeat if time permits. Keep your eyes on the copy. Compare the number of words you keyed with those you keyed in the Pretest.

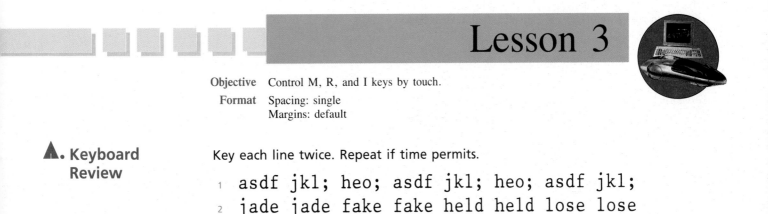

Lesson 3

Objective   Control M, R, and I keys by touch.
Format   Spacing: single
          Margins: default

A. Keyboard Review

Key each line twice. Repeat if time permits.

1 asdf jkl; heo; asdf jkl; heo; asdf jkl;
2 jade jade fake fake held held lose lose

ACADEMIC REPORTS

Reports are very commonly used communications. The format for preparing reports may differ slightly in schools and in business. The parts listed below typically appear in academic reports. The format for business reports is discussed later.

PARTS OF AN ACADEMIC REPORT

1. *Heading Information*:   At the default margins (1 inch top, 1 inch side), keyed in capital and lowercase letters. Consists of your name, your teacher's name, the class name, and the date.
   Note: The date is keyed in military style: 13 November 19—.

2. *Title*:   Centered in initial caps.

3. *Page Numbers*:   Justified at the right margin, 1/2 inch from the top of the page (line 4). Consists of the writer's last name, a space, and the page number.

4. *Parenthetical References*:   Appear in one of five formats:

   (a) If the source or author's name is given before the quote—**Example:** (157–58).

   (b) If the author's name is not given before the quote—**Example:** (Adams 157–58).

   (c) If there are two or three authors of the book or article—**Example:** (Jones, Cass, and Noel 199).

   (d) If there are four or more authors—**Example:** (Martin et al. 215–17).

   (e) If there is no author, use a shortened version of the title from where the quote was taken—**Example:** (*Critical Essays* 59).

5. *Short Quotation*:   Enclosed in quotation marks.

6. *Long Quotation*:   No quotation marks, double spaced, left margin indented 10 spaces for all lines of the quotation.

7. *Tables in Academic Reports*:

   (a) Key the table at the left margin, with double spacing and in ruled format.

   (b) Use hyphens instead of underscores for the rules.

   (c) Parenthetical references are keyed a double-space below the table.

Format.   Observe the following rules when keying academic reports:

1. *Spacing*:   Double is used throughout.

2. *Margins*:   All margins are set at default (1 inch). Page numbers are placed 1/2 inch from the top.

3. *Paragraph Indention*:   5 spaces.

---

① Chris Roberts
Mrs. Rose Dirkey
English III
18 April 19--

② Nonverbal Communications

Experts in communications have studied the effects of non-verbal communications on personal relationships. Morrison believes that we give others a nonverbal message by the clothes we wear; this communications has been called an "object language" because it refers to our use of objects such as clothing to communicate with those around us (49).

Your appearance tells a great deal about you. Emphasize your best features by dressing appropriately. You will find when you work in an office that there are varying options about what clothing is appropriate (Stewart 32).

Clothes do say something about us as individuals. If we are to convey a positive message at work, we must put some thought into the clothes that we wear. What we wear will directly impact our ability to get along with people in our work environment
④ (May, Close, and Hammer 224).

Object language also refers to the material things we possess, such as the cars we drive. We send messages out to all of those around us when we possess material items that reflect the kind of person we are (Poulding et al. 316-17).

Henderson 5 ③

"Computers seem to be everywhere today--in businesses, shcools, hospitals, government offices, transportation centers, homes--and it is difficult to imagine a time when there were no computers" (Jackson 34). ⑤

The table below shows the progression of calculating devices that ultimately led to the successful creation of the computer.
Table 1
Significant Advances in the History of Computers

Name	Invention	Date
Blaise Pascal	Mechanical adding machine	1642
Gottfried von Leibniz	Mechanical calculator	1671
Charles Babbage	Analytical engine	1850
Herman Hollerith	Punched-card machine	1887
Howard Aiken	Digital computer	1944

⑦

(Sanders 35-40)

These machines, while far from the computers we know today, were the stepping-stones to today's technology.

Many of the early inventors had the concept of how a computer would work, but the technology was not available to build these machines in their lifetimes. They were unable to see their ideas develop into reality (Dublin 37). ⑥

Some people today think that our computers will be the stepping-stones to much greater achievements than we experience

Hold Those Anchors
For **M** anchor ; L K
For **R** anchor A S D
For **I** anchor ;

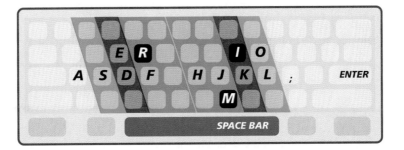

 B. **M** **Key**

Use J finger.

Key each line twice. Repeat if time permits.

3 jjj jmj jmj mjm jmj jjj jmj jmj mjm jmj
4 jmj ham ham jmj mad mad jmj mom mom jmj
5 jmj fold a hem; make a jam; less flame;
6 some messes make a mom mad; half a dome

 **C.** **R** **Key**

Use F finger.

Key each line twice. Repeat if time permits.

7 fff frf frf rfr frf fff frf frf rfr frf
8 frf err err frf for for frf far far frf
9 frf from me; for her marks; more rooms;
10 more doors are far ajar; he reads ahead

 **D.** **I** **Key**

Use K finger.

Key each line twice. Repeat if time permits.

11 kkk kik kik iki kik kkk kik kik iki kik
12 kik rim rim kik lid lid kik dim dim kik
13 kik old mill; for his risk; if she did;
14 his middle silo is loaded; more mirrors

E. **Technique Checkpoint**

Fingertips touching home keys; wrists up.

Key lines 15–16 once. Then repeat lines 3, 7, and 11.

15 his dark oak desk lid is a joke; he did
16 make a firm door from some rare red ash

 **F.** PRETEST

Key lines 17–18 for 1 minute. Repeat if time permits. Keep your eyes on the copy.

17 more sire aims roam same sale ride joke
18 mare hire elms foal lame dark aide jars

Format

1. Use 6 spaces between columns (unless there is a special reason for using more or fewer spaces).
2. Underscore all words in the column headings.
3. Sequence the items, when appropriate, by putting them in alphabetic order, putting them in numeric order, arranging them by dollar amount, and so on.
4. Use a 1-inch line to separate a footnote from the body of the table.

RULED TABLES

Ruled tables are often used for formal reports and research papers. The ruled lines (solid lines of underscores) are keyed before and after the column headings and also at the end of the table.

Format

1. Key the ruled lines the exact width of the table.
2. Single-space before each ruled line, and double-space after each ruled line.
3. If the table ends with a Total line, key a ruled line before and after the Total line.

BOXED TABLES WITH BRACED HEADINGS

Boxed tables contain both horizontal and vertical rules. The vertical rules are used to highlight the columns of the table. A braced column heading is centered over two or more columns.

Format

1. When keying a table with braced headings, determine the placement of the column headings and key them first.
2. Move the cursor above the column headings and above the horizontal ruled line.
3. Center each braced heading over the column headings it braces.
4. Horizontal rules for the braced columns should extend only over the columns that are braced.
5. Vertical rules should stop at the bracing line; they may be entered with the draw feature of your software, if available.

LEADERED TABLES

Leadered tables have keyed rows of periods between the columns. The periods ''lead'' the reader's eyes from column to column within the table.

Format

1. Key rows of solid (or spaced) periods.
2. Leave 1 blank space before the first and after the last period in each row. If you use a leader tab, the leaders may appear without spaces before and after the leader line.
3. Use at least three periods in a row of leaders.

INTERNATIONAL TREATIES AND AGREEMENTS* ↓ 3

Name	Year Adopted	Number of Countries
Common Market	1957	9
Commonwealth of Nations	1931	43
NATO	1949	15
OAS	1948	28

*Yalta not included.

SALES ANALYSIS
Borden Manufacturing Company ↓ 1

Salesperson	Units	Sales
Robert Brazinski	10	$ 427.70
Carol Dawkins	18	769.86
Janice Greene	20	855.40
Jose Herrera	17	727.09
TOTAL	65	$2780.05

SALES ANALYSIS
Borden Manufacturing Company
June 30, 19-- ↓ 1

Salesperson	1st Quarter		2d Quarter	
	Units	Gross Sales	Units	Gross Sales
Robert Brazinski	10	$ 427.70	29	$1240.33
Carol Dawkins	18	769.86	17	727.09
Janice Greene	20	855.40	28	1197.56
Jose Herrera	17	727.09	24	1026.48
Diane Keester	15	641.55	25	1069.25
Joe Yeung	19	812.63	32	1368.64
TOTAL	99	$4234.23	155	$6629.35

SUMMER SEMINAR SCHEDULE

"Time Management" .... June 7-8

"Financial Planning" .... June 11-13

"Budgeting Techniques" .... July 6-9

"Advertising Principles" ...... July 16-18

Note: If you do not use a leader tab, you must look at your work as you key the leaders to be certain you key the exact number of periods for each row.

Eyes on Copy

It will be easier to keep your eyes on the copy if you:

Review the charts for key positions and anchors.

Maintain an even pace.

Resist looking up from your copy.

Key each line twice. Repeat if time permits.

```
19  more more mire mire mere mere mare mare
20  sire sire dire dire fire fire hire hire
21  aims aims arms arms alms alms elms elms
22  roam roam loam loam foam foam foal foal
23  same same fame fame dame dame lame lame
24  sale sale dale dale dare dare dark dark
25  ride ride hide hide side side aide aide
26  joke joke jade jade jams jams jars jars
```

H. POSTTEST

Key lines 17–18 (page 8) for 1 minute. Repeat if time permits. Keep your eyes on the copy. Compare the number of words you keyed with those you keyed in the Pretest.

Lesson 4

Objective   Control T, N, and C keys by touch.
Format   Spacing: single
Margins: default

A. Keyboard Review

Key each line twice. Repeat if time permits.

```
1  asdf jkl; heo; mri; asdf jkl; heo; mri;
2  joke joke safe safe mild mild herd herd
```

Hold Those Anchors
For **T** anchor A S D
For **N** anchor ; L K
For **C** anchor A

B. **T** Key

Use F finger.

Key each line twice. Repeat if time permits.

```
3  fff ftf ftf tft ftf fff ftf ftf tft ftf
4  ftf ate ate ftf toe toe ftf kit kit ftf
5  ftf at it; for the; to them; it is the;
6  it ate at least three; that hat is flat
```

ALIGNMENT

Forms have guide words to show where to key names, dates, amounts, and so on. Forms can be ''hard formats'' (you do not alter the form when entering information) or ''boilerplate.'' When entering information on boilerplate forms, typeover mode and cursor keys must be used so that the format of the form is not changed when information is entered.

MEMOS

1. Use default side margins (1 inch).
2. Begin the guide words of the memo on line 13 (2 inches from the top edge).
3. Key the guide words in all caps, at the left margin, and double-spaced.
4. Set a tab 10 spaces from the margin (2 spaces after MEMO TO:) to key the heading information.
5. Begin the body a triple space below the last line of the heading.
6. Key any notations a double space below the body, beginning at the left margin.

BILLING FORMS

1. Align number columns on the right; center visually within the column.
2. Align word columns on the left; begin 2 spaces after the vertical rule if the form contains vertical rules.
3. Double-space; single-space turnover lines.
4. Begin *Total amount due* at the center of the description column.
5. Do not enter the symbol *$* in money columns.

OPEN TABLES

The basic format for the table is the open table.

Table Parts

1. *Title*: Centered in all capitals and bold.
2. *Subtitle*: Centered with first and main words in capital and lowercase letters.
3. *Column Headings*: Centered over the column (may be blocked at the left of word columns or at the right of number columns).
4. *Body*: The contents of the table.
   Guide Line: The longest item in each column (or column heading), plus the spaces between columns.

↓ 13

```
MEMO TO:   Chris Johnson, Department Head

FROM:      Rebecca Miller, Personnel Manager

DATE:      March 15, 19--

SUBJECT:   Interview Dates ↓₃


The interviews for the candidates who have applied for the sales
position in our Bowling Green office have been scheduled for
March 27, 28, and 29.

Please let me know if you have any conflicts with these dates by
completing and returning the enclosed form. ↓₂

[Your initials]
Enclosure
```

Ajax Manufacturing Co.
123 Main Street
Maimi Beach, FL 33124

INVOICE NO. 1892

TO: Ms. Annette Pierce   DATE: February 20, 19--
     Pierce Enterprises
     4680 First Street
     Wayne, NE 68787   TERMS: 5/10, n/30

Quantity	Description	Unit Price	Amount
12	Model CG18 secretarial desks	458.99	5,507.88
5	Model GC27 executive desks	675.84	3,379.20
12	Model EZ18 secretarial chairs	175.25	2,103.00
5	Model EZ27 executive chairs	255.55	1,277.75
	Total amount due		12,267.83

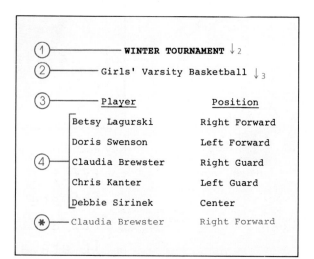

```
①————— WINTER TOURNAMENT ↓₂

②———— Girls' Varsity Basketball ↓₃

③——— Player                    Position

   ┌ Betsy Lagurski            Right Forward

   │ Doris Swenson             Left Forward

④─┤ Claudia Brewster          Right Guard

   │ Chris Kanter              Left Guard

   └ Debbie Sirinek            Center

✱——— Claudia Brewster         Right Forward
```

Hold those Anchors
For **T** anchor A S D
For **N** anchor ; L K
For **C** anchor A

 **N Key**

Use J finger.

Key each line twice. Repeat if time permits.

7 jjj jnj jnj njn jnj jjj jnj jnj njn jnj
8 jnj and and jnj not not jnj ten ten jnj
9 jnj on and on; none inside; nine tones;
10 ten done in an instant; nine kind lines

 C Key

Use D finger.

Key each line twice. Repeat if time permits.

11 ddd dcd dcd cdc dcd ddd dcd dcd cdc dcd
12 dcd arc arc dcd can can dcd ace ace dcd
13 dcd cannot act; in each car; on a deck;
14 call to cancel the tickets; act at once

E. Technique Checkpoint

Eyes on copy.
Hold home key anchors.

Key lines 15–16 once. Then repeat lines 3 (page 9), 7, and 11.

15 here is the carton of jam on this dock;
16 mail file cards to the ten nice stores;

 F. PRETEST

Key lines 17–18 for 1 minute. Repeat if time permits. Keep your eyes on the copy.

17 ink; care none this kick jets farm sail
18 sink came tone then tick jots hand rain

 **G. PRACTICE**

To Increase Skill
Keep eyes on copy.
Maintain good posture.
Speed up on the second keying of each line.

Key each line twice. Repeat if time permits.

19 ink; ink; link link rink rink sink sink
20 care care cake cake cane cane came came
21 none none lone lone done done tone tone
22 this this thin thin than than then then
23 kick kick sick sick lick lick tick tick
24 jets jets lets lets lots lots jots jots
25 farm farm harm harm hard hard hand hand
26 sail sail said said raid raid rain rain

pany address (street address plus city, state, and ZIP Code). An envelope addressed to a person at home usually includes his or her name; street address; and city, state, and ZIP Code. In either case, a courtesy title (such as Ms. or Mr.) should precede the addressee's name.

On either a small or large envelope, begin keying the addressee's name 2 inches down from the top edge (line 13). The horizontal placement of the mailing address is as follows:

On a small envelope: 2.5 inches from the left edge.

On a large envelope: 4 inches from the left edge.

Single-space the mailing address, and block all lines on the left. Leave only 1 space between the state and the ZIP Code.

Special Directions. Key an on-arrival direction (such as *Personal* or *Confidential*) 1.5 inches from the top edge (line 10) starting 1/2 inch from the left edge. Key a mailing direction (such as *Registered* or *Special Delivery*) so that it ends about 1/2 inch from the right edge (below the stamp). Use all caps; do not underscore.

Preparing Envelopes With a Computer. Many word processing programs will allow you to save time when preparing envelopes by (1) automatically addressing the envelope, (2) storing an envelope format for envelopes, (3) copying the inside address to the envelope, and (4) converting an envelope address to all capital letters.

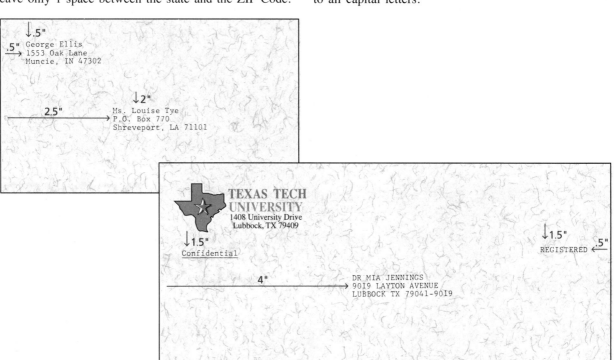

FOLDING LETTERS

For Small Envelopes, No. 6 3/4 (6 1/2 by 3 5/8 inches)

1. Fold up the bottom edge to 3/8 inch from the top edge.
2. Fold the right-hand third over to the left.
3. Fold the left-hand third over to 3/8 inch from the right edge.
4. Insert the last crease into the envelope first, with the flap facing up.

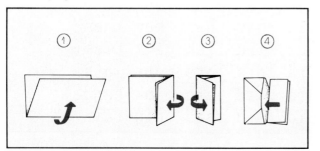

For Large Envelopes, No. 10 (9 1/2 by 4 1/8 inches)

1. Fold up the bottom third of the letter.
2. Fold the top third down to 3/8 inch from the bottom edge.
3. Insert the last crease into the envelope first, with the flap facing up.

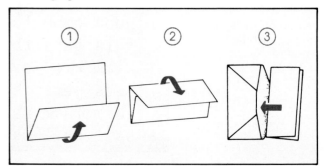

Key lines 17–18 (page 10) for 1 minute. Repeat if time permits. Keep your eyes on the copy. Compare the number of words you keyed with those you keyed in the Pretest.

Lesson 5 REVIEW

Objective Strengthen key control.
Format Spacing: single
Margins: default

Check Your Posture
Feet—apart, on floor.
Back—erect, leaning forward.
Hands—close together, fingers curved, low.
Eyes—focused on copy.

A. Keyboard Review

Key each line twice. Repeat if time permits.

1 fade home nice kite joke time loan car;
2 toes jell lace sods from jars sane the;

B. Enter/Return Key

A technique drill.

Key each line once. Return after each semicolon, and continue to key smoothly. Repeat if time permits.

3 hide from a mad animal; do not call it; [R]
4 it is not an old dresser; it is a fake; [R]
5 the jelled mold looks fine; taste some;

C. Concentration

A technique drill.

Keep eyes on copy.

Fill in the missing vowels shown at the left as you key each line once.

O 6 d- n-t ch-ke in that sm-ke; r-ll cl-ser
I 7 f-n-sh th-s s-de f-rst; -t -s th-s k-nd
E 8 h-r can- f-ll off th- f-nc-; h-r- it is
A 9 c-ncel th-t c-ke s-le; r-in is forec-st

D. PRETEST

Key lines 10–11 for 1 minute. Repeat if time permits. Keep your eyes on the copy.

10 car; heal dose sock time malt jail find
11 jam; fore rest near deer hack fill sink

TWO-PAGE LETTERS

A second-page heading for a letter should be keyed on plain paper and should include the addressee's name, the page number, and the date. Start keying the heading on line 7; use one of the styles illustrated below. Double-space after the heading before continuing the letter.

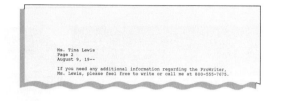

LETTER FORMATS

Modified-Block Format.   The most popular format for business letters is the modified-block format. As shown below, in this format the date line and the closing lines (complimentary closing and writer's name and/or title) begin at the center. All other lines begin at the left margin.

Modified-Block Format With Indented Paragraphs.   This format is a variation of the modified-block format in which the first line of each paragraph is indented 5 spaces.

Block Format.   In the block format, all lines begin at the left margin, as illustrated below.

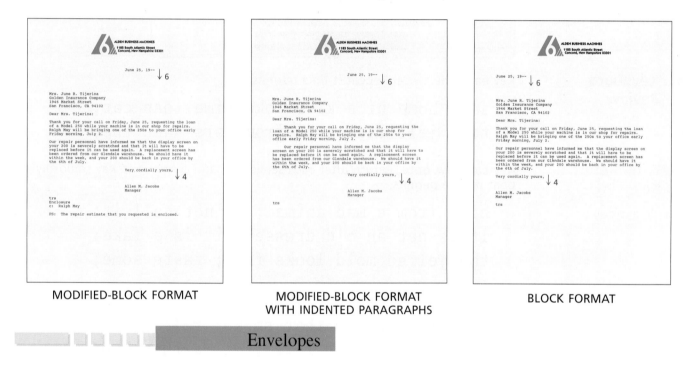

MODIFIED-BLOCK FORMAT

MODIFIED-BLOCK FORMAT
WITH INDENTED PARAGRAPHS

BLOCK FORMAT

Envelopes

ADDRESSING ENVELOPES

Every envelope should include the writer's name and return address and the addressee's full mailing address. (See the illustrations on page 343.)

Return Address.   A printed return address gives the company name; street address; and city, state, and ZIP Code. If possible, the writer's name should be keyed above the printed return address, aligned at the left with the top line of printing.

If the return address is not printed, then it should be keyed, blocked, and single-spaced, beginning 1/2 inch down (line 4) and 1/2 inch (5 spaces) in from the left edge. (**Note:** To access the 1/2-inch positions, you may have to change your software defaults.)

Mailing Address.   An envelope addressed to a person at his or her place of business generally includes the addressee's name and business title, the company name, and the complete com-

To prevent omitted letters in words:
Silently say each letter to yourself.
Strive for even rhythm.

To prevent omitted spaces between words:
Do not rest palms on keyboard.
Think "space" for each space bar stroke.
Hold thumb slightly above space bar.

Key each line twice. Keep your eyes on the copy. Repeat if time permits.

```
12  car; car; far; far; jar; jar; tar; tar;
13  heal heal seal seal meal meal deal deal
14  dose dose hose hose rose rose nose nose
15  sock sock rock rock dock dock mock mock

16  time time dime dime mime mime lime lime
17  malt malt halt halt half half calf calf
18  jail jail fail fail sail sail nail nail
19  find find hind hind mind mind kind kind

20  jam; jam; ham; ham; ram; ram; cam; cam;
21  fore fore more more tore tore core core
22  rest rest nest nest test test jest jest
23  near near fear fear hear hear dear dear

24  deer deer seer seer jeer jeer leer leer
25  hack hack lack lack sack sack tack tack
26  fill fill dill dill kill kill hill hill
27  sink sink mink mink link link oink oink
```

F. POSTTEST

Key lines 10–11 (page 11) for 1 minute. Repeat if time permits. Keep your eyes on the copy. Compare the number of words you keyed with those you keyed in the Pretest.

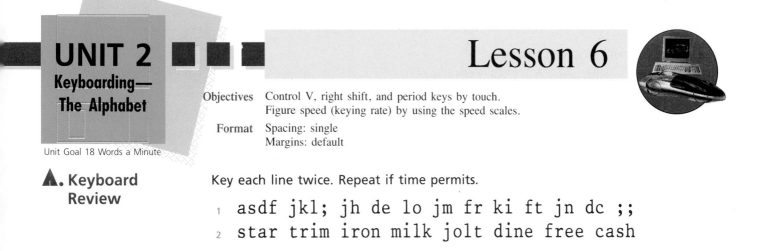

UNIT 2
Keyboarding— The Alphabet

Unit Goal 18 Words a Minute

Lesson 6

Objectives Control V, right shift, and period keys by touch.
Figure speed (keying rate) by using the speed scales.

Format Spacing: single
Margins: default

A. Keyboard Review

Key each line twice. Repeat if time permits.

```
1  asdf jkl; jh de lo jm fr ki ft jn dc ;;
2  star trim iron milk jolt dine free cash
```

BUSINESS LETTER PARTS

A business letter contains a *heading*, an *opening*, a *body*, and a *closing*.

The *heading* consists of (1) the printed letterhead and (2) the date the letter is keyed.

The *opening* includes (3) the inside address (the name and address of the party to whom the letter is being sent), and (4) the salutation. If (5) a subject line is used, it is keyed a double space below the salutation.

The *body* is (6) the message of the letter. Single-space lines; double-space between paragraphs.

The *closing* includes the following parts: (7) the complimentary closing (such as *Yours truly*, or *Cordially yours*,), which is keyed a double space below the last line of the body, (8) the handwritten signature of the person who composed the letter, (9) the writer's identification (name and title), and (10) the reference initials of the writer and/or keyboarder. Note in the first illustration that a colon is keyed after the salutation (4) and that a comma is keyed after the complimentary closing (7). This use of the colon and comma after these opening and closing lines is known as *mixed punctuation style*. If no punctuation marks are used after these lines, the style is known as *open punctuation style*.

The closing may also include the following optional parts: (11) an enclosure notation (specifying that something is enclosed with the letter), (12) a copy (*c*) notation (specifying that copies of the letter have been sent to other parties), and (13) a postscript (an added message that, when used, is always keyed as the final item in a letter). In addition, some companies include (14) the firm name, which, if used, is keyed a double space below the complimentary closing in all-capital letters.

Three additional letter parts are the attention line, the continuation-page heading, and the blind copy (*bc*) notation. The *attention line* (if used, it directs the letter to a specific person or department) can be the first line of the inside address or a separate line between the inside address and salutation. The *continuation-page heading*, used on continuation pages for long letters, indicates the addressee's name, the page number, and the date. The *bc notation* is a copy notation that appears only on the copies; the addressee does not see who has received copies.

PERSONAL-BUSINESS LETTER PARTS

A personal-business letter also has a heading, an opening, a body, and a closing, but the personal-business letter usually differs from the business letter in the following respects:

1. The letter is keyed on plain paper rather than on letterhead paper.

2. The writer's identification consists of the writer's name, street address, and city/ state/ZIP code.

3. Reference initials are omitted.

Personal-business letters may also include copy notations, enclosure notations, and so on.

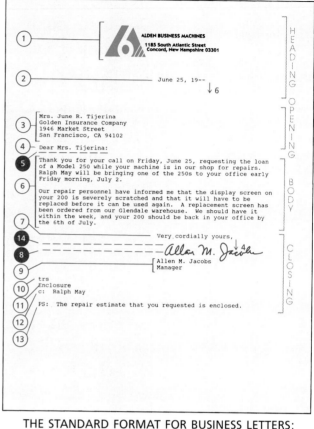

THE STANDARD FORMAT FOR BUSINESS LETTERS: MODIFIED-BLOCK STYLE

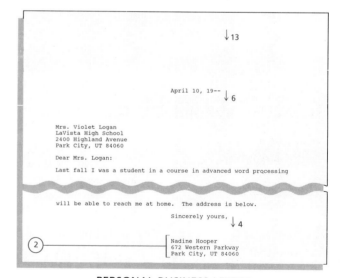

PERSONAL-BUSINESS LETTER

Hold Those Anchors
For **V** anchor A S D
For **Right Shift** anchor J
For **.** anchor ; or J

B.  **Key**

Use F finger.

Key each line twice. Repeat if time permits.

3 fff fvf fvf vfv fvf fff fvf fvf vfv fvf
4 fvf via via fvf eve eve fvf vie vie fvf
5 fvf via a van; move over; vie for love;
6 even vitamins have flavor; vote to move

C. **Right Shift Key**

Use Sem finger.

Use the right shift key to capitalize letters keyed with the left hand. To make the reach easier, curl the second and third fingers of your right hand as you complete the following three-step sequence:

① **Cap!** Keeping J finger in home position, extend Sem finger to press the right shift key; hold it down.

② **Strike!** While the shift key is still down, use the left hand to strike the letter that is to be capitalized.

③ **Home!** Release the shift key, and return finger to home position.

For capital A, you would think "Cap!" as you press the right shift, "A!" as you strike the letter, and "Home!" as fingers snap back to home position.

Key each line twice. Repeat if time permits.

7 ;;; S;; S;; ;;; C;; C;; ;;; T;; T;; ;;;
8 ;;; Sam Sam ;;; Cal Cal ;;; Ted Ted ;;;
9 ;;; Save Tom; Rick ran; Ed likes Flint;
10 Aaron and Sam moved; Vera loved Florida

D.  **Key**

Use L finger.

Key each line twice. Repeat if time permits.

11 lll l.l l.l .l. l.l lll l.l l.l .l. lll
12 l.l Dr. Dr. l.l Sr. Sr. l.l Fr. Fr. l.l
13 l.l vs. Co. St. Rd. Ave. div. ctn. std.
14 Ark. Del. Fla. Colo. Tenn. Conn. Calif.

Reference Section

Centering

Horizontal centering is used to position copy horizontally in the center of the page—that is, so that there are equal margins on both sides of the copy. Remember that the width of standard-size paper is 8 1/2 inches (85 pica spaces or 102 elite spaces).

Most word processing software packages will center material automatically in a horizontal position between margins when a function key is depressed. If not, you must place the cursor halfway between the margins and backspace once for every two characters or spaces to be centered.

Vertical centering is used to position copy between the top and the bottom margins—that is, so that there are equal margins above and below the copy. Remember, the length of standard-size paper is 11 inches (66 lines).

Many word processing software packages will center material automatically in a vertical position between the top and bottom margin when a function key is depressed. If not, follow these steps to center copy vertically on a sheet of standard-size paper:

1. Count the lines (including blanks) that the copy will occupy when keyed.
2. Subtract that number from the available number of lines on your paper.
3. Divide the difference by 2 (drop any fraction).
4. Add 1 to the result; that is the line on which you should begin.

Proofreader's Marks

Shown below are the standard proofreader's marks used in business to show changes that are to be made in draft copy. The marks with their definitions are shown in column 1. Column 2 shows an example of each mark in draft copy. Column 3 shows how the final copy should appear.

Proofreaders' Mark	Draft	Final Copy	Proofreaders' Mark	Draft	Final Copy
ss Single-space	ss first line / second line	first line / second line	Move as shown	it is (not)	it is
ds Double-space	ds first line / second line	first line / second line	Transpose	is / it so	it is not so
Move to left	let us	let us	Omit space	to gether	together
Move to right	it is so	it is so	Delete letter	error	error
5 Indent 5 spaces	5 Let it be	Let it be	Delete word	it may be	it may
Center	TITLE	TITLE	Change word (new word)	word	and so it (so)
¶ Paragraph	¶ If he is	If he is	Delete and close up	judgement	judgment
Spell out	the only ①	the only one	Don't delete	can we go	can we go
Capitalize	mrs. Wade	Mrs. Wade	Insert space	Itmay be	It may be
Lowercase letter (make letter small)	Business	business	Insert word or letter	and it (so)	and so it
			Insert punctuation mark	Shes not	She's not,
			Insert a period	other way	other way.

E. Punctuation Spacing

Space twice after a period at the end of a sentence. Do not space after the end of a line unless using word wrap.

Space once after a period used with an abbreviation and after a semicolon.

F. Technique Checkpoint

Eyes on copy.
Hold home key anchors.

G. Figuring Speed

Key each line twice. Repeat if time permits.

15 Close the door. The draft is too cold.
16 Find a match. Ask Val to start a fire.

Key each line twice. Repeat if time permits.

17 Dr. T. Vincent sees me; he made a cast.
18 East Ave. veers left; Ash Rd. is ahead.

Key lines 19–21 once. Then repeat lines 3, 7, and 11 (page 13).

19 Dr. V. Soo is on call; he asked Erv for
20 five half liters of milk. Ask Victoria
21 to deliver it to the office in her van.

① **Key for 1 minute;** then find your "average" words. Every 5 strokes (letters and spaces) counts as 1 average word. Therefore, a 40-stroke line is 8 words long; two such lines are 16 words; and so on.

② For an incomplete line, use the scale (below line 23 on this page); the number above which you stop is your word count for the incomplete line. **Example:** If you key lines 22 and 23 (see below) and start over, completing the word *task* in line 22, you have keyed 16 + 2 = 18 words in 1 minute.

H. PRETEST

Key lines 22–23 for 1 minute. Repeat if time permits. Keep your eyes on the copy.

22 jade task vice none fade mask rice hone 8
23 fame mast ride hold came fast hide fold 16
     | 1 | 2 | 3 | 4 | 5 | 6 | 7 | 8

I. PRACTICE

Build speed on repeated word patterns.

Key each line twice. Repeat if time permits.

24 jade jade fade fade fame fame came came
25 task task mask mask mast mast fast fast
26 vice vice rice rice ride ride hide hide
27 none none hone hone hold hold fold fold

J. POSTTEST

Key lines 22–23 for 1 minute. Repeat if time permits. Keep your eyes on the copy. Compare the number of words you keyed with those you keyed in the Pretest.

Table

Here is the list of businesses that I have prepared for our new contacts in the North Houston area. Please prepare a mailing list for all these company names and addresses. Give it the title NORTH HOUSTON CUSTOMER LIST, and date it today.

Target Container Company, 19784 Kuykendahl Road, 77379
Spring Manufacturing Company, 21408 Interstate 45, 77373
Williams Industries, 30131 Foster Street, 77373
Robbins Insulation, 26893 Glen Loch Drive, 77381
Dyment Industries, 26457 Greenfield Street, 77373
Southern Financial Services, 26105 Hardy Road, 77373
Shaddix Marine Company, 28471 Interstate 45, 77380
Spring Construction Company, 20763 Kuykendahl Road, 77379
Hoyt Bronson Electric, Inc., 26811 Maplewood Drive, 77373
North Metro Lumber Company, 23748 Rayford Road, 77379

Table

Prepare the following table, which summarizes our quarterly activity.

PROHELP TEMPORARY AGENCY

3d Quarter Report

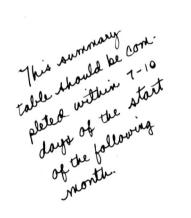

This summary table should be completed within 7-10 days of the start of the following month.

Position Filled	July ~~January~~	August ~~February~~	September ~~March~~
Data Processing	425	417	436
Word Processing	481	492	508
~~Typist~~ Office Assistant	472	504	556
Secretary	514	527	539
File Clerk	301	386	394
Data Entry Clerk	255	395	276
Desktop Publishing	27	55	67
Software Analyst	18	32	44
Computer Operator	51	63	56
Total	2,544	2,871	2,876

Form Letter

Mr. Ahlborg has decided to use the letter he dictated to you earlier as a form letter to be sent out to people who are interested in the opportunities available with ProHelp. Prepare two letters to the following individuals:

1. Joyce H. Mitchell, 13890 Queensbury Lane, Houston, TX 77079.
2. Benjamin R. Vickery, 4872 Strawberry Road, Pasadena, TX 77504.

Lesson 7

Objective Control W, comma, and G keys by touch.

Format Spacing: single
Margins: default

A. Keyboard Review

Hold Those Anchors
For **W** anchor F
For **,** anchor ;
For **G** anchor A S D

Key each line twice. Repeat if time permits.

1 sake card Rev. jest chin fail mist not;
2 Val loves that fame; Rick did not join.

B.  **W** Key

Use S finger.

Key each line twice. Repeat if time permits.

3 sss sws sws wsw sws sss sws sws wsw sws
4 sws saw saw sws own own sws was was sws
5 sws sow winter wheat; white swans swim;
6 We walked while we watched some whales.

C.  **,** Key

Use K finger.
Space once after a comma.

Key each line twice. Repeat if time permits.

7 kkk k,k k,k ,k, k,k kkk k,k k,k ,k, k,k
8 k,k an, an, k,k or, or, k,k it, it, k,k
9 k,k as soon as, two or three, if it is,
10 Van, her friend, lives in Flat, Alaska.

D.  **G** Key

Use F finger.

Key each line twice. Repeat if time permits.

11 fff fgf fgf gfg fgf fff fgf fgf gfg fgf
12 fgf get get fgf egg egg fgf leg leg fgf
13 fgf sing a song, saw a log, give a dog,
14 Gil gave a large sagging gift of games.

Dictated Letter

Key the following letter to Pamela Frazier, 10734 Riverview Way, Houston, TX 77042. The letter is unedited—watch for spelling and punctuation errors!

thank you for your request for information about prohelp. as you know from reading your local newspaper prohelp is the leading temporary agensy in the houston metropolatan area. we pride ourselves in placing more temporary workers in the workplace than any other houston placement agency. i have enclosed several broshures about the various opportunities available with prohelp. if you want imediate employment we can fullfil your need. if you want to obtain initial job training before job placement we can again meet your needs. if you would like to come in for a personall interview please complete the enclosed education/experience background questionairre. then call me at 555-4357 to arrange for your interview. sincerely v. allen ahlborg assistant director

Financial Statement

Prepare the following balance sheet. I need to send it to our auditors next week.

ProHelp

BALANCE SHEET

For the Quarter Ending September 30, 19—

ASSETS
Cash	$8,500.00	
Accounts Receivable	1,200.50	
Equipment	7,240.25	
Supplies	482.73	
Total Assets		$17,423.48

LIABILITIES
Accounts Payable	$2,275.35	
Contract Cancellation	782.90	
Total Liabilities		$ 3,058.25

EQUITY
Capital	$9,230.50	
Net Income	5,134.73	
Total Equity		14,365.23
Total Liabilities and Equity		$17,423.48

E. Technique Checkpoint

Hold home key anchors. Elbows in.

Key lines 15–17 once. Then repeat lines 3, 7, and 11 (page 15).

15 While we watched, the rival team jogged   8

16 to the edge of the field. That win was   16

17 two in a row; the team likes victories.   24

| 1 | 2 | 3 | 4 | 5 | 6 | 7 | 8

F. Counting Errors

Compare these lines with lines 18–20 below.

[1]Wamda wore [2]redsocks; Sadie wore [3]green,
[4]   Carl [5]joked with [6]Al ice, Fran, Edith.
Frank sold [7]sold Dave [8]old an washing [9]mshcone .

1. Count as an error any word that contains an incorrect character.

2. Count a word as an error if the spacing after it is incorrect.

3. Count a word as an error if the punctuation after it is incorrect.

4. Count each failure to follow directions in spacing, indenting, and so on, as an error.

5. Count a word as an error if it contains a space.

6. Count each word that is omitted as an error.

7. Count each word that is repeated as an error.

8. Count each set of transposed words as an error.

9. Count only 1 error against a word, no matter how many errors it contains.

Key each line once. Proofread carefully and note your errors.

18 Wanda wore red socks; Sadie wore green.

19 Carl joked with Alice, Fran, and Edith.

20 Frank sold Dave an old washing machine.

G. PRETEST

Take a 1-minute timing on lines 21–22. Proofread, note your errors, and figure your speed.

21 ring snow west tows ink, glow jot, hag,   8

22 king scow well down elf, crew mow, sag,   16

| 1 | 2 | 3 | 4 | 5 | 6 | 7 | 8

Key each line twice. Repeat if time permits.

H. PRACTICE

Wrists up—do not rest palms on keyboard.

Fingers curved—move from home position only when necessary.

23 ring ring wing wing sing sing king king

24 snow snow show show stow stow scow scow

25 west west went went welt welt well well

(Continued on next page)

Form Letter

I would like to send the following letter to selected businesses in the North Houston business districts, primarily around the Spring area. Prepare the letter. Omit the inside address and salutation—we'll add those parts later when we merge the content of this letter with a selected list of businesses I have prepared.

I'd like this ready by the end of the week.

HAVE YOU EVER...

1. ... found yourself short-handed when unexpected emergencies have caused a temporary reduction in your office staff?

2. ... needed an office worker who could work with a particular software package on a short-term basis?

3. ... needed some temporary help to pull you through the crunch of meeting a project deadline?

If you are like most businesses, you answered "YES" to one or all of the above questions. Pro Help Temporary Agency can assist you in eliminating staffing problems such as these. Our temporary employees are well trained in all of the latest technological software and hardware; we can respond to your request for temporary help on a moment's notice, and we guarantee our work.

If you would like to use our services, please complete and return the enclosed card, or call me direct at 555-4357 – that's 555 - HELP - for assistance in relieving any temporary staffing problems you might have. Sincerely,

Please use assistant director as my title.

26	tows tows town town gown gown down down
27	ink, ink, ilk, ilk, elk, elk, elf, elf,
28	glow glow grow grow grew grew crew crew
29	jot, jot, hot, hot, how, how, mow, mow,
30	hag, hag, rag, rag, wag, wag, sag, sag,

I. POSTTEST

Take a 1-minute timing on lines 21–22 (page 16). Proofread, note your errors, and figure your speed. Compare your performance with the Pretest.

Lesson 8

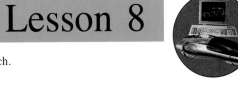

Objective Control B, U, and left shift keys by touch.

Format Spacing: single
Margins: default

A. Keyboard Review

Key each line twice. Repeat if time permits.

1 foal jive them corn wick wags logo dim,
2 Frank mailed the jewels that Coco made.

Hold Those Anchors
For **B** anchor A S
For **U** anchor ; L K
For **Left Shift** anchor F

B.  **Key**

Use F finger.

Key each line twice. Repeat if time permits.

3 fff fbf fbf bfb fbf fff fbf fbf bfb fbf
4 fbf ebb ebb fbf bag bag fbf rob rob fbf
5 fbf a back bend, a bent bin, a big bag,
6 This boat has been in a babbling brook.

B. Preview Practice

Key each line twice as a preview to the 5-minute timings below.

Accuracy 6 is temporary available tremendous experience administrative
Speed   7 have wide work lead just like some that from near that such

C. 5-Minute Timings

Take two 5-minute timings on lines 8–25. Proofread, note your errors, and figure your speed.

8 A temporary agency is a practical place to obtain work   12
9 experience, and it can quite often lead to a permanent job. 24
10 Part-time work may be just the perfect thing for you if you 36
11 are not looking for a full-time position but you would like 48
12 to get some experience that would lead to permanent work in 60
13 the near future. Part-time work can provide dozens of jobs 72
14 from which to choose; there's probably not another position 84
15 that has such a wide variety.   90

16   Many temporary positions are available in clerical and   102
17 secretarial areas. With the advent of computers in the job 114
18 market, these fields have seen tremendous growth. Numerous 126
19 jobs are now open for people to work in positions like data 138
20 entry clerk, administrative secretary, and typist. Jobs in 150
21 these fields are likely to grow for many years to come. If 162
22 you decide to work in one of these jobs, you will certainly 174
23 learn how to work with all kinds of people. These contacts 186
24 will be very helpful if you decide to change to a full-time 198
25 position.   200

| 1 | 2 | 3 | 4 | 5 | 6 | 7 | 8 | 9 | 10 | 11 | 12 SI 1.49

SIMULATION 2
Working for a Temporary Agency

You work for a temporary agency, ProHelp, in Houston, Texas. The address of ProHelp is 6389 Renwick Drive, Houston, TX 77081. Your supervisor's name is V. Allen Ahlborg. Mr. Ahlborg prefers to use the modified-block style for letters. Today is Thursday, October 10, 19—.

Priority Sheet and Work Log

Read through the entire simulation, and then complete the priority sheet. Keep an accurate work log as you complete each job.

C.  U Key

Use J finger.

Key each line twice. Repeat if time permits.

7 jjj juj juj uju juj jjj juj juj uju juj
8 juj flu flu juj urn urn juj jug jug juj
9 juj just a job, jumbo jet, jungle bugs,
10 Business students show unusual success.

D. Left Shift Key

Use A finger.

Use the left shift key to capitalize letters keyed with the right hand. To make the reach easier, curl the second and third fingers of your left hand as you complete the following three-step sequence:

① **Cap!** Keeping F finger in home position, extend A finger to press the left shift key; hold it down.

② **Strike!** While the shift key is still down, use the right hand to strike the letter that is to be capitalized.

③ **Home!** Release the shift key, and return fingers to home position.

Key each line twice. Repeat if time permits.

11 aaa Laa Laa aaa Jaa Jaa aaa Kaa Kaa aaa
12 aaa Lee Lee aaa Joe Joe aaa Kim Kim aaa
13 aaa Uncle Hal fell; Jan left; Nora ran;
14 Kate and Mona went to Ohio in November.

E. Technique Checkpoint

Keep F or J anchored when shifting.

Key lines 15–17 once. Then repeat lines 3 (page 17), 7, and 11.

15 Nan told Jake and Louise that she would   8
16 go with Kim to get bread for our lunch,   16
17 but Brent brought enough bread for all.   24
   | 1 | 2 | 3 | 4 | 5 | 6 | 7 | 8

F. PRETEST

Take two 1-minute timings on lines 18–19. Proofread, note your errors, and figure your speed.

18 bear hunk dole sum, bran rest just craw   8
19 beef just bout sun, blot vast gist bran   16
   | 1 | 2 | 3 | 4 | 5 | 6 | 7 | 8

(File name: C17.145)

Let's try to make tomorrow's edition if possible.

Use your desktop publishing software, if available, and give the highlighted sections a different point size.

Display

Use a 40-space line (2.25-inch side margins).
We have a new line of computers coming out next week, and I'd like to run an ad in the *Minneapolis Star Tribune* to announce this new product. Prepare an ad from the information I've given you below.

* * * BLAZING PERFORMANCE * * *

AT THE BEST PRICE ANYWHERE!!!

Now you can get 486 performance at a 386 price . . . from Total Computers at 4325 Edgemont Street in St. Paul. Our new Telecom Computers give you all the following features:

* **80486 32-bit processor**
* **Zero wait-state**
* **4-Mbyte RAM**
* **120-Mbyte hard drive**
* **VGA 14″ Teleview monitor**
* **2-year warranty**

ALL OF THESE FEATURES FOR ONLY $1,250

Call us now at 612-555-3875 for further information, or stop in at our Edgemont showroom to try out the all-new Telecom Computers.

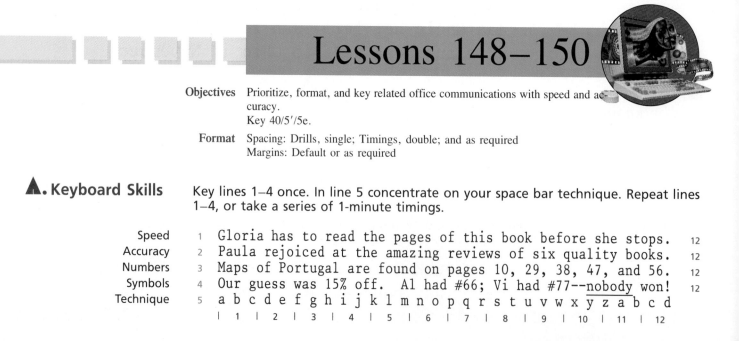

Lessons 148–150

Objectives	Prioritize, format, and key related office communications with speed and accuracy. Key 40/5′/5e.
Format	Spacing: Drills, single; Timings, double; and as required Margins: Default or as required

▲ Keyboard Skills

Key lines 1–4 once. In line 5 concentrate on your space bar technique. Repeat lines 1–4, or take a series of 1-minute timings.

Speed	1 Gloria has to read the pages of this book before she stops.	12
Accuracy	2 Paula rejoiced at the amazing reviews of six quality books.	12
Numbers	3 Maps of Portugal are found on pages 10, 29, 38, 47, and 56.	12
Symbols	4 Our guess was 15% off. Al had #66; Vi had #77--nobody won!	12
Technique	5 a b c d e f g h i j k l m n o p q r s t u v w x y z a b c d	

| 1 | 2 | 3 | 4 | 5 | 6 | 7 | 8 | 9 | 10 | 11 | 12

G. PRACTICE

Check Your Feet. They Should Be:

In front of the chair.

Firmly on the floor, square, flat.

Apart, with 6 or 7 inches between the ankles.

So placed that one foot is a little ahead of the other.

Key each line twice. Repeat if time permits.

20 bear beat beam beak bead bean been beef
21 hunk hulk bulk bunk dunk dusk dust just
22 dole doll boll bold bolt boot boat bout
23 sum, hum, gum, gun, bun, run, nun, sun,
24 bran brad bred bled blew blow blob blot
25 rest nest west best lest jest vest vast
26 just rust dust gust must mist list gist
27 craw crew crow brow brew bred brad bran

H. POSTTEST

Take two 1-minute timings on lines 18–19 (page 18). Proofread, note your errors, and figure your speed. Compare your performance with the Pretest.

Lesson 9

Objective Control Q and slash keys by touch.

Format Spacing: single

Margins: default

A. Keyboard Review

Key each line twice. Repeat if time permits.

1 club face when silk mold brag java blue
2 Jama went hiking, but Cora waved flags.

Hold Those Anchors
For **Q** anchor F
For **/** anchor J

B. Q Key

Use A finger.

Key each line twice. Repeat if time permits.

3 aaa aqa aqa qaq aqa aaa aqa aqa qaq aqa
4 aqa que que aqa qui qui aqa quo quo aqa
5 aqa half quid, quick quail, quit quest,
6 The quints squabbled on a square quilt.
7 The quartet requested squid and squash.

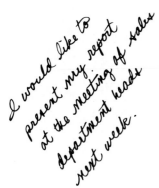

I would like to present my report at the meeting of sales department heads next week.

REPORT ON TELECOM COMPUTERS

Prepared by Shelly Bryant

Introduction

The project team for investigating the capabilities of the Telecom Computer was organized on March 1, 19—. After considerable testing of the Model 486 Telecom Computers, a survey was prepared and sent to six computer users who were responsible for testing various software packages on the Model 486. Data from this testing environment were compiled, and the results are summarized below.

Procedures → To determine satisfactory processing times for various leading software packages, all six computer users were provided with identical packages. Furthermore, identical tasks were identified for all users. For example, all 486s were required to perform multicolumn layouts, merging, spell checking, thesaurus access, headers, and footers when the word processing software was run. Similar routines were required for the spreadsheet, database, graphics, and desktop publishing packages. Five packages in each category (for a total of 25 packages) were evaluated during the testing period. Performance time for all major operations was recorded to the nearest second, with repeat trials run to verify the accuracy of all times recorded.

Findings → The findings of the desktop publishing section of this study are revealed in Table 1. Separate reports have also been prepared for the word processing, spreadsheet, database, and graphics capabilities. It should be emphasized that this report does not attempt to evaluate the effectiveness of the software packages themselves. Rather, this report reveals the speed at which the Telecom 486 can run the tested software packages. The scores revealed in Table 1 were assigned from rankings of 1 to 10, with "1" considered the slowest speed and "10" the fastest speed.

TABLE 1
Telecom 486 Performance Tests

DTP Package	User 1	User 2	User 3	User 4	User 5	User 6
Page Maker	10	9	10	8	10	10
Quark Xpress	7	8	8	9	10	9
Ready Set Go	10	10	9	10	9	10
Springboard	7	8	10	9	8	8
Ventura	10	10	9	8	10	7

Recommendations

Based on the data forwarded from each of the six testing stations, it is the recommendation of the Telecom Computer Project Team that Total Computers continue to stock the Telecom Computer, Model 486, and provide marketing support for its continued sales.

Hold Those Anchors
For **Q** anchor F
For **/** anchor J

C. / Key

Use Sem finger.
Do not space before or after a slash (diagonal).

Key each line twice. Repeat if time permits.

8 ;;; ;/; ;/; /;/ /;/ ;;; ;/; ;/; /;/ /;/
9 ;/; her/him ;/; us/them ;/; his/her ;/;
10 ;/; slow/fast, walk/ride, debit/credit,
11 The fall/winter catalog has new colors.
12 The on/off button is on the right side.

D. Technique Checkpoint

Elbows in.
Hold home key anchors.

Key lines 13–15 once. Then repeat lines 3 (page 19) and 8.

13 Quinn requested the squad to give equal   8
14 time to all junior/senior field events,   16
15 but no one entered the squat/run races.   24
   | 1 | 2 | 3 | 4 | 5 | 6 | 7 | 8

E. 12-Second Timings

Compute Speed for 12 Seconds: Multiply words keyed in 12 seconds by 5 or count each stroke as 1 word to get wam speed.

Take three 12-second timings on each line, or key each line three times. Use the scale below line 18 to determine your words a minute (wam). For example, if you stopped after the word *she* in line 16, your speed would be 20 wam.

16 Lisa can work if she makes good grades.
17 This band will march first at the game.
18 Curt ran to the goal line just in time.
   | 5   10   15   20   25   30   35   40

F. PRETEST

Take two 1-minute timings on lines 19–20. Proofread, note your errors, and figure your speed.

19 quit slot aqua vane mile quid shut walk   8
20 swat brad cube jail fate boat seek/find   16
   | 1 | 2 | 3 | 4 | 5 | 6 | 7 | 8

(File names:
T69.145 and T70.145)

I have prepared a list of the top ten customers for the month of June. Please prepare two single-spaced tables: (1) Names and addresses only; four columns—Name, Street Address, City and State, ZIP Code; arrange alphabetically by last name; open format. (2) Names and Total Monthly Purchases; two columns, arranged from largest to smallest dollar amount; leadered format; 2-inch side margins.

Key names in inverse order: last name, first name

James Sheely, 3424 Newton Ave., North Anoka, MN 55303, $4,540.

Pattie Wisner, 6300 Willow Lane, Minneapolis, MN 55430, $6,345.

Grace Liles, 645 Walnut Street, St. Paul, MN 55113, $5,000.

Dale Bowen, 204 Lawrence Drive, Elk River, MN 55330, $4,420.

Sherry Zurita, 40 Cooper Drive, Hibbing, MN 55746, $4,890.

David Graves, 9428 Wayzata Blvd., Minneapolis, MN 55426, $6,750.

Gregory Maritz, 758 Calhoun Street, Rochester, MN 55903, $3,775.

Dalores Rowe, 280 Bidwell Street, St. Paul, MN 55118, $4,895.

Emily Meadows, 230 Westwood Road, White Bear Lake, MN 55100, $5,400.

Opal Price, 129 Main Street, Jordan, MN 55352, $6,700.

Form Letter Fill-Ins

(File names:
L88A.145–L88C.145)

The winners of the drawing for June are Wisner, Liles, and Meadows. Please send each of them the form letter.

Report

(File name: R62.145)

As the chairperson of a project team that has been examining the capabilities of the new Telecom Computer, I am responsible for preparing the final report on our project. Please key the following report (page 334) that I have written.

G. PRACTICE

To Build Skill:
Key each line twice.

Speed up the second time you key the line.

Key each line twice. Repeat if time permits.

```
21  quit suit slit slid slim swim swam swat
22  slot slat flat flag quag brag brat brad
23  aqua quad luau lube tube tuba Cuba cube
24  vane vale male mall gall fall fail jail
25  mile vile Nile nice rice race face fate
26  quid ruin rude rode mode moat goat boat
27  shut/ajar mice/rats soft/hard hide/seek
28  walk/ride hike/bike cats/dogs lose/find
```

H. POSTTEST

Take two 1-minute timings on lines 19–20 (page 20). Proofread, note your errors, and figure your speed. Compare your performance with the Pretest.

Lesson 10 REVIEW

Objectives   Strengthen left- and right-shift key reaches.
Strengthen reaches on third, home, and bottom rows.
Improve speed and accuracy.

Format   Spacing: single
Margins: default

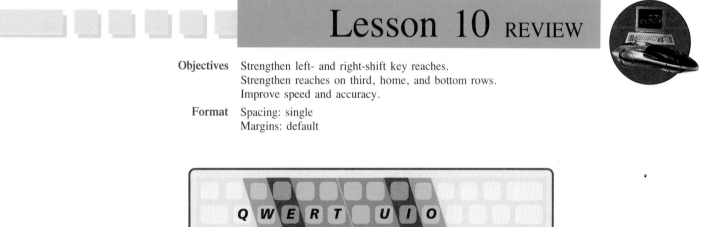

A. Keyboard Review

Key each line twice. Repeat if time permits.

```
1  sink brag quad jolt huff wave dock memo
2  Kimi Wigg holds frequent carnival jobs.
```

B. Shift Keys

Anchor **left shift** with F.

Anchor **right shift** with J.

A technique drill.

Key each line once. Keep your rhythm steady as you reach to the shift keys and back to home position. Repeat if time permits.

```
3  Otis Iris Nita Mark Uris Hans Jose Kebo
4  Fran Edie Rene Adam Vera Cara Dave Seth
```

(Continued on next page)

Congratulations! As you might recall, you signed up for our monthly drawing when you shopped at our store during the month of June. You are ① of ③ customers, during the month of June, to win a software package of your choice from a select list of our business software. Your name was one of ③ that were selected from the customers who do their computer shopping at Total Computers. ¶ Just bring the enclosed card with you to claim your prize the next time you visit Total computers. I'm also enclosing our ~~spring~~ summer catalog so that you can peruse all the ~~wonderful~~ hardware and software items we have placed on sale. We welcome your catalog orders and look forward to seeing you ~~once~~ again at Total Computers. ¶ Once again, congratulations!

(File names:
F22.145 and F23.145)

Invoices

The following customers ordered new microcomputers from Total Computers. Send each of them an invoice.

James Gorsche, 545 Lake Avenue, Alexandria, MN 58308. *Purchased an* 80486 system *with* 2-Mbyte RAM, 100-Mbyte HD, @ 1,400, *plus* 6% sales tax *and* 22.50 delivery charge.

Rose Sutherland, 290 Packard Street, Fergus Falls, MN 56537. *Purchased an* 80386 system *with both* 3.5 and 5.25 drives, @ 975, *plus* 6% sales tax *and* 21.50 delivery charge.

(File name: M15.145)

Memo With Distribution List

The following memo is to be sent to all sales department heads concerning an 8:30 a.m. meeting on July 7. The sales department heads' names are as follows: T. Abernathy, R. Cureton, S. Lopez, B. Pavratti, and K. Thompson.

This needs to be distributed as soon as possible.

A departmental meeting will be held on Tuesday, July 7, at 8:30 a.m. in Conference Room 3. The purpose of the meeting will be to discuss the projected price increase on all educational software packages. Please bring with you all pricing catalogs that we have published since the first of the year. The meeting should last about 1½ to 2 hours.

5 Jean Noel Leah Kris Mike Olla Ivan Hugh
6 Theo Eric Gino Anna Wade Burt Vida Saul

C. Concentration

A technique drill.
Keep eyes on copy.

Fill in the missing letters shown at the left as you key each line once. Repeat if time permits.

R   7 Ou- -ivers and oceans a-e being -uined.
H   8 -armful c-emicals fill muc- of t-e air.
E S   9 W- hav- lo-t u-ag- of -om- of our -oil.
E O 10 W- must w-rk t- mak- -ur w-rld cl-an-r.

D. 30-Second Timings

Compute Speed for 30 Seconds: Multiply words keyed in 30 seconds by 2 to get wam speed.

Take two 30-second timings on lines 11–12. Then take two 30-second timings on lines 13–14. Try to key with no more than 2 errors on each timing.

11 Lou Ann wanted to go down to the shore,   8
12 but Bob said it would be much too cold.   16

13 When I can go down to the shore, I will   8
14 find out if our friends can go as well.   16

| 1 | 2 | 3 | 4 | 5 | 6 | 7 | 8

E. PRETEST

Take a 1-minute timing on each line. Proofread, note your errors, and figure your speed.

Third Row   15 Walter took a ride to the quiet street.
Home Row   16 Allan had asked Donald to assist Sarah.
Bottom Row 17 Van, Mack, and Sam Baca had black vans.

| 1 | 2 | 3 | 4 | 5 | 6 | 7 | 8

F. PRACTICE
Third Row

Check Hands
Hands flat.
All fingers curved.
Hold home key anchors.

SPEED: If you made 2 or fewer errors on line 15, key lines 18–22 twice each. Repeat if time permits.
ACCURACY: If you made more than 2 errors on line 15, key lines 18–22 as a group twice. Repeat if time permits.

18 rook took cook cork work word ford fold
19 full fill file fire fore four foul fowl
20 jolt joke jets jerk jest just jugs jute
21 wire were went west jest quit quid quod
22 weed reed seed seat seal soil toil foil

C. PRACTICE

In the chart below find the number of errors you made on the Pretest (page 330). Then key each of the following designated drill lines three times.

Pretest errors	0–1	2–3	4–5	6+
Drill lines	27–31	26–30	25–29	24–28

Accuracy

24 your today exactly package checkers addresses documentation
25 often quick contain spelling functions necessary processing
26 treat hours realize addition packages preparing keyboarding
27 word using because software processor reviewing identifying

Speed

28 related rekey power merge work real ever four when what too
29 letters errors those block five jobs made word find move if
30 perform assist simple other save many more will that had or
31 prepare tables delete makes like this very also most for is

D. POSTTEST

Take another 5-minute timing on lines 6–23. Proofread, note your errors, and figure your speed. Compare your performance with the Pretest.

SIMULATION 1
Working for a
Computer Products
Store

You have recently been hired as a word processing specialist for a computer products store, Total Computers, Inc., located at 4325 Edgemont Street, St. Paul, MN 55110. The manager of the store is Shelly Bryant.

Priority Recording Sheet

Today is June 30, 19—. You have reported to work at the computer products store. In your in-basket are the jobs shown on pages 332–335. Before starting to format and key them, you should read through all the jobs to be done and decide which ones (1) are RUSH, to be done immediately; (2) are to be done promptly; or (3) may be completed when time permits. Using a priority recording sheet, which your teacher will give you, list next to each job the priority that you think it should be given.

Work Log

Ms. Bryant has asked you to keep a work log of the various jobs as you complete them. The log contains a place for you to write the time started, the time completed, the total minutes taken to complete the job, and the number of lines keyed. Many businesses use work logs to evaluate an employee's productivity (the quantity of work produced) and to allocate costs.

(File name: L87.145)

Form Letter

Each month we have a drawing for three free software packages, and those customers who have made the largest dollar purchases during the month are eligible for the drawing. Please prepare the following form letter (page 332). Block style. You supply the appropriate closing lines.

G. PRACTICE
Home Row

Check Space Bar Use
Thumb above center.

Bounce thumb off quickly.

No hesitation before or after striking.

SPEED: If you made 2 or fewer errors on line 16 (page 22), key lines 23–27 twice each. Repeat if time permits.
ACCURACY: If you made more than 2 errors on line 16 (page 22), key lines 23–27 as a group twice. Repeat if time permits.

```
23  lass lads dads gads fads fade jade wade
24  dash lash gash rash wash cash mash hash
25  gale dale sale kale hale hall fall gall
26  shad shag slag flag fled sled slid skid
27  make rake lake lark lard hard hark mark
```

H. PRACTICE
Bottom Row

Check Posture
Back straight, leaning forward.

Feet flat on floor.

Hand span from machine.

SPEED: If you made 2 or fewer errors on line 17, key lines 28–32 twice each. Repeat if time permits.
ACCURACY: If you made more than 2 errors on line 17, key lines 28–32 as a group twice. Repeat if time permits.

```
28  can, ban, van, ran, fan, man, tan, wan,
29  bend mend mind mine mice mace vase base
30  move cove cave nave vane cane mane bane
31  cone conk cons cobs cubs cabs nabs jabs
32  jamb lamb limb comb come/came name same
```

I. POSTTEST

Repeat the Pretest (page 22). Proofread, note your errors, and figure your speed. Compare your performance with the Pretest.

UNIT 3
Keyboarding— The Alphabet

Unit Goal 20 Words a Minute

Lesson 11

Objective Control P and X keys by touch.
Format Spacing: single
Margins: default

A. Keyboard Review

Key each line twice. Repeat if time permits.

```
1  blot king jars fade cave what swim quag
2  I saw black liquid vanish from the jug.
```

Lessons 145–147

Objectives Prioritize, format, and key related office communications with speed and accuracy.
Key 40/5′/5e.

Format Spacing: Drills, single; Timings, double; and as required
Margins: Default or as required.

Keyboard Skills

Key lines 1–4 once. In line 5 use your enter/return key after each word. Repeat lines 1–4, or take a series of 1-minute timings.

Speed	1 The dog and cat went to eat their food from the round dish.	12
Accuracy	2 Liza gave Max and Becky a quaint photo of a jar of flowers.	12
Numbers	3 On 10/14/92 Steven ran 38 laps; on 10/25/92 he ran 67 laps.	12
Symbols	4 Carla* and Jake* (Ryerson) paid $7.50 for 2# at $3.75 each.	12
Technique	5 at too open night am mob broke an not truck as sod drink at	

| 1 | 2 | 3 | 4 | 5 | 6 | 7 | 8 | 9 | 10 | 11 | 12 |

B. PRETEST

Take a 5-minute timing on lines 6–23. Proofread, note your errors, and figure your speed.

6   Using a word processing software package for preparing   12

7 your work is a real treat if you've ever had to rekey three   24

8 or four jobs because of errors you made. Software packages   36

9 in word processing can save you many hours of work; and the   48

10 more often you use one, the more you will realize the power   60

11 of word processing. A package like this is very quick, and   72

12 it will also assist you in identifying any errors. Most of   84

13 the packages today contain spelling checkers that will find   96

14 errors you made when keyboarding those letters, tables, and   108

15 related jobs.   111

16   When reviewing the documentation for your package, you   123

17 will find out exactly what your word processing program can   135

18 do. Most are able to merge, block, move, copy, and delete,   147

19 as well as perform many other functions. In addition, word   159

20 processing software makes it simple for you to prepare form   171

21 letters, because all you have to create is one letter. The   183

22 word processor will then merge your one letter with as many   195

23 addresses as are necessary.   200

| 1 | 2 | 3 | 4 | 5 | 6 | 7 | 8 | 9 | 10 | 11 | 12 SI 1.49 |

B. **P** Key

Use Sem finger.

Key each line twice. Repeat if time permits.

3 ;;; ;p; ;p; p;p ;p; ;;; ;p; ;p; p;p ;p;
4 ;p; ape ape ;p; pen pen ;p; nap nap ;p;
5 ;p; pen pal, perfect plot, a pale page,
6 Pat pulled a pouting pup past a puddle.
7 Please put the posies in a pail or pan.

C. **X** Key

Use S finger.

Key each line twice. Repeat if time permits.

8 sss sxs sxs xsx sxs sss sxs sxs xsx sxs
9 sxs axe axe sxs mix mix sxs tax tax sxs
10 sxs six Texans, lax taxes, vexed vixen,
11 Maxine was excited about the exit exam.
12 Examine the next box of exercise tapes.

D. Technique Checkpoint

Remember: 2 spaces at the end of a sentence; 1 space after an abbreviation.

Key lines 13–15 once. Then repeat lines 3 and 8.

13 Please fix those ripped carpets in this   8
14 duplex before next weekend. Report the   16
15 extent of the damage to Mr. Pat Dexter.   24
   | 1 | 2 | 3 | 4 | 5 | 6 | 7 | 8

E. 12-Second Timings

Take three 12-second timings on each line, or key each line three times. Try to key with no more than 1 error on each timing.

16 Pull on the tab, and the box will open.
17 Speed is good, but errors are not good.
18 Glue those pictures on the cover sheet.

         5   10   15   20   25   30   35   40

F. PRETEST

Take two 1-minute timings on lines 19–20. Proofread, note your errors, and figure your speed.

19 jell text hoax fix, quit gave slab apex   8
20 dart veal bows tops plop gate chop slag   16
   | 1 | 2 | 3 | 4 | 5 | 6 | 7 | 8

Table T68.144
Boxed format; 5 spaces between columns.

DS

Third COOPER ELECTRONICS, INC. } *bold*
Quarterly Sales Figures } *center over table*

Salesperson	Third Quarter	Second Quarter	Increase/ Decrease	Percent
J. Bethke	$58,043	$52,369	$5,665	+10.8
S. Fields	72,916	78,041*	−5,125	− 6.6
N. Meadows	41,369	36,470	4,899	+13.4
B. Robertson	42,578	35,218	7,306	+20.9
K. Symansky	51,736	50,987	749	+ 1.5
Average	$53,327	$50,617	$2,710**	+ 8.0

SS [
*Record sales for ① quarter.

**Total increases and decreases averaged.

Form F19.144 Itinerary
Display format.

ITINERARY FOR CHARLES KENYON

December 5–7, 19—

Monday, December 5

| 4:30 p.m. | Depart Atlanta Hartsfield Airport, Delta #248. |
| 6:00 p.m. | Arrive Pittsburgh. |

Tuesday, December 6

9:00 a.m.	Tour Northeast Regional Office; Manager, Sarah Crofton.
5:00 p.m.	Depart Pittsburgh Airport, Northwest #586.
7:00 p.m.	Arrive Dallas/Ft. Worth.

Wednesday, December 7

9:30 a.m.	Tour Southern Regional Office; Manager, Kenneth Sadowski.
5:45 p.m.	Depart DFW Airport, Delta #386.
8:30 p.m.	Arrive Atlanta.

Form F20.144
Invoice No. 3575. Today's date.

[*To:*] Mr. Kenneth Zachariah / CTR Industries / #239 Shady Lane / Biloxi, MS 39531 / [*Terms:*] 5/15, n/30

    5 Brass-plated hurricane lamps @ 19.95 = 99.75
    3 Rattan storage chests @ 49.50 = 148.50
    2 Fiber-optic lamps @ 39.65 = 79.30

Amount due 327.55 / Sales tax 14.74 / Delivery charges 7.50 / Total amount due 349.79

Form F21.144
Invoice No. 3576.

Today's date. Send another invoice to CTR Industries [same terms] for the following items: 4 Multi-purpose cookers @ 36.25; 7 20-piece cutlery sets @ 28.45; 5 Carbon steel woks @ 37.85. Sales tax is 5%; Delivery charges are 4.95. Calculate all totals and the total amount due.

145.00
199.15
189.25
533.40
26.67
4.95
565.02

G. PRACTICE

To Key Faster:
Read copy before keying it.

Aim for smoothness in stroking.

Key each line twice. Repeat if time permits.

```
21  jell bell ball balk bark park part dart
22  text next neat meat meal seal real veal
23  hoax coax coal cowl howl jowl bowl bows
24  fix, mix, six, sit, sits sips tips tops
25  quit quip whip ship slip flip flop plop
26  gave cave have pave page pale gale gate
27  slab slap slaw claw clan clap clop chop
28  apex Alex flex flux flax flap flag slag
```

H. POSTTEST

Take two 1-minute timings on lines 19–20 (page 24). Proofread, note your errors, and figure your speed. Compare your performance with the Pretest.

Lesson 12

Objective Control Y and hyphen keys by touch.

Format Spacing: single
Margins: default

A. Keyboard Review

Key each line twice. Repeat if time permits.

```
1  deft lack vase more hex; wing quip jibe
2  Web made quick jet flights over Paxton.
```

Hold Those Anchors
For **Y** anchor ; L K
For - anchor J

B. [Y] Key

Use J finger.

Key each line twice. Repeat if time permits.

```
3  jjj jyj jyj yjy jyj jjj jyj jyj yjy jyj
4  jyj aye aye jyj joy joy jyj yes yes jyj
5  jyj yellow yam, yard of yarn, July joy,
6  Larry made toys in May for lonely boys.
7  Shelley yearns to yodel but only yells.
```

Objectives Review open, ruled, and boxed tables.
Review an itinerary.
Review invoices.

Format Spacing: Drills, single; and as required
Margins: Default or as required

A. Keyboard Skills

Key lines 1–4 once. In line 5 concentrate on your shift technique as you capitalize each word. Repeat lines 1–4, or take a series of 1-minute timings.

Speed	1	The rain came down so fast I could not see across the road.	12
Accuracy	2	Everybody expected Jack's golf technique to win him prizes.	12
Numbers	3	On the 9th we need 4,875 bricks; on the 26th we need 3,018.	12
Symbols	4	Chris & David earned $7.75/hour loading 1,234# of #4 pines.	12
Technique	5	Cadillac Chevrolet Chrysler Ford Mercury Oldsmobile Pontiac	

| 1 | 2 | 3 | 4 | 5 | 6 | 7 | 8 | 9 | 10 | 11 | 12

B. 30-Second Timings

Take two 30-second timings on lines 6 and 7. Then take two 30-second timings on lines 8 and 9. Try to key with no more than 2 errors on each timing.

6	Take this timing to improve your speed on the keyboard; try	12
7	keying with no more than two errors on each of the timings.	24
8	To be sure you don't lose your place when keying, keep your	12
9	eyes on the copy as you move from word to word in the line.	24

| 1 | 2 | 3 | 4 | 5 | 6 | 7 | 8 | 9 | 10 | 11 | 12

Table T66.144
Standard open format.

DESKTOP PUBLISHING SKILLS

(Survey of DTP Users)

Skill	Responses	Percent
Graphics Design	68	25
Computer	62	22
Keyboarding	57	21
Word Processing	50	18
English	25	9
Journalism	14	5

Table T67.144
Standard ruled format.

CALIFORNIA MILEAGE CHART *

From	To	Miles**
Los Angeles	San Francisco	390
Sacramento	Los Angeles	380
San Diego	Eureka	810
San Diego	Sacramento	510
San Francisco	Sacramento	90

* Most direct route.
** Rounded to the nearest 10.

Hold Those Anchors
For **Y** anchor ; L K
For **-** anchor J

 **C.** **-** **Key**

Use Sem finger.
Do not space before or after hyphens.

Key each line twice. Repeat if time permits.

8 ;;; ;p- ;-; -;- ;-; ;;; ;p- ;-; -;- ;-;
9 ;p- ;-; one-third ;p- ;-; self-made ;-;
10 ;p- ;-; one-sixth ;p- ;-; part-time ;-;
11 My mother-in-law is a self-taught cook.
12 Her father-in-law saw a would-be thief.

D. **Technique Checkpoint**

Feet—on floor.
Back—straight.
Arms—elbows in.

Key lines 13–15 once. Then repeat lines 3 (page 25) and 8.

13 Positive, easy-going employees are more   8
14 likely to keep their jobs than unhappy,   16
15 contrary employees with similar skills.   24
   | 1 | 2 | 3 | 4 | 5 | 6 | 7 | 8

E. **30-Second Timings**

Take two 30-second timings on lines 16–17. Then take two 30-second timings on lines 18–19. Try to key with no more than 2 errors on each timing.

16 Set a goal to key faster every day, and   8
17 you will begin to see your speed climb.   16

18 It is nice to see your scores increase,   8
19 so push those fingers to find the keys.   16
   | 1 | 2 | 3 | 4 | 5 | 6 | 7 | 8

F. PRETEST

Take two 1-minute timings on lines 20–21. Proofread, note your errors, and figure your speed.

20 Jan, play next jury kiss boys bags quid   8
21 pan- slab cost card rope mops gape fuel   16
   | 1 | 2 | 3 | 4 | 5 | 6 | 7 | 8

Report R61.143
Bound format. Make sure the table goes on the first
page (use block protect).

DESKTOP PUBLISHING SURVEY

By [*Your name*]

Introduction

Eighty desktop publishing users responded to a recent survey conducted in the Baltimore metropolitan area. This survey was conducted by the Carmichael Research Agency.

Findings

Nine company classifications were identified by the desktop publishing users, as shown in Table 1. The greatest number of users, 35, came from the services classification. This finding supports a similar finding by Crawford,[1] [1. Don L. Crawford, "DTP in Detroit," Today's Business News, September 1992, p. 5.] which is that 45 percent of all desktop publishing users worked in the services area. Crawford[2] [2. Ibid.] also revealed that the computer training classification was the second most popular work area.

Table 1

COMPANY CLASSIFICATIONS

Classification	Users
Computer Training	12
Consulting	4
DTP Services	35
Government	10
Insurance	4
Manufacturing	3
Nonprofit Association	2
Public Relations	5
Wholesale and Distribution	5

Recommendation

It is the recommendation of this research study that additional data on the desktop publishing career field be obtained from three work area classifications—DTP Services, Computer Training, and Government—since these areas were the most popular among desktop publishing users.

Memo M14.143
Use boilerplate form.

[TO:] David Perrin / [FROM:] Karen Landers / [SUBJECT:] Computer Training Study / [DATE:] November 1, 19--

The Apex Research Group has just completed its study on computer training, and it concluded that Diversified needs to boost its computer training efforts. The Executive Board is scheduled to meet on November 29, and I have invited Apex to join our meeting to present its findings.

If you cannot attend the meeting, please appoint a replacement from your department to attend. / [your initials]

PRACTICE

Key each line twice. Repeat if time permits.

22 Jan, Dan, ran, can, man- tan- fan- pan-
23 play clay slay flay flaw flap flab slab
24 next text test best lest lost most cost
25 jury fury furl hurl hurt curt cart card
26 kiss kids lids lips laps lops lope rope
27 boys joys toys tops hops maps pops mops
28 bags wags wage wave cave cape nape gape
29 quid quip quit suit suet duet duel fuel

H. **POSTTEST**

Take two 1-minute timings on lines 20–21 (page 26). Proofread, note your errors, and figure your speed. Compare your performance with the Pretest.

Lesson 13

Objective Control Z and colon keys by touch.
Format Spacing: single

A. Keyboard Review

Key each line twice. Repeat if time permits.

1 left onyx dome quip wave jogs chin bake
2 Her big soft lynx quickly jumped waves.

Hold Those Anchors
For **Z** anchor F
For **:** anchor J

B. **Z** Key

Key each line twice. Repeat if time permits.

3 aaa aza aza zaz aza aaa aza aza zaz aza
4 aza zap zap aza zoo zoo aza zip zip aza
5 aza he zags, dazed zebras, dozing zebu,
6 Zachary ate frozen pizza in the gazebo.
7 Zircons at the bazaar blaze in the sun.

LESSON 13

Lesson 143

Objectives Reinforce skill on up and down reaches.
Review a two-page bound report with leadered table.
Review a memo.

Format Spacing: Drills, single; Timings, double; and as required
Margins: Default or as required

A. Keyboard Skills

Key lines 1–4 once. In line 5 concentrate on your shift technique as you capitalize each word. Repeat lines 1–4, or take a series of 1-minute timings.

Speed	1	I hope to get my check by at least the second of the month. 12
Accuracy	2	Jack Bowman was very excited when my quilt got first prize. 12
Numbers	3	Read pages 17, 20, 35, 46, and 89 to see the right answers. 12
Symbols	4	Interest on #237-4 (@ 12 2/3%) is $633.50; @ 14% it's $700. 12
Technique	5	Almo Anco Argo Bays Boax Bond Bush Busy Clay Dana Dice Elna

| 1 | 2 | 3 | 4 | 5 | 6 | 7 | 8 | 9 | 10 | 11 | 12 |

B. PRETEST

Take a 1-minute timing on lines 6–9. Proofread, note your errors, and figure your speed.

6 You cannot build good skills while keying if you don't 12

7 practice various reaches on the keyboard. Practice all the 24

8 reaches that are especially difficult for you when you take 36

9 your timed writings. 40

| 1 | 2 | 3 | 4 | 5 | 6 | 7 | 8 | 9 | 10 | 11 | 12 |

C. PRACTICE

SPEED: If you made 2 or fewer errors on the Pretest, key lines 10–15 twice each. Repeat if time permits.
ACCURACY: If you made more than 2 errors on the Pretest, key lines 10–12 as a group twice. Then key lines 13–15 as a group twice. Repeat if time permits.

Up Reaches
10 away card date earn fear fold argue baked cargo daily early
11 gift hold jury lets made nest films grade hours large meant
12 page plus rise seat tape vary plead rules stand theft voted

Down Reaches
13 avid balk cage disc each jobs about badly cakes coach frank
14 knee lack palm rack slab taxi packs reach score snack teach
15 very axle back calm cars sack value bales cable heavy scope

D. POSTTEST

Take a 1-minute timing on lines 6–9. Proofread, note your errors, and figure your speed. Compare your performance with the Pretest.

Hold Those Anchors
For **Z** anchor F
For **:** anchor J

C. **:** **Key**

Shift of ;.
Use Sem finger and left shift key.
Space twice after a colon.

Key each line twice. Repeat if time permits.

8 ;;; ;:; ;:; :;: ;:; ;;; ;:; ;:; :;: ;:;
9 Ms. Lia: Mr. Web: Dr. Que: Mrs. Doe:
10 Mr. Mai: Dr. Fin: Ms. Dot: Mrs. Fox:
11 To: From: Date: Subject: Attention:
12 At: When: Name: Address: Telephone:

D. Technique Checkpoint

Keep elbows close to body.
Keep eyes on copy.

Key lines 13–15 once. Then repeat lines 3 (page 27) and 8.

13 Dear Zeke: That zany Hazel visited the   8
14 zoo in this drizzle. She saw dozens of   16
15 zebras, and their lazy ways amazed her.   24
   | 1 | 2 | 3 | 4 | 5 | 6 | 7 | 8

E. 12-Second Timings

Take three 12-second timings on each line, or key each line three times. Try to key with no more than 1 error on each timing.

16 Tests are easy if you know the answers.
17 Key fast to reach the end of that line.
18 Keep your eyes on the copy as you work.

   | | | | | | | |
   5   10   15   20   25   30   35   40

F. PRETEST

Take two 1-minute timings on lines 19–20. Proofread, note your errors, and figure your speed.

19 took daze Inis face byte zing atom razz   8
20 roam gaze fond tale cure rung ship waxy   16
   | 1 | 2 | 3 | 4 | 5 | 6 | 7 | 8

G. PRACTICE

Check your posture.

Key each line twice. Repeat if time permits.

21 To: took book boom zoom loom loam roam
22 haze daze dale sale same fame game gaze

(Continued on next page)

Report R60.142
Standard format; ruled table with leaders.

DIVERSIFIED COMPUTERS, INC.

Status of computer training

The purpose of this report is to reveal the status of computer training at Diversified Computers, Inc. Computer users from all 30 District Offices supplied information for this report. The results of a questionnaire that was administered ~~to Diversified Computers employees~~ on October 10, 11, and 12 appear in Table 1 as follows:

Table 1

TYPES OF COMPUTER TRAINING _DS
(Survey conducted by Apex Research Group)

Method of Training *center over column*	Users
Individualized instruction	65*
Self-taught from documentation	52
Small-group class instruction	38*
Vendor training	32

5 spaces

SS body

center under column heading

*Training Offered by Diversified Computers.

It is apparent from the findings revealed in Table 1 ~~above~~ that Diversified Computers needs to expand its computer training effort. Of the 187 employees who received ~~computer~~ training, only 130 (55%) received that training from Diversified. ~~Vendor training was provided by Computer Training Services.~~

It is the recommendation of this group that these findings be presented ~~as soon as possible, preferably~~ at the November board meeting of Diversified Computers.

```
23  In:  Inis inns bins bind bond pond fond
24  faze face lace late mate Kate kale tale
25  By:  byte byre lyre lure sure pure cure
26  zinc zing ping ring sing sang rang rung
27  At:  atom atop stop shop whop whip ship
28  jazz razz raze rave save wave wavy waxy
```

H. POSTTEST

Take two 1-minute timings on lines 19–20 (page 28). Proofread, note your errors, and figure your speed. Compare your performance with the Pretest.

Lesson 14

Objectives Control question mark key by touch. Use caps lock to key all-capital letters.
Format Spacing: single
Margins: default

A. Keyboard Review

Key each line twice. Repeat if time permits.

```
1  gawk miff vest ploy quad zinc jinx herb
2  Dozy oryx have quit jumping big flocks.
```

Hold That Anchor
For ? anchor J

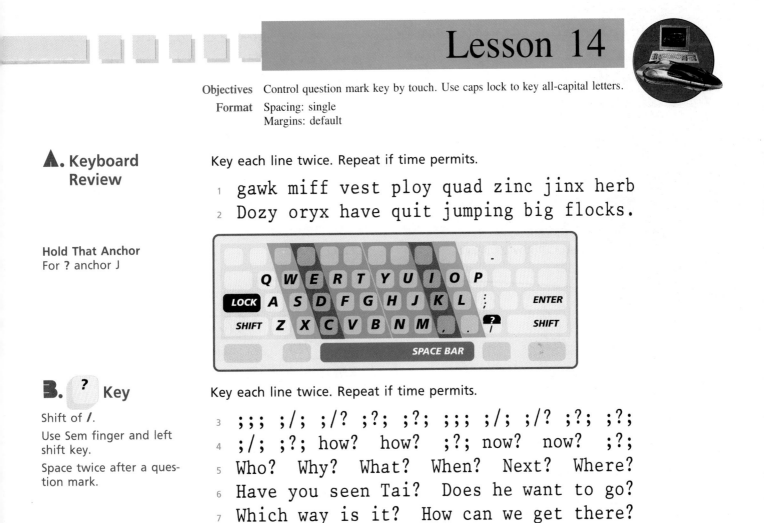

B. ? Key

Shift of /.
Use Sem finger and left shift key.
Space twice after a question mark.

Key each line twice. Repeat if time permits.

```
3  ;;; ;/; ;/? ;?; ;?; ;;; ;/; ;/? ;?; ;?;
4  ;/; ;?; how?  how?  ;?; now?  now?  ;?;
5  Who?  Why?  What?  When?  Next?  Where?
6  Have you seen Tai?  Does he want to go?
7  Which way is it?  How can we get there?
```

Letter L86.142
Modified-block style.

February 14, 19--/Harbor Furniture Company/3048 Texas Avenue/Grand Junction, CO 81504/Attention: Shipping Department/Ladies and Gentlemen:

On February 12 we received from you our most recent order for outdoor patio furniture (Invoice #2405). We appreciate the prompt, courteous service you provided so that we could have the patio furniture available for our annual Spring Festival Sale. However, a number of individual pieces were damaged in transit; and Table 1 below reveals the extent of the damage that was incurred.

The packing and crating appear to have been adequate, and I do not believe your employees damaged the furniture. There is a possibility that the personnel from Rocky Mountain Trucking, the company contracted to haul the furniture, damaged the shipment substantially on the detour route that was selected. The appropriate action, therefore, is to contact Rocky Mountain Trucking.

In the absence of any correspondence from your office, I will forward the necessary paperwork for reimbursement of approximately $275 to the trucking company. The replacement parts, however, will have to come from your warehouse./Sincerely,/Jim O'Bannion/Order Department/[Your initials]

TABLE 1

Item	Unit No.	Number of Items Damaged
7½' Pagoda Umbrella	2905-U	3 *
60" Dining Table	2863-T	1 **
21" Side Table	2847-T	2 **
18" Serving Cart	2819-A	3 *
Cushion Chaise Lounge	2938-L	4 *

* Items cannot be repaired; must be replaced.
** Items can be repaired; substitute damaged part.

C. Caps Lock Key

Use A finger.

Some parts of a document may need special emphasis. One way to emphasize (or enhance) a word or group of words is to key in ALL-CAPITAL letters. The caps lock key enables you to key words in all caps without having to shift for every letter.

To use the caps lock key:

1. Press the caps lock key. Your com-

puter may have an indicator light when the caps lock key is engaged.

2. Key the words that are to be in all caps. Only the alphabet keys will print in capitals. You will still have to press the shift key for a colon or a question mark.

3. Release the caps lock key by pressing it again.

Key each line twice.

8   Do not go to the door IF YOU ARE ALONE.
9   He finished reading GONE WITH THE WIND.
10   Was JOSE elected CLASS PRESIDENT TODAY?
11   This START/STOP SAFETY LEVER was stuck.
12   COMPUTERS scanned the FIRST-CLASS mail.

D. Technique Checkpoint

Watch those elbows and hold those anchors!

Key lines 13–15 once. Then repeat lines 3 (page 29) and 8.

13   Have you SEEN Karla? Do you know about   8
14   her TERRIBLE accident? Her car was hit   16
15   by a TRAIN. Were BOTH her arms BROKEN?   24

| 1 | 2 | 3 | 4 | 5 | 6 | 7 | 8

E. 30-Second Timings

Take two 30-second timings on lines 16–17. Then take two 30-second timings on lines 18–19. Try to key with no more than 2 errors on each timing.

16   My best friend, when I was five, called
17   last month and asked if we could visit.   16

18   We walked along that riverbank and sang   8
19   the songs we loved when we were little.   16

| 1 | 2 | 3 | 4 | 5 | 6 | 7 | 8

Review

Unit Goal 40/5'/5e

Objectives   Review business letters.
Review a two-page letter with open table.
Review a one-page report with ruled, leadered table.

Format   Spacing: Drills, single; and as required
Margins: Default or as required

▲. Keyboard Skills

Key lines 1–4 once. In line 5 concentrate on your space bar technique. Repeat lines 1–4, or take a series of 1-minute timings.

Speed | 1 | Nell has to take her time if she wants to do her best work. | 12
Accuracy | 2 | Max quickly amazed Joan Bishop with five magic card tricks. | 12
Numbers | 3 | On page 489 we read 27 lines; on page 365 we read 10 lines. | 12
Symbols | 4 | We ordered 130# of #8 stock @ $42.65 on April 7 and July 9. | 12
Technique | 5 | a 1 b 2 c 3 d 4 e 5 f 6 g 7 h 8 i 9 j 0 k , l . m / n ; o -

| 1 | 2 | 3 | 4 | 5 | 6 | 7 | 8 | 9 | 10 | 11 | 12

▣. 12-Second Timings

Take three 12-second timings on each line, or key each line three times. Try to key with no more than 1 error on each timing.

6   Your goal for this line is to key fast with only one error.
7   The short words are often keyed faster than the long words.
8   Most people can key words faster than they can key numbers.

| | | | | | | | | | | | | | |
5   10   15   20   25   30   35   40   45   50   55   60

Letter L85.142
Block style.

March 24, 19— / Mr. R. B. Gentry / 12850 Crenshaw Boulevard / Gardena, CA 90249 / Dear Mr. Gentry: / Subject: Home Security

I appreciate having the opportunity to visit with you and share with you the benefits of owning a FiveStar Home Security System. Let me share with you the two separate models we have available. We guarantee your complete satisfaction with either model. ¶ 1. Model 2098—This model is built for a one-story brick home with no basement; it is our most successful model. It is installed with a battery-pack backup. This is a complete remote system that will accommodate all of your security needs. Movement activates this system, and automatic telephone dialing is included. ¶ 2. Model 2078—This model is built for a one- or two-story brick home with a basement. Wiring is installed around every window and all entrances to your home. The price of this system will vary with the number of windows and doors in your home. ¶ If you would like further information to help you make your decision, please fill out the appropriate card and send it to me immediately. / Sincerely, / Pamela R. Davis / Sales Manager / [*Your initials*] / Enclosures

F. PRETEST

Take two 1-minute timings on lines 20–21. Proofread, note your errors, and figure your speed.

```
20  jive FLIP jamb pals wily cure sage quiz        8
21  mite slow jump cape mix; maze LASS slat        16
    |  1  |  2  |  3  |  4  |  5  |  6  |  7  | 8
```

G. PRACTICE

Speed up each time you repeat a drill line.

Key each line twice. Repeat if time permits.

```
22  jive hive hide hire tire wire mire mite
23  FLIP flop PLOP plot SLOT blot BLOW slow
24  jamb lamb limb limp lump bump pump jump
25  pals pale sale same sane vane cane cape
26  wily wild wind kind kin; fin; fix; mix;
27  cure core cove wove move more mare maze
28  sage PAGE cage CAKE bake BASE bass LASS
29  quiz quip quid quit suit skit slit slat
```

H. POSTTEST

Take two 1-minute timings on lines 20–21. Proofread, note your errors, and figure your speed. Compare your performance with the Pretest.

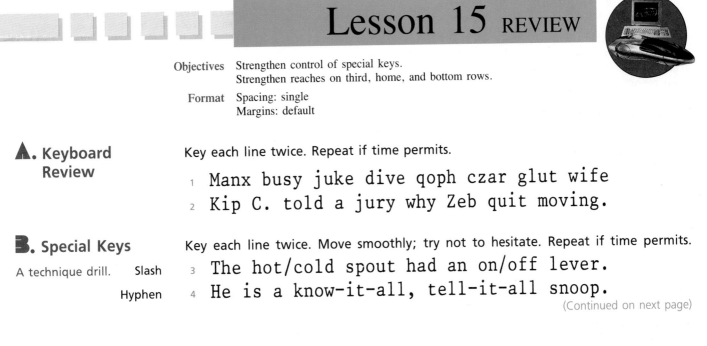

Lesson 15 REVIEW

Objectives Strengthen control of special keys.
Strengthen reaches on third, home, and bottom rows.

Format Spacing: single
Margins: default

A. Keyboard Review

Key each line twice. Repeat if time permits.

```
1  Manx busy juke dive qoph czar glut wife
2  Kip C. told a jury why Zeb quit moving.
```

B. Special Keys

A technique drill.   Slash

Hyphen

Key each line twice. Move smoothly; try not to hesitate. Repeat if time permits.

```
3  The hot/cold spout had an on/off lever.
4  He is a know-it-all, tell-it-all snoop.
```

(Continued on next page)

Example: You mentioned that three people were being considered seriously for this billing clerk position. I'm very glad to be one of those people. My bookkeeping and computer training would prove very beneficial for your company and would provide you with the administrative expertise you requested in the newspaper advertisement.

Practice. Compose and key the second paragraph for a follow-up letter. Use any one or more of the ideas suggested on page 321.

Paragraph 3

Objectives. Express greater interest in the job. Appear optimistic about the decision.

Example: My determination to become a valuable asset to your firm is greater than ever. I look forward to a favorable decision on my employment with your company.

Practice. Compose and key the final paragraph for a follow-up letter. Use any one or more of the ideas suggested on page 321.

Letter L82.140

Compose and key a complete follow-up letter using the three paragraphs you just composed. Add the following parts to complete the letter: (1) [*today's date*], (2) inside address (use your teacher's name and the address on page 314), (3) salutation, (4) complimentary closing, and (5) [*your name and return address*].

F. Job Application Integration

In this unit you learned how to prepare the papers that are necessary when you look for a part-time or full-time job: (1) a resume, (2) a letter of application, and (3) a follow-up letter. In this integrated activity, you will use the resume that you prepared in F16.134, page 308, as an enclosure for the application letter that you will be required to compose and key. In addition, you will compose and key a follow-up letter.

Letter L83.140

Compose and key a letter of application from the information provided in the classified ad in the right column. Use different content for your letter than what you used to prepare L81.136, page 314. Review the paragraphs of an application letter on pages 312–313 before composing your letter. Make a copy of the resume you prepared in F16.134, page 308, and enclose the resume with your application letter.

Form F18.140

If you are using desktop publishing, retrieve F16.134 from your disk and make one or two slight changes to your resume (that is, different point size for headings, different placement of headings, and so on) before printing a copy for the application letter.

Letter L84.140

Assume that you had a successful interview at Cordoza Industries and that you were very impressed with the company. Your follow-up letter should thank the personnel manager for the interview and reflect your positive thoughts about working for the company. (The personnel manager's name is Ms. Karen Christopher.)

Shift Keys/Colon	5	Dear Sir: Dear Jan: Dear Lori: From:
Question Mark	6	Have you? Will she? Could she? Okay?

C. Concentration

A technique drill.

Fill in the missing letters shown at the left as you key each line twice. Repeat if time permits.

G	7	Sprin- is -reen -rass and flyin- -eese.
U E	8	S-mm-r is swims-its and f-n in th- s-n.
A O	9	F-ll is c--l we-ther -nd r-king le-ves.
I N	10	W--ter -s b-g coats a-d shovel--g s-ow.
C S	11	Ea-h -ea-on i- -pe-ial in it- own way-.

D. 12-Second Timings

Take three 12-second timings on each line, or key each line three times. Try to key with no more than 1 error on each timing.

12	We do not want to be late for the game.
13	That mum corsage is larger than she is.
14	Our school colors are black and orange.

```
    5        10       15       20       25       30       35       40
```

E. PRETEST

Take a 1-minute timing on each line. Proofread, note your errors, and figure your speed.

Third Row	15	Ralph keyed quiet quips from that page.	8
Home Row	16	All fall Lake Johnna looked like glass.	8
Bottom Row	17	Can Max nab a taxicab on Bank and Main?	8

```
|  1  |  2  |  3  |  4  |  5  |  6  |  7  |  8
```

SPEED: If you made 2 or fewer errors on line 15, key lines 18–22 twice each. Repeat if time permits.
ACCURACY: If you made more than 2 errors on line 15, key lines 18–22 as a group twice. Repeat if time permits.

F. PRACTICE
Third Row

Wrists flat, palms clear of frame.

18	warm worm worn torn turn tune June dune
19	tore wore wire sire site suit quit quip
20	yarn yard ward warp wart part port tort
21	pout tout tour pour hour your sour soup
22	hype type tyke take wake rake rate fate

E. Composing Follow-Up Letters

The final step in the job application process is writing a follow-up letter. After you have had your interview, you should immediately send the interviewer a written thank-you for interviewing you. Note how each numbered paragraph of the letter shown below achieves the goals of a follow-up letter.

① In the **opening paragraph,** you should express appreciation for the interview and reaffirm your interest in the job.

② In the **second paragraph,** you may:
   a. Add new information that might be helpful in revealing your qualifications.
   b. Express pleasure at being considered a candidate for the job.
   c. Tell how you feel about the job now that the interview has been completed.

③ In the **final paragraph,** you may do any of the following:
   a. Express even greater interest in the job.
   b. Mention that you are looking forward to a favorable decision.
   c. Make yourself available for a second interview.

```
                                    May 10, 19--


Mr. Herbert A. Juneau
Director of Personnel
Apex Products Inc.
6532 Turtle Creek Boulevard
Dallas, TX 75205

Dear Mr. Juneau:

Thank you for the time you spent telling me about the billing
clerk position with Apex Products.  The interview you gave me
yesterday definitely reaffirmed my interest in working for your
company.

I was especially impressed with the Payroll Department at Apex.
The people and equipment in that department make this position
very appealing to me.

The combination of my bookkeeping experience and the in-house
training you provide for all new employees convinces me that this
position is precisely what I have been looking for.  When you
have reached your decision, I will be most eager to hear from
you.  If you desire a second interview, I would be available
after 12 noon any weekday.

                 Sincerely yours,


                 Eleanor G. Corsi
                 672 Wesley Street
                 Greenville, TX 75401
```

Before you compose and key your own follow-up letter, you will have the opportunity to work on each of the separate paragraphs necessary in a follow-up letter. Study the examples provided here and on the next page, and then compose your own paragraphs for a follow-up letter.

Paragraph 1

Objectives. Say thank you. Reaffirm interest.

Example: Thank you for the interesting time you spent with me this past Wednesday. My visit with you and the other members of your staff made me realize how very enjoyable it would be to work for your company.

Practice. Assume that the letter of application you wrote in L81.136, page 314, resulted in an interview. Compose and key the first paragraph of a follow-up letter concerning the job for which you applied.

Paragraph 2

Objectives. Strengthen your qualifications. Express pleasure to be a candidate.

(Continued on next page)

G.  PRACTICE
Home Row

Feet on floor;
back straight.

SPEED: If you made 2 or fewer errors on line 16 (page 32), key lines 23–27 twice each. Repeat if time permits.
ACCURACY: If you made more than 2 errors on line 16 (page 32), key lines 23–27 as a group twice. Repeat if time permits.

```
23  sad; lad; dad; tad; pad; mad; had; fad;
24  jail hail sail fail fall full dull lull
25  bag; sag; lag; lags legs lugs jugs jogs
26  lake make cake take bake wake rake sake
27  hall hale half calf call cell jell fell
```

SPEED: If you made 2 or fewer errors on line 17 (page 32), key lines 28–32 twice each. Repeat if time permits.
ACCURACY: If you made more than 2 errors on line 17 (page 32), key lines 28–32 as a group twice. Repeat if time permits.

H. PRACTICE
Bottom Row

Body a hand span from
machine, centered on J.

```
28  zoo, zoom boom boon boo, box, fox, lox,
29  me? in? by? TV? if? so? to? why?
30  note/tote mote/moth math/mate mute/cute
31  Mon. p.m. a.m. Inc. mfg. Nev. N.C. M.D.
32  cane bane vane vine mine mane many Manx
```

I. POSTTEST

Repeat the Pretest (page 32). Proofread, note your errors, and figure your speed. Compare your performance with the Pretest.

UNIT 4

Skillbuilding

Unit Goal 25/1'/2e*
*25 words a minute
for 1 minute with 2 or
fewer errors

Lesson 16

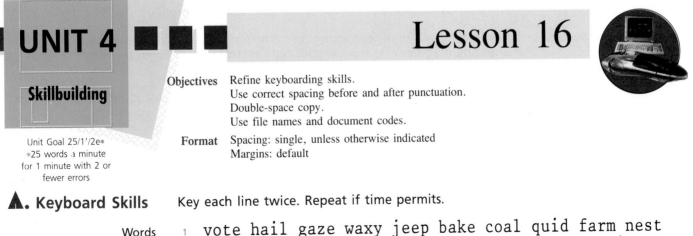

Objectives   Refine keyboarding skills.
Use correct spacing before and after punctuation.
Double-space copy.
Use file names and document codes.

Format   Spacing: single, unless otherwise indicated
Margins: default

A. Keyboard Skills   Key each line twice. Repeat if time permits.

Words   1   vote hail gaze waxy jeep bake coal quid farm nest
Speed   2   Gail has had a hard life; she must hold two jobs.
Accuracy   3   Jim, has Bev kept liquid oxygen frozen with care?

Practice Sentences	Key lines 28–29 twice each.

28 The bookcase containing magazines and software was damaged.
29 One of the packages was lost when Al's car door was opened.

3. If the subject consists of two words connected by *and* or *both . . . and*, the subject is plural and requires a plural verb.

Monday and Tuesday have been designated as holidays.
Both Chapter 5 and Chapter 9 were included on the test.

Practice Sentences	Key lines 30–31 twice each.

30 Blue and red are very popular colors found on today's cars.
31 Both the income statement and the balance sheet are needed.

4. If a subject consisting of two singular nouns connected by *and* refers to the same person or thing or is preceded by *each, every, many a,* or *many an,* a singular verb is used.

Bread and butter is his favorite snack.
Each man and woman has an equal chance of being selected.

Practice Sentences	Key lines 32–33 twice each.

32 Reading and comprehending is a skill that all should learn.
33 Many an opportunity is missed to treat other people fairly.

Pronouns

A pronoun must agree with its antecedent (the word for which the pronoun stands) in person (*I, you, her*), number (*he, they*), and gender (*he, she*).

Carol said that she was going to compete tomorrow.
The residents said that they were voting for the pool.

Practice Sentences	Key lines 34–35 twice each.

34 Doug was convinced that he placed first in the karate meet.
35 The officers believed they had reacted appropriately today.

Application Sentences	Key lines 36–45 once, correcting any errors in subject-verb agreement or pronoun-antecedent agreement. Review your copy as your teacher reads the answers. Then key lines 36–45 again.

36 Paige always complete she assignments before the deadline.
37 The small collie bark at all the people when they walks by.
38 The students writing the paper was told to finish by five.
39 One of the diskettes are cracked and won't store this data.
40 Kim and Boyd has been selected today to go to Nova Scotia.
41 Ice cream and chocolate are a favorite snack for youngsters.
42 Each rock and stone are to be picked up from Sal's driveway.
43 Many an error were overlooked when the tests were proofread.
44 The woman knew that his job performance was to be reviewed.
45 The students decided to finish they project before Monday.

B. Third Row Keys

Key each line twice. Repeat if time permits.

4 test rest pest west guest yeast roast toast totes
5 yarn yard ward word worry hurry query quirt quilt
6 We took your tire to the shop, but it was ruined.
7 Try to get an aqua shirt to wear for the picture.

C. Enter/Return Key

A technique drill.

Key each line once. Return after each semicolon and period. Continue keying smoothly. Repeat if time permits.

8 Harry met Georgette; he liked her; she liked him.
9 The play is good; it starts at seven; be on time.
10 It is windy; our leaves are flying; get the rake.
11 The days are shorter; it is cold; winter is here.

D. Punctuation Spacing

Space once after a semicolon.

Space twice after a colon.

Space twice after a period at the end of a sentence.

Space once after a period used with initials and titles.

Do not space after a period used within degrees or geographic abbreviations.

Key lines 12–21 once. Note the spacing before and after each punctuation mark. Repeat if time permits.

12 Please rake leaves; the wind has stopped blowing.
13 Todd passed the test; he studied about two hours.

14 Two people will enter the contest: Gwen and Asa.
15 Three courses are open: economics, art, and law.

16 My cat gets on the computer. She wishes to work.
17 Please turn down the radio. It is hard to think.

18 Ms. Novak and Mrs. Garcia are in the talent show.
19 Dr. R. L. Stanley was given the award by Mr. Thu.

20 Margaret has her B.S., M.B.A., and Ph.D. degrees.
21 The U.S.A. and U.K. attend the U.N. in N.Y., N.Y.

E. 12-Second Timings

Take three 12-second timings on each line, or key each line three times. Try to key with no more than 1 error on each timing.

22 Try to go faster when you repeat this drill line.
23 Next time it will be easier to finish the drills.
24 As your mind races ahead, your fingers go faster.

        5   10   15   20   25   30   35   40   45   50

B. Preview Practice

Key each line twice as a preview to the 5-minute timings below.

Accuracy 6 video matrix popularity advancement experienced application
Speed 7 have seen that just past will more than used work they over

C. 5-Minute Timings

Take two 5-minute timings on lines 8–25. Proofread, note your errors, and figure your speed.

8   We have seen a lot of changes that have taken place in 12
9   computers in just the past few years because of advances in 24
10 hardware and software. The software packages of today will 36
11 perform more difficult tasks than those used just a year or 48
12 two ago. The packages that are used today utilize graphics 60
13 and text; the packages of tomorrow will work with sound and 72
14 video, and they will also work with animation. 81

15   Printers have also experienced dozens of changes. The 93
16 daisy wheel was quite an advancement over the type bar, and 105
17 the dot matrix concept allowed us to print graphics. Laser 117
18 printers of today, though, have captured a large market for 129
19 office applications as well as for personal use. The color 141
20 laser printers of tomorrow will be speedier and smarter and 153
21 will cost less than today's models. 160

22   Networks will continue to grow in popularity. A trend 172
23 in this area will be a concept referred to as groupware, in 184
24 which two or more people work on a network at the same time 196
25 on the same project. 200

| 1 | 2 | 3 | 4 | 5 | 6 | 7 | 8 | 9 | 10 | 11 | 12 SI 1.47

D. LAB Review Subject-Verb Agreement

1. A verb must agree with its subject in number and person. The letter *s* is usually added to a verb to indicate the third person singular.

We recognize that Lou Blackwell tries his very best.
Many of the women agree with the verdict.

Practice Sentences Key lines 26–27 twice each.

26 The residents need to see why that vote was not any closer.
27 Nearly all of the employees want to attend today's meeting.

2. Phrases and clauses between a subject and verb do not affect the number of the verb. If the subject is singular, use a singular verb; if the subject is plural, use a plural verb. Use a singular verb after a phrase beginning with *one of* or *one of the*.

The quotes for the project were submitted yesterday.
One of the bombs has not been destroyed.

F. Double Spacing

All the material you have keyed so far in this course has been single-spaced. From now on, when you take a timing of 1 minute or longer, you should double-space the timing. This means there will be a blank line between each printed line. You do not have to press Enter/Return twice at the end of each line. Instead, the line spacing can be set to double (or even triple) spacing. Word wrap can be used to return each line automatically. **Note:** Some word processors do not show the text double- or triple-spaced on the screen, but it will be printed in the correct format.

G. PRETEST

Take a 1-minute timing on lines 25–27. Proofread, note your errors, and figure your speed. Format: Double spacing.

```
25  My cousin, Vera, has been exercising for a number   10
26  of weeks.  I tried to run and jump beside her for    20
27  at least one hour today.                             25
    |   1   |   2   |   3   |   4   |   5   |   6   |   7   |   8   |   9   |   10
```

H. PRACTICE

Adjacent reaches are consecutive letters that are next to each other on the same row. (we**ld**)

Jump reaches are consecutive letters on the top and bottom alphabetic rows keyed by one hand. (e**xa**m)

SPEED: If you made 2 or fewer errors on the Pretest, key each line twice.
ACCURACY: If you made more than 2 errors on the Pretest, key lines 28–30 as a group twice. Then key lines 31–33 as a group twice.

```
28  tr tray stray trend treat strut trace trips trade
29  po pole spots spore polka poker point poems polar
30  as base haste waste paste taste vases lasts fasts

31  ze size glaze craze blaze prize dozen gauze amaze
32  mu must mulch mumps music musty mushy murky munch
33  br bran brain bread break bring broth brute brush
```

I. POSTTEST

Take a 1-minute timing on lines 25–27. Proofread, note your errors, and figure your speed. Compare your performance with the Pretest.

J. File Names and Document Codes

File Names. Documents produced on computers are usually saved on disks so that they may be retrieved in order to (a) print additional copies, (b) merge with other files, (c) make changes such as adding, deleting, or rearranging information, and so on. If you have been using word processing software and have saved your daily work, you already have been using file names. Review page xvi on how to create a file name.

Document Codes. A document code is different from a file name because it is keyed on the document. The document code includes information that enables someone other than the person who keyed the document to find it on a disk. The document code may include the disk number, the file name, and/or the name or initials of the person who keyed the document. The document code in this course should reflect the following three things:

(Continued on next page)

Application Form, Page 1

EMPLOYMENT APPLICATION

PERSONAL DATA

Date: June 22, 1992

Name of applicant: Martina Valdez   Social Security No. 378-62-0495

Permanent address: 4101 Fuller Apartments, Clio, MI 48420   Phone: 313-555-2714

Temporary address: N/A   Phone: N/A

TYPE OF WORK

Type of work applying for: Secretarial

Salary expected: $1,000/month   Date available for work: Immediately

Which of the following business machines can you operate with competence?

Ten-key adding machine X	Electronic typewriter	Keypunch
Electronic calculator X	Memory typewriter X	Mimeograph X
Machine transcriber X	Word processor X	Offset
Electric typewriter X	Microfilm machine X	Photocopier X

EDUCATION

	School — Name and Location	Dates Attended	Course
Grade	Grandbriar Elementary School, Clio, MI 48420	1979-1987	N/A
High	Clio High School, Clio, MI 48420	1987-1991	Office Technology
College or Business			
Other			

HEALTH

Do you have or have you had any serious or prolonged illness? No

If so, please describe: N/A

In case of emergency, notify:

Name: Mr. & Mrs. Lee Valdez   Phone: 313-555-2578

Address: 404 Elm Street, Clio, MI 48420

Application Form, Page 1

Application Form, Page 2

EMPLOYMENT APPLICATION 2

EMPLOYMENT HISTORY

Dates of Employment	Company and Address	Position	Reason Left
June 1991-Present	Rathjen Moving Co. 471 Vienna Road Flushing, MI 48433	General office clerk	Desire secretarial position

REFERENCES

Name	Occupation	Address	Phone
Ms. Susan E. Krzyskowski	Teacher	Bus. Educ. Dept. Clio High School Clio, MI 48420	313-555-5630
Mr. Maurice W. McAllister	Office Manager	Rathjen Moving Co. 471 Vienna Road Flushing, MI 48433	313-555-5420
Ms. Audrey L. Swanson	Teacher	Economics Department Clio High School Clio, MI 48420	313-555-5499

I certify that the above statements are true and complete to the best of my knowledge. I understand that employment is contingent upon the accuracy and acceptability of the statements herein.

Date: June 22, 1992   Signature: *Martina Valdez*

Application Form, Page 2

Lessons 140/141

Objectives

Review and apply rules for subject-verb agreement and pronoun-antecedent agreement.

Format and key follow-up letters.

Reinforce all job application documents.

Key 40/5'/5e.

Format

Spacing: Drills, single; Timings, double; and as required

Margins: Default or as required

▲ Keyboard Skills

Key lines 1–4 once. In line 5 underline each word containing double letters. Repeat lines 1–4, or take a series of 1-minute timings.

Speed	1	We will try as hard as we can to start the car in the cold.	12
Accuracy	2	Two sax players in the jazz band gave a quick demo for Tom.	12
Numbers	3	Di's tabs changed from 10 and 29 to 10 and 38 to 47 and 56.	12
Symbols	4	Do it now! Pay Jake* (Adams) 10% and Pauline* (Drake) 15%.	12
Technique	5	Keep all the food in the freezer cool or it will melt fast.	

| 1 | 2 | 3 | 4 | 5 | 6 | 7 | 8 | 9 | 10 | 11 | 12

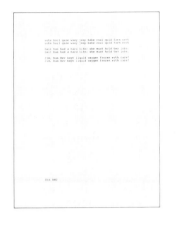

① **Type of Document.** Use the letter *D* for drills, *C* for centered jobs, *F* for forms, *L* for letters, *M* for memos, *R* for reports, and *T* for tables.

② **Document Number.** Use the lesson number if it is a drill lesson or the number of the document (as it is numbered consecutively throughout the text), followed by a period and the lesson number.

③ **Reference I.D.** Use the initials or initials and last name of the person who keys the document. Separate the Reference I.D. from the rest of the code with a space. The first part of the code can then be the same as the file name (file names cannot contain spaces).

Examples:
D16 BNOakley   (Drill lesson 16)
D16 BNO   (Drill lesson 16)
R3.61 BNO   (Report 3, Les. 61)

Place the document code at the left margin and as near the bottom of the page as your word processor allows. Each drill lesson and each document should be coded.

Footers

Most word processing programs have a footer feature which enables the user to place information at the bottom of the page or within the bottom margin. Use the footer feature for the document code.

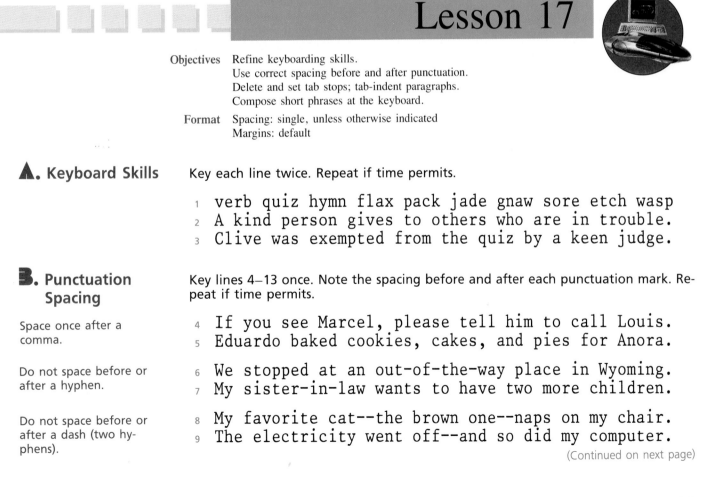

Lesson 17

Objectives Refine keyboarding skills.
Use correct spacing before and after punctuation.
Delete and set tab stops; tab-indent paragraphs.
Compose short phrases at the keyboard.

Format Spacing: single, unless otherwise indicated
Margins: default

A. Keyboard Skills

Key each line twice. Repeat if time permits.

1 verb quiz hymn flax pack jade gnaw sore etch wasp
2 A kind person gives to others who are in trouble.
3 Clive was exempted from the quiz by a keen judge.

B. Punctuation Spacing

Key lines 4–13 once. Note the spacing before and after each punctuation mark. Repeat if time permits.

Space once after a comma.

4 If you see Marcel, please tell him to call Louis.
5 Eduardo baked cookies, cakes, and pies for Anora.

Do not space before or after a hyphen.

6 We stopped at an out-of-the-way place in Wyoming.
7 My sister-in-law wants to have two more children.

Do not space before or after a dash (two hyphens).

8 My favorite cat--the brown one--naps on my chair.
9 The electricity went off--and so did my computer.

(Continued on next page)

Application Sentences   Key lines 31–40 once, providing the missing commas or semicolons. Review your copy as your teacher reads the answers. Then key lines 31–40 again.

31 Complete all the jobs, and then go on to the final chapter.
32 The new space probe looks much like a long, slender rocket.
33 Al mowed the yard, trimmed the bushes, and hoed the garden.
34 As you can see, Carmen will not be able to finish the exam.
35 Because it is warped, the diskette won't work as it should.
36 Nevertheless, you cannot take the tools out of Ed's garage.
37 Our center, Barry Sikes, scored over 50 points in the game.
38 We will attend the promotional meeting on Monday, March 17.
39 Marion finished the examination first; Ben finished second.
40 Ed wants to get an electronic typewriter; Samantha has one.

G. Filling Out Application Forms

The third step in the job application process is the completion of an application form. Most business firms have the applicant fill out an application form either before or after the interview.

Follow these suggestions when you are asked to complete such a form:

1. Be neat and accurate. Fill in the form neatly, and be sure to check for spelling and/or grammatical errors. Make corrections carefully.

2. Follow instructions. Print neatly. Try to fill in all the blanks; but if certain items do not apply to you, print "Not Applicable" or "N/A" in the space provided for your answer.

3. Do not omit continuous dates. If you are asked to supply the dates you attended high school, be sure to enter all dates—from the beginning school year to the ending school year. If you enter your years of employment, do not omit any years that you worked.

Application forms vary from one company to another, but all ask for basically the same information. The illustrations on page 318 show two sides of an application form. This form, like most others, asks the applicant to provide information as follows (note that the letters correspond to those on the illustrations):

Ⓐ **Date.** Include the month, day, and year.

Ⓑ **Personal Data.** Be sure to provide your complete permanent address (and temporary address, if applicable)—your street address, city, state, and ZIP Code.

Ⓒ **Social Security Number.** Be prepared to fill in your social security number, because every person must have one when applying for a job.

Ⓓ **Type of Work.** A company will often inquire as to the type of position you are seeking. You may also be asked a salary you expect and the date you would be available for work. If you have special machine skills, you might be asked to identify your competencies on these machines.

Ⓔ **Education.** Many application forms ask for the name of your high school as well as any colleges or business schools, the dates you attended, and the courses you completed.

Ⓕ **Health.** Answer honestly all questions on health. The questions are essential for insurance purposes, as well as to find out who should be notified in case of a medical emergency.

Ⓖ **Employment History.** Employers want to know about previous work experience. Past work experience may help you obtain a better entry-level position, so be as honest and as thorough as you can in completing this section.

Ⓗ **References.** To complete this section, use the list of references that you included in your resume. References should be people such as past employers and former teachers who can attest to your character, work habits, and potential.

Ⓘ **Signature.** DO NOT FORGET TO SIGN THE APPLICATION FORM in ink—and date it, too, if necessary.

Form F17.138
Get an application form from your teacher, and apply for a job for which you are qualified.

10 Her yes/no/yes answer was confusing to the class.
11 The wait/walk light has not been installed today.

12 Have you taken your final exams? How did you do?
13 When are you leaving? Will you have enough time?

C. Tab Key and Tab Stops

Tab Key. The tab key is used to make the cursor move to a preselected point known as a **tab stop**. On most computers, the tab key is located to the left of the Q key. Use the A finger to operate the tab key.

Default Tabs. Most word processors have preset tab stops. These are called **default tabs** and are usually set 5 spaces apart. (Some word processors have only a single 5-space default tab.) Default tabs that remain in the same place when the left margin is changed are called **absolute tabs**. Those which adjust when the left margin is moved are called **relative tabs.**

Practice: Using your A finger, press the tab key several times. Watch the cursor as you press the tab key. If it does not move at all, you do not have any default tabs. If it moves only once, you have a single default tab. If it moves each time you press the tab key, you have multiple default tabs. Press the tab key now. Then press Enter to return to the left margin.

Kinds of Tabs. Word processing software often includes four kinds of tab stops: left, right, center, and decimal.

① **Left tabs** are most commonly used for indenting paragraphs and keying tables. The cursor indents to the stop; as text is keyed, it moves to the right. (The left tab will be used in this lesson. Use of the other tabs will be practiced in later lessons.)

② **Right tabs** cause text to move to the left as it is keyed. Right tabs are frequently used to align columns of numbers on the right.

③ **Center tabs** force text to be centered from the tab stop. Center tabs are used to center headings.

④ **Decimal tabs** move text to the left until a decimal point (period) is keyed. Decimal tabs are used to align numbers on the decimal point.

Ruler. Most word processors display tab settings in a line called a **ruler** (also known as a **tab ruler, ruler line,** or **format line**). Display of the ruler and the different tab settings varies with each word processor. Some examples are shown below.

Practice: Following the directions for your software, display the ruler on the screen.

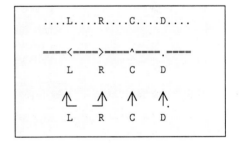

D. Deleting and Setting Tabs

Tab stops can be deleted one at a time or all at once. Similarly, tab stops can be set one at a time, and some word processors permit setting several tab stops at once.

After the appropriate tab stops are set, position the cursor at the left margin. Press the tab key with the A finger to move the cursor to the tab stop. **Note:** Some computers allow tabbing to the left as well as to the right. To move to the left, hold down the right shift key as you press the tab key.

3. Use a comma after each item in a series, except the last.

> We purchased supplies for $10, $13, and $15.
> Joe ate cookies, Jan ate doughnuts, and Kate ate chips.

4. Use a comma to set off words, phrases, or clauses that are not essential to the meaning of a sentence.

> We will, of course, approve the plan.
> Therefore, the price will increase next week.
> You will be excused, Mr. Lundeen, from our next meeting.

Practice Sentences | Key lines 23–24 twice each.

23 Candy will need more pens, pencils, and pads for the tests.
24 Gerald is, after all, the best candidate for this position.

5. Use a comma after an introductory clause that begins with *if, as, when, although, since, because,* or a similar conjunction.

> If we fail to go now, we will miss the plane.
> When it rains, our plants will drown.
> Since you paid the fee, you might as well attend.

6. Use a comma after introductory words and phrases such as *first, in my opinion, for example,* and so on.

> First, we must resolve this difficult problem.
> For example, the computer needs more disk space.

Practice Sentences | Key lines 25–26 twice each.

25 As you are aware, Dan cannot give you that information yet.
26 In my opinion, the form needs to be prepared on a computer.

7. Use commas to separate an appositive within a sentence. If the appositive appears at the end of the sentence, use only one comma.

> Mr. Nunn, our senator, will attend the session.
> I drove my new car, a Pontiac.
> Will you please see if Ms. Dunn, my attorney, is present.

Practice Sentences | Key lines 27–28 twice each.

27 Vic's new player, a Panasonic, produces high-quality sound.
28 I will use my computer, a Zenith, to do all my assignments.

Semicolons

Use a semicolon between two independent clauses when they are not joined by a conjunction.

> Mr. Blackwell is not here today; he will be here tomorrow.
> We will cut the wood; they will stain it.

Practice Sentences | Key lines 29–30 twice each.

29 Zach will get the supplies; you'll have to distribute them.
30 Yvonne moved to North Dakota; Bill moved to North Carolina.

E. Tab Practice

The abbreviations in this exercise are 2-letter state abbreviations that are always keyed in all caps.

Practice 1: Check your ruler. If you have default tabs set every 5 spaces, you are ready to begin the practice. If not, set six left tabs—one every 5 spaces. Return to your regular screen. Key lines 14–16 once. Remember to use the caps lock key.

```
14  AL    AK    AZ    AR    CA    CZ    CO
15  CT    DE    DC    FL    GA    GU    HI
16  ID    IL    IN    IA    KS    KY    LA
```

Practice 2: Clear all tab stops and set six tabs—one every 7 spaces. Rekey lines 14–16 once each; tab between abbreviations.

F. Paragraph Indentions

When a paragraph is indented, the usual indention is 5 spaces. Each indention counts as 5 strokes (1 word), the same as 5 space bar strokes would count.

G. PRETEST

Take a 1-minute timing on lines 17–19. Proofread, note your errors, and figure your speed. Format: Double spacing, 5-space tab.

```
17        Speed and accuracy will improve if your eyes  10
18  keep looking at the book and if your fingers keep  20
19  holding to their anchors.                          25
    |  1  |  2  |  3  |  4  |  5  |  6  |  7  |  8  |  9  |  10
```

SPEED: If you made 2 or fewer errors on the Pretest, key each line twice.
ACCURACY: If you made more than 2 errors on the Pretest, key lines 20–22 as a group twice. Then key lines 23–25 as a group twice.

H. PRACTICE

Double letters are the same letter keyed consecutively by the same finger. Example: ski**ll**

Alternates are a sequence of at least three letters that are keyed alternately by fingers on opposite hands. Example: **goals**

```
20  ee seek sleep beeps meets flees preen green deems
21  oo book cooks shook hoods flood blood droop snoop
22  cc occur bocci yucca hiccup soccer accord succeed

23  the cork worm vigor makes names anvil field right
24  fit paid jell girls soaps toxic chair snake shame
25  tot oaks maid bowls quake dozen bugle chant flair
```

I. POSTTEST

Take a 1-minute timing on lines 17–19. Proofread, note your errors, and figure your speed. Compare your performance with the Pretest.

J. Composing at the Keyboard

The skill of composing copy at the keyboard will allow you to create documents in your own words faster than writing them out by hand. Begin by responding to each of the questions on lines 26–30 with a short phrase—two or three words. Composition exercises will increase from phrases to sentences to paragraphs. You may look at the monitor as you compose the answers. Do not look at your hands; concentrate on each answer as you key.

Example question:
Where would you like to live?

Example response:
In Colorado

(Continued on next page)

Take a 2-minute timing on lines 6–10. Proofread, note your errors, and figure your speed.

```
 6  They paid the city, town, and county for the right to fish.   12
 7  It's time for me to go; it's time for them to go; let's go.   24
 8  Did she blame me?  Did she blame them?  Whom did she blame?   36
 9  The so-called "expert" on "bug zapping" is my neighbor Sal.   48
10  Danny made a U-turn--and got a ticket--on a one-way street.   60
```

C. PRACTICE

SPEED: If you made 4 or fewer errors on the Pretest, key lines 11–16 twice each. Repeat if time permits.
ACCURACY: If you made more than 4 errors on the Pretest, key lines 11–13 as a group twice. Then key lines 14–16 as a group twice. Repeat if time permits.

```
11  pens, turn, odor, worn, name, they, pays, them, kept, such,
12  city; paid; fish; maps; they; land; also; kept; coal; lame;
13  juror's zebra's widow's buyer's uncle's citizen's visitor's

14  What?  Give?  When?  Shake?  Fight?  Where?  Bored?  Score?
15  "keypad" "formats" "courseware" "standalone" "text editing"
16  double-space--walkie-talkie--half-and-half--president-elect
```

D. POSTTEST

Take another 2-minute timing on lines 6–10. Proofread, note your errors, and figure your speed. Compare your performance with the Pretest.

E. Concentration

A technique drill.

Key lines 17–20 twice as a group. Keep your eyes on the copy.

```
17  accommodation lackadaisical weatherproofed environmentalist
18  objectionable bougainvillea characteristic hyperventilation
19  philosophical discombobulate identification thoughtlessness
20  filibustering nonenforceable reconnaissance departmentalize
```

**F. LAB Review
Commas**

1. Use a comma to separate two independent clauses when they are joined by the conjunction *and, but, or,* or *nor* into one compound sentence.

The software worked very well, and we may purchase additional copies.
Chapter 15 is on desktop publishing, and Chapter 11 is on hardware.

2. Use a comma to separate two adjectives that modify the same noun.

She was a very honest, capable person.
Daniel fired the loud, powerful rifle.

Practice Sentences

Key lines 21–22 twice each.

```
21  The software is powerful, but it does not have a thesaurus.
22  The tall, modern building on Fifth is our new headquarters.
```

Remember to key the document code after the last exercise.

26 *Who is your best friend?*
27 *What is your favorite song?*
28 *What cities or countries would you like to visit?*
29 *Who is a past president of the United States?*
30 *What books have you enjoyed reading?*

Lesson 18

Objectives   Refine keyboarding skills.
Use correct spacing before and after punctuation.
Compose short phrases at the keyboard.

Format   Spacing: single, unless otherwise indicated
Margins: default

A. Keyboard Skills

Key each line twice. Repeat if time permits.

Words   1   doze hawk yelp quit glib mend safe tact jinx rave
Speed   2   We all must be good friends to have good friends.
Accuracy   3   We have quickly gained sixty prizes for best jam.
| 1 | 2 | 3 | 4 | 5 | 6 | 7 | 8 | 9 | 10

B. Bottom Row Keys

Key each line twice. Repeat if time permits.

4   Zeb, nab, cab, can, man, mane vane cane came name
5   Manx zinc comb numb xenia cabin mavin venom nizam
6   Maxine gave Barbara five dozen Xavier Cafe menus.
7   Beverages from six machines have no fizz in them.

C. Caps Lock Key

A technique drill.

Key each line twice. Use the caps lock key for all-cap words. Repeat if time permits.

8   Station KSST usually plays COUNTRY/WESTERN music.
9   When we were in NEW YORK, we saw a BROADWAY play.
10   AUGUST has been the HOTTEST month I can remember.
11   Marci was EMBARRASSED when she DROPPED her plate.

D. Tab Key

A technique drill.

Set four tabs—one every 10 spaces. Key each line once; tab between words. Repeat if time permits.

12	If	you	want	to	improve
13	your	skill,	you	can.	Watch
14	your	posture;	anchor	your	fingers;
15	and	think	where	those	keys
16	are.	You	can	do	it.

Letter L80.136

Compose and key a complete letter of application using the four paragraphs you just composed. Add the following parts to complete the letter: (1) [*today's* *date*], (2) inside address: Ms. Joyce Talltrees / Human Resources Department / The Eldon Corporation / 1873 South Broadway / [*your city, state, ZIP Code*], (3) salutation, (4) complimentary closing, (5) [*your name and return address*], and (6) enclosure notation.

Letter L81.136

Compose and key a letter of application from the information provided in one of the two classified ads below. Select the ad that most closely resembles the type of position for which you would like to apply and for which you are better qualified.

DATA ENTRY CLERK

Southwest Oil & Gas Company has an opening for a data entry clerk.

This is an entry-level position within our Accounting Department. Qualifications include dependability and willingness to learn. Applicant must have had some training in using data entry and/or word processing equipment and software.

Excellent benefits include a comprehensive medical and dental program, disability income protection, and free parking.

If interested, send a letter of application and resume to:

PERSONNEL DEPARTMENT
SOUTHWEST OIL & GAS COMPANY
504 STANLEY PLACE
TEMPE, AZ 85281

SOGCO is an Equal Opportunity Employer

SECRETARY

The Dallas Morning News has an opening in the Data Processing Department for a secretary.

All interested applicants must key 50 wam, must have wp skills, and must have at least two years of secretarial training and/or experience. Ability to use transcribing equipment helpful but not required. You must be a self-motivator and work with little or no supervision.

We offer excellent working conditions and company benefits.

Send a letter of application and resume to:

PERSONNEL OFFICE
THE DALLAS MORNING NEWS
2400 ABRAMS ROAD
DALLAS, TX 75214

An Equal Opportunity Employer

Lessons 138/139

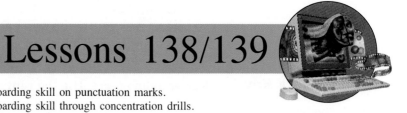

Objectives	Reinforce keyboarding skill on punctuation marks.
	Reinforce keyboarding skill through concentration drills.
	Review and apply comma and semicolon rules.
	Fill out an application form.
Format	Spacing: Drills, single; Timings, double; and as required
	Margins: Default or as required

Keyboard Skills

Key lines 1–4 once. In line 5 use your tab key to advance from one word to the next through the entire line. Repeat lines 1–4, or take a series of 1-minute timings.

Speed	1	The paper might run low before we can finish that next job. 12
Accuracy	2	Brown jars prevented the mixture from freezing too quickly. 12
Numbers	3	The five packages arrived 10, 29, 38, 47, and 56 days late. 12
Symbols	4	Molly chose #1 (a boat) and #3 (a truck)--Hurrah for Molly! 12
Technique	5	lap 111 cot 222 map 333 see 444 buy 555 not 666

| 1 | 2 | 3 | 4 | 5 | 6 | 7 | 8 | 9 | 10 | 11 | 12 |

E. Punctuation Spacing

Key lines 17–26 once. Note the spacing before and after each punctuation mark. Repeat if time permits.

Semicolon	17	Their cat hid upstairs; she is afraid of thunder.
Colon	18	Her dress has three colors: navy, red, and aqua.
Period: end of sentence	19	We went to the zoo. We saw baby lions and seals.
Period: abbreviations	20	Dr. G. L. Evans received a grant for his project.
Period: Countries	21	Harrison and Daniel took a trip across the U.S.A.
Comma	22	Kirstin has three dogs, five cats, and one horse.
Hyphen	23	The down-and-out prizefighter won his last fight.
Dash	24	Mom was upset--very upset--about the broken dish.
Slash	25	The March/April issue of your journal came today.
Question Mark	26	Did you enjoy your time off? Did you sleep late?

F. 30-Second Timings

Take two 30-second timings on lines 27–28. Then take two 30-second timings on lines 29–30. Try to key with no more than 2 errors on each timing.

```
27  Seven of us rode the bus down to the shelter last   10
28  Saturday and helped serve meals to many homeless.   20

29  It was hard work, but we enjoyed being able to do   10
30  something to help solve this problem in our city.   20
    |  1  |  2  |  3  |  4  |  5  |  6  |  7  |  8  |  9  |  10
```

G. PRETEST

Take a 1-minue timing on lines 31–33. Proofread, note your errors, and figure your speed. Format: Double spacing, 5-space tab.

```
31        Look up in the western sky and see it filled   10
32  with majestic pinks and reds as the sun begins to   20
33  set behind those clouds.                            25
    |  1  |  2  |  3  |  4  |  5  |  6  |  7  |  8  |  9  |  10
```

H. PRACTICE

Left and right reaches are a sequence of at least three letters keyed by fingers on either the left or the right hand. (lease, think)

SPEED: If you made 2 or fewer errors on the Pretest, key each line twice.
ACCURACY: If you made more than 2 errors on the Pretest, key lines 34–36 as a group twice. Then key lines 37–39 as a group twice.

```
34  rat warts wages gears diets hired stage table get
35  ear moves greet enter crank rests vases exact tag
36  age cages bears carts force serve wheat raged was

37  mop alike fills unite moods equip loose mopes lip
38  hip pours allow pound joked nouns pumps looms him
39  joy tunic moors alone polka input union mouth hop
```

1. **Introduction.** Tell the reader the purpose of the letter, the job you are applying for, and how you learned of the job.

2. **Second paragraph.** Give special consideration to the qualifications you have that make you especially valuable in this position and the skills you have that can help the employer and the company. Refer to the resume you are enclosing.

3. **Third paragraph.** Mention special skills that set you apart from other applicants. (Are you exceptionally well organized? Do you work well with people?)

4. **Final paragraph.** Restate your interest in the job and your desire for an interview. Indicate when you will be available. Include your home phone number so that the employer can reach you easily.

Letter L79.136
Key the letter of application shown on page 312. Modified-block style (see page 99 for preparing a personal-business letter).

Composing a Letter of Application

Before you compose and key your own complete letter of application, you will have the opportunity to work on each of the separate paragraphs necessary in a letter of application. Read and study the examples provided in the following paragraphs, and then compose individual paragraphs for your own letter of application.

Paragraph 1

Objectives. Specify the job applied for, and mention how you found out about it.

Example: I would like to apply for the position of office assistant for your company. My high school English teacher, Ms. Lorie Gold, informed me of this opening.

Practice. Compose and key the first paragraph for a letter of application in which you are applying for the position of office assistant. Add any information that you think is necessary.

Paragraph 2

Objective. List relevant skills.

Example: The experience I gained as an office clerk for my father's insurance agency qualifies me for the office assistant position in your company. As stated on the enclosed resume, most of my duties involved daily use of keyboarding, filing, and communications skills. These skills would be especially beneficial to your company.

Practice. Compose and key the second paragraph for a letter of application. Include specific clerical office skills you possess that would be beneficial to the company.

Paragraph 3

Objective. Convince the reader that you have special skills. Sell yourself!

Example: My computer skills and my English skills are well above average, and I feel that I could perform any of the jobs I would be called upon to do with a minimum of error and with a high degree of competence.

Practice. Compose and key the third paragraph for a letter of application. Identify in this paragraph any special skills that you have.

Paragraph 4

Objectives. Restate your interest in the position. Arrange an interview. Give your telephone number.

Example: It would be a pleasure to work for your company as an office assistant. If you wish to interview me for this position, please telephone me at 301-555-4774 any weekday after 3 p.m.

Practice. Compose and key the fourth paragraph for a letter of application. Review the illustration on page 312 to find out what information you should include in this paragraph.

Take a 1-minute timing on lines 31–33 (page 40). Proofread, note your errors, and figure your speed. Compare your performance with the Pretest.

J. Composing at the Keyboard

Key the document code when you have finished.

Answer the questions on lines 40–45 with three or four words. Do not look at your hands. Repeat if time permits.

40   *What are your favorite foods?*
41   *What are three large cities in the United States?*
42   *What are three jobs you would enjoy doing?*
43   *What is your favorite television program?*
44   *What are two of your favorite holidays?*
45   *What are three of your favorite sports?*

Lesson 19

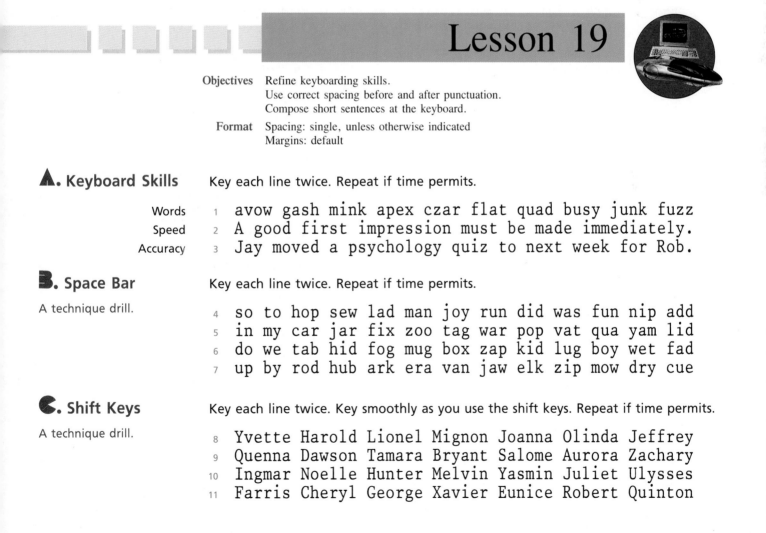

Objectives	Refine keyboarding skills.
	Use correct spacing before and after punctuation.
	Compose short sentences at the keyboard.
Format	Spacing: single, unless otherwise indicated
	Margins: default

A. Keyboard Skills

Key each line twice. Repeat if time permits.

Words   1   avow gash mink apex czar flat quad busy junk fuzz
Speed   2   A good first impression must be made immediately.
Accuracy   3   Jay moved a psychology quiz to next week for Rob.

B. Space Bar

A technique drill.

Key each line twice. Repeat if time permits.

4   so to hop sew lad man joy run did was fun nip add
5   in my car jar fix zoo tag war pop vat qua yam lid
6   do we tab hid fog mug box zap kid lug boy wet fad
7   up by rod hub ark era van jaw elk zip mow dry cue

C. Shift Keys

A technique drill.

Key each line twice. Key smoothly as you use the shift keys. Repeat if time permits.

8   Yvette Harold Lionel Mignon Joanna Olinda Jeffrey
9   Quenna Dawson Tamara Bryant Salome Aurora Zachary
10   Ingmar Noelle Hunter Melvin Yasmin Juliet Ulysses
11   Farris Cheryl George Xavier Eunice Robert Quinton

The circled numbers refer
to explanations on page
313.

May 22, 19--

Mr. Samuel Davis
A to Z Contractors, Inc.
4701 Hanna Drive
Memphis, TN 38128

Dear Mr. Davis:

① One of your employees, Chris Corsi, mentioned that you have a
secretarial position available at A to Z Contractors, Inc. I
would like to be considered as an applicant for this position.

② My keyboarding rate of 65 words a minute and my extensive
background in computers will enable me to serve your company as a
competent office worker. In addition, I possess a knowledge of
filing procedures and have received special training on telephone
usage, as you will see in the enclosed resume.

③ In addition to these specific office skills, I have also been an
active participant at several regional competitions for
parliamentary procedure. These activities have provided me with
valuable human relations and oral presentation skills.

④ I am definitely interested in working for A to Z Contractors. I
will telephone your office on June 4 to arrange for an interview
with you at your convenience. If you wish to speak to me before
that date, please telephone me at 901-555-1212.

Sincerely,

Janice L. Dale

Janice L. Dale
2110 Ellen Lane
Memphis, TN 38109

Enclosure

D. Tab Key

A technique drill.

Set four tabs—one every 10 spaces. Key each line once; tab between words. Repeat if time permits.

12 When	you	key,	use	the
13 correct	form.	It	is	easier
14 when	you	form	the	proper
15 habits.	Then	you	do	not
16 have	to	break	bad	ones.

E. Concentration

A technique drill.

Fill in the missing vowels as you key each line once. Repeat if time permits.

17 D- y-u ke-p yo-r ey-s on th- c-py y-u ar- key-ng?
18 Y-u m-st le-rn to th-nk wh-re all thos- k-ys ar-.
19 Ret-rn to th- h-me k-ys aft-r y-u go up -nd d-wn.
20 E-ch d-y thos- fing-rs w-ll m-ve a l-ttl- f-st-r.
21 On- d-y so-n yo-r f-ng-rs w-ll fly ov-r th- k-ys.

F. Punctuation Spacing

Key lines 22–26 once. Note the spacing before and after each punctuation mark. Repeat if time permits.

22 My favorite program is on; please turn on the TV.
23 We must talk to two people: Consuela and Carlos.
24 Accounting is a good course. I am taking it now.
25 Mrs. Y. O. Bickford and her son, B. J., are home.
26 Professor Jim Bell, Ph.D., is from Santa Fe, N.M.

G. 12-Second Timings

Take three 12-second timings on each line, or key each line three times. Try to key with no more than 1 error on each timing.

27 Make it a habit to be on time for class and work.
28 Good school habits will soon be good work habits.
29 Make up your mind to do the best that you can do.

```
    5    10    15    20    25    30    35    40    45    50
```

H. PRETEST

Take a 1-minute timing on lines 30–32. Proofread, note your errors, and figure your speed. Format: Double spacing, 5-space tab.

30   Have you tried to get a project completed by   10
31 a school deadline only to realize that you simply 20
32 are not able to finish?   25

```
  |  1  |  2  |  3  |  4  |  5  |  6  |  7  |  8  |  9  | 10
```

I. PRACTICE

Up reaches are consecutive letters on the home row and third row keyed by one hand. (task)

SPEED: If you made 2 or fewer errors on the Pretest, key each line twice.
ACCURACY: If you made more than 2 errors on the Pretest, key lines 33–35 as a group twice. Then key lines 36–38 as a group twice.

33 lo love ploys locks lobes block flock clock glove
34 gr gray grain grave groan grass grade grows great
35 ea zeal lease eases plead beast means treat seats

(Continued on next page)

5. Use figures for exact or approximate amounts of money.

The house was priced at $125,000.
We spent nearly $25,000 to air-condition the building.

6. Spell out indefinite numbers and amounts of money.

It seemed that thousands of people attended the exhibit.
The company lost many millions of dollars.

Practice Sentences   Key lines 36–37 twice each.

36   Sharon will spend about $3,500 for her new computer system.
37   Many thousands of dollars may soon be spent on these tasks.

7. Generally spell out all ordinal numbers that can be expressed in one or two words. A hyphenated number counts as one word.

The five hundredth anniversary of the discovery of America was in 1992.

8. Spell out street names from *First* through *Tenth;* use figures above *Tenth.* Also use figures for all house numbers except *One.* (Use *st, d,* and *th* except in dates when the day follows the month.)

We need to pick up the merchandise at 193 Tenth Street.
Mirabel lives at One East 68th Street.

Practice Sentences   Key lines 38–39 twice each.

38   Bernard will celebrate his fifteenth birthday on August 22.
39   The fire trucks rushed to the huge fire at 158 27th Street.

Application Sentences   Key lines 40–47 once, correcting errors in number style. Review your copy as your teacher reads the answers. Then key lines 40–47 again.

40   Heidi expects about forty to 45 students to sign up for class.
41   40 copies will be needed for the meeting next Wednesday.
42   Shall I do my shopping on 5th Avenue or on Fourth Street?
43   James and Sarah will fly to Spain on February 23d at ten p.m.
44   The cost of the new office furniture we purchased was nine hundred dollars.
45   It may cost a few 1,000,000 dollars for us to repay the debt.
46   The fall program began at ten o'clock and ended at one fifteen p.m.
47   Could we meet at 10:30 a.m., or would eleven o'clock be better?

F. Letters of Application

The resume is a summary of your skills and experience. When you send your resume to a prospective employer, you must, of course, send a cover letter—the *letter of application.* Together, the resume and the letter of application are your introduction to the company.

Limit your letter of application to one page—about four paragraphs, as shown in the letter on page 312. Note the exact purpose of each paragraph.

(Continued on page 313)

Down reaches are consecutive letters on the home row and bottom row keyed by one hand. (call)

36	sc scar scoot scold scent scant scare scone scrap
37	nk pink links blank honks sinks plank crank drink
38	av lava raven brave avoid shave favor avert paved

J.  POSTTEST

Take a 1-minute timing on lines 30–32 (page 42). Proofread, note your errors, and figure your speed. Compare your performance with the Pretest.

K. Composing at the Keyboard

Eyes on the monitor.

Answer the questions in lines 39–43 with complete sentences; repeat the question in each response. (See the example below.) Each sentence must have a subject and a predicate. Single-space each response, but double-space between responses.

Example question:
In which month do the leaves start to fall?

Example response:
The leaves start to fall in September.

39 *What are you going to do when you finish high school?*
40 *What is one way a computer can help you?*
41 *Why is good appearance important for a job interview?*
42 *What can pets teach us?*

Key the document code.

43 *Why are hurricanes dangerous?*

Lesson 20

Objectives	Refine keyboarding skills.
	Use correct spacing before and after punctuation.
	Compose short sentences at the keyboard.
Format	Spacing: single, unless otherwise indicated
	Margins: default

A. Keyboard Skills

Key each line twice. Repeat if time permits.

Words   1 plum waxy next qoph brag skit clod fizz jilt itch
Speed   2 It is good to meet new people as soon as you can.
Accuracy 3 Cover the oozy liquid wax before Jack mops again.

B. Alphabet Review

Key each line twice. Repeat if time permits.

4 equip gaudy whack major veins toxic quartz baffle
5 venom shady squaw fudge zebra spill jacket matrix
6 banjo rhyme affix quack laugh steep heaven wizard
7 Jinx lazy fingers; be quick to move them up/down.

 **PRACTICE**

In the chart below find the number of errors you made on the Pretest (page 309). Then key each of the following designated drill lines three times.

Pretest errors	0–1	2–3	4–5	6+
Drill lines	27–31	26–30	25–29	24–28

Accuracy

24 job seem research companies extremely confidence employment
25 can and employer interview difficult profitable conceivable
26 task you'll realize continue positive searching application
27 may take inquire complete guarantee successful professional

Speed

28 business finding sellers during first every about make your
29 officers however details nature steps going match hunt much
30 products success perform secure there apply until more must
31 occasion between people decide skills isn't right good have

 **POSTTEST**

Take another 5-minute timing on lines 6–23 (page 309). Proofread, note your errors, and figure your speed. Compare your performance with the Pretest.

E. LAB Review Numbers

1. Spell out numbers from 1 through 10; use figures for numbers above 10. However, any number that begins a sentence is spelled out.

   Only three buildings were constructed.
   Send 11 fliers and 28 brochures today.
   Seventeen printers were ordered for our department.

2. In technical copy and for emphasis, use figures for numbers.

   We must delete 13 lines in the copy.
   We have to add 3 liters of water to the solution.

Practice Sentences

Key lines 32–33 twice each.

32 Joe played six records that were recorded by three artists.
33 Today she ran 4.1 miles, which is equal to 6.63 kilometers.

3. In business writing, use figures for dates.

   The event is scheduled for August 10, 1999.

4. In business writing, use figures for most periods of time. If there are no minutes, omit the colon and zeros. (Use *a.m., p.m., noon, midnight,* or *o'clock.*)

   It is now 47 minutes after our scheduled departure 10:30 a.m.
   The session began at 7 o'clock.
   The flights are scheduled at 8 p.m. and 12 midnight.

Practice Sentences

Key lines 34–35 twice each.

34 I am going to see the play Cats at 8 o'clock on January 24.
35 At 12 noon we will leave home to make our 1:30 p.m. flight.

C. Shift Keys

A technique drill.

Key each line twice. Key smoothly as you use the shift keys. Repeat if time permits.

8 Kameko Latham Justin Pascal Hayley Isabel Nokomis
9 Winona Vernon Zenina Felice Elliot Carlos Timothy
10 Oliver Irving Phoebe Margot Javier Ursula Leilani
11 Samuel Warden Gwynne Regina Donata Arthur Querida

D. Tab Key

A technique drill.

Set four tabs—one every 10 spaces. Key each line once; tab between words. Repeat if time permits.

12 Keep   your   eyes   on   the
13 copy   as   you   press   the
14 tab.   Keep   it   smooth   as
15 you   glide   across   the   line.
16 Reach   for   the   right   keys.

E. Concentration

A technique drill.

Fill in the missing vowels as you key each line once. Repeat if time permits.

17 Ke-p y-ur elb-ws r-lax-d and cl-se to y-ur s-des.
18 K-ep b-th fe-t on th- flo-r, on- aft-r th- oth-r.
19 Ke-p yo-r b-ck er-ct, b-t le-n yo-r b-dy forw-rd.
20 K-ep y-ur h-ad up -nd t-rned tow-rd th- textb--k.
21 K--p all f-ng-rs curv-d -nd y--r wr-sts up a b-t.

F. Punctuation Spacing

Key lines 22–26 once. Note the spacing before and after each punctuation mark. Repeat if time permits.

22 If Kimball can go tomorrow, we will go then also.
23 That fly-by-night business was selling old disks.
24 Their flowers--especially the tulips--are lovely.
25 Their park has roads as well as hike/bike trails.
26 Have you seen my gloves? Are they in the drawer?

G. 30-Second Timings

Take two 30-second timings on lines 27–28. Then take two 30-second timings on lines 29–30. Try to key with no more than 2 errors on each timing.

27 Standing up for what you believe is not easy when   10
28 you seem to be the only one who takes that stand.   20

29 If you know that you are right, speak up. Others   10
30 will soon take courage and join your brave stand.   20
   | 1 | 2 | 3 | 4 | 5 | 6 | 7 | 8 | 9 | 10

H. PRETEST

Take a 1-minute timing on lines 31–33. Proofread, note your errors, and figure your speed. Format: Double spacing, 5-space tab.

31   There are fewer golf courses in Clark County   10
32 than in Milton County. One reason is the lack of   20
33 rich soil to grow grass.   25
   | 1 | 2 | 3 | 4 | 5 | 6 | 7 | 8 | 9 | 10

Lessons 136/137

Objectives Review and apply number-usage rules.
Format and key letters of application.
Key 40/5'/5e.

Format Spacing: Drills, single; Timings, double; and as required
Margins: Default or as required

▲. Keyboard Skills

Key lines 1–4 once. In line 5 use your enter/return key after each word. Repeat lines 1–4, or take a series of 1-minute timings.

Speed	1	This unit is built to help you with all of your job skills.	12
Accuracy	2	Poor Jack was vexed about my long and quite hazy falsehood.	12
Numbers	3	On 12/26/93 I read 47 want ads; on 12/30/93 I read 58 more.	12
Symbols	4	On 5/1/93 it was $.75; on 5/2/93 (a day later) it was $.85.	12
Technique	5	You have to strike the keys very rapidly to beat the clock.	

| 1 | 2 | 3 | 4 | 5 | 6 | 7 | 8 | 9 | 10 | 11 | 12

B. PRETEST

Take a 5-minute timing on lines 6–23. Proofread, note your errors, and figure your speed.

6   Finding a job can be an extremely difficult and tiring   12
7   task. As difficult as it may seem, however, there are some   24
8   positive steps you can take to make your job hunt much more   36
9   profitable.   38
10   First, you must realize that not every job application   50
11   you complete is going to guarantee employment. Not only is   62
12   it conceivable that many people may apply for the same job,   74
13   it is also possible that you may decide that this job isn't   86
14   the right one for you. You will have to continue searching   98
15   until you secure a good match between you and the employer.   110
16   Second, do some research on companies that you want to   122
17   interview. Inquire about who their executive officers are,   134
18   what kind of business they do, how successful they are, and   146
19   the nature of their major products and best-sellers.   156
20   Third, be a professional during your interview. Dress   168
21   for the occasion, brush up on your people skills, and build   180
22   your confidence by going over the details of your interview   192
23   so that you'll perform your very best.   200

| 1 | 2 | 3 | 4 | 5 | 6 | 7 | 8 | 9 | 10 | 11 | 12 SI 1.50

Discrimination reaches are keys that are commonly substituted and easily confused. (**wear**)

SPEED: If you made 2 or fewer errors on the Pretest, key each line twice.
ACCURACY: If you made more than 2 errors on the Pretest, key lines 34–36 as a group twice. Then key lines 37–39 as a group twice.

34 asa flask aside sails saved masks sadly trash sas
35 fgf frogs foggy gaffe fugue golfs goofs fight gfg
36 ewe weeks fewer sewer sweat swell sweet weans wew

37 ioi spoil toils lions coins joins soils boils oio
38 mnm hymns money names numbs minor lemon means nmn
39 klk locks block flock keels kills kilts kilns lkl

Take a 1-minute timing on lines 31–33. Proofread, note your errors, and figure your speed. Compare your performance with the Pretest.

J. POSTTEST

K. **Composing at the Keyboard**

Key the document code.

Answer the questions on lines 40–44 with complete sentences; repeat the questions in each response. Single-space each response, but double-space between responses.

40 *Why is it important to have friends?*
41 *Who are two people who have been in the news this week?*
42 *What are two cities that are state capitals?*
43 *Why do we have insurance on our automobiles?*
44 *What are two qualities you like about a teacher?*

UNIT 5

Keyboarding— Numbers and Symbols

Unit Goal 27/2'/4e

Lesson 21

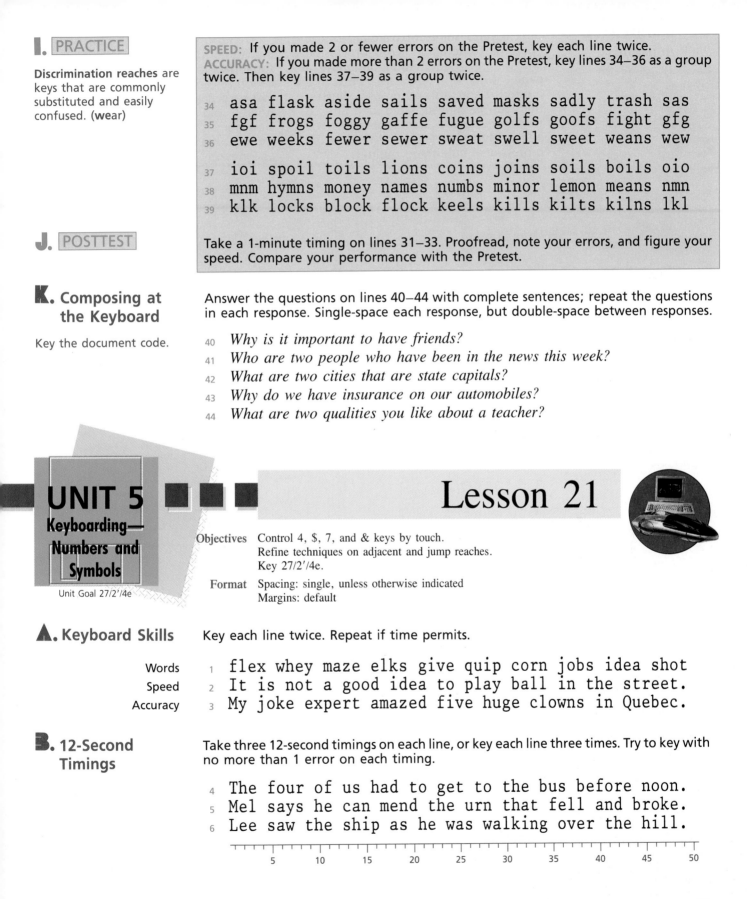

Objectives Control 4, $, 7, and & keys by touch.
Refine techniques on adjacent and jump reaches.
Key 27/2'/4e.

Format Spacing: single, unless otherwise indicated
Margins: default

A. Keyboard Skills

Key each line twice. Repeat if time permits.

Words
Speed
Accuracy

1 flex whey maze elks give quip corn jobs idea shot
2 It is not a good idea to play ball in the street.
3 My joke expert amazed five huge clowns in Quebec.

B. 12-Second Timings

Take three 12-second timings on each line, or key each line three times. Try to key with no more than 1 error on each timing.

4 The four of us had to get to the bus before noon.
5 Mel says he can mend the urn that fell and broke.
6 Lee saw the ship as he was walking over the hill.

5	10	15	20	25	30	35	40	45	50

F. Using Desktop Publishing

Desktop publishing software allows the operator to combine word processing and graphics together in designing a page. With this software, both the printed characters and graphic illustrations can be moved, sized, and altered to create a page that approaches the quality that is often found only in the professional publishing business.

Desktop publishing can be used by individuals to produce high-quality personal papers such as resumes and application letters. When used correctly, the software can produce professional results. If you have this software in your classroom, you can use it to provide a professional touch to your next assignment.

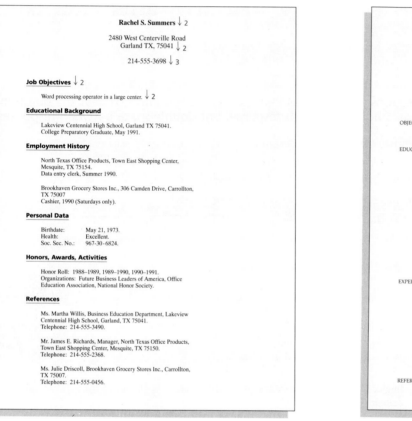

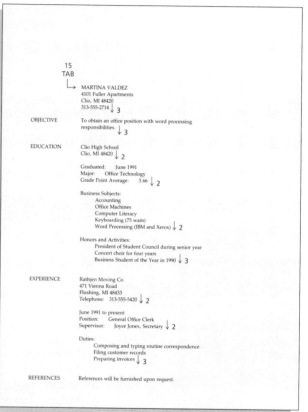

Form F16.134

Prepare a resume for yourself, using the guidelines introduced on pages 306 and 307 and the illustration appearing on page 306. Include all sections that are pertinent and applicable to your background and experience. Do not include a section if you have no entries to place in that section. Use your keyboarding teacher's name as one of your three references.

If you are using desktop publishing software, create the resume with your word processing software. Save it as F16.134, and import it into your desktop publishing software. To highlight the various sections

of the resume, complete the following steps:

1. Draw a single line around the entire resume.
2. Boldface your name, address, and telephone number.
3. Boldface and underscore all side headings.
4. Use the following point sizes:
   Your name: 18-point
   Your address and telephone number: 14- or 16-point
   Side headings: 14- or 16-point
   Text in the resume: 12-point

Hold Those Anchors
For **4 $** anchor A
For **7 &** anchor ;

To Practice Top Row Reaches:
Key each reach slowly to feel the distance and direction of the reach.
Then key it again more smoothly.

C.  **Key**

4 Use F finger.

Key each line twice. Repeat if time permits.

7 frf fr4f f4f 444 f4f 4/44 f4f 44.4 f4f 44,444 f4f
8 44 foes, 44 films, 44 flukes, 44 folders, or 4.44
9 I see 4 swans, 4 geese, and 44 ducks on the lake.

$ Shift of 4. Do not space between $ and the number.

10 frf fr4 f4f f4$f f$f f$f $4 $44 $444 f$f f4f $444
11 $4, 4 fans, $44, 44 fish, $444, 444 fellows, $444
12 He paid $4 for the pears and $44 for the oranges.

D.  **Key**

7 Use J finger.

Key each line twice. Repeat if time permits.

13 juj ju7j j7j 777 j7j 7/77 j7j 77.7 j7j 77,777 j7j
14 77 jets, 77 jumps, 77 jokers, 77 joggers, or 7.77
15 Tony will perform June 4 and 7, not July 4 and 7.

& Shift of 7.
Space before and after the ampersand.

16 juj ju7 j7j j7&j j&j j&j j& &j& ju7& j&j j7j ju7&
17 7 jars & 7 jugs & 7 jewels & 7 jurors & 7 jungles
18 He thinks he paid $47 & $74 instead of $44 & $77.

E. **Technique Checkpoint**

Keep eyes on copy while keying numbers and symbols.

Key lines 19–22 once. Then repeat lines 7, 10, 13, and 16.

19 C & R Shoe Store has the casual shoes on sale for 10
20 $44, but Toe & Heel is still charging $74 for the 20
21 same shoes. I paid $47 for a pair of dress shoes 30
22 at His & Hers last week, but I wish I had waited. 40
     | 1 | 2 | 3 | 4 | 5 | 6 | 7 | 8 | 9 | 10

F. PRETEST

Take a 1-minute timing on lines 23–25. Proofread, note your errors, and figure your speed. Format: Double spacing, 5-space tab.

23   Each of us should try to eat healthful food, 10
24 get proper rest, and exercise moderately in order 20
25 to face life with more enthusiasm.   27
     | 1 | 2 | 3 | 4 | 5 | 6 | 7 | 8 | 9 | 10

Alternative Formats for Resumes

The illustration below shows some alternative formats for the sections of a resume. The basic format may be changed by using one or more of the alternative features.

(A) The name, address, and telephone number are blocked at the left to start in the same printing position as each of the entries in the major sections of the resume.

(B) Section headings are keyed in all capitals.

(C) Pertinent business courses are identified in the education section.

(D) No references are given; instead, a statement is made that references will be sent upon request.

```
                             15
                             TAB
                              ↓
                             MARTINA VALDEZ
                             4101 Fuller Apartments
                             Clio, MI 48420
                             313-555-2714 ↓ 3

(A) → OBJECTIVE           To obtain an office position with word processing
                          responsibilities. ↓ 3

(B) → EDUCATION           Clio High School
                          Clio, MI 48420 ↓ 2

                          Graduated:  June 1991
                          Major:  Office Technology
                          Grade Point Average:  3.66 ↓ 2

                          Business Subjects:
                               Accounting
                               Office Machines
                               Computer Literacy
                               Keyboarding (75 wam)
                               Word Processing (IBM and Xerox) ↓ 2

                          Honors and Activities:
                               Student Council President during senior year
                               Concert choir for four years
                               Business Student of the Year in 1990 ↓ 3

(C) → EXPERIENCE          Rathjen Moving Co.
                          471 Vienna Road
                          Flushing, MI 48433
                          Telephone:  313-555-5420 ↓ 2

                          June 1991 to present
                          Position:  General Office Clerk
                          Supervisor:  Joyce Jones, Secretary ↓ 2

                          Duties:
                               Composing and keying routine correspondence
                               Filing customer records
                               Preparing invoices ↓ 3

(D) → REFERENCES          References will be furnished upon request.
```

Form F15.134
Key the resume shown above.

PRACTICE

SPEED: If you made 2 or fewer errors on the Pretest, key each line twice.
ACCURACY: If you made more than 2 errors on the Pretest, key lines 26–28 as a group twice. Then key lines 29–31 as a group twice.

Adjacent Reaches

26 er were every veers verge sewer error steer loner
27 op open opera moped hoped opine scoop sloop slope
28 tr tree tried troop train truth stray strip strum

Jump Reaches

29 ve even every veers vests verge verbs heave leave
30 ex flex exams exits exist exalt exact vexed Texas
31 on upon onion spoon phone wrong honor ozone front

Take a 1-minute timing on lines 23–25 (page 46). Proofread, note your errors, and figure your speed. Compare your performance with the Pretest.

H. POSTTEST

I. 1-Minute Alphanumeric Timing

Take one 1-minute timing on lines 32–34. Proofread, note your errors, and figure your speed. Format: Double spacing, 5-space tab.

32   Please take a $47 check to Rent & Run Videos   10
33 to get movies and snacks for the 44 girls who are   20
34 staying here from 4 p.m. to 7 a.m.   27
   | 1 | 2 | 3 | 4 | 5 | 6 | 7 | 8 | 9 | 10

J. 2-Minute Timings

To figure words-a-minute speed, divide the total number of words keyed by 2. Errors, however, are not divided.

35   Getting up in the morning is quite a job for   10
36 me. I grab my jacket and race for the yellow bus   20
37 just in time to miss it. Five more minutes would   30
38 have done it. Next time I will not doze so long.   40
39 Can I still make it? Maybe I will beat the bell;   50
40 at least I can try.   54
   | 1 | 2 | 3 | 4 | 5 | 6 | 7 | 8 | 9 | 10 SI 1.10

Lesson 22

Objectives   Control 3, #, 8, and ∗ keys by touch.
             Refine keyboarding skills.
             Key 27/2'/4e

Format   Spacing: single, unless otherwise indicated
         Margins: default

A. Keyboard Skills

Key each line twice. Repeat if time permits.

Speed   1 It will be time for us to stop when the sun sets.
Accuracy   2 Jeff Mendoza quickly plowed six bright vineyards.

(Continued on next page)

Resumes

Once you have identified a job you want to apply for, your first step is to prepare a *resume*—a summary of your training, background, and qualifications for the job.

A resume contains different sections, depending on what information you want to include about your education, experience, personal background, and so on. The resumes illustrated at the right and on page 307 show the basic information to include. Read directions A through G for formatting resumes. Follow the margin settings, spacing directions, and tab setting shown below the illustration at the right.

(A) **Heading.** For easy identification, begin the resume with your name, address, and telephone number, including your area code. (Center each line.)

(B) **Objective.** This is a statement of your job preference. It indicates to a prospective employer the type of job you are seeking.

(C) **Education.** If you have little business experience, list your education after your objective. The education section should begin with the highest level of education you have completed—that is, all items should be listed in *reverse* chronological order (the most recent first). For each entry you should include the name and address of the school, any diplomas earned and the years in which you earned them, the year you graduated, and your major area of study.

(D) **Experience.** If your experience is stronger than your education, include it after your objective. If not, place the experience section after the education section. For each job you include, give the name, address, and telephone number of the company; the dates of employment; your job title(s); and the name and title of your supervisor, if not included in the references section. You may also want to include a brief description of the duties you performed.

(E) **Personal Data.** By law, employers cannot ask certain questions—for example, an applicant's age. Thus many applicants choose *not* to include a personal data section. If you do choose to include a personal data section, you might wish to list such items as your height, weight, social security number, health, birth date, and marital status. If used, this section should be placed after the education and experience sections.

(F) **Honors, Awards, and Activities.** Achievements mentioned in this section may give you an "edge"

over other applicants. You should include your participation in clubs and organizations, any honors and awards you have received, and any special recognitions you have earned. You may also want to include your scholastic placement in your graduating class (such as "top 10 percent").

(G) **References.** The final section of a resume lists the names, job titles, addresses, and telephone numbers of at least three persons who can tell a prospective employer what kind of worker you are. For this reason most people use teachers, former supervisors, and former employers as references. Before you use anyone as a reference, you *must* get permission from each individual to use his or her name. Another option for the references section is simply to include this statement: "References will be furnished upon request."

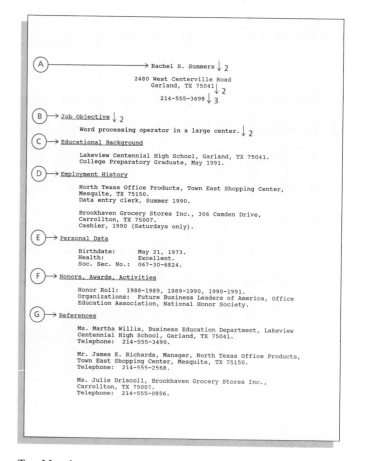

Top Margin:	*On page 1, 9 lines; on continuation pages, 6 lines.*
Left/Right Margins:	*1-inch.*
Bottom Margin:	*6 to 9 lines.*

Single-space within each entry; double-space as indicated. Use 5-space tab.

| Numbers | 3 | Lines 44, 47, and 74 were right; line 77 was not. |
| Symbols | 4 | Alpha & Beta pays $4, $4.77, and $7.44 for dimes. |

Hold Those Anchors
For **3 #** anchor A or F
For **8 ∗** anchor ;

B. **Key**

3 Use D finger.

Shift of 3. Do not space between the number and the #.

Key each line twice. Repeat if time permits.

5 ded de3d d3d 333 d3d 3/33 d3d 33.3 d3d 33,333 d3d
6 33 dots, 33 dimes, 33 dishes, 33 daisies, or 3.33
7 Draw 3 circles, 33 squares, and 3,333 rectangles.

8 ded de3 d3d d3#d d#d d#d #3 #33 #333 d#d d3d #333
9 #3, 3 dogs, #33, 33 dots, #333, 333 ditches, #333
10 Is Invoice #733 for 433#, 344#, or 343# of fruit?

C. **Key**

8 Use K finger.

∗ Shift of 8. Do not space between the word and the ∗ (asterisk).

Key each line twice. Repeat if time permits.

11 kik ki8k k8k 888 k8k 8/88 k8k 88.8 k8k 88,888 k8k
12 88 kegs, 88 kilns, 88 knocks, 88 kickers, or 8.88
13 The zoo has 33 zebras, 38 monkeys, and 88 snakes.

14 kik ki8 k8k k8∗k k∗k k∗k ∗8 ∗88 ∗888 k∗k k8k ∗888
15 ∗8, 8 keys, ∗88, 88 kits, ∗888, 888 kimonos, ∗888
16 This manual∗ and this report∗ are in the library.

D. Technique Checkpoint

Keep eyes on copy while keying numbers and symbols.

Key lines 17–20 once. Then repeat lines 5, 8, 11, and 14.

17 We found 38 references for Project #88. However, 10
18 the most important magazine∗ was not on Stack #33 20
19 or Stack #38. We asked the librarian on duty for 30
20 help; she said to look on page 383 of this book.∗ 40
| 1 | 2 | 3 | 4 | 5 | 6 | 7 | 8 | 9 | 10

 PRETEST

Take a 1-minute timing on lines 21–23. Proofread, note your errors, and figure your speed. Format: Double spacing, 5-space tab.

21   Do you brood when you make errors on papers? 10
22 It would be better to figure out what causes them 20
23 and to look for corrective drills. 27
| 1 | 2 | 3 | 4 | 5 | 6 | 7 | 8 | 9 | 10

Practice Sentences	Key lines 16–17 twice each.

16 Pat lived in the Midwest before she moved south to Florida.
17 The flood was severe in the northern section of the county.

4. Capitalize official titles that precede names, but do not capitalize titles that follow names.

The lecture on global warming was given by Professor James Hill.
We asked Mayor Jennings to attend the opening ceremonies.
Barbara Caulfield, mayor of Central City, was the guest speaker.

5. Capitalize names of days, months, holidays, and religious days. Do not capitalize the names of the seasons.

I believe that Mother's Day is on a Sunday in May.
We hold our conferences in the fall and winter.

Practice Sentences	Key lines 18–19 twice each.

18 Paulette Ashland, senator from West Virginia, did not vote.
19 On Monday we do not have school because of President's Day.

6. Capitalize a noun followed by a number or a letter that indicates sequence. However, do not capitalize the nouns *line*, *note*, *page*, *paragraph*, *size*, and *verse*.

Please refer to Exhibit A in Chapter 5 on page 7.
We copied note 1 and paragraph 2 in Section 1.

Practice Sentences	Key lines 20–21 twice each.

20 As you can see, Chart 4 in Part Four on page 17 is missing.
21 She will order size 10 on Invoice 2704 as note 3 indicated.

Application Sentences	Key lines 22–29 once, providing the missing capitals. Review your copy as your teacher reads the answers. Then key lines 22–29 again.

22 james and i grew up in montana, and every april we go home.
23 they knew that captain furgeson drove his ford on the trip.
24 the accident occurred on the west side of east 56th street.
25 i moved to the south right after the new office was opened.
26 the military representative, colonel hayden, spoke to them.
27 in the fall they will celebrate thanksgiving on a thursday.
28 i think verse 5 on page 238 of chapter X is the most vivid.
29 bob's assignment was to complete lines 22–25 in lesson 134.

E. Applying for a Job

Now that you are near the end of your first keyboarding course, you may soon be looking for a part-time or full-time job. In applying for a job, you will need to use your keyboarding skills (1) to prepare a resume, (2) to compose a letter of application, (3) to prepare a follow-up letter. You will also need to complete an application form. Each of these tasks is discussed on the following pages.

F. PRACTICE

SPEED: If you made 2 or fewer errors on the Pretest, key each line twice.
ACCURACY: If you made more than 2 errors on the Pretest, key lines 24–26 as a group twice. Then key lines 27–29 as a group twice.

Double Letters

24 tt Otto otter utter butte witty putty jetty attar
25 ll bill hills chill shell smell small stall allay
26 rr errs error berry terry carry worry furry hurry

Alternates

27 is down gland blame cycle eland signs clang prune
28 so hair roams handy title slack boney snake spent
29 go idle shape flaps whale shake their quake slant

G. POSTTEST

Take a 1-minute timing on lines 21–23 (page 48). Proofread, note your errors, and figure your speed. Compare your performance with the Pretest.

H. Number and Symbol Practice

Key each line once. Repeat if time permits.

30 38 cubs, 37 clubs, 34 stubs, 33 shrubs, 83 doubts
31 83 aims, 87 maids, 84 raids, 88 braids, 73 brains

32 78 inks, 48 links, 43 minks, 83 brinks, 33 drinks
33 34 cans, 88 canes, 73 manes, 84 cranes, 78 planes

before a number means "number"; # after a number means "pounds."

34 #4 blue, 8# roast, $3 paint, 77 books,* 3 & 4 & 8
35 #8 tree, 7# boxes, $4 horse, 38 lists,* 7 & 3 & 4

36 The geometry test grades were 88, 87, 84, and 83.
37 Seek & Find Research sells this book* for $37.84.

I. 1-Minute Alphanumeric Timing

Take one 1-minute timing on lines 38–40. Proofread, note your errors, and figure your speed. Format: Double spacing, 5-space tab.

38   Wheatly & Kingsly sent Statement #3887 to us 10
39 for closing the sale of our home at 43 Ryan Road; 20
40 that other law firm* charges $748.   27
   | 1 | 2 | 3 | 4 | 5 | 6 | 7 | 8 | 9 | 10

J. 2-Minute Timings

Take two 2-minute timings on lines 41–46. Proofread, note your errors, and figure your speed. Format: Double spacing, 5-space tab.

41   While you work, be sure to keep your eyes on 10
42 the text. If you quit looking at the words, your   20
43 eyes just may lose their spot and zip back to the   30
44 wrong line. As you read your timing, it will not   40
45 make sense because of the words that are missing.   50
46 Every error adds up.   54
   | 1 | 2 | 3 | 4 | 5 | 6 | 7 | 8 | 9 | 10 SI 1.11

B. 30-Second Timings

Take two 30-second timings on lines 6 and 7. Then take two 30-second timings on lines 8 and 9. Try to key with no more than 2 errors on each timing.

6 A resume should be prepared without error; an employer will   12
7 look very closely at the quality of work put into a resume.   24

8 When you go for a job interview, obtain as much information   12
9 as you can about the company and the people who work there.   24
    | 1 | 2 | 3 | 4 | 5 | 6 | 7 | 8 | 9 | 10 | 11 | 12

C. "OK" Timings

Take two 30-second "OK" (errorless) timings on lines 10–11. Then take two 30-second "OK" timings on lines 12–13. Goal: No errors.

10 Hazel hurt her elbow when she jumped quickly from the taxi,   12
11 and the fall also gave her a sore shoulder until Wednesday.   24

12 The six jet-black vans zipped quietly through the wet road,   12
13 but they were not able to finish the entire course in time.   24
    | 1 | 2 | 3 | 4 | 5 | 6 | 7 | 8 | 9 | 10 | 11 | 12

D. LAB Review Capitalization

In Units 7 through 18 you completed 24 LABs (Language Arts for Business) that presented modern rules of punctuation and style. In this unit you will review many of these LABs and will complete exercises related to them. Learning activities will be introduced through (1) brief reviews of the rules, (2) examples of each rule, (3) sentence practice for each rule, and (4) sentence applications of all the rules.

1. Capitalize every proper noun and the first word of every sentence. Also capitalize the pronoun *I*.

Proper nouns:	Major Andrews	Salt Lake City	Pontiac
Common nouns:	major	city	car

Complete sentence: She and I bought the same brand of microcomputer.

Practice Sentences

Key lines 14–15 twice each.

14 We moved to Arizona in May; in January we moved to Georgia.
15 Dr. Lander does not believe that I flew to Spain and Italy.

2. Capitalize *north, south, east,* and *west* when they refer to specific regions, are part of a proper noun, or are within an address.

Shirley lived in the North until 1992. (Specific region.)
Sam worked for the West Side Shopping Center. (Part of proper noun.)
Jan's new address is 340 South Maple Avenue. (Part of address.)

You must face east when taking the picture. (General direction.)
Ron's office is on the east side of the city. (General location.)

3. Capitalize *northern, southern, eastern,* and *western* when they refer to specific people or regions, not when they refer to general locations or directions.

Karen worked for Northern Realty Company.
Karen sold most of the homes in the southern part of the county.

Lesson 23

Objectives   Control 2, @, 9, and (keys by touch.
Refine keyboarding skills.
Key 27/2'/4e.

Format   Spacing: single, unless otherwise indicated
Margins: default

A. Keyboard Skills

Key each line twice. Repeat if time permits.

Speed   1 The goal of trade schools is to teach job skills.

Accuracy   2 Lazy Jaques picked five boxes of oranges with me.

Numbers   3 The answer is 87 when you add 43 and 44 together.

Symbols   4 Invoices #37 and #84 from T & V Supply were $834.

Hold Those Anchors
For **2 @** anchor F
For **9 (** anchor J

B. @/2 Key

2 Use S finger.

Key each line twice. Repeat if time permits.

5 sws sw2s s2s 222 s2s 2/22 s2s 22.2 s2s 22,222 s2s

6 22 sips, 22 sites, 22 swings, 22 signals, or 2.22

7 The class used 22 disks, 23 ribbons, and 24 pens.

@ Shift of 2. @ means "at." Space once before and after an @.

8 sws sw2 s2s s2@s s@s s@s @2 @22 @222 s@s s2s @222

9 @2, 2 sets, @22, 22 sons, @222, 222 sensors, @222

10 They bought 2 pens @ $2.23 and 4 markers @ $8.72.

C. (/9 Key

9 Use L finger.

Key each line twice. Repeat if time permits.

11 lol lo9l 19l 999 19l 9/99 19l 99.9 19l 99,999 19l

12 99 laps, 99 loops, 99 lilies, 99 lifters, or 9.99

13 Hugh said 99 times not to ask for the 99 flavors.

(Shift of 9. Space once before an opening parenthesis; do not space after it.

14 lol lo9 19l 19(1 1(1 1(1 (9 (99 (999 1(1 19l (999

15 (9, 9 logs, (99, 99 lots, (999, 999 latches, (999

16 lo9((99((9 lo9(1 lo(9(9(9 (9(9(9 1(lo9(o19(

Table T65.133
Boxed table. Single spacing; 3 spaces between columns.

Continental Oil Company
Current Recommendations

Company	Earnings Last Year	Earnings This Year	Earnings Next Year*	Percent Yield
Apex Corp.	$ 4.26	$ 4.63	$ 5.38	0.3
Craytech, Inc.	3.50	3.78	4.18	1.8
Global Corp.	2.28	2.98	3.28	2.7
Manchester Corp.	2.40	3.74	4.33	2.5
Mexcal Petroleum	9.51	11.20	12.25	1.4
Textonic, Inc.	6.28	6.83	7.33	2.6
Union Int'l.	2.50	3.41	4.23	0.6

* Anticipated

UNIT 19
Lab Review and Applying for a Job

Unit Goal 40/5'/5e

Lessons 134/135

Objectives   Review and apply capitalization rules.
Format and key resumes.
Use desktop publishing software, if available.

Format   Spacing: Drills, single; and as required
Margins: Default or as required

▲. **Keyboard Skills**   Key lines 1–4 once. In line 5 concentrate on shift key techniques as you capitalize each word. Repeat lines 1–4, or take a series of 1-minute timings.

Speed	1	We could not get the stick off the top of the roof for her.	12
Accuracy	2	Sixteen black crows frequently seized Jim's huge grapevine.	12
Numbers	3	I saw 10 planes, 29 cars, 38 trains, 47 buses, and 56 jets.	12
Symbols	4	Chris* paid 3% more for the $8.50 table (which was ruined).	12
Technique	5	One Three Five Seven Nine Eleven Thirteen Fourteen Fifteen.	

| 1 | 2 | 3 | 4 | 5 | 6 | 7 | 8 | 9 | 10 | 11 | 12

D. Technique Checkpoint

Keep eyes on copy while keying numbers and symbols.

Key lines 17–20 once. Then repeat lines 5, 8, 11, and 14 (page 50).

17 The shift of the 9 key is the (, but the (has to   10
18 have the other one before it can be used. On the   20
19 other hand, the shift of the 2 is @, and @ can be   30
20 used all by itself. Can you key 2 and 9 quickly?   10
    | 1 | 2 | 3 | 4 | 5 | 6 | 7 | 8 | 9 | 10

E. 30-Second Timings

Take two 30-second timings on lines 21–22. Then take two 30-second timings on lines 23–24. Try to key with no more than 2 errors on each timing.

21 We will go to the fair in the city for lunch, and   10
22 we will stay to hear the band and see the parade.   20

23 The desk was moved over to the left side, but all   10
24 of us who work at the desk liked it on the right.   20

F. PRETEST

Take a 1-minute timing on lines 25–27. Proofread, note your errors, and figure your speed. Format: Double spacing, 5-space tab.

25   Were you in the biology group that mixed the   10
26 ragweed seeds with the vegetable seeds? That was   20
27 why Jon and Kim sneezed all month.   27
    | 1 | 2 | 3 | 4 | 5 | 6 | 7 | 8 | 9 | 10

G. PRACTICE

SPEED: If you made 2 or fewer errors on the Pretest, key each line twice.
ACCURACY: If you made more than 2 errors on the Pretest, key lines 28–30 as a group twice. Then key lines 31–33 as a group twice.

Left Reaches

28 gas bread verge dated cease refer feast crest bar
29 saw vests vexed graze tread seeds tests weeds far
30 car crate beast farce wears serve grace wards tab

Right Reaches

31 nip pupil hippo imply nippy unpin jumpy oomph pop
32 oil plink pulpy holly puppy lumpy milky nylon mom
33 hum pylon minim union jolly ninon mummy Yukon you

H. POSTTEST

Take a 1-minute timing on lines 25–27. Proofread, note your errors, and figure your speed. Compare your performance with the Pretest.

I. 1-Minute Alphanumeric Timing

Take one 1-minute timing on lines 34–36. Proofread, note your errors, and figure your speed. Format: Double spacing, 5-space tab.

34   Tours #72 and #43 will begin at noon and are   10
35 scheduled to end at 3:28 p.m. If you want to pay   20
36 now, the total cost for two is $9.   27
    | 1 | 2 | 3 | 4 | 5 | 6 | 7 | 8 | 9 | 10

Key each line twice as a preview to the 5-minute timings below.

Accuracy 5 next unit quick popular impulse powerful computer megahertz
Speed 6 what more than many look only that most have also will them

C. 5-Minute Timings

Take two 5-minute timings on lines 7–24. Proofread, note your errors, and figure your speed.

7 Just what makes a computer more powerful than another? 12
8 The reasons are many, but let's look at only a few that are 24
9 the most popular. Quick and powerful computers have a fast 36
10 clock speed, which is measured in megahertz. The very fast 48
11 computers run at around 33 megahertz, which also makes them 60
12 very powerful. 63
13 A powerful computer can also store a lot of data. The 75
14 term that's used to describe the storage unit of a computer 87
15 is known as random-access memory. Memory can vary from one 99
16 computer to another, but you should try to get at least one 111
17 million bytes of memory. 116
18 The next factor that can determine the power and speed 128
19 of your computer is measured by the number of bits that can 140
20 be processed at one time. A bit is the smallest measure or 152
21 impulse inside the computer; it takes eight of them to make 164
22 a byte. Many computers today process data at a speed of 16 176
23 bits or higher. It won't be long before a larger number of 188
24 bits will be used to process data. 195

| 1 | 2 | 3 | 4 | 5 | 6 | 7 | 8 | 9 | 10 | 11 | 12 SI 1.47

Table T64.133
Boxed table. Single spacing; 7 spaces between columns.

ANALYSIS OF FIRST-QUARTER SALES

Branch	Computers	Word Processors	Totals
Boston	186	58	244
Detroit	843	429	1,272
Houston	1,107	967	2,074
Milwaukee	639	240	879
Oklahoma City	908	624	1,532
San Francisco	927	597	1,524

LESSON 133

Take two 2-minute timings on lines 37–42. Proofread, note your errors, and figure your speed. Format: Double spacing, 5-space tab.

37	The man got on the subway and set his bag of	10
38	glass jars on the floor with care. His feet were	20
39	bound in squalid rags; his hands were gloved with	30
40	plastic. His sad, dull eyes gave him the look of	40
41	an exile; he had no home, for he was a citizen of	50
42	the lonely streets.	54

| 1 | 2 | 3 | 4 | 5 | 6 | 7 | 8 | 9 | 10 SI 1.13

Lesson 24

Objectives Control 1, !, 0, and) keys by touch.
Refine keyboarding skills.
Key 27/2'/4e.

Format Spacing: single, unless otherwise indicated
Margins: default

A. Keyboard Skills

Key each line twice. Repeat if time permits.

Speed 1 The big lake was filled with wild ducks or geese.
Accuracy 2 Ten foxes quickly jumped high over twelve zebras.
Numbers 3 Mrs. Hernandez said to read pages 29, 38, and 47.
Symbols 4 Hit & Miss Hardware had #8 nails @ $2.39 a pound.

Hold Those Anchors
For **1 !** anchor F
For **0)** anchor J

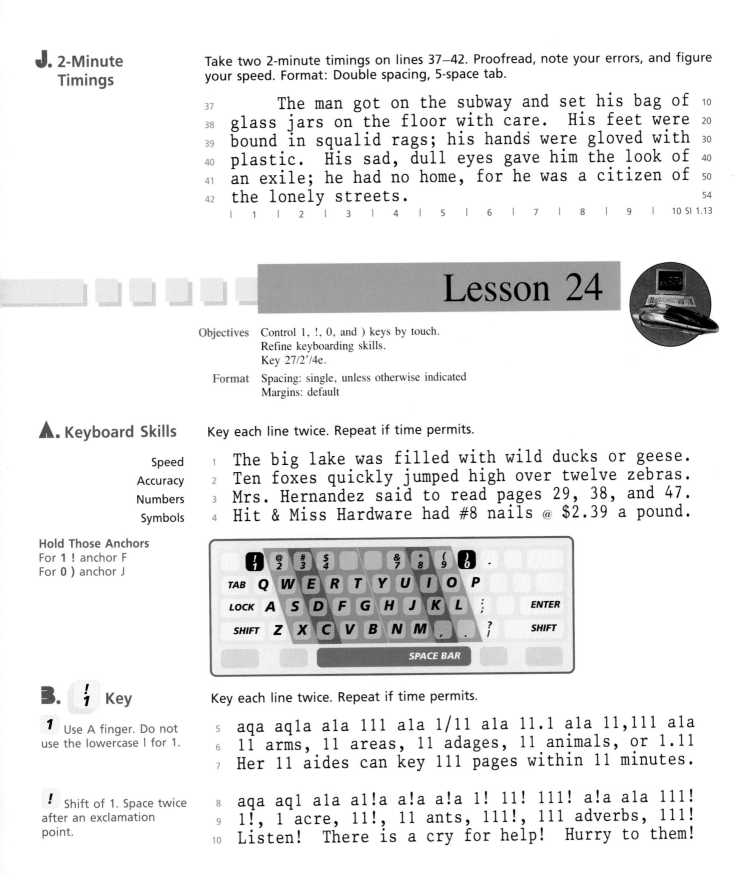

B. ¹⁄₁ Key

1 Use A finger. Do not use the lowercase l for 1.

Key each line twice. Repeat if time permits.

5 aqa aq1a a1a 111 a1a 1/11 a1a 11.1 a1a 11,111 a1a
6 11 arms, 11 areas, 11 adages, 11 animals, or 1.11
7 Her 11 aides can key 111 pages within 11 minutes.

! Shift of 1. Space twice after an exclamation point.

8 aqa aq1 a1a a1!a a!a a!a 1! 11! 111! a!a a1a 111!
9 1!, 1 acre, 11!, 11 ants, 111!, 111 adverbs, 111!
10 Listen! There is a cry for help! Hurry to them!

 **Boxed Tables**

A boxed table contains vertical lines between columns as well as horizontal lines. The standard format for ruled tables is used to format boxed tables. (See Lesson 56, page 133.) Use a black pen and a ruler to draw in the vertical lines after you print the table.

Note: You may use line draw to create the horizontal and the vertical lines. For horizontal lines, return once before and once after the line. For vertical lines, leave an uneven number of spaces between columns—5, 7, and so on—as the vertical line will occupy a space. (In some programs, line draw cannot be used for vertical lines when the copy is double-spaced. Use single spacing and an extra hard return at the end of each line to achieve double spacing.)

Table T63.132
Boxed table. Single spacing; 5 spaces between columns.

ESTIMATED PASSENGER TRAFFIC AT WORLD AIRPORTS

Airport	City	International Miles	Domestic Miles
Heathrow	London	28,568,017	2,822,324
J. F. Kennedy	New York	11,490,342	11,056,238
Frankfurt-Main	Frankfurt	9,634,230	4,329,812
De Gaulle	Paris	7,550,932	853,834
Kastrup	Copenhagen	6,795,902	1,680,867

Lesson 133

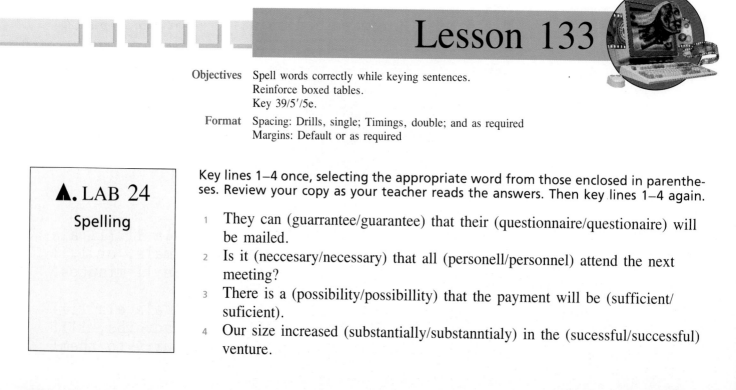

Objectives Spell words correctly while keying sentences.
Reinforce boxed tables.
Key 39/5'/5e.

Format Spacing: Drills, single; Timings, double; and as required
Margins: Default or as required

▲. LAB 24

Spelling

Key lines 1–4 once, selecting the appropriate word from those enclosed in parentheses. Review your copy as your teacher reads the answers. Then key lines 1–4 again.

1 They can (guarrantee/guarantee) that their (questionnaire/questionaire) will be mailed.
2 Is it (neccesary/necessary) that all (personell/personnel) attend the next meeting?
3 There is a (possibility/possibillity) that the payment will be (sufficient/suficient).
4 Our size increased (substantially/substanntialy) in the (sucessful/successful) venture.

C.  Key

0 Use Sem finger. Do not use the capital O for 0.

) Shift of 0 (zero). Space once after a closing parenthesis; do not space before it.

D. Technique Checkpoint

Keep eyes on copy; hold home key anchors.

E. 12-Second Timings

F.  PRETEST

G.  PRACTICE

Up Reaches

Key each line twice. Repeat if time permits.

11 ;p; ;p0; ;0; 000 ;0; 1.00 ;0; 20.0 ;0; 30,000 ;0;
12 300 parts, 700 planks, 800 parades, 900 particles
13 Can you add these: 10, 90, 20, 80, 30, 70, & 40?

14 ;p; ;p0 ;0; ;0); ;); ;);););;);;; ;); ;0;);;;
15 ;0; ;0) ;); ;); 10) 20) 30) 40) 70) 80) 90) 1001)
16 That car (the convertible) is her favorite color.

Key lines 17–20 once. Then repeat lines 5, 8 (page 52), 11, and 14.

17 Follow these steps when keying symbols: (1) cap, 10
18 (2) strike, and (3) home. Keep your eyes on your 20
19 copy! Move smoothly as you shift and reach for 1 30
20 or 0. Concentrate! Learn to make those reaches! 40

Take three 12-second timings on each line, or key each line three times. Try to key with no more than 1 error on each timing.

21 They have a lot of work to do before they can go.
22 If it does not rain, we will go to his new house.
23 Those girls held a social to pay for their visit.

| 5 | 10 | 15 | 20 | 25 | 30 | 35 | 40 | 45 | 50 |

Take a 1-minute timing on lines 24–26. Proofread, note your errors, and figure your speed. Format: Double spacing, 5-space tab.

24   Dave and I took our backpacks and started up 10
25 the old mountain trail. About sunset, we stopped 20
26 to set up camp and have a hot meal. 27

| 1 | 2 | 3 | 4 | 5 | 6 | 7 | 8 | 9 | 10 |

SPEED: If you made 2 or fewer errors on the Pretest, key each line twice.
ACCURACY: If you made more than 2 errors on the Pretest, key lines 27–29 as a group twice. Then key lines 30–32 as a group twice.

27 il pail trail child spill build drill filed lilac
28 st step casts start nasty blast stone guest stair
29 ho shot homes holly hover shove phone chose shock

(Continued on next page)

Lesson 132

Objectives Identify frequently misspelled words while keying sentences.
Reinforce financial statements.
Format and key a boxed table.

Format Spacing: Drills, single; and as required
Margins: Default or as required

▲. LAB 24

Spelling

Key lines 1–4 once. Then repeat lines 1–4, or take a series of 1-minute timings. (The spelling words are underlined.)

```
1   The questionnaire is to be sent out no later than tomorrow.    12
2   Their prices increased substantially in the past two weeks.    12
3   This year's bazaar was extremely successful, thanks to you.    12
4   We have a sufficient number of items for the grand opening.    12
    |  1  |  2  |  3  |  4  |  5  |  6  |  7  |  8  |  9  |  10  |  11  |  12
```

B. 12-Second Timings

Take three 12-second timings on each line, or key each line three times. Try to key with no more than 1 error on each timing.

```
5   He can key a form, a memo, and a table by the end of class.
6   Be sure that you check all your work before you hand it in.
7   Check for the right spelling in all the words that you use.
        5    10    15    20    25    30    35    40    45    50    55    60
```

Table T62.132 Balance Sheet

Use .75-inch side margins. Calculate totals.

Major Touch Cleaners
Balance Sheet
December 31, 19--

Assets

Cash	$ 12,000.00
Accounts Receivable	500.00
Equipment	77,000.00
Supplies	250.00
Total Assets	

Liabilities

Loans Payable	$ 4,000.00
Income Tax Payable	2,500.00
Total Liabilities	6,500.00

Partners' Equity

J. Fillmore, Capital	$ 45,000.00
M. Fillmore, Capital	38,250.00
Total Equity	
Total Liabilities and Equity	

Down Reaches

```
30  av have shave paved waved knave avert gavel ravel
31  ca camp scamp scale cable carve catch recap pecan
32  ab able about abate cable cabin habit labor squab
```

H. POSTTEST

Take a 1-minute timing on lines 24–26. Proofread, note your errors, and figure your speed. Compare your performance with the Pretest.

I. 1-Minute Alphanumeric Timing

Take one 1-minute timing on lines 33–35. Proofread, note your errors, and figure your speed. Format: Double spacing, 5-space tab.

```
33      Lucy said to buy a dozen (12) pumpkin pies @   10
34  $1.97 from the deli at 483 Willow Road.  However,  20
35  they had only 10 left when I went.                 27
    |  1  |  2  |  3  |  4  |  5  |  6  |  7  |  8  |  9  |  10
```

J. 2-Minute Timings

Take two 2-minute timings on lines 36–41. Proofread, note your errors, and figure your speed. Format: Double spacing, 5-space tab.

```
36      When you must deal with an angry person, the   10
37  best thing to do is just listen; you must not get  20
38  angry too.  Stay calm, and try to help him or her  30
39  realize that you hear what is being said.  Do not  40
40  expect a swift change to your point of view; this  50
41  is not a quick job.                                54
    |  1  |  2  |  3  |  4  |  5  |  6  |  7  |  8  |  9  |  10 SI 1.14
```

Lesson 25

Objectives   Control 5, %, 6, and ^ keys by touch.
Refine keyboarding skills.
Key 27/2'/4e.

Format   Spacing: single, unless otherwise indicated
Margins: default

A. Keyboard Skills

Key each line twice. Repeat if time permits.

Speed   1 The team and band are ready for the game tonight.
Accuracy 2 Six heavy guys jumped for a waltzing quarterback.
Numbers   3 The top five winners were 17, 43, 20, 89, and 33.
Symbols   4 Our shop (A & V) has #10 envelopes* @ $.25 a doz.

Table T60.131 Balance Sheet
Use .75-inch side margins

The Aztec Club ↓2
BALANCE SHEET ↓2
For the Year Ending June 30, 19-- ↓3

ASSETS
Supplies on Hand $279.70
Cash in Bank 526.69
Accounts Receivable 214.52
    Total Assets .... $1,020.91 ↓2

LIABILITIES
Accounts Payable $314.08
Refunds on Memberships 123.10
    Total Liabilities .... $ 437.18 ↓2

EQUITY
Capital $415.75
Profit from Club Activities 167.98
    Total Equity 583.73
      Total Liabilities and Equity ... $1,020.91

Table T61.131 Income Statement
Use default margins.

Lawler and Smith, Inc. ↓2
SUMMARY INCOME STATEMENT ↓3

SALES .... $43,412.87 ↓2

COST OF GOODS SOLD
Beginning Inventory.................... $31,226.48
Inventory Purchases 14,436.08
Total Available $45,662.56
Ending Inventory 28,573.08
    Cost of Goods Sold .... 17,089.48 ↓2

GROSS PROFIT ON SALES .... $26,323.39 ↓2

EXPENSES
Selling Expense $13,122.40
Rent Expense 3,547.98
Heat and Light 2,580.02
Depreciation of Equipment 1,098.98
    Total Expenses .... 20,349.38 ↓2

NET INCOME BEFORE TAXES .... $ 5,974.01

Hold Those Anchors
For **5 %** anchor A
For **6 ^** anchor ;

Reach Guide
Because 5 and 6 are long reaches, they are the hardest to control. Concentrate on them and master them so that all the number keys will be easy for you.

B.  **Key**

5 Use F finger.

Key each line twice. Repeat if time permits.

5 ftf ft5f f5f 555 f5f 5/55 f5f 55.5 f5f 55,555 f5f
6 55 fins, 55 facts, 55 fields, 55 futures, or 5.55
7 We saw 55 sheep, 15 goats, 155 cows, and 5 bulls.

% Shift of 5. The % is used in statistical data. Do not space between number and %.

8 ftf ft5 f5f f5%f f%f f%f 5% 55% 555% f%f f5f 555%
9 5%, 5 foes, 55%, 55 fees, 555%, 555 fiddles, 555%
10 Our meal is 20% starch, 25% fat, and 55% protein.

C.  **Key**

6 Use J finger.

Key each line twice. Repeat if time permits.

11 jyj jy6j j6j 666 j6j 6/66 j6j 66.6 j6j 66,666 j6j
12 66 jaws, 66 jokes, 66 judges, 66 jackets, or 6.66
13 The averages were 96.36, 86.56, 81.66, and 76.46.

^ Shift of 6. The ^ (caret) is used for the function of exponentiation in some programming languages.

14 jyj jy6 j6j j6^j j^j j^j ^j ^jj ^jjj j^j j6j ^jjj
15 6^, 6 jigs, 66^, 66 jabs, 666^, 666 jigsaws, 666^
16 Our math test had these problems: 5^2, 3^4, 8^3.

D. Technique Checkpoint

Keep eyes on copy while keying numbers and symbols.

Key lines 17–20 once. Then repeat lines 5, 8, 11, and 14.

17 Mrs. Gibson said to work problems 5 and 6 on page 10
18 55, but I worked problems 5 and 6 on page 66. Do 20
19 you understand how to find 15% of 56 or 6% of 65? 30
20 Will you explain how to find 136^5 and 75^6 also? 40
   | 1 | 2 | 3 | 4 | 5 | 6 | 7 | 8 | 9 | 10

E.  **Alphabet Review**

Key each line once. Repeat if time permits.

21 aa alas also after again bb bake blow begin black
22 cc came coat charm clear dd drop door dream dated

23 ee ever each eager enemy ff five foal frame flute
24 gg game give grate guard hh hope hall heavy human

25 ii iced into ideal ionic jj jail joke jewel juice
26 kk keep kick knife knock ll long lace lower lever

(Continued on next page)

Objectives   Recognize frequently misspelled words while keying sentences.
Format and key financial statements.

Format   Spacing: Drills, single; and as required
Margins: Default or as required

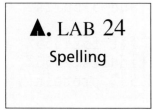

A. LAB 24

Spelling

Key lines 1–4 once. Then repeat lines 1–4, or take a series of 1-minute timings. (The spelling words are underlined.)

1   Tim can <u>guarantee</u> that you will be satisfied with our work.   12
2   Do you <u>believe</u> that it is <u>necessary</u> to be there at 10 a.m.?   12
3   They have enough <u>personnel</u> to finish all jobs by Wednesday.   12
4   There is a <u>possibility</u> that they will postpone the meeting.   12

| 1 | 2 | 3 | 4 | 5 | 6 | 7 | 8 | 9 | 10 | 11 | 12

Words containing double letters are frequently misspelled in written communications. Study the list below to improve your spelling of these words.

guarantee   necessary   personnel   possibility
questionnaire   substantially   successful   sufficient

B. Formatting Financial Statements

Periodic financial statements help businesses to analyze cash flow, profit and loss, and other important financial data. Among the monthly, quarterly, or yearly statements that are commonly used are the balance sheet and the income statement (see page 299).

Because it is important to compare a current financial statement with past statements, they should be formatted consistently.

To format financial statements:

1. Use a 2-inch top margin and default side margins. (If the statement is very wide, make the margins narrower, or change the font to a smaller size.)

2. Position the money columns only 2 spaces apart (not 6) for easier reading. Set a left leader tab for the first money column; set a decimal tab for the second money column.

3. Key major entries in all caps. Double-space before major entries.

4. Capitalize the first letter of each major word in subentries.

5. Indent subentries 5 spaces from the left margin.

6. Indent *Total* lines 5 spaces from the beginning of the line above.

7. Underline separate groups of numbers that must be added or subtracted. Remember: The underlines must be as wide as the longest entry including the dollar sign. Activate the underline function and space to the start of the shorter numbers.

8. Use a double underline under selected total lines.

Double Underline   Some word processing software allows you to select either a single or a double underline.

Line Draw   Some word processing software contains a feature called **line draw** that enables the user to draw a variety of lines: single lines, double lines, thin lines, thick lines. Unlike lines made with the underline feature, lines drawn with the line draw feature occupy a separate horizontal line.

27 mm mope mail merit music nn name none never night
28 oo over open order occur pp pure pain piece plump
29 qq quit quad quest quote rr roar rain rhyme rural
30 ss sing soap saber sense tt time talk tooth trait
31 uu ugly upon usual until vv vase vine vocal vivid
32 ww west warm wince wrong xx axis exit xenon x-ray
33 yy year yank young yield zz zany zinc zebra zonal

F. Number and Symbol Review

Key each line once. Repeat if time permits.

34 63 maps, 96 snaps, 56 traps, 15 drapes, 46 grapes
35 75 lots, 58 plots, 61 slots, 50 floats, 68 cloaks

36 35 hams, 64 trams, 95 slams, 26 flames, 67 blames
37 85 ails, 60 sails, 69 nails, 54 snails, 74 trails

38 (1) 23% of $17, (2) 2^9, (3) 15 @ $.81, (4) Wait!
39 (5) the key,* (6) A & W, (7) 65 @ $.10, (8) 40^3*

40 He rented 65 tables, 392 chairs, and 4,078 vases.
41 Mona said 2^3 and 20% of 40 have the same answer.

42 Eve collected 89 leaves, 93 bugs, and 74 flowers.
43 A & Z billed us for 97 pens @ $.23 on Invoice #8.

44 The 473 people were served 980 rolls by 12 girls.
45 Neat & Clean (formerly #1 Laundry) is in Memphis.

G. 1-Minute Alphanumeric Timing

Take one 1-minute timing on lines 46–48. Proofread, note your errors, and figure your speed. Format: Double spacing, 5-space tab.

46   Mandy ran 10.84 miles last week, and Michele   10
47 ran 9.76 miles. They are training for the 5K run   20
48 that is scheduled for November 23.   27
   | 1 | 2 | 3 | 4 | 5 | 6 | 7 | 8 | 9 | 10

H. 2-Minute Timings

Take two 2-minute timings on lines 49–54. Proofread, note your errors, and figure your speed. Format: Double spacing, 5-space tab.

49   Those who can run fast for a short time make   10
50 good sprinters. Those who excel in long runs can   20
51 be good distance racers. To win a race, you have   30
52 to join those contests which use your skills. Do   40
53 not quit if you fail. Analyze your strengths and   50
54 then win with them.   54
   | 1 | 2 | 3 | 4 | 5 | 6 | 7 | 8 | 9 | 10 SI 1.14

E. Distribution Lists in Memos

Because of the number of people who might be receiving a memo, it is not always possible to enter their names in the space provided at the top of the memo after the guide words *MEMO TO:*. In this instance the names should be placed at the bottom of the memo. To format a distribution list in a memo:

1. Key the words *See distribution below* after the guide words *MEMO TO:* at the top of the memo.
2. Key the word *Distribution:* at the left margin a triple space below the last notation. Underline the word (but not the colon).
3. Begin the list of names, arranged alphabetically, at the left margin, a double space below the word *Distribution:*.

```
MEMO TO:   See distribution below

FROM:      J. R. Toomey

DATE:      May 5, 19--

SUBJECT:   Computers in Education Conference
```

```
map is attached to help you find your way through the downtown
area.  We know this is going to be one of the finest meetings we
have ever held, and we look forward to seeing you there.

rs
Attachment

Distribution:

T. Adams
R. Collins
D. Herrera
L. Lopez
B. Poranski
K. Sandell
B. Thompson
```

Memo M12.130
Use a boilerplate memo form. Today's date.

[Distribution:] N. Booker, L. Edigner, R. Lopez, B. McNeill, W. Mooney, J. Symarek, R. Wong / [*FROM:*] Gail Morgan / [*SUBJECT:*] Annual Goals / Attached is a draft of our annual goals. I hope you will all have an opportunity to review the draft prior to our meeting on the 16th. I look forward to any suggestions or ideas you may have. ¶ My sincere thanks to those of you who sent in materials from which this draft was prepared. See you Friday morning in Conference Room 216. / [*Your initials*] / Attachment

F. Routing Lists for Memos

A routing list is used to send the same memo to several persons. To be sure that all addressees read the memo, each person initials his or her name and passes the memo on to the next person on the list. The last person on the list often returns the memo to the person who circulated it.

A routing list is formatted very much like a distribution list.

To format a routing list:

1. Key the words *See below* after the guide words *MEMO TO:*.
2. Key the word *Route:* over the list instead of the word *Distribution:*.
3. Key four underscores after each name to allow each person to write his or her initials.

Memo M13.130
Use a boilerplate memo form. Today's date.

[Route:] Adrian Abriatti, Lisa Doran, John Gilbert, Gary Jenkins, Carla Stander, Ruth Walters / [*FROM:*] Christian Reynolds / [*SUBJECT:*] Promotion List / Enclosed is the promotion list for the Northeast Division. As you are aware from the comments made at the last meeting, only 80 percent of all recommended promotions were granted. ¶ Please check the list to see if all your respective personnel promotions are included. Pass the list on to the next person on the list until all managers have had the opportunity to review the names. Then return this list to me. / [*Your initials*] / Enclosure

Level 2

Goals

1. Demonstrate speed and accuracy on straight copy with a goal of 32 words a minute for 3 minutes with 5 or fewer errors.
2. Demonstrate an ability to use the numeric keypad and special symbols on the keyboard.
3. Demonstrate an ability to locate and correct errors.
4. Demonstrate an ability to center material horizontally and vertically on a page.
5. Demonstrate an ability to understand proofreader's marks by making appropriate corrections in text copy.
6. Demonstrate basic formatting skills on enumeration, outlines, single-page and multipage academic reports, personal-business letters, and business letters.
7. Apply rules for correct use of word division and capitalization in written communication.

In sports medicine, the computer is used in a variety of ways. The two most common are indirect calorimetry and biomechanics. Indirect calorimetry involves metabolic measurements that indicate how hard a person is exercising. Biomechanics is an analysis of human motions. Athletes use biomechanics to improve their performance.

Take a 5-minute timing on lines 6–22. Proofread, note your errors, and figure your speed.

```
 6        Have you ever felt run-down, tired, and fatigued?  The    12
 7   symptoms just mentioned are experienced by many of us these    24
 8   days.  They adversely affect our job performance, limit the    36
 9   time we can spend with our families and friends, and affect    48
10   our health.  The paragraph that follows gives a few ways to    60
11   minimize these problems as we become more active persons in    72
12   all our activities.                                            76
13        It is essential that we get plenty of sleep so that we    88
14   are rested when we get up each morning.  We must eat a good   100
15   breakfast so that we can build up energies for the day that   112
16   follows.  Physical exercise is needed, and it might well be   124
17   the one most important ingredient in building up our energy   136
18   reserves.  We should participate in exercise that increases   148
19   our breathing rates appreciably, makes our hearts beat more   160
20   quickly, and causes us to perspire.  Such exercise helps us   172
21   to increase our energies and become healthier people.  Life   184
22   will be more enjoyable if we can focus on these actions.      195
     |  1  |  2  |  3  |  4  |  5  |  6  |  7  |  8  |  9  |  10  |  11  |  12  SI 1.48
```

In the chart below find the number of errors you made on the Pretest. Then key each of the following designated drill lines three times.

Pretest errors	0–1	2–3	4–5	6+
Drill lines	26–30	25–29	24–28	23–27

Accuracy

```
23   have tired exercise fatigued important enjoyable ingredient
24   beat ever energies physical essential mentioned appreciably
25   felt down increase possible breakfast breathing experienced
26   just many suggests minimize healthier paragraph performance
```

Speed

```
27   family people times limit today rate ways with they and the
28   become health build sleep these help well that more our job
29   person active heart thing cause life take must most all get
30   things plenty focus might quite each beat make part for day
```

Take another 5-minute timing on lines 6–22. Proofread, note your errors, and figure your speed. Compare your performance with the Pretest.

Lesson 26

Objectives Control 4, 5, 6 and 1, 2, 3 on the numeric keypad.
Refine symbol-key skills.
Refine composing-at-the-keyboard techniques.
Key 30/2'/4e.

Format Spacing: Drills, single; Timings, double
Margins: Default

▲. Keyboard Skills

Key each line twice. Repeat if time permits.

Speed   1 Cheryl may wish to sell this land if she owns it.
Accuracy 2 Skip was quite vexed by the jazzman from Cologne.
Numbers 3 Key the date as 6/3/97 or 6-3-97 or June 3, 1997.
Symbols 4 When H & L orders it at a 5% discount, #8 is $10.

B. Numeric Keypad

The **home keys** for the numeric keypad are **4, 5,** and **6.** Numeric keypads often have a raised dot on the 5 key to help your fingers stay in the correct position. Place your J K L fingers on 4 5 6.

Most computers have a separate enter key on the numeric keypad; use the Sem finger to control it. Otherwise, use the J finger to control the regular enter/return key.

C.

Keys

Use J K L fingers.

Keep eyes on copy.

This exercise will appear as one long column of numbers.

Enter each line of numbers below. Keep your eyes on the copy, and use the proper finger for each key. Press Enter once after each three-digit number. Press Enter twice before starting the next line of numbers. Repeat if time permits.

5	444	555	666	445	446	554	556	664	665	456
6	455	466	544	566	644	655	454	545	565	656
7	464	646	456	465	546	564	645	654	465	546

8	444	445	446	455	466	456	454	465	464	444
9	555	554	556	544	566	546	545	564	565	555
10	666	664	665	644	655	645	646	654	656	666

D.

Keys

Use J K L fingers.

Accuracy is very important when entering numbers. When you finish, proofread carefully.

Enter each line of numbers below. Keep your eyes on the copy, and use the proper finger for each key. Press Enter once after each three-digit number. Press Enter twice before starting the next line of numbers. Repeat if time permits.

11	414	141	411	144	441	114	444	414	525	636
12	525	252	522	255	552	225	555	525	636	414
13	636	363	633	366	663	336	666	636	414	525

(Continued on next page)

Memo M11.129
Use a boilerplate memo form. Fit the names in the space available. Use today's date.

[*MEMO TO:*] Tina Bonds, Terry Fowler, Steve Moore, Tracie Shelton / [*FROM:*] Royce Manders / [*SUBJECT:*] Annual Meeting / The annual conference of the Association for Computer Dealers (ACD) will be held in Los Angeles during the week of September 10, 19—. As area support representatives, you might like to know about some of the sessions we have planned for this year's meeting, and I have attached a copy for your information. We hope you will be able to pass this information around to the various computer users in your area. / [*Your initials*] / Attachment

Table T59.129
Prepare the following information to be sent as the attachment to the above memo. Arrange it in three columns with the headings *Date, Time,* and *Topic.* Single-space the items; double-space between the items. Provide a suitable title.

September 10, 8:30-9:30 a.m., ''Laser Printer Upgrades''
September 10, 2:00-3:00 p.m., ''Network Use: It Doesn't Come Easy''
September 10, 5:00-6:00 p.m., ''High-Speed Modems—The Right Touch''
September 11, 1:00-2:00 p.m., ''Graphics in the Fast Lane for the 1990s''
September 11, 3:00-4:15 p.m., ''What Price Do You Pay for Enough Power?''
September 12, 6:30-7:45 p.m., ''Why Your Company Needs a 32-Bit Machine''

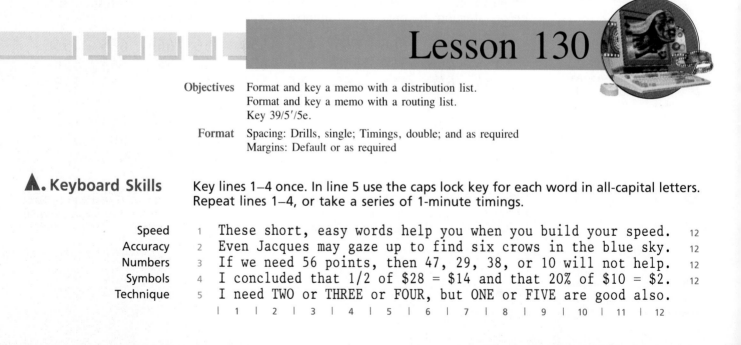

Lesson 130

Objectives   Format and key a memo with a distribution list.
Format and key a memo with a routing list.
Key 39/5'/5e.

Format   Spacing: Drills, single; Timings, double; and as required
Margins: Default or as required

▲. Keyboard Skills

Key lines 1–4 once. In line 5 use the caps lock key for each word in all-capital letters. Repeat lines 1–4, or take a series of 1-minute timings.

Speed	1	These short, easy words help you when you build your speed.	12
Accuracy	2	Even Jacques may gaze up to find six crows in the blue sky.	12
Numbers	3	If we need 56 points, then 47, 29, 38, or 10 will not help.	12
Symbols	4	I concluded that 1/2 of $28 = $14 and that 20% of $10 = $2.	12
Technique	5	I need TWO or THREE or FOUR, but ONE or FIVE are good also.	

| 1 | 2 | 3 | 4 | 5 | 6 | 7 | 8 | 9 | 10 | 11 | 12

14	414	415	416	144	155	166	145	146	541	641
15	525	524	526	255	244	266	254	256	452	652
16	636	634	635	366	355	344	364	365	463	563

E. Technique Checkpoint

Keep eyes on copy.
Use proper fingers.
Concentrate on accuracy.

Enter each line of numbers below. Keep your eyes on the copy, and use the proper finger for each key. Press Enter once after each three-digit number. Press Enter twice before starting the next line of numbers. Repeat if time permits.

17	456	546	645	564	654	123	213	312	231	321
18	144	145	146	255	254	256	366	365	364	153
19	441	451	461	552	542	562	663	653	643	624
20	412	413	414	415	416	412	423	434	445	456
21	521	523	524	525	526	512	523	534	545	556
22	631	632	634	635	636	612	623	634	645	656

F. Symbol Review

Key each line twice. Repeat if time permits.

23 Luke has a sister (his oldest) who lives in Rome.
24 Rachel bought 17 doughnuts @ $.15 from Yum & Yum.
25 Henry needed a loan at 12%, but the rate was 16%.
26 We found #4 blue dye, but there was no #2 yellow.
27 Look! There has been a car accident on Loop 281!

G. 12-Second Timings

Take three 12-second timings on each line, or key each line three times. Try to key with no more than 1 error on each timing.

28 All of my homework is done, and my room is clean.
29 Now I can do what I want for the next four hours.
30 It would be nice to take the dog for a long walk.

5	10	15	20	25	30	35	40	45	50

H. 2-Minute Timings

Remember to key the document code when this lesson is completed.

Take two 2-minute timings on lines 31–36. Proofread, note your errors, and figure your speed.

31 Just before school is out in the spring, the 10
32 seniors start to realize that they must make some 20
33 plans for their lives. Most, though, do not know 30
34 exactly what type of job they want or which major 40
35 they might choose in school. What they should do 50
36 is to move toward goals that equip them for life. 60

| 1 | 2 | 3 | 4 | 5 | 6 | 7 | 8 | 9 | 10 SI 1.14 |

I. Composing at the Keyboard

Respond to the questions on lines 37–39 with three or four short sentences. Keep your eyes on the screen as you compose the sentences; do not look at your hands.

37 *What are four facts about your state?*
38 *What are three things you like about a good friend?*
39 *What are four reasons why we should say "no" to illegal drugs?*

B. 12-Second Timings

Take three 12-second timings on each line, or key each line three times. Try to key with no more than 1 error on each timing.

5 The wall will come down if they do not fix it at this time.
6 We need to take a rest if we want to finish this job today.
7 They can eat their meal in the next small town on the road.

5	10	15	20	25	30	35	40	45	50	55	60

C. Concentration

A technique drill.

Key lines 8–11 once, reading the words from right to left. Keep your eyes on the copy, and strive for complete concentration.

8 lazily; exercises keyed having from habits jerky acquire We
9 forces that practice by habits bad such overcome can we but
10 taught. been we've as smoothly, keying on concentrate to us
11 copy. the on concentrate must we backwards, lines keying By

D. Multiple Addressees in Memos

A memo that is being sent to several people should contain all the names in the heading (do not use a copy notation). To format multiple addressees in memos:

1. Insert the names after the guide words *MEMO TO:*, separating each name with a comma.
2. Be sure to leave 1 blank line (a double space) between the last name and the next line of the heading.

Note: If the memo is being prepared on a form, the names must fit in the space available. Use an initial instead of a first name to save space when several names need to be inserted or when the amount of space is limited.

```
MEMO TO:  T. Blake, J. Gainer, C. Thomas   DATE:  February 29, 19--
   FROM:  Audrey Dupont
SUBJECT:  Work Schedule
```

```
MEMO TO:  Teresa Blake, John Gainer,   FROM:  Audrey Dupont
          Charlotte Thomas
SUBJECT:  Work Schedule             DATE:  February 29, 19--
```

Memo M10.129

Use a boilerplate memo form. Fit the names in the space available. (Remember to use typeover mode for the heading information.) Use today's date.

[*MEMO TO:*] Irving Gold, Nona Osborne, Peggy O'Neal / [*FROM:*] Peter Karingada / [*SUBJECT:*] Course Approval / All new-course requests were approved at this month's curriculum meeting; however, we have to make some changes in our request for an additional 12 microcomputers for our word processing lab. It was suggested that we obtain new bids for our microcomputers, as our request was based on bids that we received last August. ¶ Please have your revised bids ready for next month's meeting. / [*Your initials*]

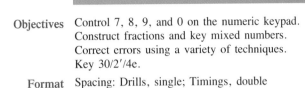

Objectives Control 7, 8, 9, and 0 on the numeric keypad.
Construct fractions and key mixed numbers.
Correct errors using a variety of techniques.
Key 30/2'/4e.

Format Spacing: Drills, single; Timings, double
Margins: Default

A. Keyboard Skills

Key each line twice. Repeat if time permits.

Speed   1   We kept our financial records for the first year.

Accuracy   2   Taxi drivers quickly zip by the jumble of wagons.

Numbers   3   Registers 10, 29, 38, 47, and 56 did not balance.

Symbols   4   The reference book* was $29 after a 25% discount.

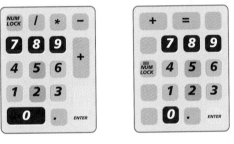

B.  Keys

Use J K L fingers.

An error in a number is not as obvious as an error in a word. Concentrate on accuracy as you enter the numbers.

Enter each line of numbers below. Keep your eyes on the copy, and use the proper finger for each key. Press Enter once after each three-digit number. Press Enter twice before starting the next line of numbers. Repeat if time permits.

5	474	747	477	744	447	774	444	417	528	639
6	585	858	588	855	558	885	555	528	639	417
7	696	969	699	966	669	996	666	639	417	528
8	417	418	419	147	148	149	744	745	746	747
9	527	528	529	257	258	259	854	855	856	858
10	637	638	639	367	368	369	964	965	966	969

C.  0 Key

Use right thumb.

Enter each line of numbers below. Keep your eyes on the copy, and use the proper finger for each key. Press Enter once after each three-digit number. Press Enter twice before starting the next line of numbers. Repeat if time permits.

11	400	401	402	403	404	405	406	407	408	409
12	500	510	520	530	540	550	560	570	580	590
13	600	690	580	470	630	520	410	407	508	609
14	700	701	702	703	704	105	106	107	108	109
15	800	801	802	803	804	205	206	207	208	209
16	900	901	902	903	904	305	306	307	308	309

Letters L77.128 and L78.128
Form letters. Modified-block style.

(1) Create the base letter from the copy below. Save the document as L77.128. (2) Create a merge file for the three people listed below, if you have this capability. (3) Prepare letters for each of the three people. (4) Save each of the letters; if using separate file names, use L78A.128, L78B.128, and L78C.128.

November 1, 19— / (Name 1) / (Street Address) / (City, State ZIP Code) / Dear (Last Name): / A colleague of yours, (Name 2), recommended your name to me as a person who might be willing to help me with a research study I am conducting on computer technology at West Georgia College. ¶ Your input will help me reach my goal for the number of respondents I hope to include from (State). In addition, your expertise in (Area) will provide helpful information in this area of computer technology. ¶

Please use the enclosed preaddressed envelope to return the enclosed questionnaire to me. I look forward to including you as one of the participants in my study and hope to hear from you before December 1. / Sincerely, / Donald L. Crawford / Professor / [*Your initials*] / 2 Enclosures

L78A Mr. Raymond Bentley / 24 South Walnut Street / Stillwater, OK 74074 / Mr. Bentley / (Name 2) Clint Hale / (State) Oklahoma / (Area) word processing

L78B Ms. Dorothy Garcia / 1130 Lee Highway / San Angelo, TX 76903 / Ms. Garcia / (Name 2) Marcia Adams / (State) Texas / (Area) databases

L78C Dr. Charlotte Luna / 2350 Palomas Drive / Albuquerque, NM 87118 / Dr. Luna / (Name 2) Robert Kingsford / (State) New Mexico / (Area) desktop publishing

Lesson 129

Objectives   Spell words correctly while keying sentences.
Reinforce keyboarding skill through concentration drills.
Format memos with multiple addressees.
Reinforce tables.

Format   Spacing: Drills, single; and as required
Margins: Default or as required

▲.LAB 23

Spelling

Key lines 1–4 once, selecting the appropriate word from those enclosed in parentheses. Review your copy as your teacher reads the answers. Then key lines 1–4 again.

1   We would like to (accomodate/accommodate) the request of every (employe/employee).
2   We (appreciate/appreceate) all the work you did on the (curicullum/curriculum) guide.
3   The (correspondence/correspondance) must be sent in (approximately/aproximmately) one month.
4   The violator will be (assesed/assessed) an (appropriate/apropriate) fee by Friday.

D. Technique Checkpoint

Keep eyes on copy.
Use proper fingers.
Concentrate on accuracy.

Enter each line of numbers below. Keep your eyes on the copy, and use the proper finger for each key. Press Enter once after each three-digit number. Press Enter twice before starting the next line of numbers. Repeat if time permits.

```
17  751  962  873  503  321  734  520  731  113  791
18  263  701  228  673  339  491  301  552  677  319
19  207  553  910  442  406  662  123  456  789  654
20  540  498  664  205  764  880  969  121  494  757
21  919  228  337  486  785  513  487  980  225  428
22  853  167  755  119  909  704  945  326  830  350
```

E. Constructing Fractions

To construct a fraction, use the slash key.

Use the numbers across the top of the keyboard as you key each line twice. Repeat if time permits.

```
23  1/3, 3/4, 4/7, 6/10, 5/12, 9/14, 17/18, and 11/20
24  Now add 1/5, 2/5, 1/10, and 3/10; my answer is 1.
25  Other fractions are 7/12, 44/75, 8/31, and 16/23.
26  Can you add 2/3, 1/4, 3/4, 11/12, 7/12, and 1/24?
```

F. Keying Mixed Numbers

Mixed numbers are whole numbers with fractions. Space once between the number and the fraction.

Key each line twice. Repeat if time permits.

```
27  Key:  3 7/8, 9 5/12, 47 1/2, 56 4/5, and 99 2/17.
28  My room is 12 2/3 feet wide and 14 1/2 feet long.
29  This glass holds 8 1/2 oz; that one holds 10 1/4.
30  Delcie worked 7 1/4 days of the last 2 1/2 weeks.
```

G. 2-Minute Timings

Key the document code when this lesson is completed.

Take two 2-minute timings on lines 31–36. Proofread, note your errors, and figure your speed.

```
31      The end of a semester would be just great if   10
32  it were not for the tests.  It is a joy to finish   20
33  the term and have all the courses done.  The only   30
34  shadow is exams.  Some students, though, like the   40
35  tests, since they show how much has been learned.   50
36  What is a puzzle to one is quite clear to others.   60
     |  1  |  2  |  3  |  4  |  5  |  6  |  7  |  8  |  9  |  10 SI 1.17
```

H. Correcting Errors

In Lesson 28 you will begin to *format* (arrange) documents. Before saving or printing a document, you should carefully proofread it and correct any errors.

It is very easy to correct errors using word processing software. Most programs offer a variety of features that will aid you in proofreading and producing accurate documents.

One such feature is a **spell checker**. A spell checker "proofreads" a document and highlights misspelled words. Some spell checkers even suggest possible correct spellings; all the user has to do is select the appropriate word. A spell checker, however, cannot find errors such as keying *from* instead of *form* or *their* instead of *there*. The user still must proofread a document carefully after using the spell checker.

Other features that aid in correcting errors in **editing** (correcting, changing, rearranging) documents are explained on page 62.

(Continued on next page)

Take a 5-minute timing on lines 5–21. Proofread, note your errors, and figure your speed.

```
 5        The way the computer works is quite a mystery to some,    12
                      1                           2
 6   for it is able to execute its tasks at a speed difficult to    24
              3                      4
 7   comprehend.  To understand how a computer works is not that    36
          5              6                            7
 8   complicated when you realize that it is like a light switch    48
                  8                        9
 9   that is turned on or off.  Computers store data in millions    60
            10                 11                          12
10   of cells, each of which is capable of holding an electrical    72
                          13                     14
11   charge.  When the cells are being charged with electricity,    84
                 15                     16
12   characters such as letters, numbers, or special symbols are    96
         17                18                   19
13   being stored in the memory of the computer.                  105
                  20              21

14        Each cell that is used to store data in the computer's  117
                      22                           23
15   memory is called a byte.  A byte is only one character; and   129
                24                   25
16   if you wanted to store a five-letter word in the computer's   141
          26                27                        28
17   memory, you would need five bytes of memory.  Moving data a   153
                  29                         30
18   character at a time appears to be a slow, tedious task that   165
              31          32
19   would take forever to complete.  However, computers work at   177
         33              34                     35
20   the speed of light; and the processing of millions of bytes   189
                  36                37
21   takes just a matter of seconds.                              195
           38              39
     |  1  |  2  |  3  |  4  |  5  |  6  |  7  |  8  |  9  |  10  |  11  |  12  SI 1.45
```

In the chart below find the number of errors you made on the Pretest. Then key each of the following designated drill lines three times.

Pretest errors	0–1	2–3	4–5	6+
Drill lines	25–29	24–28	23–27	22–26

Accuracy

```
22   quite appears charged realize mystery electrical comprehend
23   some however capable millions complete character understand
24   able tedious special numbers execute processing electricity
25   switch current difficult computer's complicated five-letter
```

Speed

```
26   appears turned moving speed works light that when like data
27   holding letter wanted store cells which each with such used
28   seconds symbol called tasks being would only word need five
29   matters stored memory works takes bytes work time slow take
```

Take another 5-minute timing on lines 5–21. Proofread, note your errors, and figure your speed. Compare your performance with the Pretest.

① Delete or Backspace. If the error is noticed immediately, use the delete or backspace key to remove the incorrect character(s); then key the correct text. **Note:** Some computers have both a delete key, which deletes the character at the cursor, and a backspace key, which deletes the character to the left of the cursor.

Practice: Key the sentence below as shown. Delete the letters in color immediately after you key them.

```
Wee hearrd a loneley woolf howwl.
```

② Insert. If a letter, word, space, or line has been omitted, use the arrow keys to move the cursor to the correct position, and then simply key the text using the insert mode.

Practice: Key the sentence below.

Make sure you are in insert mode. Position the cursor on the first letter of <u>will</u> and key <u>and Jeremy</u> ; then position the cursor on the first letter of <u>contest</u> and key <u>and ensemble</u> .

```
Kay will enter the solo contest.
```

③ Typeover. The typeover (or overstrike) mode allows one letter or word to be replaced by another. The insert mode cannot be used while the typeover mode is being used.

Practice: Key the sentence below.

Change to typeover mode; then position the cursor on the first letter of <u>Joe</u> and key <u>Kay</u>. Use arrow keys (do not space) to position the cursor on the first letter of <u>bus</u>, and key <u>new mall</u>.

```
Joe walked to the bus stop again.
```

④ Word Delete. Some word processors permit deleting one word at a time.

Practice: Key the sentence below.

Use the word delete feature to delete <u>Lou,</u> and <u>Tad,</u> .

```
We paid Tom, Lou, Ken, Tad, and Ben.
```

⑤ Line Delete. Most word processors have a feature that allows deleting one line at a time or deleting from the cursor to the end of the line.

Practice: Key the following lines exactly as shown. (Tap the enter/return key at the end of each line.)

Use the line delete feature to delete the second line. Then move the cursor to the <u>c</u> in <u>computers</u> in the first line and delete the rest of that line.

```
We enjoyed learning the history of computers; it has
helped us understand and appreciate the importance of
the great men and women who have contributed to the
development of computers.
```

⑥ Block Delete. This feature should be used if a large amount of text needs to be deleted.

Practice: Key the four lines in the line delete practice above. Mark the text to be blocked; then block-delete all the text.

Correction Practice: Key the 2-minute timing paragraph (lines 31–36) on page 61 at your fastest rate. Then use all the features of your word processing software to proofread and correct the copy.

	L76A	L76B	L76C
	Ms. Faye Hays	Mr. Alvin Morgan	Mr. Lloyd Blair
	450 Marshall Avenue	212 Rockview Court	318 Culloden Court
	Charlotte, NC 28211	Charlotte, NC 28211	Charlotte, NC 28214
	Ms. Hays	Mr. Morgan	Mr. Blair
	$75.45	$102.35	$82.40
	March 15	March 20	March 25

March 1, 19-- ↓₆

(Name)
(Street Address)
(City, State ZIP Code)

Dear (Last Name):

We want to thank you for your bus*i*ness with us at our Shannon Mall store. Your agreement states that your (1st) quarterly payment of (Amount) is due on (Date). For your convenience a coupon book is ~~attached~~ *enclosed* that you can use to make *this* payment and all future payments.

Be sure to place Simonson's mailing address in the ~~window~~ part of the envelope that is *also* enclosed for your use in mailing us *your* payment. ¶ We appreciate your business and hope to serve your appliance needs in the coming years. / Sincerely, / William Renfrow / Accounts Receivable / [Your initials] / 2 Enclosures

Lesson 128

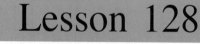

Objectives   Identify frequently misspelled words while keying sentences.
Reinforce form letters with inserts.
Key 39/5'/5e.

Format   Spacing: Drills, single; Timings, double; and as required
Margins: Default or as required

▲. LAB 23
Spelling

Key lines 1–4 once. Then repeat lines 1–4, or take a series of 1-minute timings. (The spelling words are underlined.)

```
1  We were assessed a late fee of $15 for our overdue payment.      12
2  Marlin has not yet received the correspondence from Denise.      12
3  Our business curriculum might include a keyboarding course.      12
4  She was the only employee in our department to be promoted.      12
   |  1  |  2  |  3  |  4  |  5  |  6  |  7  |  8  |  9  |  10  |  11  |  12
```

Lesson 28

Objectives   Improve technique on the tab key.
Refine techniques on adjacent and jump reaches.
Center items horizontally (across) on a page.

Format   Spacing: Drills, single; Timings, double; and as noted
Margins: Default

A. Keyboard Skills

Key each line twice. Repeat if time permits.

Speed   1   The boys said their job was to cut down the bush.
Accuracy   2   Having Ben wait, Joel quickly fixed many zippers.
Numbers   3   Now read this new order: 10, 29, 38, 47, and 56.
Symbols   4   Buy 15# of seed (rye grass) @ $1.59 a pound soon.

B. Tab Key

A technique drill.

Set 8 tabs every 6 spaces. Tab between numbers and words. Repeat if time permits.

5	55	fin	88	kit	33	dot	66	ham	77
6	99	log	22	saw	11	ant	44	fog	66
7	75	jug	19	quo	35	eat	13	axe	40
8	94	oar	68	yak	46	ran	26	win	82
9	20	sip	57	gnu	01	pea	83	ice	79

C. PRETEST

Take a 1-minute timing on lines 10–12. Proofread, note your errors, and figure your speed.

10   If they have any extra fruit and milk, would   10
11   you deliver them to the annex? I must buy twenty   20
12   stamps tomorrow to mail out my food drive fliers.   30
     | 1 | 2 | 3 | 4 | 5 | 6 | 7 | 8 | 9 | 10

D. PRACTICE

SPEED: If you made 2 or fewer errors on the Pretest, key lines 13–18 twice each. Repeat if time permits.
ACCURACY: If you made more than 2 errors on the Pretest, key lines 13–15 as a group twice. Then key lines 16–18 as a group twice. Repeat if time permits.

Adjacent Reaches

13   ui suit fruit quint squid guilt quilt fluid guide
14   we west tower power swept tweed jewel dowel fewer
15   lk milk talks yolks sulks hulks stalk silky balky

(Continued on next page)

Take a 1-minute timing on lines 5–8. Proofread, note your errors, and figure your speed.

```
 5        You can get a better grade in your courses if you will    12
 6    allow enough time to find and delete or erase any errors as    24
 7    you prepare the final draft.  A neat paper can impress many    36
 8    of your readers.                                               39
      |  1  |  2  |  3  |  4  |  5  |  6  |  7  |  8  |  9  | 10  | 11  | 12
```

SPEED: If you made 2 or fewer errors on the Pretest, key lines 9–14 twice each. Repeat if time permits.
ACCURACY: If you made more than 2 errors on the Pretest, key lines 9–11 as a group twice. Then key lines 12–14 as a group twice. Repeat if time permits.

Left-hand Reaches

```
 9    add bar bag era few best data acted beads brass cards caves
10    get raw sat sea tea cage case debts defer edges erase faces
11    bed beg eve fat war debt rest fewer grade refer seats state
```

Right-hand Reaches

```
12    him hop ill boil clip coil cool fill full allow ample ankle
13    ink inn joy gulp hill hold hole hook hope built child chips
14    mop oil pin hung hunt jump like lime lips clips color drill
```

Take a 1-minute timing on lines 5–8. Proofread, note your errors, and figure your speed. Compare your performance with the Pretest.

Set a tab every 10 spaces. Key lines 15–20 once; as you key the lines, keep your eyes on the copy as you depress the tab key to move from word to word. Then repeat lines 15–20.

```
15    the       sit       bat       map       pie       did
16    baud      boot      disk      user      copy      pack
17    media     entry     fixed     ports     track     until
18    system    direct    screen    impact    liquid    prints
19    display   compute   sources   minutes   process   writers
20    computer  literacy  bootable  literate  software  accuracy
```

In some form letters, words or phrases within the paragraphs may vary. Individual words within a paragraph can be treated as field identifiers and can be placed in the body whenever the codes for those field identifiers are called for in the merge process. Stop codes are particularly useful for inserting information in the body if the merge file feature is not available.

Letters L75.127 and L76.127

Format a form letter from the copy on page 291. Field identifiers are marked with parentheses ( ). Note that there are two data fields within the body of the letter. Save the document as L75.127.

Create a merge file for the three people whose names and addresses appear on page 291. Prepare letters for each of the three people as you did before. (**Note:** If you do not have a merge function, prepare the letters without the merge file.)

Save the documents; if using separate file names, use L76A.127, L76B.127, and L76C.127.

```
16  ex exam exert exile exist extra exact annex vexed
17  mp jump stamp mumps imply plump ample champ swamp
18  mo more money among movie smoke mouse month emote
```

E. POSTTEST

Take a 1-minute timing on lines 10–12 (page 63). Proofread, note your errors, and figure your speed. Compare your performance with the Pretest.

F. Horizontal Centering

Text is centered horizontally by positioning the cursor at the midpoint between the left and right margins and backspacing once for every two letters or spaces. For example:

Matthew Hunt

Do not backspace for a letter that is left over.

Stephanie Tolar

Word processors have a **center feature** that centers text automatically between margins. Some word processors require

that the text be keyed before the centering command is given; others require that the centering command be given before the text is keyed; and still others will accept both methods.

Note: Word processors vary in the ways they center copy. Some do not "backspace" for the extra letter, some do, and others center on a half space. Examples:

| Hunt | Hunt | Hunt |
| Tolar | Tolar | Tolar |

Practice: Center the following terms horizontally using the centering command.

```
bold
extra large
italics
large
outline
shadow
```

Line-Spacing Commands Word processors permit various line-spacing commands such as single, double, and triple spacing to be placed in a document. If no command is given, single spacing is usually the default spacing. Some word processors will not display double- or triple-spaced text on the screen, so the document cannot be seen with the correct spacing until it is printed.

Top Margin Commands A top margin command can also be placed in a word processing document. This instructs the printer to advance the paper a specified number of lines or inches before printing the text.

(Date)
↓6

(Name)

(Street Address)

(City, State ZIP Code)

(Salutation):

Congratulations! You are a winner in the Bold journey contest sponsored by Outdoor Magazine. As you know, you have qualified ~~for~~ to attend the Outdoor Adventure camp this summer at Big Branch, Utah. Outdoor magazine is proud to award you this all-expenses-paid vacation, and we hope that you are looking forward to ~~to~~ joining the other 71 high school students across the country who are also winners. ¶ Next week we will send ~~send~~ you all the details concerning your travel plans, equipment, and the type of clothing you should bring. ¶ We look forward to seeing you at big branch. / Sincerely, / Brandon T. Dillard / Editor in Chief / [*Your initials*]

Lesson 127

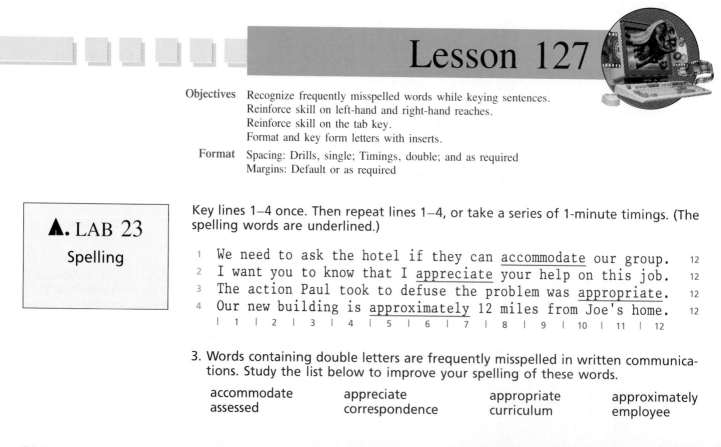

Objectives Recognize frequently misspelled words while keying sentences.
Reinforce skill on left-hand and right-hand reaches.
Reinforce skill on the tab key.
Format and key form letters with inserts.

Format Spacing: Drills, single; Timings, double; and as required
Margins: Default or as required

▲. LAB 23
Spelling

Key lines 1–4 once. Then repeat lines 1–4, or take a series of 1-minute timings. (The spelling words are underlined.)

1 We need to ask the hotel if they can <u>accommodate</u> our group.   12
2 I want you to know that I <u>appreciate</u> your help on this job.   12
3 The action Paul took to defuse the problem was <u>appropriate</u>.   12
4 Our new building is <u>approximately</u> 12 miles from Joe's home.   12
   | 1 | 2 | 3 | 4 | 5 | 6 | 7 | 8 | 9 | 10 | 11 | 12

3. Words containing double letters are frequently misspelled in written communications. Study the list below to improve your spelling of these words.

accommodate	appreciate	appropriate	approximately
assessed	correspondence	curriculum	employee

The job number C1.28 refers to Centering Job 1, Lesson 28. Use this job number as the file name and as part of your document code.

Centering C1.28

Format the following terms by centering them in a single column on one page. Set a 2-inch top margin and double-spacing commands. Leave 5 blank lines (return three times) between each group. When you finish, key the document code at the bottom left. Key C1.28 followed by a space and your initials or name. Example: C1.28 TAJ or C1.28 TAJones.

database	Assembler	Charles Babbage
desktop publishing	BASIC	Herman Hollerith
graphics	COBOL	John Napier
spreadsheet	FORTRAN	Blaise Pascal
word processing	Pascal	John von Neumann

Centering C2.28

Center horizontally; double-space; 2-inch top margin; key document code.

EBCDIC and ASCII codes are used to represent letters, numbers, and special characters in the computer.

Centering C3.28

Center horizontally; double-space; 2-inch top margin; key document code.

You are cordially invited to attend The National Honor Society reception at 2:30 p.m. Friday, November 30 Mason High School Library

Lesson 29

Objectives	Control ' and '' keys while holding anchors.
	Refine number-key skills.
	Refine horizontal centering techniques.
	Key 30/2'/4e.
Format	Spacing: Drills, single; Timings, double; and as noted
	Margins: Default

▲. Keyboard Skills

Key each line twice. Repeat if time permits.

Speed	1	This firm may make a profit now that they own it.
Accuracy	2	Two jobs require packing five dozen axes monthly.
Numbers	3	We cut this twine 9 1/2, 7 3/4, and 6 5/8 inches.
Symbols	4	Jefferson got a 15% discount on the 24# of bread.

Letter L71.126

Block style. Prepare the base form letter. Use field identifiers or stop codes if available. Otherwise, begin the body on line 26.

Date ↓6

Name
Street Address
City, State ZIP Code

Salutation:

We are delighted that homes in our newest subdivision, Sun City Estates, are now available for sale. I know that this area is especially appealing to you. ¶ I have enclosed three of our popular floor plans, all of which meet the following specifications: a minimum of 1,700 square feet, hardwood floors, and solid wood doors. These homes are built on the "Good Cents" plan to minimize your heating and air-conditioning bills. ¶ Call me at 555-3484 if you'd like to visit Sun City Estates. I would be happy to walk you through our models. / Sincerely, / Johnnie Martinez, Agent / [*Your initials*] / 3 Enclosures

▶. Filling in Form Letters

If you have a merge file function:

1. Key the addresses into the merge file.

2. Retrieve the form letter and prepare a letter for each person in the file, following the procedures for your software.

3. Save the documents.

Note: Many companies save only the base form letters—they do not save those which have been addressed.

If you do not have a merge function:

1. Retrieve the form letter.

2. Move to line 13 and key the date. (If you used stop codes, the cursor will be at the correct position.)

3. Move down an inch to line 19; key the inside address. (If you used stop codes, the cursor will move to the correct position as soon as you complete the date.)

4. Move to line 24; key the salutation.

5. Save the documents. Use a separate file name for each letter.

Letter L72.126

Retrieve and fill in the form letter L71.126. Use today's date and the information below. Save the letters; if using separate file names, use L72A.126, L72B.126, and L72C.126.

L72A Ms. Jennifer Gray / 1239 Meadow Lane / Albuquerque, NM 87125 / Dear Ms. Gray

L72B Mr. Kendall Watson / 2398 San Mateo Boulevard, NE / Albuquerque, NM 87110 / Dear Mr. Watson

L72C Dr. C. W. Patterson / 5310 Central Avenue East / Albuquerque, NM 87108 / Dear Dr. Patterson

Letters L73.126 and L74.126

Form letters. Modified-block style. Use today's date.

(1) Create the base letter from the copy on page 289. Save the document as L73.126. (2) Create a merge file for the three people listed below if you have this capability. (3) Prepare letters for each of the three people. (4) Save each of the letters; if using separate file names, use L74A.126, L74B.126, and L74C.126.

L74A Mr. Stan Cepekski / P.O. Box 1893 / South Gate, CA 90280 / Dear Mr. Cepekski

L74B Ms. Sally Ramando / 115 Crawford Street / Dalton, GA 30720 / Dear Ms. Ramando

L74C Mrs. Melissa Calvano / 102 Dominion Drive / Westlake, OH 44145 / Dear Mrs. Calvano

Hold Those Anchors

For ' anchor J

For " anchor J

B.  , Key

Next to ; key. Use Sem finger.

Do not space before or after an apostrophe within a word.

C.  " Key

Shift of ' key. Use Sem finger.

Key each line twice. Repeat if time permits.

```
5  ;'; ;'; ''' It's Lynn's job to get Mia's lessons.
6  Isn't Ron here?  Where's Lori?  Wasn't Ray going?
7  It's not I.  We're so happy.  Aren't you pleased?
```

Key each line twice. Repeat if time permits.

```
8   ;"; ;"; """ "Over here," Sue cried.  "I am here."
9   The signals are "red" for stop and "blue" for go.
10  "Wait!" they shouted.  The painting was a "fake."
```

D. Quotation Marks

Quotation marks are used in pairs. Often the second quotation mark is used with another punctuation mark, as shown in lines 11–15 below.

Follow these rules when using quotation marks with other punctuation:

1. Place commas and periods *before* the second quotation mark (see A, B).

2. Place colons and semicolons *after* the second quotation mark (see C, D).

3. Place question marks and exclamation points *before* the second quotation mark *only if* the entire quotation is a question or an exclamation (see E). In all other cases, place the question mark or exclamation point *after* the second quotation mark (see F, G).

Practice: Key lines 11–15 once. Format: Double spacing, 5-space tab.

```
11       "Good morning,"[A] said Tina.  "Come in."[B]
12       I did as she "offered":[C] I went in.  She
13  said that I seemed "excited";[D] she listened.
14       "What's your news?"[E] she asked.  "Tell me!"[E]
15  Did she already "know"?[F]  I think she "guessed"![G]
```

E. Technique Checkpoint

Keep eyes on copy while keying apostrophes and quotation marks.

Key lines 16–19 once. Then repeat lines 5 and 8.

```
16  People don't use "please" or "thank you" as often   10
17  as they used to.  Is it that they don't "care" or   20
18  "feel," or is it that they're too "busy" or can't   30
19  "remember" to be courteous?  We all should "try."   40
    |  1  |  2  |  3  |  4  |  5  |  6  |  7  |  8  |  9  | 10
```

UNIT 18
Advanced Formatting

Unit Goal 39/5'/5e

Lesson 126

Objectives Format and key form letters.
Prepare merge files for form letters.

Format Spacing: Drills, single; and as required
Margins: Default or as required

A. Keyboard Skills

Key lines 1–4 once. In line 5 use your tab key to advance from one word to the next through the entire line. Repeat lines 1–4, or take a series of 1-minute timings.

Speed
1 The road to the left is the right one to take on our drive.   12
Accuracy
2 Wolf gave Jake an extra dozen quarts, but he can't pay him.   12
Numbers
3 Dayle should use car 47, 38, 29, or 10 if 56 laps are left.   12
Symbols
4 With 5% error he can guess #32's and #48's price--honestly!   12
Technique
5 own rod for lap cot map cow jam wit hem dog pan
   | 1 | 2 | 3 | 4 | 5 | 6 | 7 | 8 | 9 | 10 | 11 | 12

B. "OK" Timings

Take two 30-second "OK" (errorless) timings on lines 6–7. Then take two 30-second "OK" timings on lines 8–9. Goal: No errors.

6 Max and Kay reviewed the subject before giving Phil a quiz,   12
7 and then they scheduled the quiz for Thursday of next week.   24

8 The jovial men expressed a welcome to big Fritz; and before   12
9 they knew it, Gwendolyn quickly joined in to wish him well.   24
   | 1 | 2 | 3 | 4 | 5 | 6 | 7 | 8 | 9 | 10 | 11 | 12

C. Form Letters

A form letter is a base letter that can be sent to a number of people. Form letters used to be duplicated, but microcomputers allow a company to store a form letter and fill it in when it is needed. When the finished letter is printed out, it looks like it was personally written, not duplicated.

To format a form letter, you must allow room for the date, the inside address, and the salutation. Following standard formatting rules, the date begins on line 13 (2 inches from the top edge), and the inside address begins 6 lines below—on line 19 (3 inches down). Assuming the address is 4 lines long, begin the salutation on line 24—4 lines plus 1 blank line. Begin the body a double space below the salutation—on line 26.

Merge Feature

Many word processors have a **mail merge** file (sometimes called an **address** file). The names and addresses of the people to whom letters will be sent can be inserted into this file, and the form letters can be automatically addressed. For automatic addressing, you must insert a command that identifies every field that requires information from the merge file. The field identifiers differ in each software package. Two common identifiers are the asterisk (*) and the parentheses. These field identifiers are positioned where you want the information printed.

Stop Codes

Some word processing programs do not have a merge feature but have a feature that enables you to put codes in a document that will stop the printer at the codes. After the required information is filled in, the printer continues to print, stopping at each code, until the document is completed.

F. Keyboard and Keypad Number Review

Use the numbers across the top of the keyboard as you key lines 20–24 twice each. When you finish, switch to the numeric keypad and enter only the three-digit numbers once. Proofread carefully.

```
20  ju7j 711 712 713 714 715 fr4f 406 407 408 409 400
21  ki8k 811 812 813 814 815 de3d 306 307 308 309 300
22  lo9l 911 912 913 914 915 sw2s 206 207 208 209 200
23  ;p0; 011 012 013 014 015 aq1a 106 107 108 109 100
24  jy6j 611 612 613 614 615 ft5f 506 507 508 509 500
```

G. 2-Minute Timings

Take two 2-minute timings on lines 25–30. Proofread, note your errors, and figure your speed.

```
25      When you work with people every day, you get   10
26   to know the things that bring them joy.  You also  20
27   find out quickly what they do not like.  A bit of  30
28   extra effort in a dozen small ways will make your  40
29   office a pleasant place in which to work.  Try to  50
30   do or say at least one thoughtful thing each day.  60
```
| 1 | 2 | 3 | 4 | 5 | 6 | 7 | 8 | 9 | 10 SI 1.17

H. Titles

A title is usually set apart from the copy below it. The most common way to display a title is to key it in all caps. Follow a title with 2 blank lines (↓3). If a document is to be double-spaced, do not change to double spacing until after you have keyed the title and spaced down three times.

Centering C4.29
Center horizontally; double-space; 2-inch top margin; key document code.

Centering C5.29
Center horizontally; double-space; 2-inch top margin; key document code.

```
MEANINGS OF STATE NAMES↓3
Colorado:  Red
Nevada:  Snow-clad
North Dakota:  Friend
Wisconsin:  Grassy place
Florida:  Flowery Easter
Kansas:  South wind people
Indiana:  Land of the Indians
Connecticut:  Long river place
Alaska:  Land that is not an island
```

```
QUALITIES EMPLOYEES SHOULD HAVE↓3
Competent job skills
Dependability
Good human relations skills
Honesty
Loyalty to the company
Positive attitude
Promptness
Trustworthiness
Willingness to learn
```

Level 6

The computer has become an indispensible tool for the graphic artist. Whether the product is a magazine, a book, a poster, a diagram, or a motion picture, a computer was probably used to create part or all of the product.

Goals

1. Demonstrate keyboarding speed and accuracy on straight copy with a goal of 40 words a minute for 5 minutes with 5 or fewer errors.
2. Correctly proofread copy for errors and edit copy for revision.
3. Apply production skills in keyboarding and formatting copy for business documents from a variety of input modes.
4. Correctly spell words containing double letters, and review all language arts rules presented in Levels 2 through 5.
5. Complete and compose documents required for a job application sequence.
6. Prioritize and make appropriate formatting decisions while completing two simulations.

Lesson 30

Objectives
Refine keyboarding skills.
Count vertical lines on a page.
Center material vertically (up and down) on a page.
Reinforce horizontal centering.

Format
Spacing: Single unless otherwise noted
Margins: Default

A. Keyboard Skills

Key each line twice. Repeat if time permits.

Speed
1 We will be out for spring break in two more days.

Accuracy
2 Jon's wacky quip amazed but vexed his girlfriend.

Numbers
3 Your fingers can now find 10, 29, 38, 47, and 56.

Symbols
4 He saw Jane's new car. It's not "up" but "down"!

B. Quotation Marks and Apostrophes

Key each line twice. Repeat if time permits.

5 It's amazing how fast a pet can "train" an owner.
6 Most of us wouldn't swap our pets for "anything."

7 "We can't go," wailed Cathy. "There's no money."
8 "Why don't you earn the money?" Cathy's dad said.

9 Wouldn't it be nice if we didn't make any errors?
10 Our teacher shouts, "Keep your eyes on the copy!"

C. Keyboard Number Review

Use the numbers across the top of the keyboard as you key lines 11–17 twice each.

11 We found the pictures on pages 8, 41, 53, and 92.
12 Josh counted 75 cats, 60 dogs, 8 mice, and 1 rat.
13 Those fruitcakes weigh 4 lb, 3.5 lb, and 2.75 lb.
14 The high today was around 89, but the low was 56.
15 My license number is 08246319; yours is 41283902.
16 My vases are 3 3/8, 5 1/2, and 9 1/4 inches tall.
17 It took Nicolas 3 1/4 hours to walk 10 2/3 miles.

D. 30-Second Timings

Take two 30-second timings on lines 18–19. Then take two 30-second timings on lines 20–21. Try to key with no more than 2 errors on each timing.

18 The first thing you need to know before you buy a   10
19 computer is how it will be used most of the time.   20

20 Will you be using a database, a spreadsheet, or a   10
21 word processor? A computer must meet your needs.   20

| 1 | 2 | 3 | 4 | 5 | 6 | 7 | 8 | 9 | 10 |

Report R58.125 Agenda

Center horizontally.

```
        CREDIT UNION WORKSHOP
    Hammond's Building, room 278  ] DS
         Oct. 15, 19-
```

8:00	Opening Remarks
	Garrik Henderson
8:15	Mortgage Loans
	Denise Fairfield-bryant
9:00	Checking/Savings Accounts
	Mary Decker & Dave Smith
10:00	Certificates of Deposit
	Russell Latimer
11:00	Mutual Funds
	Celeste Giovanicci
12:00	Luncheon and Speaker
	Brenda Fairmeadows

Report R59.125

Unbound format with footnote.

COMPUTER SURVEY

By [*Your Name*]

It has been evident from the research that has been conducted over the past month that we must update our computer services in all our district offices. Our current inventory of computers in the four district offices is shown in Table 1.

TABLE 1

District Computer Usage

District	Purchase Date	Number
Eastern	1980	13
Northern	1982	7
Southern	1979	5
Western	1983	9

Brian Dunwoody stated in his recent article that "enhancements in software packages have made obsolete those computers that were purchased in the early 1980s because of their small memory capacities."[1] We are in a position today that demands that we update the hardware that has been identified in Table 1 so that we can continue to run our current word processing, spreadsheet, and database software packages.

---

1. Brian Dunwoody, "Where Is Software Going?" The Software Gazette, July 1990, p. 21.

Letter L70.125

Dictated coupon letter. Modified-block style.

[*Today's date*] mr c w cyphert 214 seminole street bradford pa 16701 dear sir we can now supply a selection of PENN NEWS covers in a size and format suitable for framing a set of three covers all by famous artists now is available (*paragraph*) these are full-color prints enlarged to 9″ by 12″ on heavy coated paper without the magazine logo the set includes the following: philadelphia harbor (april issue) salmon creek (july issue) and gettysburg (september issue) the price is $3 per set delivered (*paragraph*) clip the coupon below fill it in and attach your check make your check or money order payable to the pennsylvania state commission sincerely harvey laird jr executive director [*Your initials*]

- -

pennsylvania state commission
p.o. box 1011
harrisburg pa 17108

enclosed is a check for $_____ for _____ set(s) of the three covers of PENN NEWS

please send to _____
          name

          _____
          address

          _____
          city   state   zip

E. Vertical Spacing

Most word processors have a default value of 6 lines to an inch. Standard printer paper is 11 inches long, so there are $11 \times 6 = 66$ lines on a page. Most word processors permit making changes in the lines per inch. In this book, you will use the default of 6 lines per inch unless directed otherwise.

```
 ─  1    single double triple
 ─  2    single ------ ------
 ─  3    single double ------
 ─  4    single ------ triple
 ─  5    single double ------
 1  6    single ------ ------
```

F. Vertical Centering

For material to look centered, the top and bottom margins must be approximately the same. To place copy in the vertical center of a page, follow these steps:

1. Count the lines (including blanks) that the copy will occupy when keyed.
2. Subtract that number from the available number of lines on your paper.
3. Divide the difference by 2 (drop any fraction). This is your top margin.
4. Add 1 to the result; that is the line on which you should begin.

Example 1: To center 12 single-spaced lines on a full sheet of paper (66 lines), begin on line 28. $[66 - 12 = 54; 54 \div 2 = 27; 27 + 1 = 28]$

Example 2: To center 8 double-spaced lines on a full sheet, 15 lines are needed for the copy (8 keyed, 7 blank); begin on line 26. $[66 - 15 = 51; 51 \div 2 = 25\ 1/2;$ drop the fraction; $25 + 1 = 26]$

Practice: Center these lines vertically and horizontally. Use double spacing.

> To center double-spaced
> lines vertically,
> → you must count every
> keyed line and all
> the blank lines.

Check: After printing, fold paper from top to bottom. The crease should be in the center, close to the point indicated by the arrow.

Center Page

Some word processors have a feature that will automatically center copy vertically on the page.

Centering C6.30
Center vertically and horizontally. Double-space.

DIFFICULT WORDS TO SPELL↓₃
acknowledgment
believe
changeable
congratulate
develop
embarrass
February
grammar
hors d'oeuvre
receive

Centering C7.30
Center vertically and horizontally. Double-space.

FREQUENTLY USED
FOREIGN EXPRESSIONS↓₃

ad hoc
alma mater
etc.
habeas corpus
laissez-faire
per se
vice versa

Form F13.124 Invoice

Use today's date. If a form is not available, set up as a table. Calculate all totals and total amount due.

[*Invoice No.*] 1466 / [*To*] Lillian's Gifts / 389 Drury Lane / Topeka, KS 66604 / [*Terms*] n/60
 4 Cylindrical floor spotlights @19.85
13 Stoneware canisters @ 42.75
 6 Sewing baskets @ 16.99
 3 Canvas log carriers @ 9.50
Sales tax 34.45 / Shipping 12.00

Memo M9.124

Use boilerplate form. Use hanging-indented format for the enumerated items. Indent the table 10 spaces from each margin.

[*MEMO TO:*] Alex Chaney / [*FROM:*] Katherine Lee / [*DATE:*] July 16, 19— / [*SUBJECT:*] Omaha Report / Deborah Kellerman was a real delight to visit with on my recent trip to Omaha! I expressed to her your sincere congratulations on a job well done in achieving the tremendous sales increases throughout the Omaha division.

Ms. Kellerman is a very organized and thorough manager. She plans well and shares her ideas with the district managers. If I were to pinpoint any specific actions she has taken to turn around the Omaha area, I would have to mention the following:

1. She has established an excellent routine of identifying long-term (annual), intermediate (quarterly), and short-term (weekly) sales estimates for each of the districts.

2. She has implemented an excellent program of recognition for top sales performers.

3. She has concentrated her efforts on establishing a goodwill communications link with major division customers.

4. She motivates her managers.

5. She meets our competition aggressively and positively.

In addition to listing the above reasons for Ms. Kellerman's success, I would have to point out that the following district managers have also played a key role in Omaha's success:

Manager	District
Alexa North	Cheyenne District
Richard Spiers	Pierre District
John Collum	Sioux Falls District

All in all, this division has made some positive moves in the past 18 months, and they are to be commended for a fine job. / [*Your initials*]

Form F14.124 Itinerary
Display format.

ITINERARY FOR
R. T. SANDERS
FEBRUARY 2-4, 19--
FEBRUARY 2
2:30 p.m. DEPART MINNEAPOLIS, N.W. FLIGHT 230.
3:15 p.m. ARRIVE CHICAGO, O'HARE.
ACCOMMODATIONS: AIRPORT HILTON, GUARANTEED RESERVATION.
7:00 p.m. MEET WITH SHARON O'DONNELL, DISTRICT MANAGER.
FEBRUARY 3
9:00 a.m. DEPART CHICAGO, O'HARE, N.W. FLIGHT 402.
11:30 a.m. ARRIVE BALTIMORE.
1:45 p.m. ATTEND REGIONAL MEETING, HOLIDAY INN, CONQUISTADOR ROOM.
3:30 p.m. TOUR ANNAPOLIS PLANT ACCOMPANIED BY KEN LESTER.
ACCOMMODATIONS: HOLIDAY INN.
FEBRUARY 4
8:30 a.m. DEPART BALTIMORE, N.W. FLIGHT 731.

Lesson 31

Objectives Control _, =, and + keys while holding anchors.
Underline copy using the underline function.
Spread-center text.
Use a variety of print enhancements.
Reinforce horizontal and vertical centering.

Format Spacing: Single unless otherwise noted
Margins: Default

A. Keyboard Skills

Key each line twice. Repeat if time permits.

Speed 1 There may be snow or sleet in the forecast today.
Accuracy 2 Zed quickly jumped five huge barrels to warn Max.
Numbers 3 My five favorite numbers are 7, 33, 9, 8, and 40.
Symbols 4 He shouted, "Wait!" (There was no use; we left.)

Hold Those Anchors

For __ anchor J

For ± anchor J

B. ⎯ Key

Shift of - (hyphen).
Use Sem finger.

The underscore key on a computer can only be used in a blank space and is usually used only to draw lines.

To underline a word or a group of words, it is necessary to use a code to begin the underlining and one to end it. The code varies with the software used. Some word processors display the underline on the screen; others do not. A color monitor may show the underlined text in a different color.

Do *not* underline the punctuation or the space following an underlined word or phrase. (**Exception:** If the punctuation is part of a title—as in Oklahoma!—then the punctuation *is* underlined.) Normally, the punctuation or spaces *within* a group of words are underlined. If your word processor does not automatically do that, you may key an underscore between each word.

Key each line twice. Use the underscore key. Repeat if time permits.

Use 4 underscores for the blank line.

5 ;p⁻ ;p_ ;_; ;_; _;_ __;_ _⁻_ _⁻_ ;p⁻ ;p_ ;_; ;p_
6 Fill in the blank: There are ____ U.S. Senators.

Key each line twice. Use your word processor underline code. Repeat if time permits.

7 I did not see her take a pen, but I know she did.
8 Did they have an opportunity to see My Fair Lady?
9 Seven of us went to see the play Where's Charley?
10 There was no excuse for rudeness and bad manners.

Take two 5-minute timings on lines 8–24. Proofread, note your errors, and figure your speed.

```
 8        Just what should you look for when you want to buy new      12
 9   computer equipment?  There are many things to consider, and      20
10   you want to make a good choice because a computer must last      36
11   you for years and years.  Price is an important feature for      48
12   any purchase, and computers are no exception.  When you are     60
13   ready to purchase, shop around extensively for the best buy     72
14   on that particular brand or model.  The size of a computer,     84
15   in terms of how fast it runs and how much memory it has, is     96
16   also very important.  These two features are very critical,    108
17   because you want some assurance that your computer will run    120
18   many of the large software packages on the market today and    132
19   in the future.  You should also try to find a computer that    144
20   has both standard diskette and micro diskette drives.  Dual    156
21   drives give the system more versatility.  As with any large    168
22   item of purchase, make certain that your new computer has a    180
23   good warranty so that it can be returned and/or repaired if    192
24   it is defective.                                               195
     |  1  |  2  |  3  |  4  |  5  |  6  |  7  |  8  |  9  |  10  |  11  |  12  SI 1.45
```

Report R57.124 Minutes of a meeting

The Business Club
MINUTES OF THE MONTHLY MEETING
March 7, 19—

ATTENDANCE

The March meeting of the Business Club was held on March 7, 19—, in Room 124 of the Business Building. The meeting was called to order by Danielle Waters, President, at 3:15 p.m. and was adjourned at 4:30 p.m. All members except Gary Hagen and Marion Alborg were present.

UNFINISHED BUSINESS

The secretary read the minutes of the last meeting, and they were approved as read. The treasurer reported a balance of $78.25 in the Club account as of the end of February. There was no further unfinished business.

NEW BUSINESS

A car wash will be held on March 20 in the Brookings Shopping Center. All Club members are urged to help with this project and are to report to the shopping center at 8:30 a.m. on March 20. Notices will be posted in the local newspaper, at the Food Store, and at Ward's Drugstore.

Allen Meyer, Secretary

Hold Those Anchors

For __ anchor J

For = + anchor J

C.  Key

+ is shift of =.
Next to hyphen. Use Sem finger.

Key each line twice. Repeat if time permits.

11 ;=; === ;=; === = A = 95, B = 85, C = 75, D = 65.
12 ;+; +++ ;+; +++ 3 + 15 + 31 + 48 + 67 + 73 = 237.
13 Yes, 4 + 4 = 8 and 7 + 7 = 14; but 2 + 39 = what?

D. Technique Checkpoint

Space once before and after the + and the =.
Hold anchors while making long reaches.

Key lines 14–17 once. Then repeat lines 5 (page 70), 11, and 12.

14 If 5 + 7 = 12 and 7 + 5 = 12, what will 6 + 6 be? 10
15 Make the line 12 underscores long: _____ . 20
16 If 4 + 4 = 8 and 8 + 8 = 16, how much is 16 + 16? 30
17 The Daily Mirror said that 15 students were hurt. 40
   | 1 | 2 | 3 | 4 | 5 | 6 | 7 | 8 | 9 | 10

E. 12-Second Timings

Take three 12-second timings on each line, or key each line three times. Try to key with no more than 1 error on each timing.

18 Walking can pick you up if you are feeling tired.
19 Your heart and lungs can work harder as you walk.
20 It may be that a walk is often better than a nap.
         5   10   15   20   25   30   35   40   45   50

F. Spread Centering

A formatting technique.

To give added emphasis to a centered display line, spread it by leaving 1 space between letters and 3 spaces between words, like this:

THIS   IS   SPREADING

Practice: Spread-center the line above and the line below.

SPREAD WORDS FOR EMPHASIS

G. Print Enhancements

Note: From now on, use all caps and bold for titles.

You have learned three ways to emphasize text—all caps, underlining, and spread centering. Word processing software offers many other ways.

Most have expanded and compressed print options. Some offer a variety of **fonts** (styles of print) and features such as bold, italics, or shadow.

If your word processor and printer have these capabilities, experiment with the two lines above using different print enchancements.

☐OFFICE TECHNOLOGY CONFERENCE☐
August 7, 19--

8:30	Registration	Lobby
9:00	Vendor Demonstration of Biotech System	Computer Room
10:15	Coffee	Lobby
11:30	Display of BioTech Software	Gallery
12:00	Lunch	Dining Room
1:30	Records Management and the Computer Speaker: Jack Bellari, Systems Analyst	Conference A
2:30	Coffee	Lobby
2:45	Networking Marilyn Gowdy Coordinator Speaker: Alice Davis, WP Supervisor	Computer Room
4:00	Questions and Answers Leader: Joseph Ogarkov, Programmer	Conference C
4:30	Discussion and evaluation	Conference C

Lessons 124/125

Objectives Review keying itineraries, memos, minutes of meetings, invoices, agendas, reports, tables, and letters.
Review keying footnotes.
Review use of a boilerplate form.
Key 39/5′/5e.

Format Spacing: Drills, single; Timings, double; and as required
Margins: Default or as required

A. Keyboard Skills

Key lines 1–4 once. In line 5 backspace to underline each word containing double letters immediately after keying it. Repeat lines 1–4, or take a series of 1-minute timings.

Speed	1	That round key that you gave me will not fit into the door.	12
Accuracy	2	Jock was pleased to qualify in the men's bike extravaganza.	12
Numbers	3	You must set tabs at 10, 29, 38, 47, and 56 for this table.	12
Symbols	4	Just 4% of #56 ($2.36) and 3% of #78 ($1.90) were used now.	12
Technique	5	Will all good people on Kellog Street stamp their feet too?	

| 1 | 2 | 3 | 4 | 5 | 6 | 7 | 8 | 9 | 10 | 11 | 12

B. Preview Practice

Key each line twice as a preview to the 5-minute timings on page 283.

Accuracy	6	flexible computer assurance equipment defective extensively
Speed	7	there thing years price ready brand model terms these comes

Reveal Codes

When special functions (such as underlining, boldface, tab) are used in a document, function codes are placed in the document. Some programs place the codes on the work screen; others "hide" the codes. The **reveal codes** function displays the hidden codes.

It is important to reveal the codes whenever you are inserting or deleting special functions or to check to make sure any special function codes are correctly placed in the document.

H. Displays

A variety of display techniques are used to make items like announcements, invitations, and advertisements look attractive. To format a display:

1. Center the material vertically and horizontally.

2. Use a combination of display techniques—some lines in all capitals, some lines in capitals and lowercase letters, some lines in expanded or compressed print, some lines in a different font, some words in bold and/or underlined, and so on.

Centering C8.31 Invitation
Display format. Follow the enhancements shown. Double-space. If time permits, key the job again using different techniques.

WELCOME BACK TO SCHOOL ↓₃
Big Sandy Student Council
cordially invites you
to a reception
M O N D A Y
2 to 4 p.m.
in the
<u>Wildcat Library</u>

Centering C9.31 Announcement
Display format. Follow the enhancements shown. If time permits, key the job again using different techniques.

It's <u>Not</u> Just Another Garage Sale!
This <u>is</u> the BIG one.
Five families have combined
years of treasures.

Saturday from 8 a.m. to 8 p.m.
Corner of Black Walnut and Ash
D O N ' T   M I S S   I T !

Lesson 32

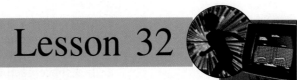

Objectives   Control [ ], { }, and 〈 〉 keys while holding anchors.
Create special symbols.
Block-center text horizontally.
Reinforce vertical centering.

Format   Spacing: Single unless otherwise noted
Margins: Default

A. Keyboard Skills

Key each line twice. Repeat if time permits.

Speed   1 A traffic jam caused us to be late to work today.
Accuracy   2 Expectedly, Madge quit her zoo job in five weeks.
Numbers   3 Rita saw 47 boys, 38 girls, 29 men, and 56 women.
Symbols   4 There were <u>only</u> seventeen #2 pencils @ $.03 left!

C. Agendas

An agenda may be a list of topics to be discussed at a meeting, or it may be a formal program of a meeting.

To format an agenda that is a list of topics:

1. Use the hanging-indented format for enumerations.

2. Arrange the topics in a logical sequence.

To format an agenda that is a formal program:

1. Use a columnar format (like the format for itineraries).

2. Arrange the time information in the first column.

3. Leave 3 to 6 spaces between columns.

4. Arrange the descriptive information in the second column. Begin individual entries (topic, speaker's name, room number) at the tab stop.

5. Use a line length appropriate for the program. If the descriptive information is very short, center the program horizontally as you would a table.

```
                        ↓ 2"

           COMPUTER CONFERENCE ↓ 2

       Hillsboro Resort Inn--Cleveland ↓ 2

              January 6, 19-- ↓ 3

   8:30     Computers in the Workplace
            Christopher Haynes / Alexander Room ↓ 2

   9:30     Coffee Break

  10:00     Networking--The Future of Computers
            Regina Wollencheck / Saturn Room

  11:00     Desktop Publishing--Myth or Miracle?
            Fay Laney / Franklin Room

  12:00     Lunch / Ballroom A

   1:00     Teleconferencing Roundtables
            Steven Pullman / Ballroom B
            Karen Kline / Ballroom C
```

Report R55.123 Agenda

Key the illustration above. Center horizontally; 6 spaces between columns.

D. Programs With Justified Right Margins

If the speaker's name or the room number is keyed in a third column, the program will look more attractive if the right margin is justified (ends evenly). To format programs with the right margin justified:

1. Arrange the time and descriptive material in columns 1 and 2 as in programs that are not justified.

2. Backspace each item in the third column from the right margin or use a right tab.

3. When the space between columns is wide, use leaders to fill in the space. Also use leaders if items in the description column are very different in length [as in Report R56.123 (page 282)]. Leave 1 space after the last word in column 2 and 1 space before the first word in column 3. **Note:** Some software may not leave this space.

Right Justify   Some word processing programs have a **right justify** feature that will automatically justify copy at the right margin. In addition, some programs automatically right justify when the dot leaders feature is used. In other programs, you may have to set a right tab for the last column in order to get justified copy with dot leaders.

Report R56.123

Prepare the agenda on page 282. Default margins; 3 spaces between columns 1 and 2; leaders between columns 2 and 3. Right justify.

Hold Those Anchors

For [ ] anchor J

For { } anchor J

For ⟨ anchor ;

For ⟩ anchor ; or J

B.  **Keys**

Use Sem finger.
{ is shift of [.
} is shift of].

Brackets are used (1) to enclose a correction or insertion in quoted material and (2) to enclose a parenthetical element within a larger parenthetical element.

Braces are used in mathematical expressions {(0,0), (1,1), (2,2)} and to enclose comments in Pascal programming language {This program averages grades.}.

Key each line once. Repeat if time permits.

5 ;[; [[[;[; [[[;];]]] ;];]]] [page 9], [pause]
6 "I love our state. [Applause.] Vote for Jones."
7 (We do not know if she is from Flint [Michigan].)

8 :{: {{{ :{: {{{ :}: }}} :}: }}} {(-8, 9)}, {Loop}
9 Is the correct solution set to No. 7 {(4, 2, 6)}?
10 {This program reads and alphabetizes last names.}

C. **Keys**

Use K finger for ⟨ (less than). ⟨ is shift of comma.
Use L finger for ⟩ (greater than). ⟩ is shift of period.

Key each line once. Repeat if time permits.

11 k⟨k k⟨k ,⟨, ,⟨, k,⟨ k,⟨ ⟨⟨⟨ ⟨,⟨ ,⟨, 4 ⟨ 5, 8 ⟨ 10
12 4 ⟨ 5 and 6 ⟨ 7 and 8 ⟨ 9 and 10 ⟨ 11 and 12 ⟨ 13
13 If A ⟨ B and B ⟨ C, then the solution is B = 155.

14 1⟩1 1⟩1 .⟩. .⟩. 1.⟩ 1.⟩ ⟩⟩⟩ ⟩.⟩ .⟩. 16 ⟩ 9, 3 ⟩ 2
15 Z ⟩ Y and N ⟩ M and K ⟩ J and 33 ⟩ 29 and 54 ⟩ 42
16 Todd said (X - Y) ⟩ 15, but Laura thought Z ⟩ 15.

D. Technique Checkpoint

Do not space after [and { or before] and }.

Do space before and after ⟨ and ⟩.

Key lines 17–20 once. Then repeat lines 5, 8, 11, and 14.

17 "If we give up, [pause] there can be no freedom." 10
18 (How can she [Jane] leave without the documents?) 20
19 K. Harmdierks wrote {(5,0), (0,-5)} on the board. 30
20 {This program determines if X ⟩ Y and if NN ⟨ M.} 40
| 1 | 2 | 3 | 4 | 5 | 6 | 7 | 8 | 9 | 10

E. 30-Second Timings

Take two 30-second timings on lines 21–22. Then take two 30-second timings on lines 23–24. Try to key with no more than 2 errors on each timing.

21 Try to practice keying at a steady pace; practice 10
22 those drills evenly and smoothly without pausing. 20

23 I hope Pam takes a plane that will get here after 10
24 four so that I can go to the airport to meet her. 20
| 1 | 2 | 3 | 4 | 5 | 6 | 7 | 8 | 9 | 10

send someone to the conference. After further discussion, it was agreed that Mr. King and his assistant, Paul Carruthers, would represent Computer Visions at the conference.

Mr. Fang announced that a joint meeting of the Computer Services Department and the New Products Department is to be scheduled after the first of the year. The purpose of the meeting is to outline the five-year plan that is due at regional headquarters on May 1, 19__. A copy of the guidelines for the five-year plan is attached.

Jean Carr, Secretary

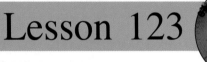

Lesson 123

Objectives   Select the correct spelling of words while keying sentences.
Format and key agendas.
Format and key programs with justified right margins.
Reinforce use of leaders.

Format   Spacing: Drills, single; and as required
Margins: Default or as required

A. LAB 22
Spelling

Key lines 1–4 once, selecting the appropriate word from each pair enclosed in parentheses. Review your copy as your teacher reads the answers. Then key lines 1–4 again.

1   The company (acquesition/acquisition) was based on Paul's (recommendation/reccomendation).
2   It was our (decision/desision) to make full (utilisation/utilization) of the estate.
3   (Congradulations/Congratulations) on the very fine (orientasion/orientation) that you gave.
4   The (commission/comission) will print the second (edision/edition) of its report.

B. 30-Second Timings

Take two 30-second timings on lines 5 and 6. Then take two 30-second timings on lines 7 and 8. Try to key with no more than 2 errors on each timing.

```
5   One type of report is an agenda; it's used to inform people    12
6   of all the items that may be discussed at a future meeting.    24

7   The minutes of a meeting are also a kind of report; minutes    12
8   are a record of the proceedings of a meeting for reference.    24
    |  1  |  2  |  3  |  4  |  5  |  6  |  7  |  8  |  9  | 10  | 11  | 12
```

F. Special Symbols

Many keys on the keyboard can be used to represent special symbols. Some are keyed "as is," some are keyed above the line, and others are keyed below the line. The most common of these special symbols are shown below.

Most software programs, when used with certain printers, allow the user to create many other symbols such as the paragraph mark (¶), the cent sign (¢), and foreign language characters.

Practice: Key the examples in the third column, following the procedures given in the column labeled "Keystrokes." Center the material horizontally and vertically. Use double spacing.

Symbols	Keystrokes	Examples
Roman numerals	Capitals of I, V, X, L, C, D, and M.	Chapter XVIII
Feet and inches	For feet, apostrophe; for inches, quotation mark.	Mary is 5' 2".
Minutes, seconds	For minutes, apostrophe; for seconds, quotation mark.	Time: 3' 15"
Times, by	Small letter x; space before and after.	What is 5 x 6?
Minus	Single hyphen; space before and after.	140 − 56 = 84
Ellipsis	Three periods, spaced apart (but four periods if one or more words are omitted at the end of the sentence).	He . . . also He I
Superscript	Raise the number or letter above the line by using superscript code (if software and printer have this capability).	$8^2 + 6^2 = 100$
Degrees	Small letter o, keyed as superscript.	$32^\circ F$ (or $0^\circ C$)
Subscript	Lower the number or letter below the line by using subscript code (if software and printer have this capability).	H_2O is water.

G. Block Centering

To center a group of lines (not each line separately), use the following block-centering procedure:

1. Select the longest line in the group and center that line. Do not use a title as the longest line—titles are centered separately.
2. Note the position where the longest line begins; set a tab stop at that point.
3. Begin all lines, except for the title, at this tab stop.

Practice: Block-center each group of lines in the next column. Begin on line 26, and leave 5 blank lines between each group. Double-space.

Centering a block

of lines is called

block centering.

↓ 6

ITEMS TO BE CENTERED

↓ 3

Titles

Tables

Displays

E. Minutes of a Meeting

Minutes of a meeting are saved in a three-ring binder. To format minutes:

1. Set margins for a bound report.
2. Key the title on line 7 of page 1. Key page numbers on line 7 of additional pages.
3. Single space.
4. Key side headings in all-capital letters. Double-space before and after side headings.
5. Start the closing (secretary's name and title) at the center. Leave 3 blank lines for the signature.

↓ 7
The Business Club
MINUTES OF THE MONTHLY MEETING
[Today's Date] ↓ 3

ATTENDANCE

The monthly meeting of The Business Club of Walsh High School was held in Room 19, Mario Falohetti presiding. The meeting began at 3:15 and closed at 4 p.m. All officers, all members except Jeff Gates and Harriet Larkin, and the sponsor were present.

UNFINISHED BUSINESS

The secretary read the minutes of the last meeting, and they were approved as read. The treasurer stated that there was $28.75 in the Club account as of the end of the month. That was all the unfinished business.

year. A copy of each of the resolutions is attached to and becomes part of these minutes. ↓ 4

Martha Wolf, Secretary

Report R54.122
Minutes of a meeting.

Computer Services Department
MINUTES OF THE MONTHLY MEETING
September 20, 19__

ATTENDANCE

The September meeting of the Computer Services Department was held on September, 20, 19__, in Room 136 of Computer Visions Inc. The meeting began at 9:30 a.m. and was adjourned at 11:30 a.m. Michael Fang, Department Head, presided at the meeting. All personnel were present.

UNFINISHED BUSINESS

The secretary read the minutes of the August meeting. After one minor change suggested by Peter Salinski was accepted, the minutes were approved.

Helen Graff presented a report on the facsimile machine installation. Rewiring should be finished by November 1, and the system will be activated the following week. A follow-up report will be given at the October meeting.

NEW BUSINESS

Bernard King discussed the telecommunications conference to be held January 2-6, 19__. His position was that in light of Computer Visions' interest in this area, we should

(Continued on next page)

Block Centering C10.32

Format the three groups of terms by block-centering each group. Set a 2-inch top margin. Double-space. Leave 5 blank lines between each group.

daisy wheel printer
dot matrix printer
ink jet printer
laser printer
thermal printer
↓6

laptop computer
pixel
semiconductor
superconductor
telecommunications
↓6

download
dump
master file
peripheral
window

Centering C11.32

Center vertically; block-center horizontally. Double-space. Spread-center and bold the title. If time permits, key the job again using special print features of your word processor.

SPECIAL TELEPHONE FEATURES
Automatic Callback
Call Forwarding
Call Restriction
Call Timing
Call Waiting
Conference Calls
Speed Calling

Lesson 33

Objectives	Reinforce number and symbol keys.
	Reinforce centering skills.
	Key 30/2'/4e.
Format	Spacing: Drills, single; Timings, double; and as noted
	Margins: Default

A. Keyboard Skills

Key each line twice. Repeat if time permits.

Speed 1 The main office wants this payment by next month.
Accuracy 2 Quickly object to Wes dumping five toxic hazards.
Numbers 3 Mark read the winning numbers: 157, 869, and 23.
Symbols 4 Pencil & Paper has 2 reference manuals* @ $14.98.

B. Keyboard Number Review

Keep eyes on copy.
Key smoothly.

Use the numbers across the top of the keyboard as you key each line twice. Proofread; note your errors.

5 we 23 ye 63 per 034 you 697 quit 1785 wrote 24953
6 to 59 of 94 top 590 eye 363 tour 5974 quite 17853
7 it 85 re 43 rip 480 toy 596 root 4005 power 09234
8 up 70 at 15 pit 085 rot 405 tier 5834 queue 17373
9 or 94 pi 08 row 492 two 529 tire 5843 witty 28556

Take a 5-minute timing on lines 5–21. Proofread, note your errors, and figure your speed.

5	Reports are some of the most popular documents used in	12
6	business offices. They're placed near the top of hard-copy	24
7	documents that are produced and used in business today. As	36
8	you have often seen in this course, reports are prepared in	48
9	many unique styles. Their styles might vary in the margins	60
10	that are used, in the type size that is used, in the choice	72
11	of side and paragraph headings, in the spacing that is used	84
12	in the report, in the way that references are cited, and in	96
13	the number of spaces that are used for setting tabs.	106
14	Regardless of the format that's used, reports are very	118
15	important to running a business. They are used for various	130
16	reasons, but here are some of the most major ones. Reports	142
17	are often used to keep records of past performance; reports	154
18	are excellent for a status check on current jobs. They are	166
19	also used to propose solutions for any problems that exist.	178
20	Finally, reports are often needed to give direction for the	190
21	company's future years.	195

| 1 | 2 | 3 | 4 | 5 | 6 | 7 | 8 | 9 | 10 | 11 | 12 SI 1.43

C. PRACTICE

In the chart below find the number of errors you made on the Pretest. Then key each of the designated drill lines three times.

Pretest errors	0–1	2–3	4–5	6+
Drill lines	25–29	24–28	23–27	22–26

Accuracy

22 copy running setting reports problems excellent performance
23 hard various spacing popular company's references solutions
24 near records margins prepared direction important paragraph
25 most current offices business headings documents regardless

Speed

26 propose placed course status space today often most near to
27 problem unique styles reason their style might used that is
28 finally choice report that's cited major keeps have seen of
29 company number spaces format check exist years this type in

D. POSTTEST

Take another 5-minute timing on lines 5–21. Proofread, note your errors, and figure your speed. Compare your performance with the Pretest.

C. Symbol Review

Key each line once. Repeat if time permits.

$ 10 My special rates are $15, $27, $36, $48, and $59.
@ 11 They sold 8 bananas @ $1.39 and 6 apples @ $1.28.
  12 Buy 8 @ $.70 and 8 @ $.80; the total will be $12.

13 Carpet remnants were #37, #45, #98, #60, and #21.
% 14 Rates went up from 2% to 4%, 5% to 7%, 8% to 10%.
  15 Their #8 and #9 sizes are 36% to 46% higher here.

: 16 Times listed: 2:01, 1:56, 2:47, 10:29, or 11:38.
& 17 Pair them as follows: 10 & 29, 38 & 47, 56 & 65.
* 18 Which is the right date: 1919,* 1943,* or 1955?*
  19 S & L* arrived at 12:30; P & I* arrived at 12:45.

= 20 Grades: A = 100, B = 92, C = 83, D = 74, F = 65.
+ 21 Hollie added 91 + 82 + 73 + 65 + 50; she got 361.
( ) 22 He listed items (10), (65), (74), (83), and (92).
  23 Lisa, did you know that (6 + 6)(7 + 7) = 12 x 14?

! 24 Oh! No! Up! Yes! Here! Down! There! Shout!
' 25 It's not that he can't speak; it's that he won't.
" 26 "Look at it go!" she exclaimed. "Isn't it fine!"
_ 27 Please find Call of the Wild or Return of Lassie.
  28 "Let's buy tickets!" yelled Jo. "It's Oklahoma!"

D. 2-Minute Timings

Take two 2-minute timings on lines 29–34. Proofread, note your errors, and figure your speed.

29   Have you ever wished to live in a castle and 10
30 be part of those exciting times? Long ago moats, 20
31 or deep ditches, were dug to help guard against a 30
32 raid. The donjon, or keep, was a tall tower that 40
33 held the living quarters, since it was hard to be 50
34 seized. Guarding the grounds took a lot of time. 60

| 1 | 2 | 3 | 4 | 5 | 6 | 7 | 8 | 9 | 10 SI 1.21

Centering C12.33
Center vertically and horizontally. Double-space.

EARLY PRESIDENTS AND THEIR WIVES↓3
George and Martha Washington
John and Abigail Adams
Thomas and Martha Jefferson
James and Dolley Madison
James and Elizabeth Monroe
John Quincy and Louise Adams

Centering C13.33
Center vertically and horizontally. Double-space.

TIPS FOR DESIGNING NEWSLETTERS↓3
Identify the market.
Determine the purpose.
Plan the layout.
Leave adequate white space.
Avoid a cluttered look.
Use graphics effectively.
Use no more than two typefaces.

```
26  degree demand others after often while open many for can go
27  that's judged worker there doors these wish also who but on
28  people person school right thing prime find jobs may the is
29  listed reason skills along going being will than one get of
```

D. POSTTEST

Take another 5-minute timing on lines 5–21 (page 276). Proofread, note your errors, and figure your speed. Compare your performance with the Pretest.

E. Single-Spaced Business Reports

Single spacing is used in a business report when the report is long and the originator wants as few pages as possible. To format in this style:

1. Use default (1-inch) margins.
2. Begin the title 1 1/2 inches from the top (line 10).
3. Single-space; double-space between paragraphs.
4. Double-space before and after side headings if they are used. Side headings may be changed to paragraph headings if the report does not have both side headings and paragraph headings.
5. Use a half blank line where you would normally use a full blank line if your software provides for vertical half spacing.

Note: Desktop publishing software will allow you to make additional refinements in line spacing by adjusting the "leading" (space) between individual lines and paragraphs.

Report R53.121

Retrieve Report R49.119 and make the following changes: (1) delete the first sentence in the first paragraph; (2) delete the final sentence in the paragraph entitled *Telephone Lines;* (3) block delete the information following footnote 2 in the paragraph entitled *Fiber-Optic Cables;* (4) block delete the paragraphs entitled *Microwave Transmissions* and *Satellite Transmissions;* (5) block delete the long quotation; (6) block delete the section entitled *Careers in Telecommunications.* Renumber the footnotes as needed and reformat in single-spaced style.

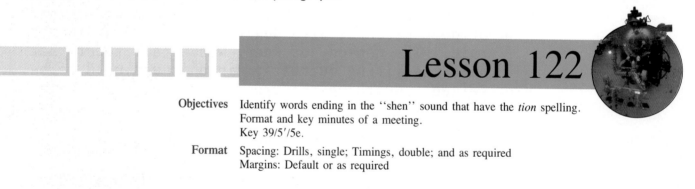

Lesson 122

Objectives   Identify words ending in the "shen" sound that have the *tion* spelling.
Format and key minutes of a meeting.
Key 39/5'/5e.

Format   Spacing: Drills, single; Timings, double; and as required
Margins: Default or as required

A. LAB 22

Spelling

Key lines 1–4 once. Then repeat lines 1–4, or take a series of 1-minute timings. (The spelling words are underlined.)

```
1  The 8th edition of Gregg Typing will be used for the class.   12
2  An orientation class may be held for all transfer students.   12
3  It is my recommendation that all of the charges be dropped.   12
4  Maximum utilization will be made of all second-floor rooms.   12
   |  1  |  2  |  3  |  4  |  5  |  6  |  7  |  8  |  9  |  10  |  11  |  12
```

Centering C14.33
Center vertically; block-center. Double-space.

PLANETS
Earth
Jupiter
Mars
Mercury
Neptune
Pluto
Saturn
Uranus
Venus

Centering C15.33
Center vertically; block-center. Enlarge title. Double-space.

MAJORS IN VISUALLY HANDICAPPED EDUCATION↓3

Florida State University

Eastern Michigan University

University of Michigan

Western Michigan University

D'Youville College, New York

The University of Toledo

Kutztown University, Pennsylvania

Northern State College, South Dakota

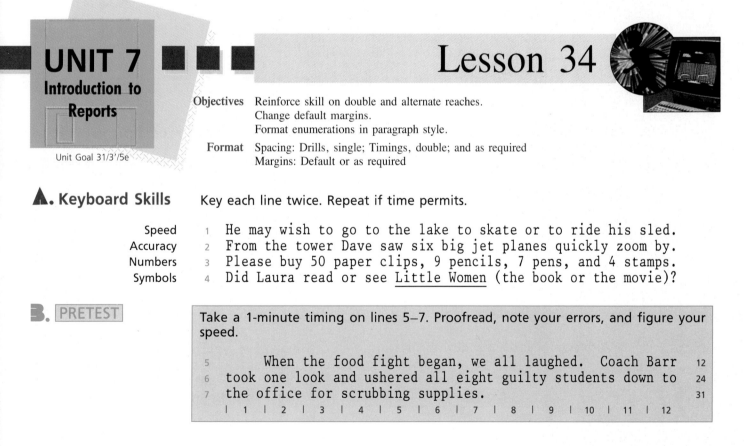

UNIT 7
Introduction to Reports

Unit Goal 31/3'/5e

Lesson 34

Objectives   Reinforce skill on double and alternate reaches.
Change default margins.
Format enumerations in paragraph style.

Format   Spacing: Drills, single; Timings, double; and as required
Margins: Default or as required

A. Keyboard Skills

Key each line twice. Repeat if time permits.

Speed   1   He may wish to go to the lake to skate or to ride his sled.
Accuracy   2   From the tower Dave saw six big jet planes quickly zoom by.
Numbers   3   Please buy 50 paper clips, 9 pencils, 7 pens, and 4 stamps.
Symbols   4   Did Laura read or see <u>Little Women</u> (the book or the movie)?

B. PRETEST

Take a 1-minute timing on lines 5–7. Proofread, note your errors, and figure your speed.

5   When the food fight began, we all laughed. Coach Barr   12
6   took one look and ushered all eight guilty students down to   24
7   the office for scrubbing supplies.   31
     | 1 | 2 | 3 | 4 | 5 | 6 | 7 | 8 | 9 | 10 | 11 | 12

2. Words that end in *sion* or *tion* are frequently misspelled in written communications. Study the list below to improve your spelling of these words.

acquisition	commission	congratulations	decision
edition	orientation	recommendation	utilization

B. PRETEST

Take a 5-minute timing on lines 5–21. Proofread, note your errors, and figure your speed.

```
 5        Finishing high school can open up many doors for those      12
 6   who wish to go on to complete a two- or four-year degree in      24
 7   college, and it may also open up opportunities to those who      36
 8   wish to find jobs after high school.  Jobs that may require      48
 9   advanced training will often demand more than a high school      60
10   degree, but there are also good jobs that are open to those      72
11   high school graduates who seize that opportunity.               82
12        Employers look for the right skills when they hire the      94
13   high school graduate.  One thing that's judged is whether a     106
14   person has exceptional people skills.  They want to know if     118
15   the person they are going to hire is able to get along with     130
16   people.  Of all the reasons for failing at a job, not being    142
17   able to get along well with co-workers is often listed as a     154
18   prime reason for failure.  It is thought by many that these     166
19   skills are essential on the job.  Another criterion that is     178
20   watched carefully is how well a worker can communicate with     190
21   others while on the job.                                        195
     |  1  |  2  |  3  |  4  |  5  |  6  |  7  |  8  |  9  |  10  |  11  |  12  SI 1.40
```

C. PRACTICE

In the chart below find the number of errors you made on the Pretest. Then key each of the following designated drill lines three times.

Pretest errors	0–1	2–3	4–5	6+
Drill lines	25–29	24–28	23–27	22–26

Accuracy

```
22   those seize whether require advanced training opportunities
23   two- high capable colleges graduates finishing communicates
24   can watched getting complete employers carefully co-workers
25   up judged failing criterion four-year essential exceptional
```

(Continued on next page)

If you made 2 or fewer errors on the Pretest (page 77), key lines 8–13 twice each. Repeat if time permits.
ACCURACY: If you made more than 2 errors on the Pretest (page 77), key lines 8–10 as a group twice. Then key lines 11–13 as a group twice. Repeat if time permits.

Double Reaches

8 ff chaff stiff bluff affix scuff cliff offer sniff stuff ff
9 oo looks shoot loose noose scoop droop boost moose stool oo
10 rr carry tarry berry hurry worry merry marry sorry furry rr

Alternate Reaches

11 hangs thigh fight hairy eight laugh sight gland rigid widow
12 towns chair girls chant clams snaps prowl worms flame their
13 prism signs usher clamp ogled frown light growl other heist

D. POSTTEST

Take a 1-minute timing on lines 5–7 (page 77). Proofread, note your errors, and figure your speed. Compare your performance with the Pretest.

E. Changing Default Margins

Word processors have **word wrap,** which automatically drops the cursor down to the next line and returns it to the left margin without the user having to press Enter/Return. Therefore, line-ending decisions are made by the software.

When text is keyed using word wrap, it can be reformatted by changing the left and right margin settings. Some word processors set margins by the side margin width, and others use the line length. Some use inches; others use spaces. When spaces are used, the settings will differ depending on the type size being used. The chart below shows the various measures used for setting margins.

Inch margins	1	1.5	2
Inch line	6.5	5.5	4.5
10 pitch/12 point Space margins	10	15	20
Space line	65	55	45
12 pitch/10 point Space margins	12	18	24
Space line	78	66	54
(round to	80	65	55)

Margins are usually changed through a **format** command; the exact procedures will differ depending on the software you use.

In this course, whenever you are told to use default margins, the default is assumed to be 1 inch, and the type-size default is assumed to be 10 pitch/12 point (65-space line).

(Continued on next page)

Report R51.120

Prepare a contents page for your report. Begin with *I. Connections Used in Telecommunications;* use the side and paragraph headings in the report for the rest of the contents.

■. Cover Page

A cover page contains the title of the report, the name of the writer, the name of the person for whom the report was prepared, and the date. For academic reports, it also contains the name of the course.

To format a cover page:

1. Center the report title and the writer's name in the upper 33 lines of the page.
2. Center the name of the person for whom the report was prepared (teacher), and/or the person's title or company (or the course name), and the date in the lower 33 lines of the page.

Note: To center copy in both halves of the page, change your page length to 5.5 inches or 33 lines. Key the copy for the top half of the page and use the center page command. Use a hard page break. Then key the copy for the bottom half of the page and use the center page command.

Report R52.120

Prepare a cover page for your report. Use your name, your keyboarding teacher's name, and today's date.

```
COMPUTER SYSTEMS DESIGN
By Philip A. Johnson




- - - - - - - - - - - - - - - - - - - - - -




Joan Malcolm
Technology Forecasting Inc.
October 19, 19--
```

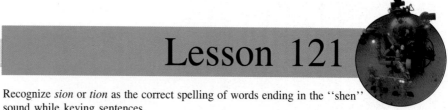

Lesson 121

Objectives Recognize *sion* or *tion* as the correct spelling of words ending in the "shen" sound while keying sentences.
Format and key a single-spaced business report.
Key 39/5'/5e.

Format Spacing: Drills, single; Timings, double; and as required
Margins: Default or as required

▲. LAB 22

Spelling

Key lines 1–4 once. Then repeat lines 1–4, or take a series of 1-minute timings. (The spelling words are underlined.)

```
1  An acquisition was made by the agent representing the firm.   12
2  Lorenzo earned a large commission on the sale of the house.   12
3  We extended our congratulations to Maria on her high marks.   12
4  It is the board's decision to release the information soon.   12
   | 1 | 2 | 3 | 4 | 5 | 6 | 7 | 8 | 9 | 10 | 11 | 12
```

Practice

1. Key the two paragraphs below. Use default margins. Double-space between paragraphs.
2. Set 1.5-inch side margins (5.5-inch line). Key the two paragraphs again from your screen copy. Notice the difference in line length.
3. Set 2-inch side margins (4.5-inch line). Key the two paragraphs once more from your screen copy. Again note the shorter line length.

Have you noticed that the timings and drills in each lesson end at the same place? This is no coincidence. Each line has been made to end at a certain point by writing and rewriting it so that all the lines are blocked at the right margin.

The reason that the lines are written to end evenly is to help you check for accuracy when you proofread your work. A line, other than the last one of a paragraph, that does not end evenly must contain an error. You can look for this quickly.

F. Enumerations

An enumeration is a series of numbered or lettered words, phrases, or sentences. An enumeration may be in paragraph style, where paragraphs are indented and begin with a number or a letter.

To format paragraph enumerations:

1. Set margins appropriate for the length of the enumerated items.
2. Center the enumeration vertically if it is on a page by itself, or leave a 2-inch top margin (begin on line 13).
3. Follow the numbers or the letters with a period and 2 spaces.
4. Indent the first line 5 spaces from the left margin. Turnover lines block at the left margin.

Paragraph enumerations may be double-spaced or single-spaced. If single spacing is used, leave 1 blank line between paragraphs.

Review: Formatting Titles

1. Center the title over the copy.
2. Key the title in all caps and bold.
3. Triple-space after the title ($\downarrow$ 3).

Some jobs have arrows and numbers to help you space vertically. For example, $\downarrow$ 3 means "go down 3 lines." (Leave 2 lines blank, and key text on the third line.)

Report R1.34 Enumeration

Paragraph style. Format: 1.5-inch side margins, 2-inch top margin, 5-space tab, single spacing.

BENEFITS OF DESKTOP PUBLISHING $\downarrow$ 3

1. The need for outside help is eliminated; all elements of document production are kept within the business.

2. Security of documents is easier to control, since people outside the business are not involved.

3. Updates and changes can be made easily and quickly.

4. All phases of publishing are kept within the business, giving greater control over costs and deadlines.

C. Bibliography

A bibliography is an alphabetic listing of all the books and articles consulted by the writer, including all references cited in the footnotes. A bibliography is very similar in format to a "Works Cited" page.

To format a bibliography:

1. Center the heading BIBLIOGRAPHY on a clean sheet of paper, beginning on line 13.

2. Triple-space after the heading before entering the first line in the bibliography.

3. Use the same margins as used in the report or term paper. Begin each entry at the left margin, and indent continuation lines 5 spaces. (See page 161 for hanging indents.)

4. Use single spacing for turnover lines, but double-space between entries.

5. Do not number the entries.

6. List the entries in alphabetic order by the authors' *last* names. For an entry that has no author, alphabetize the title of the article or book. When alphabetizing titles, disregard *The, A,* and *An.*

7. Use six hyphens to avoid repeating an author's name after his or her first listing. (See the illustration.) When an author has more than one title listed, arrange titles alphabetically.

8. Separate items within each entry with commas.

9. Use page numbers only if the material is part of a larger work (such as a magazine article). Use the range of pages for the entire work.

10. Number the bibliography page the same way the other pages of the report are numbered.

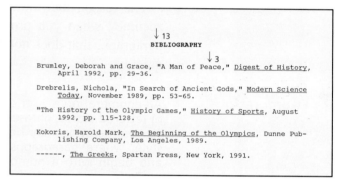

Report R50.120

Prepare a bibliography for Report R48.118 (pages 270–272), using the footnote references for your bibliographic entries. Make the following change and additions: (1) *Change the page reference for Larkins to* pp. 16–18. (2) *Add:*

Peter A. McWilliams, <u>A Short Course in Telecommunications</u>, 2d ed., Prelude Press, Los Angeles, 1989.
<u>Forecasting the Future: Special Report</u>, Pembroke Press, New York, 1991.

D. Table of Contents

A table of contents is an outline of the headings in a report and the page references to them.

To format a table of contents:

1. Center the title CONTENTS on line 13. (You may spread-center the title if you wish.)

2. Use the same margins as those used in the report.

3. Follow outline format, but do not use bold on roman numeral lines.

4. Use leaders (rows of periods) to connect the headings with the numbers. Leave 1 space between the words and the start of the leaders and 1 space between the end of the leaders and the *longest* page number. (Leaders should all end at the same spot.)

Note: If your software has a leader tab, set the tab at the point where you want the final column to end (it will be aligned at the right).

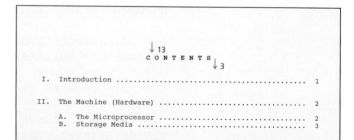

Report R2.34 Enumeration
Paragraph style. Format: 1.5-inch side margins, 2-inch top margin, 5-space tab, double spacing.

BETTER COMMUNICATION

Here are three practical suggestions to help make your conversation more interesting and effective:

1. Listen attentively. Almost all of us need to be better listeners. Don't be preoccupied with your own thoughts.

2. Ask the right questions. Good questions show a genuine interest in the other person.

3. Learn how to disagree. It isn't what you say but how you say it that often makes all the difference.

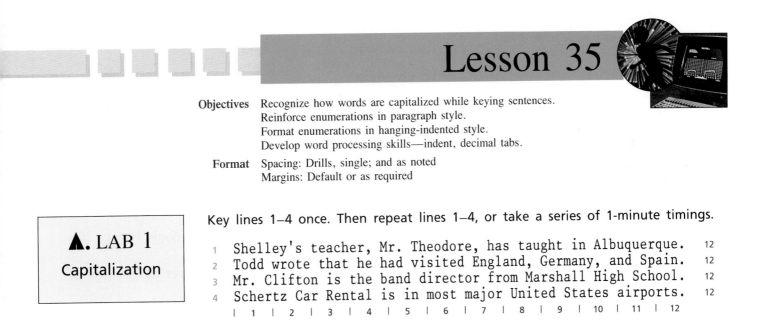

Lesson 35

Objectives Recognize how words are capitalized while keying sentences.
Reinforce enumerations in paragraph style.
Format enumerations in hanging-indented style.
Develop word processing skills—indent, decimal tabs.

Format Spacing: Drills, single; and as noted
Margins: Default or as required

▲. LAB 1
Capitalization

Key lines 1–4 once. Then repeat lines 1–4, or take a series of 1-minute timings.

```
1  Shelley's teacher, Mr. Theodore, has taught in Albuquerque.   12
2  Todd wrote that he had visited England, Germany, and Spain.   12
3  Mr. Clifton is the band director from Marshall High School.   12
4  Schertz Car Rental is in most major United States airports.   12
   | 1 | 2 | 3 | 4 | 5 | 6 | 7 | 8 | 9 | 10 | 11 | 12
```

1. Capitalize the first word of every sentence.

This winter has been one of the most severe in recent history.

2. Capitalize a proper noun (the official name of a person, place, or thing) and the pronoun *I*: Mr. Theodore, Albuquerque, England, Marshall High School. **Note:** Common nouns such as *museum, high school,* and *city* are also capitalized when they are part of proper names: Carnegie Museum, Patterson High School, New York City.

Jara and I always watch the Thanksgiving Day parade in Chicago.

Take two 30-second "OK" (errorless) timings on lines 5–6. Then take two 30-second "OK" timings on lines 7–8. Goal: No errors.

```
5  Vi mixed the grape juice for my party, and then she quickly   12
6  prepared ice cream topped by our huge, frozen strawberries.   24

7  When Zeth requested a bill, did Jack pay for fixing my van,   12
8  or did he indicate that he would be back on Tuesday to pay?   24
   |  1  |  2  |  3  |  4  |  5  |  6  |  7  |  8  |  9  | 10  | 11  | 12
```

Report R49.119
Continue the report you started in Lesson 118, pages 270–272.

Lesson 120

Objectives Select the correct spelling of words ending in silent *e* while keying sentences.
Format and key a bibliography.
Format and key a table of contents.
Format and key a cover page.

Format Spacing: Drills, single; and as required
Margins: Default or as required

A. LAB 21

Spelling

Key lines 1–4 once, selecting the appropriate word from each pair enclosed in parentheses. Review your copy as your teacher reads the answers. Then key lines 1–4 again.

1 The (absence/abcense) of the (juvinile/juvenile) was noted by the teacher today.
2 The (maintainance/maintenance) (schedual/schedule) should be met if we're to succeed.
3 The (mortgage/morgage) is (adaquate/adequate) to cover the loan on our new home.
4 The two (seperate/separate) teams were (eligable/eligible) for the play-off game.

B. 12-Second Timings

Take three 12-second timings on each line, or key each line three times. Try to key with no more than 1 error on each timing.

```
5  The chair and the desk have to be moved right to the front.
6  The lawn is green and dry, and it must be cut at this time.
7  A pen will break if you press on the point for a long time.
   |    5    10    15    20    25    30    35    40    45    50    55    60
```

B. 30-Second Timings

Take two 30-second timings on lines 5–6. Then take two 30-second timings on lines 7–8. Try to key with no more than 2 errors on each timing.

```
5  If you have documents which need to be sent to another city   12
6  immediately, you should consider using a facsimile machine.    24

7  After scanning a document page, a fax machine sends signals    12
8  to a receiving fax machine, which then makes an exact copy.    24
   | 1 | 2 | 3 | 4 | 5 | 6 | 7 | 8 | 9 | 10 | 11 | 12
```

Report R3.35 Enumeration

Paragraph style. Format: Default side margins, 2-inch top margin, 5-space tab, single spacing.

```
                 CAPITALIZATION RULES

     A.  Capitalize the first word of a sentence, an expression
used as a sentence, and a quoted sentence.
     B.  Capitalize an independent question within a sentence and
each item displayed in a list or an outline.
     C.  Capitalize each line in a poem unless the style of the
poem itself is different.
     D.  Capitalize the first word of the salutation and the
complimentary closing of a letter.
     E.  Do not capitalize the first word after a dash or a
parenthesis unless it is a proper noun or the first word of a
quoted sentence.
```

C. Indent/Temporary Left Margin

Sometimes copy has to be displayed, or "set off," within the body of a document. One way to display copy is to indent a paragraph 5 to 10 spaces from the left margin. Many word processing software programs allow the user to set an indent or a temporary left margin. After the command is entered, all lines following that command will be indented the number of spaces given in the command. Procedures vary with each word processor. **Practice:** Set 1.5-inch side margins and a 6-space tab stop. Then key the lines below using your word processor's temporary left margin feature for turnover lines.

```
ONE:  Indenting turnover lines is called "hanging
      indention" and is used for special displays such
      as outlines and enumerations.

TWO:  Using the automatic indent or temporary left
      margin feature is an easy way to indent these
      turnover lines automatically.
```

D. Hanging-Indented Enumerations

Horizontal and vertical placement of enumerations is the same, regardless of style. The difference is in the way the paragraphs are displayed. For hanging-indented style:

1. The numbers or letters begin at the left margin and align on the period. Two spaces follow the period. If a number has more than one digit (such as 10), space in from the left margin for the numbers with fewer digits.

2. Turnover lines are indented and align with the first word in the line above. (The numbers or letters stand by themselves.) Set a tab for the indent.

3. Hanging-indented enumerations are always single-spaced. If any item takes more than one line, leave a blank line between all items.

TABLE 1

Transmission Speeds in Telecommunications

Speed	Bits per Second	Example
Low	40 to 300	Telegraph
Medium	300 to 9,600	Telephone
High	Over 9,600	Fiber optics*

Source: Beryl Robichaud et al., Introduction to Information Processing, 4th ed., McGraw-Hill, New York, 1989, p. 163.

*Also includes microwave and satellite communications.

Careers in Telecommunications

Telecommunications is such a fast-moving, high-technology career field that job openings are available in many of the larger industries in this country— including the "airlines, retail outlets, high-tech factories, and even fast-food chains."[5] [5. James L. Shefter, Telecommunications Careers, Franklin Watts, New York, 1988, p. 17.] Those who enter this exciting career field can expect generally high salaries because of the high demand for people with telecommunications background and training. Job openings are available for people who have attended shop classes in high school or who have taken vocational courses in high school to prepare them as technicians to work with circuit boards, control boxes, power supplies, and other equipment that is used for the transmission of electronic data. Opportunities are also available in areas such as drafting, programming, and repair work. Once you obtain an entry-level position, you can often obtain advanced training and education through company-sponsored programs. Thus you can advance in your job within the telecommunications career field through a dual program of job-related experience and company-sponsored training.

Conclusion

Telecommunications is an exciting career field that offers a number of advantages to those who enter its many areas. Scientific breakthroughs in the coming years will lead to even more sophistication in the hardware used to transmit information. Career opportunities are likely to follow this same course of progressive movement to guarantee job opportunities for years to come.

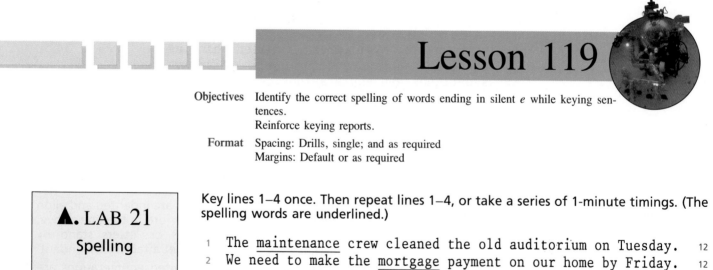

Lesson 119

Objectives Identify the correct spelling of words ending in silent *e* while keying sentences.
Reinforce keying reports.

Format Spacing: Drills, single; and as required
Margins: Default or as required

▲. LAB 21
Spelling

Key lines 1–4 once. Then repeat lines 1–4, or take a series of 1-minute timings. (The spelling words are underlined.)

1	The <u>maintenance</u> crew cleaned the old auditorium on Tuesday.	12
2	We need to make the <u>mortgage</u> payment on our home by Friday.	12
3	Our coach will <u>schedule</u> the next game by Wednesday evening.	12
4	She must <u>separate</u> the new textbooks from the old textbooks.	12

| 1 | 2 | 3 | 4 | 5 | 6 | 7 | 8 | 9 | 10 | 11 | 12 |

Decimal Tabs

Some word processors allow the setting of decimal tabs that can be used whenever items are to align on the period—the **decimal point**. (A left tab aligns on the left.)

A decimal tab can be used in enumerations to align on the period. However, this is not necessary unless the number contains more than one digit or if a **proportional font** (characters are different widths) is used.

Use indent/temporary left margin feature if available.

Report R4.35 Enumeration

Hanging-indented style. Format: Default side margins, 2-inch top margin, 4-space indent.

HANGING-INDENTED ENUMERATION

A. A hanging-indented enumeration can be a set of steps, a series of numbered or lettered words or statements, or a list of items.

B. It is arranged so that the numbers or letters stand by themselves in the margin.

C. Each number or letter is followed by a period, and the period is followed by two spaces.

D. All lines that do not start with a number or a letter are indented.

E. Single-space, but if any item takes more than one line, leave a blank line between items.

Lesson 36

Objectives   Identify how words are capitalized while keying sentences.
Reinforce enumerations in hanging-indented style.
Format outlines.
Compose paragraphs at the keyboard.
Key 31/3'/5e.

Format   Spacing: Drills, single; Timings, double; and as required
Margins: Default or as required

▲. LAB 1
Capitalization

Key lines 1–4 once. Then repeat lines 1–4, or take a series of 1-minute timings.

1   This work was done best by a Spanish company, El Periodico.   12
2   Mrs. Jazarian, our supervisor, is going to Tibet next year.   12
3   The Hawaiian hula group will be featured at the Oil Palace.   12
4   The French student will visit the Grand Canyon in February.   12
   | 1 | 2 | 3 | 4 | 5 | 6 | 7 | 8 | 9 | 10 | 11 | 12

nology used in business offices today. This report will describe how it works and provide the reader with a background in understanding how important it is to the office of the future.

Connections Used in Telecommunications

As mentioned above, information in a telecommunications system flows from one point to another via telephone lines or specially designed cables. Microwaves and satellites can also be used in a telecommunications link.[1] [1. Beryl Robichaud et al., Introduction to Information Processing, 4th ed., McGraw-Hill, New York, 1989, pp. 160, 163.] Let us look at each of these methods for linking a sending station and a receiving station together.

Telephone Lines. This method of linking a sender and a receiver together should be no stranger to us, for telephone lines have been used for over 100 years for this specific purpose. The difference is that now the lines are insulated better so that there is less outside interference when messages are sent. The real advantage of using telephone lines is that the telephone lines that are already in place can then be used to transmit information.

Coaxial Cables. This method of transmission uses a wire that is very similar to that which is used for cable television. The wire that actually carries the transmission is very well insulated—even better insulated than telephone lines. Thus the message is clearer and is sent faster.

Fiber-Optic Cables. One of the newest technologies used to transmit information in a telecommunications system is fiber optics. With fiber optics technology, a voice or data is transmitted "by means of a laser light beam flashing through tiny glass fibers no thicker than a human hair."[2] [2. Ibid., p. 160.] These fiber-optic cables are capable of handling over 200,000 conversations at one time, and new technology will soon allow them to handle over 500,000 conversations at one time.[3] [3. Sarah E. Hutchinson and Stacy C. Sawyer, Computers, The User Perspective, 2d ed., Richard D. Irwin, Home-

wood, Ill., 1990, p. 422.] At this rate, you would be transmitting messages at the rate of over 100 million characters per second.

Microwave Transmissions. Microwaves can be used to transmit information from a sending station to a receiving station. With this connection, obviously, no wires are used for the transmission because the information is sent via microwaves from one antenna to another. This method of sending information is much faster and cheaper than using telephone lines and coaxial cables, but it does require that relay stations be positioned no more than 30 miles apart to transmit information.

Satellite Transmissions. These days we are accustomed to watching some television programs that are broadcast from different locations around the globe. This is possible because of satellite transmission, and such transmission is also possible in telecommunications. This method of sending information is used only by large international companies, however, because it is very expensive.

Telecommunications Hardware

Data created by a computer must be transformed into a format that will allow it to be sent over telephone wires or over cable lines. The equipment that is used to make this transformation is known as a modem.

A modem takes computer-generated data, converts it into a format that will allow it to travel along a telephone line, and then converts it back to a computer format when it reaches another computer. This procedure is called modulation/demodulation.[4] [4. Cheryl Larkins, "Communications Hardware in the Office," The Data Chronicle, February 1990, p. 17.]

Modems transmit data at speeds that average about 2,400 bps (bits per second), which is equivalent to around 300 characters per second. Various speeds of transmission are summarized in Table 1 below.

(Continued on next page)

LESSON 118

B. Preview Practice

Key each line twice as a preview to the 3-minute timings below.

Accuracy 5 next flying contest checked members qualify excited Arizona
Speed   6 their there they held the for and big jet by if of to so go

C. 3-Minute Timings

Take two 3-minute timings on lines 7–14. Proofread, note your errors, and figure your speed.

Using Speed Markers

The raised numbers in this timing are speed markers. At the end of the timing, the number you reach will tell your "wam" speed because the total words have already been divided by 3. For example, if your timing were to end on the last letter of *checked* on line 13, your speed would be 26 wam.

```
                    1              2              3              4
 7      Ten members of our club hope to win first place in the    12
            5              6              7              8
 8   contests next month; if they win a first or second place in   24
            9             10             11             12
 9   their contests, they will move up to the state level, which   36
           13             14             15             16
10   will be held in March.  The top three who win in each state   48
           17             18             19             20
11   contest will qualify for the last big contest in April.  We   60
           21             22             23             24
12   are so excited; this year, Tucson, Arizona, will be host of   72
           25             26             27             28
13   this contest.  We have checked the cost of flying there and   84
           29             30             31
14   will have to wash a lot of cars to go by jet.                 93
   |  1  |  2  |  3  |  4  |  5  |  6  |  7  |  8  |  9  |  10  |  11  |  12  SI 1.19
```

Report R5.36 Enumeration
Hanging-indented style. Format: Default side margins, 2-inch top margin, 4-space indent.

TELECOMMUNICATIONS

1. Computers can be used for communication by connecting them with telephone lines, microwaves, or satellites.
2. A modem is a device that is used to connect a computer to telephone lines.
3. Computers must have special software to enable them to be used for communication.
4. Many different databases, which provide current, up-to-date information on almost any subject, are available to computers.
5. Another way to use telephone lines for communication is the transmission of pages of text and graphics by facsimile machines.

Take a 1-minute timing on lines 5–8. Proofread, note your errors, and figure your speed.

```
 5        We will need to bring all kinds of food to the dinner,    12
 6   and we also need to bring with us forks and spoons and cups    24
 7   for everyone.  She will drive from the busy city to a field    36
 8   for that day.                                                  39
     |  1  |  2  |  3  |  4  |  5  |  6  |  7  |  8  |  9  |  10  |  11  |  12
```

C. PRACTICE

SPEED: If you made 2 or fewer errors on the Pretest, key lines 9–14 twice each. Repeat if time permits.
ACCURACY: If you made more than 2 errors on the Pretest, key lines 9–11 as a group twice. Then key lines 12–14 as a group twice. Repeat if time permits.

Double Reaches

```
 9   nn funny cannon cannot dinner manner runner winner channels
10   oo good wood room soon proof spoon foods tooth groom booths
11   tt kitty bottle button attach cattle fitted attacks attends
```

Alternate Reaches

```
12   duck duty bush busy city clay audit blend civic cycle field
13   dock down both bowl buck burn flaps girls goals panel risks
14   dial corn cork body also auto rocks spent their tight vivid
```

D. POSTTEST

Take a 1-minute timing on lines 5–8. Proofread, note your errors, and figure your speed. Compare your performance with the Pretest.

E. Bound Reports

In a bound report, the left margin must be 1 1/2 inches wide to allow for binding on the left. This format change can be accommodated by either (1) changing the left margin or (2) using a command that provides a page offset. **Note:** Only the left margin changes; the right margin remains 1 inch wide—the minimum width for side margins.

F. Long Quotes in Business Reports

In academic reports, you learned that long quotes were double-spaced and indented 10 spaces. In business-report style, long quotes should be single-spaced and indented 5 spaces from both the left and right margins.
Reset both margins before and after keying the long quotation.

Double Indent

Some software programs have a double indent feature (sometimes called the quote feature) that indents the copy from both margins. If this feature is available, you will not have to change margin settings.

Variable Spacing

Changing from double spacing to single spacing before a long quote may require that you use a Line Format command to change your line spacing. You will have to change your line spacing back again to resume double spacing.

Report R48.118
Bound report with footnotes. Begin preparing the report, and continue in Lesson 119.

TELECOMMUNICATIONS
By [*Your name*]

Telecommunications, or data communications, refers to the use of the telephone or specially designed cables to transmit information from one location to another. Telecommunications had its beginning over 100 years ago, for it was on March 10, 1876, that Alexander Graham Bell used a telephone to utter those now famous words, "Mr. Watson, come here; I want you." Data communications is associated closely with computers and the high tech-

(Continued on next page)

D. Outlines

Note: Some word processing software packages have an outline feature.

Use indent/temporary left margin and decimal tab features if available.

To format an outline, follow these rules:

1. Either use the same margins as those used in the paper that was outlined, or set your margins so that the outline will be centered horizontally.

2. Center the outline vertically, or use a 2-inch top margin (line 13).

3. Align the periods after roman numerals. Space forward for the shorter numerals, or use a decimal tab.

4. Use single spacing, but triple-space before and double-space after a line that begins with a roman numeral.

5. Indent each subdivision 4 more spaces:

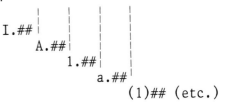

6. Use initial caps and bold for entries that begin with a roman numeral. Bold the roman numeral.

Report R6.36 Outline

Format: 1.5-inch side margins, 2-inch top margin, 4-space decimal tab, 4 additional left tabs (3 spaces, 4 spaces, 4 spaces, 4 spaces).

DISTRIBUTING INCOMING MAIL ↓3

I. Sort the Mail. ↓2

    A. Sort the mail by addressees.
    B. Sort the mail by priority.
       1. Priority, overnight, and fax mail are first.
       2. Personal and confidential mail are second.
       3. Telegrams and special delivery are third.
       4. First-class and interoffice mail are next.
       5. Second- and third-class mail are last.
          a. This may be magazines or brochures.
          b. This may also include "junk" mail. ↓3

II. Check the Contents. ↓2

    A. Remove letters from the envelopes.
    B. Attach enclosures.
       1. Do not use metal clips on magnetic media.
          a. Plastic clips are safe to use.
          b. Tape may be used.
       2. Use caution when stapling enclosures. ↓3

III. Stamp the Date and Time on Correspondence.

Practice: Before you begin the two practice exercises, you must learn how the footnote feature in your software program operates. In some programs you do *not* key the text reference or footnote numbers—the program automatically inserts the numbers.

Use default side margins, a 5-space tab, and double spacing. Use default top and bottom margins of 1 inch. Use the illustration on page 268.

Footnotes on a Full Page

1. Depress the enter/return key until the line indicator shows that you are on line 45 (8.33 inches). Because of the default 1-inch top margin, this is actually line 52 from the top edge of the paper.
2. Key *the year 1871.*
3. Follow the procedure for the footnote feature in your software, and key the footnote information.
4. Key the final sentence of the text.

5. Follow the procedure for the footnote feature, and key the footnote information.

Footnotes on a Partial Page

1. Block the lines you have keyed, and copy them at the top of the next page. The copy should appear on lines 1 and 3 (lines 7 and 9 from the top edge of the paper).
2. Print both pages.

On the first page, the text copy should appear at the bottom of the page, starting on line 52. Your software should have placed the footnotes at the bottom of the page, separated from the text by a divider line, leaving a 1-inch bottom margin.

On the second page, the two lines of text should print on lines 7 and 9 at the top of the page; the footnotes (and the divider line) should appear at the bottom of the page in the exact position that they appeared on the first page.

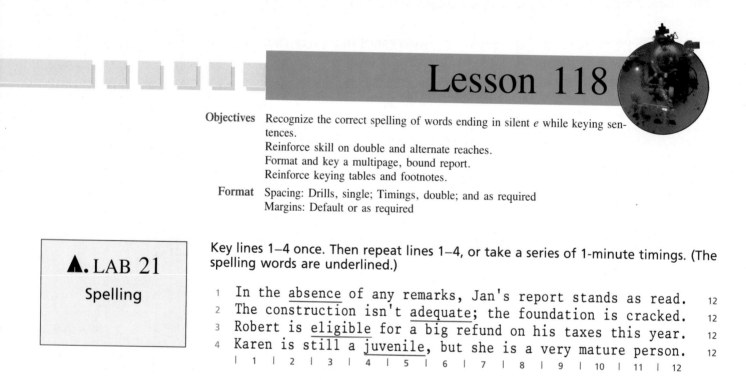

Lesson 118

Objectives Recognize the correct spelling of words ending in silent *e* while keying sentences.
Reinforce skill on double and alternate reaches.
Format and key a multipage, bound report.
Reinforce keying tables and footnotes.

Format Spacing: Drills, single; Timings, double; and as required
Margins: Default or as required

▲ LAB 21

Spelling

Key lines 1–4 once. Then repeat lines 1–4, or take a series of 1-minute timings. (The spelling words are underlined.)

```
1  In the absence of any remarks, Jan's report stands as read.     12
2  The construction isn't adequate; the foundation is cracked.      12
3  Robert is eligible for a big refund on his taxes this year.      12
4  Karen is still a juvenile, but she is a very mature person.      12
   |  1  |  2  |  3  |  4  |  5  |  6  |  7  |  8  |  9  | 10  | 11  | 12
```

1. Words that end in silent *e* are frequently misspelled in written communications. Study the list below to improve your spelling of these words.

absence	adequate	eligible	juvenile
maintenance	mortgage	schedule	separate

E. Composing at the Keyboard

Remember these points as you compose at the keyboard:

1. Organize your ideas mentally—do not write them down.
2. Use the correct format for the document you are composing.
3. Try to key a final copy of the document on the first try.
4. You may look at the text you are composing; keep your eyes on the screen—not on the keys.
5. Proofread and edit if necessary.

Compose Paragraph Practice

Compose an answer in paragraph form to two of the questions below. Have at least four sentences in each paragraph. If time permits, compose an answer to the third question. Format: Double spacing, 5-space tab.

1. What do you think you will be doing five years from now?
2. What are four things you would like to change about yourself?
3. Who are four people in history you would most like to meet? Why?

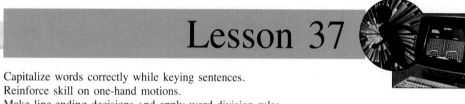

Lesson 37

Objectives Capitalize words correctly while keying sentences.
Reinforce skill on one-hand motions.
Make line-ending decisions and apply word division rules.
Reinforce outlines.

Format Spacing: Drills, single; Timings, double; and as required
Margins: Default or as required

▲. LAB 1
Capitalization

Key lines 1–4 once, providing the missing capitals. Review your copy as your teacher reads the answers. Then key lines 1–4 again.

mr. and mrs. boltz wrote that they had visited los angeles.

we took ms. verhetsel and ms. mikesa to the airport monday.

we saw the american flag flying at our embassy in scotland.

has mr. coby been to the top of the sears tower in chicago?

B. PRETEST

Take a 1-minute timing on lines 5–7. Proofread, note your errors, and figure your speed.

```
5        His debut as a racer revealed hours of practice on the   12
6   track.  After nineteen laps, he was ninth; but he completed   24
7   that race by winning second place.                            31
    |  1  |  2  |  3  |  4  |  5  |  6  |  7  |  8  |  9  | 10 | 11 | 12
```

Report R47.117
Endnotes. Standard format.

1. Beryl Robichaud et al., <u>Introduction to Information Processing</u>, 4th ed., McGraw-Hill, New York, 1989, pp. 160, 163.
2. Ibid., p. 160.
3. Sarah E. Hutchinson and Stacy C. Sawyer, <u>Computers, The User Perspective</u>, 2d ed., Richard D. Irwin, Homewood, Ill., 1990, p. 422.
4. Cheryl Larkins, ''Communications Hardware in the Office,'' <u>The Data Chronicle</u>, February 1990, p. 17.
5. James L. Shefter, <u>Telecommunications Careers</u>, Franklin Watts, New York, 1988, p. 17.

F. Footnotes

When a text reference for a footnote is placed in the text, the footnote must be placed in the correct position at the bottom of the same page. If more than one footnote is used on a page, each follows in sequence at the bottom of the page. To format footnotes:

1. Plan ahead to determine the number of lines you must "save" at the bottom of the page for the footnotes. As you enter each reference in the text, estimate the number of lines for each footnote.
2. Change to single spacing after the last line of the text; key a 2-inch line beginning at the left margin. This line separates the footnotes from the text.
3. Double-space, indent 5 spaces, and key the foot-

note number followed by a period, 2 spaces, and the reference. Single-space turnover lines, and begin them at the left margin, as shown in the illustration below.

Note: Some style manuals indicate the use of a superscript number (without a space) in footnotes as well as in text references. Example:

[1]Barbara Anne Hemsley

4. Double-space between footnotes.
5. Always place footnotes at the bottom of the page—even on the last page of a report, which may have only a few lines of text. The bottom margin below the footnote should be a minimum of 6 lines or a maximum of 9 lines.

Footnote Feature

Many word processing programs have a footnote feature that will automatically place footnotes at the bottom of the page on which they are referenced. An underline will accompany the footnotes to separate them from the text of the report. In some programs, the footnote feature can be used for endnotes as well as footnotes.

```
45   the year 1871.¹  This unique invention was not accepted until
46
47   the turn of the century, when Bobbsfield moved to England.²
48                                                              ↓1
49   ─────────────────────────────────── ↓2
50       1.   Barbara Anne Hemsley, "The Distant Land," The National
51   Outlook, April 1991, pp. 215-216.↓2
52
53       2.   Ibid., p. 217. ■
─ ─ ─ ─ ─ ─ ─ ─ ─ ─ ─ ─ ─ ─ ─ ─ ─ ─ ─ ─ ─ ─ ─ ─ ─ ─ ─ ─ ─ ─ ─ ─

     B:\R48                          Doc 1    Pg 1    Ln 45      Pos 35
```

C. PRACTICE

SPEED: If you made 2 or fewer errors on the Pretest (page 85), key lines 8–13 twice each. Repeat if time permits.
ACCURACY: If you made more than 2 errors on the Pretest (page 85), key lines 8–10 as a group twice. Then key lines 11–13 as a group twice. Repeat if time permits.

Left Reaches

8 gates fasts error decks crews bases award reeds craze saves
9 verse abate react areas based crate debts erect facet tears
10 safes avert crave waste dares erase taxes baste reads creed

Right Reaches

11 polly onion plump jolly ninny lumpy nylon nippy jumpy milky
12 joint point humor humid mount hound pound mound honor hippo
13 mumps jumps mills links pools plums minks nouns hooks holly

D. POSTTEST

Take a 1-minute timing on lines 5–7 (page 85). Proofread, note your errors, and figure your speed. Compare your performance with the Pretest.

E. Line-Ending Decisions

When you key text, the end of each line should be as close to the right margin setting as possible. That means that after you have completed a document, while you are proofreading and editing it, you should check the margin line endings.

Sometimes you may find that changing your right margin by 2 or 3 spaces will make the right margin look more even. Other times you will have to divide a long word to make the line end closer to the margin.

Hyphenation Feature

Many word processors have a hyphenation feature that will divide words at the end of lines or will highlight those words so that the user can insert a hyphen at the appropriate division point. Therefore, it is often necessary to decide whether to complete a word or to divide it.

F. Word Division Rules

Unless there is more than a half inch of space at the end of a line, do not divide a word. If it is necessary, however, follow the rules given below.

Absolute Rules

1. Divide only between syllables. If you are not sure where a syllable ends, use a dictionary. Never guess, for some words are tricky.

   Examples: syl-la-ble   prod-uct   chil-dren   knowl-edge
   pres-ent (a gift)   pre-sent (to make a gift)

2. Do not divide:
   a. A word pronounced as one syllable: *shipped, strength, tire.*
   b. Any contraction: *couldn't, can't, o'clock.*
   c. Any abbreviation: *dept., UNICEF, a.m.*
   d. The last word on a page.

(Continued on next page)

Practice: Key the sentences below, placing the superscripts in their proper position (and font, if necessary).

Note: If your software does not have a superscripts feature, place the text reference in parentheses on the same line as the text. Example:

```
occupation.(1)
```

```
Legal assistants will be the fastest-growing occupation.¹ How-
ever, computer training will be the most popular offering.²
```

D. References

Book Reference. The full publication information for a book is as follows: Author, <u>book title</u> [*underlined*], publisher, place of publication, year of publication, page number if reference is being made to a specific page.

```
John Speer, Flying, Aviation Books, Inc., New York, 1991, p. 10.
```

Magazine Article. The full publication information for a magazine is as follows: Author [*if known*], "article title" [*in quotes*], <u>name of magazine</u> [*underlined*], volume number [*if applicable*], date, page number.

```
Beth Zeiman, "The Friendly Skies," Pilot's Quarterly, Vol. 6,
Spring 1992, p. 88.
```

Two References in a Row. When referring to a book or magazine article that is the same as the one immediately preceding, shorten it by using the abbreviation *Ibid.* (meaning "in the same place"). Add a page number if the page is different.

```
Ibid., p. 86.
```

Two References in the Same Work. When referring to a book or magazine article fully identified in an earlier reference—but *not* the one immediately preceding—shorten the notation as follows: Author's surname, page number.

```
Speer, p. 11.
```

E. Endnotes

Endnotes are used instead of footnotes and are placed at the end of the report. They are similar in format to the List of Works Cited.

To format endnotes:

1. Use the same margins as used in the report.
2. Follow the paragraph format for enumerations (see page 79).
3. Number the endnotes page the same way the other pages of the report are numbered.
4. Center the heading NOTES on line 13.

Note: Some academic style manuals indicate the use of a superscript number (without a space) in endnotes as well as in text references.

```
                    ↓ 13
                  NOTES ↓ 3

    1.  "The History of the Olympic Games," History of Sports,
August 1992, p. 116.

    2.  Ibid., p. 119.

    3.  Harold Mark Kokoris, The Greeks, Spartan Press, New
York, 1991, p. 79.

    4.  Deborah and Grace Brumley, "A Man of Peace," Digest of
History, April 1992, p. 31.

    5.  Kokoris, p. 88.
```

Preferred Rules		Preferred	Avoid
3.	Divide a compound word between the whole words that it contains. Similarly, divide a hyphenated compound word after the hyphen.	business- men under- stand father- in-law clerk- typist	busi- nessmen un- derstand fa- ther-in-law clerk-typ- ist
4.	Divide after a one-letter syllable unless it is part of a suffix. Divide between two consecutive, separately pronounced vowels.	sepa- rate simi- lar radi- ation valu- able	sep- arate sim- ilar rad- iation valua- ble
5.	Divide after a prefix or before a suffix.	super- sonic legal- ize	su- personic le- galize
6.	Avoid dividing separate parts that must be read as units such as dates, personal names, and street names.	May 14, / 1998 Ms. Teri / Ward 319 Ash / Lane	May / 14 Ms. / Ward 319 / Ash Lane

Word Division Practice 1

As you key lines 14–16, insert a hyphen at the correct division point if the word can be divided.

14 laughs settle instant worthwhile children doesn't knowledge

15 worthy signed planned UNESCO p.m. steamed stop mfg. leading

16 swims eight service shouldn't raising courts bamboo carload

Word Division Practice 2

Use your automatic hyphenation feature as you key the paragraph below. If your word processor does not have an automatic hyphenation feature, key the paragraph. Then go back and insert a hyphen and a space at the appropriate division point. If you make the correct line-ending decisions, all lines except the last will end evenly. Format: Double spacing, 1.75-inch side margins.

17 A wholesome diet is a must if you are to have good health.

18 If you do not know much about nutrition, then you should start

19 learning--now. Eating habits can destroy good health or can

20 help you attain good health, so be sure to eat wholesome food

21 at every meal. If you would like to read some information on

22 nutrition, visit your library or your local bookstore. Also,

23 be sure to learn how vitamin supplements ensure that we receive

24 the minimum daily requirements of vitamins and minerals.

Table T58.116
Retrieve Table T57.116 and format it as a ruled table; delete the leaders, 20 spaces between columns.

UNIT 17
Formal Business Reports

Unit Goal 39/5'/5e

Lesson 117

Objectives   Format and key text references.
Format and key endnotes.
Format and key footnotes.

Format   Spacing: Drills, single; and as required
Margins: Default or as required

A. Keyboard Skills

Key lines 1–4 once. In line 5 use your enter/return key after each word. Repeat lines 1–4, or take a series of 1-minute timings.

Speed	1	On this line you should attempt to key at a very fast rate.	12
Accuracy	2	Jack will exhibit very quaint games for Buzz's fall parade.	12
Numbers	3	On 12/30/89 Rick sold 46 tickets, and then he soon sold 57.	12
Symbols	4	Does it cost $2.34, or do 36# (@ $.17/pound) cost 20% more?	12
Technique	5	Press enter (or return) after every word; eyes on the copy.	

| 1 | 2 | 3 | 4 | 5 | 6 | 7 | 8 | 9 | 10 | 11 | 12

B. 30-Second Timings

Take two 30-second timings on lines 6 and 7. Then take two 30-second timings on lines 8 and 9. Try to key with no more than 2 errors on each timing.

6 Our water pipe broke late last spring, and we have not been   12
7 able to get it fixed so that our swimming pool can be used.   24

8 We would like to go swimming as soon as the sun is out, but   12
9 we cannot swim beyond the safe water lines near the cliffs.   24

| 1 | 2 | 3 | 4 | 5 | 6 | 7 | 8 | 9 | 10 | 11 | 12

C. Text References

In Lesson 67 you formatted reports with run-in references, which indicate to the reader the source of the statement cited. Run-in references were formatted in parentheses within the body of the report.

Another way to format references is to place all the notes at the end of the report. References formatted in this way are called *endnotes*.

A third way to format references is to place the notes at the bottom of the same page on which they occur, similar to what you did with the "footnotes" in tables in Lesson 115.

Whether endnotes or footnotes are used, the presence of a reference must be indicated in the body of the report. To indicate the presence of a reference in the body, key a superscript (raised) number immediately following the appropriate word, phrase, or sentence.

Superscripts

Many word processing programs have a superscript feature that raises the number (or letter) above the line. Some programs print the superscript in the same size as the text, while others reduce the size of the superscript.

Report R7.37 Outline
Format: 1.5-inch side margins, 2-inch top margin. Set appropriate tab stops.

MAKING FRIENDS ↓3

I.   Join an Organization↓2

     A.   School Clubs
          1.   Business Professionals
               of America
          2.   Thespians
     B.   Out-of-School Groups
          1.   Candy Stripers
          2.   4-H Club↓3

II. Find a Pen Pal↓3

III. Take Up a Sport↓2

     A.   Join a neighborhood team
     B.   Form a new team
          1.   Tennis
          2.   Soccer
          3.   Golf

Report R8.37 Outline
Retrieve Report R7.37, and edit it by making the following changes.

Under   I. B. Out-of-School Groups

Insert 3. Computer Clubs
            a. Local
            b. National

Under   **II. Find a Pen Pal**

Insert A. Join a pen pal club
            B. Write to servicemen and
               servicewomen overseas

Under   III. B. Form a new team

Insert Three sports you like or are
            interested in (**delete** *Tennis,
            Soccer,* and *Golf*).

ADD   **IV. Be a Friendly Person**
            A. Be a good listener
            B. Smile

Lesson 38

Objectives Apply word division rules.
            Format one-page academic reports

Format   Spacing: Drills, single; and as required
            Margins: Default

▲. Keyboard Skills

Key lines 1–4 once. Then follow the instructions in line 5.

Speed	1	We may make a nice profit if all of the work is done right.
Accuracy	2	Last week Jed McVey was quite busy fixing the frozen pipes.
Numbers	3	They counted 47, 38, 29, and 10; we counted 56, 47, and 38.
Symbols	4	Note that 4# is 4 pounds, #7 is No. 7, and 9% is 9 percent.
Technique	5	Rekey lines 1–4 and underline all of the three-letter words.

Form F11.116 Invoice

Use today's date. Calculate all totals and total amount due. If a form is not available, set up as a table.

[*Invoice No.*] 5438 / [*To*] Larry Hanfield, Contractor / 378 Crestview Lane / Hyden, KY 41749 / [*Terms*] 2/10, n/30

6   24-inch bifold doors w/frosted glass @ 83.75

3   Oak corner wall cabinets (24 × 24 × 30) @ 119.99

3   Thermoplastic bathtub wall kits @ 135.89

5   Oak medicine cabinets with beveled mirror door @ 152.99

Delivery charges 81.40

Form F12.116 Itinerary

Display format.

ITINERARY FOR PAUL CUNNINGHAM
October 2–4, 19—

Sunday, October 2

4:50 p.m.	Depart Dallas, DFW Airport, Delta Air Lines Flight 748, dinner served.
7:30 p.m.	Arrive Atlanta Airport.
8:00 p.m.	Depart Atlanta Airport, Delta Air Lines Flight 556.
9:15 p.m.	Arrive Lexington.
	Accommodations: Sheraton Inn, guaranteed reservation.

Monday, October 3

9:00 a.m.	Meet with Chris Bloomfield, Schofield Hall, University of Kentucky.
1:00 p.m.	Convention at Rupp Arena.

Tuesday, October 4

9:25 a.m.	Depart Lexington, Delta Air Lines Flight 983, snack served.
11:14 a.m.	Arrive Dallas, DFW Airport.
2:30 p.m.	Meeting with Kathryn Davis.

Table T57.116

Use 2-inch side margins (45-space line); double spacing.

Use this year and next year.

BUSINESS CLUB OFFICERS

(19 -- to 19 --)

Marie Herraro	President *
Anthony Westmoreland	Vice President *
James Knutson	Secretary **
Marsha Landers	Treasurer
Frances Abernathy	Reporter

* 2-year term.

** Title changed to Corresponding Secretary next year.

B. "OK" Timings

This version of a 30-second timing is used to build accuracy on alphabetic copy. Your goal is to maintain your 30-second speed but to key without error. Take two 30-second "OK" timings on lines 6–7. Then take two 30-second "OK" timings on lines 8–9.

```
 6  Some students begin to excel just by having peace and quiet   12
 7  as they work.  First analyze your study habits for success.   24

 8  When keying, work to exceed your last speed by bending your   12
 9  fingers just enough to zip to the key, moving very quickly.   24
    |  1  |  2  |  3  |  4  |  5  |  6  |  7  |  8  |  9  |  10 |  11 |  12
```

C. Word Division Practice

Key lines 10–19. When you reach the underlined word or phrase in each sentence, decide whether it may be divided. If it may be divided, do so at the best division point; return, and complete the sentence. If it should not be divided, key it; return, and complete the sentence. Your teacher will give the correct answers when you finish; repeat any sentences you missed. Format: Double-space between sentences.

10 First place was given to the <u>centerpiece</u> made of pinecones.

11 Please try to keep the books <u>separated</u> into two different stacks.

12 Can you believe that our <u>graduation</u> is only five months away?

13 Mr. Tortellini was the only <u>eyewitness</u> to the bank robbery.

14 The ambulance driver notified <u>Dr. John Hammel</u> of the accident.

15 We followed Harry to a house at <u>845 Eden Drive</u> in Morrisville.

16 Marissa Liebmann took her <u>mother-in-law</u> shopping in Dallas.

17 When the water pipe burst, we asked <u>Mr. Cagle</u> to come immediately.

18 It seemed that Michael became a <u>superstar</u> almost overnight.

19 Their wedding has been set for <u>August 5</u> in Springfield, Missouri.

D. One-Page Academic Reports

There are many formats for reports. The one illustrated on page 90 is a simple, basic style for academic reports.

1. All margins (top, bottom, and side) are 1 inch, which are generally the default (preset) margins.

2. Double-space the entire report.

3. Key your name at the left margin, followed by your teacher's name, the class name, and the date.
Note: The date is keyed in military style: 13 November 19--

4. Center the title, and use *initial caps*, which means to capitalize the first letter of each important word.

5. Indent paragraphs 5 spaces.

Production Practice. Set 1-inch side margins; 1-inch top margin; 5-space tab. Double-space. Use the report illustrated on page 90. Key the 4 lines of the heading. Center and key the title. Then key the first three lines of the report. Check your work against the illustration. Delete this practice, and repeat it.

Academic Report R9.38
Key the report on page 90. Standard format.

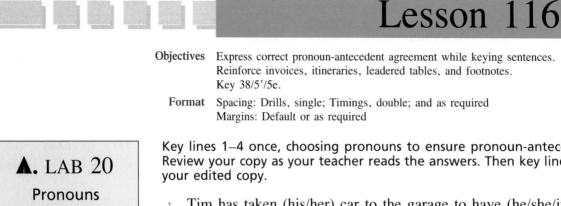

Lesson 116

Objectives   Express correct pronoun-antecedent agreement while keying sentences.
Reinforce invoices, itineraries, leadered tables, and footnotes.
Key 38/5'/5e.

Format   Spacing: Drills, single; Timings, double; and as required
Margins: Default or as required

▲. LAB 20
Pronouns

Key lines 1–4 once, choosing pronouns to ensure pronoun-antecedent agreement. Review your copy as your teacher reads the answers. Then key lines 1–4 again from your edited copy.

1   Tim has taken (his/her) car to the garage to have (he/she/it) repaired.
2   In April Mr. and Mrs. Sanchez sold (his/her/their) home to Claudette.
3   All the teachers expressed (his/her/their) concerns about this issue.
4   Joan Carson said (he/she/they) would submit (his/her/their) resignation tomorrow.

▐. Preview Practice

Key each line twice as a preview to the 5-minute timings below.

Accuracy   5   extra purchased important principles recognized permissible
Speed   6   been made even more that what make just one the and for our

◖. 5-Minute Timings

Take two 5-minute timings on lines 7–22. Proofread, note your errors, and figure your speed.

7   The topic of ethics has always been a critical one for   12
8   the office, and the advent of computer software has made it   24
9   even more critical. Broadly speaking, ethics refers to the   36
10   way in which we conduct ourselves in the things that we do.   48
11   It concerns what we believe is right on the basis of morals   60
12   or common principles. Ethics in using software quite often   72
13   centers on the topic of copying. It's not legal for you to   84
14   make extra copies of software unless you're making a backup   96
15   copy of software that you have purchased. To make one copy   108
16   of software for use at home or one copy of software for use   120
17   at your office is permissible, just as long as you paid for   132
18   the original software that you have copied. A site license   144
19   will permit you to get additional copies to use. By paying   156
20   the software company for a site license, you can make those   168
21   extra copies of the software to use on a site. This method   180
22   of making copies is recognized as an important one.   190

| 1 | 2 | 3 | 4 | 5 | 6 | 7 | 8 | 9 | 10 | 11 | 12 SI 1.45

1-inch
margins
Double
spacing

Chris Roberts

Mrs. Rosa Pirkey

English III

15 April 19--

Title
centered,
initial caps

Human Relations in the Business World

Being able to work well with other people is one of the most important attributes a person with a business career can have. Office workers should consider themselves to be team members with a single goal of working together for the good of the company.

Knowing oneself helps in understanding others. Most people have many needs in common. They want their basic physical and emotional needs met; they want to be safe and comfortable, and they want to be liked and accepted. These needs can provide a foundation for getting to know, accept, and like others.

Courtesy is an important key to getting along with others. Learning and using co-workers' names is imperative, as well as giving sincere compliments and offering to help out when critical deadlines must be met.

If all employees believe that they are working toward one common goal of success for their business, they will begin to act and respond as team members. This will, in turn, lead to good human relations and higher productivity.

ONE-PAGE ACADEMIC REPORT

LESSON 38

D. Tables With Footnotes

A footnote is used in a table to provide explanatory notes or comments on the information in the table. It appears at the bottom (or the "foot") of the table and is formatted in unruled and ruled tables as follows:

Tables Without Ruled Lines.

1. Separate the footnote from the body of the table with a 1-inch underline.
2. Single-space before keying the underline; double-space after it.
3. Key an asterisk or some other symbol at the beginning of a footnote to indicate its use in the table.
4. Key short footnotes beginning at the left margin; single-space between footnotes.
5. Indent the first line of long (two-line) footnotes 5 spaces; key turnover lines beginning at the left margin; double-space between footnotes. (Do not mix styles in the same table—if one footnote is long, use the long format for all footnotes.)

Tables With Ruled Lines.

1. Key the footnote a double space below the final rule.
2. Follow Steps 3 through 5 under "Tables Without Ruled Lines."

Note: If a note at the bottom of a table explains where the information used in the table originated, it is called a *source note*. A source note is keyed exactly like a table footnote, except the word *Source:* precedes the note instead of an asterisk or some other symbol.

Table T54.115
Single spacing; 2.25-inch side margins (40-space line).

BUSINESS CONTEST WINNERS

Top Five Contestants

Name	Points
Kathy Westberg	254*
Allen Samuelson	237
Richard Olson	219
Carol Grove	191**
Linda Levang	191**

*Highest score in district.
**Tied for 4th place.

Table T55.115
Single spacing; 2-inch side margins (45-space line).

ALFRED B. NOBEL PRIZES

(Area and Year First Awarded to U.S.A.)

Chemistry	1914
Economics	1970
Literature	1930
Peace	1906*
Physics	1907
Physiology or Medicine	1930

Source: 1989 World Almanac.

*Theodore Roosevelt was the first U.S.A. Nobel Peace Prize winner.

Table T56.115
Retrieve Table T55.115 and make the following changes: (1) *Change the subtitle to* First Awarded to U.S.A. (2) *Delete the leaders; 6 spaces between columns.* (3) *Add the names of the recipients: chemistry,* Theodore W. Richards; *economics,* Paul A. Samuelson; *literature,* Sinclair Lewis; *peace,* Theodore Roosevelt; *physics,* Albert A. Michelson; *physiology or medicine,* Karl Landsteiner. (4) *Add column heads:* Area, Recipient, Year. (5) *Delete the footnote (retain the source note).*

Academic Report R10.38
Standard format.

Dawn Lauren Soeder
Mrs. M. Lynn Gorman
Office Administration
13 November 19—

Dressing for an Interview

It has been said that there is only one chance to make a good first impression. If your appearance is sloppy, the interviewer may assume that your work will also be sloppy.

A woman should wear a dress, suit, or skirt and blouse, preferably in a neutral color such as navy, gray, or black. Color can be added through accessories. The important thing to remember is to use moderation—in skirt length, jewelry, shoe heels, and so on. Resist the urge to wear fad items.

A man should wear a neutral-colored suit. Color can be added with a tie, but do not choose distracting patterns or sizes.

Common sense should be the guide, but if you do not feel confident in choosing proper attire, find a book at the library that describes how to dress for success. When you have decided what to wear, ask the opinion of someone whose judgment you trust.

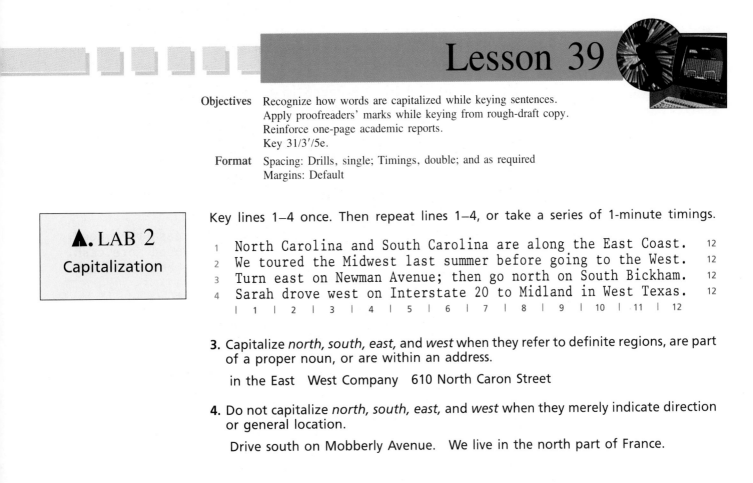

Lesson 39

Objectives Recognize how words are capitalized while keying sentences.
Apply proofreaders' marks while keying from rough-draft copy.
Reinforce one-page academic reports.
Key 31/3'/5e.

Format Spacing: Drills, single; Timings, double; and as required
Margins: Default

▲. LAB 2
Capitalization

Key lines 1–4 once. Then repeat lines 1–4, or take a series of 1-minute timings.

```
1  North Carolina and South Carolina are along the East Coast.   12
2  We toured the Midwest last summer before going to the West.   12
3  Turn east on Newman Avenue; then go north on South Bickham.   12
4  Sarah drove west on Interstate 20 to Midland in West Texas.   12
   |  1  |  2  |  3  |  4  |  5  |  6  |  7  |  8  |  9  | 10  | 11  | 12
```

3. Capitalize *north, south, east,* and *west* when they refer to definite regions, are part of a proper noun, or are within an address.

in the East   West Company   610 North Caron Street

4. Do not capitalize *north, south, east,* and *west* when they merely indicate direction or general location.

Drive south on Mobberly Avenue.   We live in the north part of France.

Table T53.114
Use 1.75-inch side margins (50-space line); single spacing. Use closed leaders unless using dot leaders function.

DISCOVERY SPACE MISSIONS, 1983–1985

(Commander and Date)

Henry Hartsfield, Jr.	08-30-83
Frederick Hauck	11-08-84
Thomas Mattingly	01-24-85
Karol Bobko	04-12-85
John Lounge	08-27-85

Lesson 115

Objectives Identify correct pronoun-antecedent agreement while keying sentences.
Improve technique on the space bar.
Format and key tables with footnotes.
Review leadered tables.

Format Spacing: Drills, single; and as required
Margins: Default or as required

A. LAB 20
Pronouns

Key lines 1–4 once. Then repeat lines 1–4, or take a series of 1-minute timings. (The pronouns are underlined.)

1 Greg has placed his diskette in the sleeve inside his desk. 12
2 Marcia or Janet has taken her computer disk to be repaired. 12
3 The bus drivers knew that their schedules had been changed. 12
4 Terry and I have agreed to pick up our groceries by 11 a.m. 12
| 1 | 2 | 3 | 4 | 5 | 6 | 7 | 8 | 9 | 10 | 11 | 12

B. 12-Second Timings

Take three 12-second timings on each line, or key each line three times. Try to key with no more than 1 error on each timing.

5 Jane will sell four lots when they find the cash they need.
6 They will sell him some more lots when they need more cash.
7 Jane will give them back the money they gave her last week.
5   10   15   20   25   30   35   40   45   50   55   60

C. Space Bar

A technique drill.

Key lines 8–12 once; do not pause before or after striking the space bar. Then key lines 8–12 a second time, trying to maintain a consistent stroking speed as you progress through each line.

8 a b c d e f g h i j k l m n o p q r s t u v w x y z a b c d
9 1 2 3 4 5 6 7 8 9 0 1 2 3 4 5 6 7 8 9 0 1 2 3 4 5 6 7 8 9 0
10 ad ax am an as at be by do go my he hi ho if in is it ma me
11 nab net nip not nut pat pen pit pow put ran red rip rot run
12 sat sew sip sob sun tap ten tin tot tub yap yes yip yow zip

Take a 3-minute timing on lines 5–12. Proofread, note your errors, and figure your speed.

```
                      1                2                3                4
5        People who fly a great deal often suffer from jet lag.       12
              5              6               7              8
6    Our bodies are programmed to work on a fixed rhythm; and if      24
            9            10              11             12
7    we go quickly from one time zone to another, that rhythm is      36
          13             14              15             16
8    disturbed.  If you were to fly from New York to London, you      48
             17            18             19             20
9    would find that you would want to sleep when it was time to      60
            21            22              23             24
10   work.  You would not want food when others were eating.  By      72
           25              26              27             28
11   the end of the day, you would be spent.  Your rhythms would      84
              29              30             31
12   right themselves, though, after several days.                    93
     |  1  |  2  |  3  |  4  |  5  |  6  |  7  |  8  |  9  |  10  |  11  |  12  SI 1.21
```

In the chart below find the number of errors you made on the Pretest. Then key each of the following designated drill lines two times.

Pretest errors	0–1	2–3	4–5	6+
Drill lines	16–20	15–19	14–18	13–17

Accuracy

```
13   New York find great rhythm London people another programmed
14   want your often would sleep bodies suffer quickly disturbed
15   when food time fixed right though others several themselves
16   zone work deal from were after spent eating rhythms suffers
```

Speed

```
17   other quick often them food that ever not fix one end we of
18   finds sleep great when deal days gram new ten are the go be
19   wants other spent zone time jets from hem her lag not to if
20   would works after body your whom were eat pen fly was on by
```

Take another 3-minute timing on lines 5–12. Proofread, note your errors, and figure your speed. Compare your performance with the Pretest.

E. Proofreaders' Marks

When corrections must be made in copy, professional writers, editors, proofreaders, and those who key documents use proofreaders' marks.

These symbols are quick and easy to use, and they make keying from a rough draft easier and faster. Study the proofreaders' marks shown below.

Proofreaders' Mark		Draft	Final Copy	Proofreaders' Mark		Draft	Final Copy
∧	Insert (word, letter)	he may^not^ know	he may not know	ℐ	Delete	a bad dream	a dream
¶	Make new paragraph	¶When it is	When it is	∩	Transpose	how you can	how can you
≡	Capitalize	John sheraton	John Sheraton	⌒	Omit space	red wood	redwood

In the chart below find the number of errors you made on the Pretest (page 260). Then key each of the following designated drill lines three times.

Pretest errors	0–1	2–3	4–5	6+
Drill lines	24–28	23–27	22–26	21–25

Accuracy

21 is exist message selection computer comparison presentation
22 are common variety software referred supported relationship
23 it's because writers although choosing recognize frequently
24 pie format written graphic excellent information understand

Speed

25 reader sliced number chart their other items they most line
26 manner pieces change kinds graph looks right will used work
27 better reveal period today three often makes that when want
28 support report choice print forms parts like this show over

D. POSTTEST

Take another 5-minute timing on lines 5–20. Proofread, note your errors, and figure your speed. Compare your performance with the Pretest.

E. Leaders

Leaders (rows of periods) are used to lead the eye across a page, usually from one column to another. They are often used in tables to spread a table to fill a specific line length, or they are used when the entries in the first column vary greatly in length. Leaders are especially helpful in financial statements, tables of contents, and programs.

Leaders usually appear in one of two formats: (1) as a series of continuous dots with no space between each dot [*closed leaders*] or (2) as a series of dots with a blank space between each dot [*open leaders*]. Open leaders must align, so it is easier to key closed leaders. To key leaders:

1. Set tab stops for the table.
2. Find the point where the final period on each line of leaders will be keyed. There should be 1 blank space between the last period and the beginning of the longest item in the next column.

3. Key the first item in the first line, space once, and key the line of periods. Remember to stop 1 space before the longest item in the next column.

Note: If using open leaders, you may have to space twice before the line of periods in order to make the dots align.

4. Key the first item in the next column.
5. Repeat Steps 3 and 4 for each line.

```
        1 SPACE

August↓................. 986
September↑............. 1,092
        1 SPACE
August↓. . . . . . . . . 986
September ↑. . . . . . . .↑1,092

    2 SPACES        1 SPACE
```

Dot Leaders

Some word processing programs have a feature called **dot leaders** that will automatically print leaders from one column to another. In some programs, the default tab stop for dot leaders is a right tab. To align copy on the left, you must change the tab stop to a left tab. Most dot leaders use open (spaced) leaders. In some programs, you must space once after each entry in the first column before pressing the tab key in order to ensure that there will be at least one space separating words in the first column from the row of periods.

Academic Report R11.39
Standard format.

(Student)

(Teacher)

(Class)

(Date)

Body Language

Your facial expressions, posture, and gestures may speak so loudly that your words can not be heard by your listeners. body language is a powerful communicator. How do you react when a person whom to you are talking smiles--or frowns? A smile usually indicates that the listener agrees and accepts what is being said. a frown, on the other hand, mean may disagreement or even a hostility. Your eye contact can also create an exciting impression. A person who looks you in eye the shows interest or sincerity in what is being said, while someone who does not make eye contact seems just to have no interest in the conversation. Also, it is difficult to trust some one who you cannot you look in the eye.

A person with good posture seems more much confident than one who is slouches or slumps. people may doubt the abilities of one who will not stand up or sit up straight. nervous gestures should be avoided because they give may others the the impression of boredom or impatience. Always avoid tapping pens or pencils, swinging your legs, or shuffling your feet. however, hand good gestures while speaking may be useful in your making a point or keeping your listeners' attention.

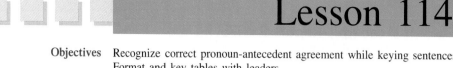

Lesson 114

Objectives   Recognize correct pronoun-antecedent agreement while keying sentences.
Format and key tables with leaders.
Key 38/5′/5e.

Format   Spacing: Drills, single; Timings, double; and as required
Margins: Default or as required

▲. LAB 20
Pronouns

Key lines 1–4 once. Then repeat lines 1–4, or take a series of 1-minute timings. (The pronouns are underlined.)

```
1  Boyd found his computer books on the desk next to the door.   12
2  Paula and I are ready to take our exam scheduled for 9 a.m.    12
3  The students hope that they can get passes to today's game.    12
4  The Smiths and Carsons will go to their sons' tennis match.    12
   |  1  |  2  |  3  |  4  |  5  |  6  |  7  |  8  |  9  | 10  | 11  | 12
```

A pronoun must agree with its *antecedent* (the word or words for which the pronoun stands) in person *(I, you, he)*, number *(he, they)*, and gender *(he, she)*.

Frank said that *he* could do the job alone.
The *managers* believe that *they* will settle this matter today.

B. PRETEST

Take a 5-minute timing on lines 5–20. Proofread, note your errors, and figure your speed.

```
            Information that is presented in a graph or a chart is    12
 6  frequently referred to as graphics.  Many writers like this      24
 7  manner of presentation because they recognize that a reader       36
 8  will better understand their message when it's supported by       48
 9  graphics.  Although many kinds of graphics exist today, the       60
10  three most common are the pie chart, the bar chart, and the       72
11  line chart.  The computer software of today is able to make       84
12  and print all three of these graphics forms in a variety of       96
13  formats to be used in reports and other written work.            107
            A pie chart looks like a pie that has been sliced into   119
15  several pieces.  It's used often to reveal the relationship      131
16  of parts to a whole.  A bar chart is an excellent choice if      143
17  you want to show a comparison of a limited number of items.      155
18  But if you want to show changes over a long period of time,      167
19  use a line chart.  Make the right selection in choosing the      179
20  chart that will support everything that you have written.        190
    |  1  |  2  |  3  |  4  |  5  |  6  |  7  |  8  |  9  | 10  | 11  | 12  SI 1.43
```

Lesson 40

Objectives Identify how words are capitalized while keying sentences.
Format multipage academic reports.
Key 31/3'/5e.

Format Spacing: Drills, single; Timings, double; and as required
Margins: Default

▲. LAB 2
Capitalization

Key lines 1–4 once. Then repeat lines 1–4, or take a series of 1-minute timings.

1 Montreal, Quebec, is north of New York and west of Vermont. 12

2 Joel has been planning a trip to the South and the Midwest. 12

3 He will zip to North Carolina for the election on Saturday. 12

4 Max has moved from 402 West Mockingbird to 963 South Pecan. 12

| 1 | 2 | 3 | 4 | 5 | 6 | 7 | 8 | 9 | 10 | 11 | 12

B. Preview Practice

Key each line twice as a preview to the 3-minute timings below.

Accuracy 5 next express citizens politics campaign questions published

Speed 6 through paper sure then city with ask too the and for to is

C. 3-Minute Timings

Take two 3-minute timings on lines 7–14. Proofread, note your errors, and figure your speed.

7   High school is not too soon for a student to be active 12

8 in politics. First, keep up with the news each day so that 24

9 you can know what the issues are. Next, express your point 36

10 of view and ask questions; write letters to be published in 48

11 the paper. If you choose to be more active, then you might 60

12 want to join a campaign team to help a friend win a post in 72

13 your school, city, or state government. As a good citizen, 84

14 you will be sure to speak through your votes. 93

| 1 | 2 | 3 | 4 | 5 | 6 | 7 | 8 | 9 | 10 | 11 | 12 SI 1.19

Database Software

All kinds of information can be stored by those using database software. The advantage of using a database is that the information in the database can be retrieved and sorted in a variety of ways. Database software can be used to create tables, mailing lists, and mailing labels. If part of an integrated software package, the database can be used as merge files.

Sort

Some word processing programs have a sort feature that enables the user to re-arrange data that has been prepared as a table.

Table T50.113

Open format. Use 4 spaces between columns; double spacing. If you are using a microcomputer with database software, enter the names and addresses below. Then prepare the data as a 5-column table and save it. The information in the database will be used again in Tables T51 and T52.

SELECTED CUSTOMER ADDRESS LIST
(California Region)

Last Name	First Name	Address	City	ZIP
Beasley	David	5687 Rincon Dr.	Whittier	90606
Coggins	Betty	2780 Buchanan St.	San Francisco	94123
Fernandez	Ruben	11599 Campbell Ave.	Riverside	92505
Hamby	Carol	247 Park Ave.	Santa Cruz	95068
Hashikawa	Doris	903 Florida St.	Vallejo	94590
Lansdell	Clayton	8734 Calder Ln.	Walnut Creek	94598
McDaniel	Danielle	3567 Sepulveda Blvd.	Los Angeles	90034
McDaniel	Darryl	6598 Cheery Ave. S.	Fresno	93725
Polaski	Edward	2689 Cowper St.	Palo Alto	94306
Thompson	Jeanean	5078 Pasadena Ave.	Sacramento	95841

Table T51.113

Retrieve and reformat Table T50.113, arranging the items alphabetically by city. If you are using a microcomputer with database software, conduct a sort to achieve the correct arrangement.

Table T52.113

Retrieve and reformat Table T50.113 again, arranging the items numerically by ZIP Code, with the lowest number first. If you are using database software, conduct a sort to achieve the correct arrangement.

D. Multipage Academic Reports

Academic reports of two or more pages are formatted in much the same manner as one-page reports. The two differences are numbering pages and determining page breaks.

To format multipage academic reports:

1. Place the writer's last name on line 4 followed by the page number on all pages of the report. This "header" information should end at the right margin.

2. Leave at least two lines of a paragraph at the bottom of a page, and carry at least two lines to the top of a new page. (A three-line paragraph would have to be keyed all on one page.)

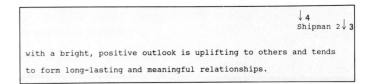

↓ 4
Shipman 2 ↓ 3

with a bright, positive outlook is uplifting to others and tends to form long-lasting and meaningful relationships.

**Page Headers
Page Numbering**

Most word processors have a feature that allows text to be keyed in a document once and then printed automatically at the top of each page. Text that appears at the top of each page of a document is called a **header.** Headers usually print in the top margin. However, some word processors insert the header on the first line below the top margin.

A header is frequently used with the **page numbering** feature, which automatically counts and prints each page number of a document. The page numbering feature can be separate or part of the header.

Page Breaks

Another feature of word processors is **automatic page break,** which calculates the end of each page of a document. This is known as a **soft page break.** The calculation can be changed by setting different top and bottom margins. The user can place **hard page breaks** in a document, which force pages to end before the break that would be calculated by the software.

**Widow/Orphan
Protection**

The **widow and orphan protection** feature is used in long documents. A **widow** is the last line of a paragraph that has been carried to the top of another page. An **orphan** is the first line of a paragraph that has been left alone at the bottom of a page. The widow and orphan protection feature changes the page break to prevent widows and orphans in the printout.

View Document

Many word processing programs allow the user to see how the document will look before printing it. Using the **view document** function places an image of the full page, in reduced form, on the screen. The user can check for correct alignment, page breaks, and total appearance of the document.

Production Practice. Use 1-inch side and bottom margins, double spacing, and a 5-space tab.

1. Set a header for your last name and the page number to begin 1/2 inch from the top edge, ending at the right margin.
2. Key your name 1 inch from the top.
3. Space down 8 inches from the top (document line 43, page line 49), and key the second paragraph of Report

R12.40 (page 96). If you do not have widow and orphan protection, calculate the page ending and use a hard page break.

4. Use the view document function, if available, or print a copy of the Production Practice. Did the word processor place the header at the top of both pages? Did it leave at least two lines at the bottom and carry at least two lines to the next page?

Objectives Reinforce tables.
Introduce use of database software.
Introduce use of a sort command.

Format Spacing: Drills, single; and as required
Margins: Default or as required

▲. Keyboard Skills

Key lines 1–4 once. In line 5 practice shifting techniques as you capitalize each word. Repeat lines 1–4, or take a series of 1-minute timings.

Speed	1	If I get a pay raise by the first of the week, I will work. 12
Accuracy	2	The old, gray boxer won seven unique prizes from lazy Jack. 12
Numbers	3	With 20 laps completed, Car #1735 and Car #4689 were ahead. 12
Symbols	4	Interest on #71-A36 (@ 8 3/4%) is $17.50; @ 9% it's $18.00. 12
Technique	5	Abac Adel Alma Alto Carl Clyo Cobb Eden Elko Eton Gray Hull

| 1 | 2 | 3 | 4 | 5 | 6 | 7 | 8 | 9 | 10 | 11 | 12

ᗷ. "OK" Timings

Take two 30-second "OK" (errorless) timings on lines 6–7. Then take two 30-second "OK" timings on lines 8–9. Goal: No errors.

6 Jack bought five exquisite bronze bowls at Pam's yard sale,   12
7 and he proudly displayed them at an antique show yesterday.   24

8 The jovial men expressed a quick welcome to Fritz, and then   12
9 they proceeded to bring up thirteen issues to be discussed.   24

| 1 | 2 | 3 | 4 | 5 | 6 | 7 | 8 | 9 | 10 | 11 | 12

Table T49.113
Ruled format, 6 spaces between columns, double spacing, change default margins.

SALES REPORT
Week of January 9, 19--

Customer Number	Customer Name	Date	Amount	Salesperson Number
2017	Acker, Grady	01/09/--	$168.95	3
2027	McCall, Moses	01/09/--	82.75	2
2035	Harris, Tina	01/10/--	110.40	2
2006	Cohen, Nadine	01/10/--	78.32	1
2044	West, Gregory	01/11/--	143.95	4
2015	Pruitt, R. C.	01/12/--	37.80	3
2025	Dickson, Madge	01/13/--	110.15	1
2020	Manitou, Doug	01/13/--	78.26	2
2039	Bishop, Carlotta	01/13/--	65.99	2
2023	Whirley, Tony	01/15/--	123.75	4

Academic Report R12.40
Standard format. Header: Shipman [#]. Title: A Positive Attitude

[ ] means fill in appropriate information
/ means hard return
¶ means new paragraph

Brad Shipman / Miss Meredith Hunt / Information Processing / *[Today's date]*

   A positive attitude is one of the most important qualities anyone can possess. How day-to-day situations are handled affects a person's health, personal relationships, and work. While it may seem that some people are born with bad attitudes, researchers say that negative attitudes can be turned into positive ones if the desire to change is strong enough. ¶ Attitude can affect an individual's health. Anyone who has practiced a lifetime of negative thinking will experience much more harmful stress than someone who does not perceive every challenge in life as a crisis. Having to deal with harmful stress on a daily basis can lead to health problems ranging from chronic fatigue to magnification of allergy symptoms and, in some cases, to heart disease. ¶ Although it has been said that misery loves company, few people choose to be in the company of someone who is constantly complaining and seems angry at the world. The ability to make and keep friends is closely linked with attitude. A person with a bright, positive outlook is uplifting to others and tends to form long-lasting and meaningful relationships. ¶ Employees who never seem satisfied on the job will not be as productive as those who enjoy their work and see themselves as part of the company team. Advancement in a career is often dependent on management's recognition of an employee's productivity and value to the company; therefore, it pays to be positive. ¶ A positive attitude can be developed by consciously making an effort to find some humor in troublesome situations. This may mean having to laugh at oneself, but most people need to take themselves less seriously. Another step in changing from negative to positive thinking is improvement of self-esteem. A person who has difficulty being positive toward others usually has a poor self-image. An additional strategy for developing a positive attitude is to focus on the needs of others by finding one kind thing to do for someone else each day. ¶ A positive attitude is contagious. After it has been developed, it can easily be shared with others.

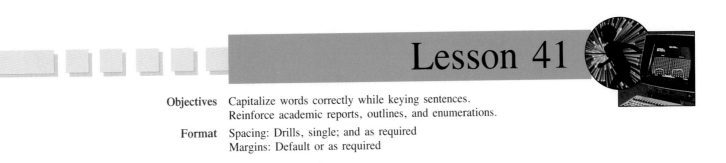

Lesson 41

Objectives Capitalize words correctly while keying sentences.
Reinforce academic reports, outlines, and enumerations.

Format Spacing: Drills, single; and as required
Margins: Default or as required

▲. LAB 2
Capitalization

Key lines 1–4 once, providing the missing capitals. Review your copy as your teacher reads the answers. Then key lines 1–4 again.

1 we visited the ozarks on our way to the northeast last may.
2 we attended west side high school, which is west of dallas.
3 the southern railroad runs north from mexico to washington.
4 the southern headquarters are on east oak drive in atlanta.

Accuracy

21 one the create dozens package sequence possible information
22 can that letter office features because processing database
23 its used sorted example display packages software addresses
24 quite delete merged examples columnar versatile spreadsheet

Speed

25 major tools moved place some word name user one the can its
26 other types items store your with sort make use all and lot
27 these merge today ways data soft from base ware are for any
28 names table makes many also easy most sort name way add day

D. POSTTEST

Take another 5-minute timing on lines 5–20 (page 256). Proofread, note your errors, and figure your speed. Compare your performance with the Pretest.

Form F9.112 Itinerary
Display format.

ITINERARY FOR MAYOR VALDEZ
October 24–27, 19—

Monday, October 24

7:10 p.m.   Depart Kennedy International Airport,
TNA Flight 455 to Geneva, Switzerland.

Tuesday, October 25

10:15 a.m.   Arrive Geneva, Switzerland.
Accommodations: Hotel Geneva.

3:00 p.m.   Tour watch factory.

Wednesday, October 26

9:00 a.m.   Train to Bern.

1:00 p.m.   Visit Castle of Chillon.

6:20 p.m.   Train to Zurich.
Accommodations: Schweiz Hotel.

Thursday, October 27

8:40 a.m.   Tour Swiss Credit Bank.

3:05 p.m.   Depart Zurich, TNA Flight 611 to New York.

6:05 p.m.   Arrive Kennedy International Airport.

Form F10.112 Invoice
Use today's date. If a form is not available, set up as a table. Calculate all totals and total amount due.

[*Invoice No.*] 867 / [*To*] Thor Manufacturing Co. / 2041 Hawthorne Boulevard / Torrance, CA 90503 / [*Terms*] 2/10, n/30 / 1 Decorative showcase, Style 6784, all glass with metal trim @ 876.50 / 3 Glass shelves with beveled edges, Style 8257 @ 88.00 / 2 Round tables, Style 8407, 22″ diameter, plastic top with metal base @ 72.90 / 4 Revolving display racks, Style 441R, aluminum, brown, @ 102.50 / Delivery charges 75.00

Take two 30-second timings on lines 5–6. Then take two 30-second timings on lines 7–8. Try to key with no more than 2 errors on each timing.

```
 5   It is important to plan your time wisely.  You should start   12
 6   by making a list of all the things which you must get done.   24

 7   Next, decide what things must be done first and what things   12
 8   can wait.  Group the tasks that are alike, and get started.   24
     |  1  |  2  |  3  |  4  |  5  |  6  |  7  |  8  |  9  | 10  | 11  | 12
```

Academic Report R13.41
Standard format. Use your last name for the header. Use your name, your teacher's name, your class, and today's date for the heading.

Reference Materials

To work efficiently in today's office, it is necessary to know where to find many kinds of information. Therefore, it is very important that office workers know what kinds of reference materials have the information needed and how to use those resources.

Even though many word processors have spell checkers and automatic hyphenation, office workers still must make the final decision on accuracy. A word-division manual is a quick reference for spelling and word division. Because it does not have definitions of the words, it is smaller and quicker to use than a dictionary.

A dictionary may be used to look up words that are not found in a word-division manual. It gives not only divisions of words but also definitions, pronunciations, and derivations.

A thesaurus is a book that can be used to find words of similar meanings (synonyms). If you are using the same word too many times in a letter or report, replacements can be found in a thesaurus. Some word processors have their own thesauruses to suggest substitutes for overused words in a document. An additional reference for synonyms is a crossword puzzle dictionary.

The obvious use for a ZIP Code directory is to find the correct ZIP Codes for addressing mail. Another important use, however, is to find the correct spelling of cities and towns that are not listed in a dictionary.

An atlas is a book of maps and mileage tables. This information can be used for making telephone calls to other time zones, planning trips, making itineraries, or working with various real estate transactions.

An office reference manual is a necessity for any office worker. It covers such topics as grammar, usage, and style; business correspondence guidelines; dictation and keyboarding techniques; word division; and abbreviations. Solutions to most of the day-to-day problems of an office worker can be found in a reference manual.

Lesson 112

Objectives Correct errors in subject-verb agreement while keying sentences.
Reinforce itineraries and invoices.
Key 38/5′/5e.

Format Spacing: Drills, single; Timings, double; and as required
Margins: Default or as required

▲. LAB 19
Subject-Verb
Agreement

Key lines 1–4 once, correcting any errors in subject-verb agreement. Review your copy as your teacher reads the answers. Then key lines 1–4 again.

1 For no obvious reason, each runner and jogger have blisters.
2 Both the student and the teacher has worked on the report.
3 Sherry and Thomas is to represent our class in Washington.
4 Jennifer and Boyd has a new car to drive to the next meet.

B. PRETEST

Take a 5-minute timing on lines 5–20. Proofread, note your errors, and figure your speed.

5 A database is one of the major software tools that can 12
6 be used in dozens of ways in an office. This package is so 24
7 versatile in its use because all of its data can be sorted, 36
8 moved, and merged with many other types of software. Also, 48
9 it's easy to add a lot of items or to delete a lot of items 60
10 of your choice. Because of these features, the database is 72
11 quite a popular software package in many offices today. 83
12 The information in a database can be merged with other 95
13 software packages. Some of the merges are with spreadsheet 107
14 and word processing software. The names and addresses in a 119
15 database, for example, can be merged with a letter and used 131
16 in the inside address of the letter. Also, it's quite easy 143
17 to create a table or a display from all of the data because 155
18 the database stores it in columnar format. One of the most 167
19 used features of a database is the sort. The sort makes it 179
20 possible for the user to place records in any sequence. 190

| 1 | 2 | 3 | 4 | 5 | 6 | 7 | 8 | 9 | 10 | 11 | 12 SI 1.44

C. PRACTICE

In the chart below find the number of errors you made on the Pretest. Then key each of the following designated drill lines (page 257) three times.

Pretest errors	0–1	2–3	4–5	6+
Drill lines	24–28	23–27	22–26	21–25

Report R14.41 Outline
Format: 1-inch side margins, 2-inch top margin. Set appropriate tab stops.

Refer to the proofreaders' marks on page 92 if necessary.

Body Language

I. Facial Expressions Say as Much as Words.

    A. Smiling and frowning are forms of communication.

    B. Eye contact creates many impressions.

        1. Good eye contact expresses interest and sincerity.

        2. Poor eye contact indicates disinterest or dishonesty.

II. Posture Makes a statement.

    A. Good posture shows confidence and alertness.

    B. poor posture may cause others to doubt your own abilities.

III. Gestures Can Be Negative or Positive.

    A. Nervous gestures may indicate boredom or impatience.

        1. avoid tapping pens or pencils.

        2. Avoid swinging legs or shuffling feet.

    B. Using hand gestures while speaking may be useful.

Report R15.41 Enumeration
Hanging-indented style. Format: 1-inch side margins, 2-inch top margin, 4-space indent.

ADVANTAGES OF CENTRALIZED Word PROCESSING

1. Equipment costs are reduced because it is purchased only for the centralized area--not for all of the departments in a company.

2. Several operators can work on a long, detailed project at one time, thus completing it faster.

3. documents used repetitively throughout the company cannot be stored in a central location.

4. The many levels of positions in the centralized department provide advancement opportunities for employees.

Form F8.111 Itinerary
Display format.

ITINERARY FOR RAYMOND R. BLACK
November 11-13 19__

Monday, November 11
    8:30 a.m.   Leave for airport.
    10:00 a.m.   Delta Flight 704 to Chicago.

    11:50 a.m.   Arrive O'Hare International; met by Karen Calendar, District Manager, North Central Division.
        Accommodations: Executive Inn Airport, single-room reservation guaranteed.

    3:30 p.m.   Meet with sales representatives for briefing on new products, Prescott Room.

    7:00 p.m.   Dinner at Candle House Restaurant, 2415 N. Vine Street. Reservation made for seven people.

Tuesday, November 12
    9 a.m.-noon   Tour of New Products Division, Mount Prospect plant, with Ms. Calendar.

    12 noon   Lunch with Adam Wesley, V.P. for New Products.

    Afternoon   Meet with Milwaukee Division managers, Carter Room adjacent to Prescott Room.

Wednesday, November 13
    9:30 a.m.   Leave for O'Hare.
    11:15 a.m.   Delta Flight 409 to Atlanta, lunch served.
    1:05 p.m.   Arrive Atlanta.

Objectives Format a personal-business letter.

Format Spacing: Drills, single; and as required
Margins: Default or as required

A. Keyboard Skills

Key lines 1–4 once. Then do what line 5 tells you to do. Repeat lines 1–4, or take a series of 1-minute timings.

Speed | 1 | The group of friends met at the mall and went to the movie. | 12
Accuracy | 2 | Jeff Waxmann quickly moved our gear by the Amazon campsite. | 12
Numbers | 3 | Some important years were 1492, 1620, 1776, 1865, and 1945. | 12
Symbols | 4 | Louis (Jones, not Bishop) owns 50% of Lou & Eve's Ski Shop. | 12
Technique | 5 | Key line 3 again, and boldface or underline the years.

| 1 | 2 | 3 | 4 | 5 | 6 | 7 | 8 | 9 | 10 | 11 | 12

B. 12-Second Timings

Take three 12-second timings on each line, or key each line three times. Try to key with no more than 1 error on each timing.

6 We saw a sad little dog sitting in an old chair in a ditch.
7 She came to our home and hid under some boards in the yard.
8 She became our pet and lived a happy life for twelve years.

5   10   15   20   25   30   35   40   45   50   55   60

C. Personal-Business Letters

A letter from an individual to a business is called a personal-business letter (see the illustration on page 100), and it has these standard parts:

Date Line. The month, day, and year are the first part of a personal-business letter.

Inside Address. This includes the name and address of the business or person to whom the letter is being sent.

Salutation. The salutation is a greeting such as *Dear Mr. Corley.*

Body. The body contains the message of the letter.

Complimentary Closing. This is a phrase such as *Yours truly* or *Sincerely yours.*

Signature. The writer's signature is handwritten on the letter with black or blue ink.

Writer's Identification. The writer's keyed name and address are the last part of the letter.
Note: Placing the writer's return address below the keyed name is becoming popular. (An alternative style is to key the return address immediately above the date.) If the return address is placed below the keyed name, it does not interfere with addressing envelopes automatically.

(Continued on page 101)

B. Itineraries (display)

Another format for itineraries—a display format—is shown below. To prepare an itinerary in display format:

1. Use default margins. Set tabs 5 spaces and 25 spaces from the left margin.
2. Begin the heading on line 13, or center the itinerary vertically.
3. Double-space after the heading to begin the body. (Because the day/date information is to the left, it will look like more than a double space between the heading and body.)
4. Beginning at the left margin, key the day, month, and date. Underline and bold the day/date information.
5. Double-space after the day/date information. Indent all time notations 5 spaces from the left margin. Use local time for all time notations. Align times on the colon—space in for the hours *1* to *9*.
6. Use the indent feature to move to the event section of the itinerary so that turnover lines will indent automatically.
7. Single-space individual notations; double-space between events.

Form F7.111 Itinerary
Display format.

ITINERARY FOR PAULETTE BJORG ↓2
April 13–16, 19— ↓2

Wednesday, April 13 ↓2

7:30 a.m.   Registration in Ballroom 1. Registration packet and program provided. ↓2

8:00 a.m.   Complimentary breakfast—2d-floor dining room. Meet Christy Blanchard for breakfast. ↓2

9:00 a.m.   Technology sessions (repeated at 1:00 p.m. and 3:00 p.m.). ↓2

Thursday, April 14

9 a.m. to noon   Network presentations—Meeting Room 4.

2 p.m. to 5 p.m.   Artificial Intelligence presentation—Meeting Room 7.

Friday, April 15

9:30 a.m.   Roundtable discussions—moderator for Session 16 in Ballroom 2.

1:15 p.m.   Software demonstration—attend demonstrations in Meeting Rooms 10 and 12.

8:00 p.m.   Hospitality Night in hotel gardens.

Saturday, April 16

10:00 a.m.   Business meeting and critical issues task force report—Ballroom 1.

1:00 p.m.   Luncheon (tickets provided in registration packet).

3:00 p.m.   Meet with Planning Committee for next year's convention.

	↓ 13
Date Line	December 3, 19--
	↓ 6

In address blocks, use the two-letter state abbreviation, or spell out the name of the state (*GA* or *Georgia*). Two-letter abbreviations are used only with ZIP Codes and are keyed in capital letters with no periods or space between the letters. Leave 1 space between the state and the ZIP Code.

Inside Address	Mr. J. J. Smiddy South Hunter High School 1400 Rincon Road Savannah, GA 31419 ↓2
Salutation	Dear Mr. Smiddy: ↓2

Body

Single-space the body; double-space between paragraphs.

Thank you for allowing me to observe your business classes last week. It was a pleasure to watch the excitement and enthusiasm of the students as they learned how to make word processors and databases work together to print professional business letters. ↓2

It was encouraging to see students coming in after school in order to learn the advanced features of integrated software and to work on their computerized accounting assignments. Today's students are working to prepare for business careers, and I am convinced that teaching them is the right career for me. ↓2

My student-teaching experience with you next semester is going to be an exciting challenge; I am truly looking forward to it. ↓2

Complimen- tary Closing	Sincerely yours,
	↓4
Signature	*Ms. Julie Fowler*
Writer's Identification (name and address)	Ms. Julie Fowler 35 Preston Way Garden City, GA 31408

PERSONAL-BUSINESS LETTER
BLOCK STYLE WITH MIXED PUNCTUATION

Form F6.110 Itinerary
If a form is not available, set up as a table with 4 spaces between columns.

Itinerary for T. L. Brazinski
May 7-8, 19--

May 7 3:15 p.m. Depart New York, La Guardia, American Flight 238 to St. Louis.

3:30 p.m. Arrive St. Louis; met by Brandon Williams, St. Louis University.
Accommodations: Embassy Suites, guaranteed reservation No. 183-34-001.

May 8 7:00 a.m. Breakfast with Brandon Williams, hotel restaurant.

8:30 a.m. Interview with Dr. Carole Adams, Department Chair, Information Systems, School of Business, Room 235.

9:30 a.m. Tour of Information Systems Department.

10:30 a.m. Interview with departmental faculty, Room 240.

12 noon Lunch with Dean Carrington, School of Business, Colorado Room, University Center.

2:30 p.m. Depart St. Louis, American Flight 262 to New York.

4:45 p.m. Arrive New York, La Guardia.

Lesson 111

Objectives Identify correct subject-verb agreement while keying sentences.
Format and key display itineraries.

Format Spacing: Drills, single; and as required
Margins: Default or as required

▲. LAB 19
Subject-Verb Agreement

Key lines 1–4 once. Then repeat lines 1–4, or take a series of 1-minute timings. (Subjects and verbs are underlined.)

1 Each car and driver has a chance to win the car race today.   12
2 Ms. Fletcher and Mr. Pryor from Boston have arrived by car.   12
3 Both Frank and Helen are taking the advanced calculus test.   12
4 Peanut butter and jelly makes a good sandwich for children.   12
   | 1 | 2 | 3 | 4 | 5 | 6 | 7 | 8 | 9 | 10 | 11 | 12

To format a personal-business letter:

1. Use standard paper (8.5 by 11 inches).

2. Use 1-inch side margins.

3. Begin the date 2 inches from the top (line 13).

4. Key the inside address 1 inch (6 lines) below the date at the left margin.

5. Key the salutation a double space below the inside address.

6. Begin the body a double space below the salutation. Single-space paragraphs, but double-space between them.

7. Begin the complimentary closing a double space below the body.

8. Key the writer's identification 4 lines below the complimentary closing.

Letters can be formatted in a variety of styles. The letter illustrated on page 100 is shown in block style with mixed punctuation.

Block Style. This style is popular because it is easy to use. All parts of the letter begin at the left margin.

If line 1 in your software is the first line **after** the top margin, you must subtract the number of lines in the top margin from 13 to determine the starting line (13 − 6 = 7; key the date on line 7).

Mixed Punctuation. This is the most commonly used punctuation style. A colon follows the salutation, and a comma follows the complimentary closing. Use mixed punctuation unless told otherwise.

Production Practice. Single spacing. 1-inch side margins. Use the letter illustrated on page 100.

1. Space down 2 inches and key the date. Space down 1 inch. Key the inside address. Double-space and key the salutation. Check your work; then delete the practice.

2. Repeat 1. above using today's date and your teacher, school, and school address for the inside address and salutation. Check your work; then delete the practice.

3. Key the last paragraph in the letter beginning on line 1. Double-space; key the complimentary closing; then space down 4 lines and key the writer's name and address. Check your work; then delete the practice.

4. Repeat 3. above using your name and address as the writer's. Check your work; then delete the practice.

Date Insert

Some word processing programs have a feature that automatically inserts the current date into a document. If you use this feature, you must make sure that the date is correct when you start up the computer. You may even be able to change the format (like the military-style date you used in academic reports).

Personal-Business Letter L1.42
Block style. Mixed punctuation.
Key the letter illustrated on page 100.

/ means hard return
¶ means new paragraph

Personal-Business Letter L2.42
Block style. Mixed punctuation.

[*Today's date*] / Mrs. Shari Davis / 5200 Rosewood / Knoxville, TN 37924 / Dear Mrs. Davis: / Your presentation at the Kimberlin Garden Club last Tuesday evening was one of the most enjoyable our club has ever had. ¶ The interesting facts

(Continued on next page)

E. Itineraries (columnar)

An *itinerary* is an outline of the details of a planned trip. It includes departure and arrival times, meeting times, flight plans, hotel reservations, and other essential information.

An itinerary can be prepared in a number of different formats. In its simplest format, the information is arranged in columns on plain paper or on a printed form. The columns are *DATE*, *TIME*, and *EVENT*.

Heading. The heading includes the person's name and the inclusive dates of the trip.

1. In all caps, on line 7, center the words *ITINERARY FOR* followed by the person's name. (If plain paper is being used, begin the heading on line 13 or vertically center the itinerary.)
2. Double-space and center the dates of the trip.

Body. Key the body line by line (as if you were keying a table).

1. Begin a double space below the column headings.
2. Approximately center the date and time information in the columns. Abbreviate the month if necessary.

3. Use the indent feature to move to the "Event" column in case any item has a turnover line.
4. Single-space entries, but double-space before beginning a new date.
5. Underline words that identify special items such as accommodations and reminders.

For itineraries longer than one page, enter page numbers on all pages except the first, beginning on line 7 at the right margin.

```
                    ↓7
                ITINERARY FOR M. J. DONALDSON   ↓2
                    December 10-13, 19--

DATE          TIME               EVENT

↓2
Dec. 10      9:35 a.m.    Depart Memphis, United Air Lines Flight 433,
                          lunch served.
             1:02 p.m.    Arrive San Francisco, San Francisco
                          International Airport.
             5:30 p.m.    Depart hotel for Chinatown visit.
                          Hotel: Mark Hopkins Hotel, One Nob Hill.
                                                              ↓2
Dec. 11      9:00 a.m.    Convention at Mark Hopkins Hotel.
                          Reminder: Call Pat Wolton to confirm dinner
                          arrangements for Tuesday.

Dec. 12      9:00 a.m.    Convention at Mark Hopkins Hotel.
             7:00 p.m.    Dinner with Pat Wolton.

Dec. 13      10:30 a.m.   Depart hotel for airport.
             12:00 noon   Depart San Francisco, San Francisco
                          International Airport, United Air Lines Flight
                          700, lunch served.
             7:15 p.m.    Arrive Memphis.
```

Form F5.110 Itinerary

If a form is not available, set up as a table with 4 spaces between columns.

```
            ITINERARY FOR MICHELLE PRINCETON
                    May 4-6, 19--


    DATE        TIME                  EVENT


    May 4      9:10 a.m.    Depart Kansas City, American Flight 248.
               10:15 a.m.   Arrive Minneapolis; met by Warren Miller
                            from the Twin Cities office.

               12:15 p.m.   Lunch with T. R. Evans, 3M Corporation.
               2:00 p.m.    Conference with Minneapolis staff.
               6:30 p.m.    Dinner with Warren Miller.
                            Motel: Holiday Inn, Interstate 94 West.

    May 5      9:00 a.m.    Presentation, "Technology's Impact on
                            Records Management," ARMA Conference,
                            Executive Inn, St. Paul.
               10:30 a.m.   Attend ARMA sessions.
               1:30 p.m.    Working sessions with ARMA participants.
               6:30 p.m.    Kodak Trade Show, Convention Center.

    May 6      9:35 a.m.    Depart Minneapolis, American Flight 154.
               10:45 a.m.   Arrive Kansas City.
```

combined with your delightful sense of humor held the audience's attention every minute. In addition, the lovely plants you brought were outstanding examples of what all of us can accomplish if we use the right techniques. ¶ Would you consider coming back as a guest lecturer for the Kimberlin Garden Symposium in July? I will call you next Monday to discuss the details. / Sincerely yours, / Ms. Kelly Brown / 306 Bluebird Lane / Kimberlin Heights, TN 37920

Lesson 43

Objectives   Recognize how words are capitalized while keying sentences.
             Reinforce skill on up and down reaches.
             Apply proofreaders' marks while keying from rough-draft copy.
             Edit documents using block commands.
             Reinforce personal-business letters.

Format   Spacing: Drills, single; Timings, double; and as required
             Margins: Default or as required

A. LAB 3
Capitalization

Key lines 1–4 once. Then repeat lines 1–4, or take a series of 1-minute timings.

1 We waited with Senator Sam Bentson to see Governor Simpson.   12
2 The rabbi, David Rabicoff, introduced us to Major Houlihan.   12
3 Seven letters were addressed to Mr. and Mrs. Dustin Soeder.   12
4 Our mayor, Lorna Weitzel, asked Senator Lingle for funding.   12
   | 1 | 2 | 3 | 4 | 5 | 6 | 7 | 8 | 9 | 10 | 11 | 12

5. Capitalize official titles when they come before personal names.

   We asked Mrs. Maples to introduce Professor Ledbetter at the meeting.

6. Do not capitalize official titles when the name that follows is in apposition and is set off by commas.

   The president, Pamela Harris, gave the agenda to the secretary, Cara White.

B. PRETEST

Take a 1-minute timing on lines 5–7. Proofread, note your errors, and figure your speed.

5   Talk around the table was that huge debts were tallied   12
6 by the team; the coach denied it, of course. She called it   24
7 a hoax--only a sham; there were no tabs.   32
   | 1 | 2 | 3 | 4 | 5 | 6 | 7 | 8 | 9 | 10 | 11 | 12

Objectives Recognize correct subject-verb agreement while keying sentences.
Reinforce skill on adjacent and jump reaches.
Format and key columnar itineraries.

Format Spacing: Drills, single; Timings, double; and as required
Margins: Default or as required

▲. LAB 19
Subject-Verb Agreement

Key lines 1–4 once. Then repeat lines 1–4, or take a series of 1-minute timings. (Subjects and verbs are underlined.)

```
1  Karen and Brad are expected to practice for the track meet.   12
2  Both David and Theresa are very good at debugging programs.    12
3  Every pen and pencil in my classroom was used for the test.    12
4  Cheesecake and cherries is one of Phil's favorite desserts.    12
   | 1 | 2 | 3 | 4 | 5 | 6 | 7 | 8 | 9 | 10 | 11 | 12
```

4. If the subject consists of two words connected by *and* or by *both . . . and*, the subject is plural and requires a plural verb.

Mr. Johnson and *Mr. Bruce have received* promotions.
Both the *collection* and the *distribution* of mail *are* to be expanded.

5. If a subject consisting of two nouns connected by *and* refers to the same person or thing or is preceded by *each, every, many a,* or *many an,* a singular verb is used.

Corned beef and cabbage is our Monday special.
Each boy and girl *has* a ticket to the game.

B. PRETEST

Take a 1-minute timing on lines 5–8. Proofread, note your errors, and figure your speed.

```
5        Reading a book during a weekend is a wise choice.  You   12
6  can increase your word power even by reading popular books.    24
7  Enjoy yourself; join a number of those who choose to read a    36
8  good book.                                                     38
   | 1 | 2 | 3 | 4 | 5 | 6 | 7 | 8 | 9 | 10 | 11 | 12
```

C. PRACTICE

SPEED: If you made 2 or fewer errors on the Pretest, key lines 9–14 twice each. Repeat if time permits.

ACCURACY: If you made more than 2 errors on the Pretest, key lines 9–11 as a group twice. Then key lines 12–14 as a group twice. Repeat if time permits.

Adjacent Reaches

```
9   po pond port pour pound pouch poach point polka power polar
10  oi soil toil boil hoist point joist poise spoil avoid noise
11  we weak wean wept weave wedge sweat weigh weary dowel sweet
```

Jump Reaches

```
12  in bind find grin brain cabin cling brink drain faint grain
13  um numb jump lump chump mumps crumb gummy stump thumb bumpy
14  ce cede cell cent cease hence sauce grace niece cedar cello
```

D. POSTTEST

Take a 1-minute timing on lines 5–8. Proofread, note your errors, and figure your speed. Compare your performance with the Pretest.

SPEED: If you made 2 or fewer errors on the Pretest (page 102), key lines 8–13 twice each. Repeat if time permits.
ACCURACY: If you made more than 2 errors on the Pretest (page 102), key lines 8–10 as a group twice. Then key lines 11–13 as a group twice. Repeat if time permits.

Up Reaches

8 ta talk tame tack taste tally tales taped tanks taffy table
9 ly only rely July tally bully reply folly lymph apply lycra
10 de deal dews dean delve depot defer death debts demur denim

Down Reaches

11 ax hoax flax waxy taxes borax axles taxis waxen axiom flaxy
12 m; ham; ram; jam; prom; ream; team; loam; warm; sham; seem;
13 bs cabs hubs tubs cribs knobs curbs grabs verbs swabs herbs

D. POSTTEST

Take a 1-minute timing on lines 5–7 (page 102). Proofread, note your errors, and figure your speed. Compare your performance with the Pretest.

E. Proofreaders' Marks

More proofreaders' marks are illustrated below. Study them; then apply your knowledge in L3.43 (page 104), a rough-draft personal-business letter.

Proofreaders' Mark	Draft	Final Copy	Proofreaders' Mark	Draft	Final Copy
Delete and close up	arguement	argument	Insert punctuation	if its ready	if it's ready,
Don't delete	our two copies	our two copies	Move left	she fell	she fell
Insert space	tothe right	to the right	Move right	The crown	The extra
Make it a period	until now	until now.	Move as shown	two extra pages	two pages

Block Move

Block move is a function that allows copy in one location in a document to be moved to another location without rekeying it. The text is deleted from one place and inserted in another.

Block Copy

Block copy is a function that allows text to be duplicated and placed in another location within the document. The original text remains in its place, and the copy of the text appears in the new position.

Practice. (a) Key the six lines below. **(b)** Use the block move function to move the lines so that they are in the following order: 2, 5, 4, 6, 1, 3. **(c)** Copy lines 1, 3, and 5 two lines below the practice. **(d)** Copy lines 2, 4, and 6 two lines below the copies of 1, 3, and 5.

1. Discussion of interest sessions.
2. Roll call.
3. Viewing of keynote speaker video.
4. Reading of treasurer's report.
5. Reading and approval of minutes.
6. Presentation of membership report.

Form F1.109 Invoice
Use today's date. If a form is not available, set up as a table.

[*Invoice No.*] 338 / [*To*] Skyway Ski Resort / P.O. Box 7 / Stowe, VT 05672 / [*Terms*] 2/10, n/30

1	Transfer case gear, Model 776W	295.00	295.00
3	Plastic flexible tubing	79.95	239.85
1	Overhaul gasket set, No. 37-4037, for Model 776W	22.50	22.50
	Total amount due		557.35

Form F2.109 Invoice
Use today's date. If a form is not available, set up as a table.

[*Invoice No.*] 1096 / [*To*] Mr. Martin Teldair / Grant Enterprises / 4769 Wood Avenue / Boston, MA 02136 / [*Terms*] n/30

12	Model 2481 18-speed all-terrain bikes	185.75	2,229.00
7	Model 2250 foam-padded seats	22.33	156.31
15	Model 2469 12-speed trail bikes	145.95	2,189.25
8	Model 2168 26-inch bike tires	45.95	367.60
	Total amount due		4,942.16

D. Adjustments To Invoices

Adjustments such as delivery charges, sales taxes, and discounts are entered before *Total amount due*. First enter *Amount due* (a subtotal) a double space below the last entry. Then enter the adjustment line (or lines) single-spaced below *Amount due*, with a rule under the last adjustment entry. Double-space and then enter *Total amount due*.

```
Amount due           343.35
Sales tax 6%          20.60
Delivery charges      15.00

Total amount due     378.95
```

Form F3.109 Invoice
Use today's date. If a form is not available, set up as a table.

[*Invoice No.*] 2709 / [*To*] Ms. Shelly Landman / M & M Industries / 5893 Fairmount Street / Tucson, AZ 85712 / [*Terms*] n/45

6	Model 73445 polyester sleeping bags, blue	54.75	328.50
6	Model 73445 polyester sleeping bags, red	54.75	328.50
12	Model 36422 nylon backpacks, assorted colors	22.90	274.80
4	Model 98633 lightweight pup tents	164.95	659.80

Amount due 1,591.60 / Discount 20% −318.32 / Sales tax 5% 63.66 / Total amount due 1,336.94

Form F4.109 Invoice
Send another invoice (No. 2714) to M & M Industries, same terms, for the following items: 6 Campstoves, Model BT30 @ 59.95 / 2 Camptents, Model ND72 @ 215.95 / 12 Campside tool kits, Model TL05 @ 19.95. Discount is 20%; sales tax is 5%. Calculate all totals and total amount due.

Personal-Business Letter L3.43
Block style. Mixed punctuation.

February 17, 19-- ↓ 1 inch

Mr. James Wigington, Personnel Director
Baird and Kovacs Agency
4368 Wildwood Circle
Glassboro, nj 08028

Dear Mr. Wigington:

Miss Rhonda Hunt, an accountant in your agency, told me me about a summer job opening her in department; I would like to apply for that position.

I am now completing my sophomore year as an accounting major at Glassboro State College and will be available for employment from June 4 through August 31. During this current school year, I have worked as a part-time bookkeeper in the business administration department of the college.

You can contact me at my home telephone number, 555-4097, after 4 p.m. Monday through Friday. I would happy be to come for an interview at your convenience.

Yours truly,

↓ 4

Kevin Hodge
739 Ridge Road
Glassboro, NJ 08028

Personal-Business Letter L4.43
Edit Letter L3.43, making the following changes:

1. Block delete the inside address and salutation; insert the following information in their place:

   Mrs. Elizabeth Henderson / Director of Human Resources / The Makah Insurance Agency / 5903 Quinault Boulevard / Yakima, WA 98901 / Dear Mrs. Henderson:

2. Move the phrase *as an accounting major* in paragraph 2 to follow *Glassboro State College.*

3. Move the first sentence in paragraph 3 so that it is the last sentence in the paragraph.

4. Block delete the writer's name and address; insert the following information in its place:

   Miss Rayna Harris / 1405 Northcutt Drive / Yakima, WA 98901

C. Invoices

An *invoice* is a bill sent by one company or organization for materials it sold or services it rendered to another company or organization. Invoices vary in size, length, and complexity, but all contain the same information.

Heading. The common heading information includes the name and address of the purchaser and the date. It may also include an invoice number, if not preassigned; a customer number; a salesperson name or number; and the terms of the sale. Guide words are used to identify what information is required.

Body. The body of the form is arranged in columns. Information in the body includes the quantity, description, unit price, and total amount. Some invoices also include a catalog or stock number. Double-space between entries; single-space entries that take more than one line. Do not use the symbol $ in money columns.

Total Amount Due. Some invoices include a "Total amount due" line. If not, the line must be added to the form. Begin the "Total amount due" line a double space below the body, at the center of the "Description" column.

On the microcomputer, invoices will be in one of two forms:

1. An image of the form will appear on the screen, and you use the tab key to move from one **field** (area in which information is filled in) to another. Printing may be done on a preprinted form, or the form may be printed along with the information.

2. Field names will appear on the screen, usually as a list of items. The tab key is used to move from field to field. The information is printed on a preprinted form.

These forms are "hard formats"—you will not alter the form if you are in insert mode or when you depress Enter/Return. You can also create a boilerplate form, but you must remember to use typeover mode to fill in the information and use the cursor keys to move from column to column and line to line. When creating a boilerplate form, you should set tabs so that fill-ins in the top half of the form use the same tabs as fill-ins in the bottom half of the form. Information in number columns should align on the right and be approximately centered in the column. Information in description columns should align on the left.

Ajax Manufacturing Co.
123 Main Street
Maimi Beach, FL 33124

INVOICE NO. 1892

TO: Ms. Annette Pierce   DATE: February 20, 19--
     Pierce Enterprises
     4680 First Street
     Wayne, NE 68787   TERMS: 5/10, n/30

Quantity	Description	Unit Price	Amount
12	Model CG18 secretarial desks	458.99	5,507.88
5	Model GC27 executive desks	675.84	3,379.20
12	Model EZ18 secretarial chairs	175.25	2,103.00
5	Model EZ27 executive chairs	255.55	1,277.75
	Total amount due		12,267.83

Forms Software

There are a number of forms software programs. Some of these programs allow you to create "hard-format" forms and to fill them in. Other programs aid you in filling in preprinted forms. Using a sample of the form, the program prints a grid on the form. You use the grid to determine where to key the information so that it will appear on the form in the proper place.

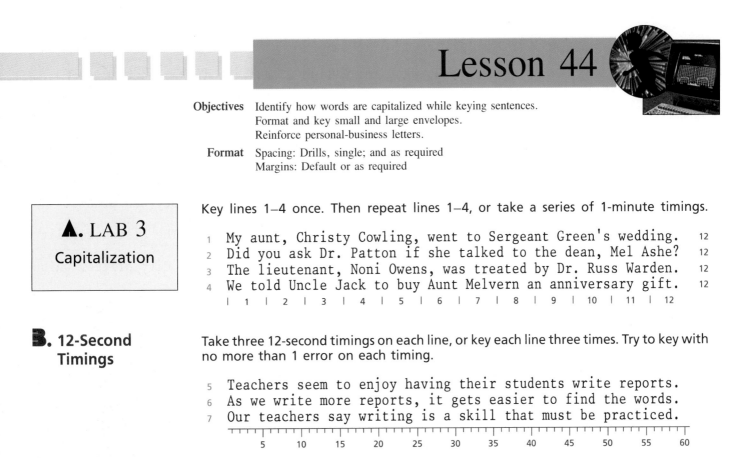

Lesson 44

Objectives Identify how words are capitalized while keying sentences.
Format and key small and large envelopes.
Reinforce personal-business letters.

Format Spacing: Drills, single; and as required
Margins: Default or as required

A. LAB 3
Capitalization

Key lines 1–4 once. Then repeat lines 1–4, or take a series of 1-minute timings.

1 My aunt, Christy Cowling, went to Sergeant Green's wedding. 12
2 Did you ask Dr. Patton if she talked to the dean, Mel Ashe? 12
3 The lieutenant, Noni Owens, was treated by Dr. Russ Warden. 12
4 We told Uncle Jack to buy Aunt Melvern an anniversary gift. 12
| 1 | 2 | 3 | 4 | 5 | 6 | 7 | 8 | 9 | 10 | 11 | 12

B. 12-Second Timings

Take three 12-second timings on each line, or key each line three times. Try to key with no more than 1 error on each timing.

5 Teachers seem to enjoy having their students write reports.
6 As we write more reports, it gets easier to find the words.
7 Our teachers say writing is a skill that must be practiced.

    5   10   15   20   25   30   35   40   45   50   55   60

C. Envelopes

Two addresses appear on envelopes—the writer's return address and the mailing address (where the letter is being sent). Follow the guidelines below. Refer to the illustrations on page 106.

Return Address. If the return address is not printed on the envelope, it should be keyed 1/2 inch down (line 4) and 1/2 inch (5 spaces) from the left edge. Change the default top margin to 1/2 inch and the default left margin to 1/2 inch.

Mailing Address. Begin the mailing address 2 inches down from the top edge (line 13). The horizontal placement of the mailing address will depend on the size of the envelope. Set a tab for the mailing address.

1. For small envelopes (No. 6 3/4), begin the mailing address 2.5 inches from the left edge.
2. For large envelopes (No. 10), begin the mailing address 4 inches from the left edge.

Note: In all addresses, key the city, state, and ZIP Code on one line. Remember to leave 1 space between the state and the ZIP Code.

Special Directions. Special directions are keyed 1.5 inches down from the top edge (line 10).

1. Begin an **on-arrival direction** (such as *Personal* or *Confidential*) at the reset left margin (1/2 inch). Use capital and small letters underlined.
2. Begin a **mailing direction** (such as *Registered* or *Special Delivery*) so that it ends about 1/2 inch from the right edge (below the stamp). Use all caps; do not underline.

You will have to change the default right margin when you address a large envelope with a mailing direction.

Envelope Shortcuts. The computer offers many ways to save time in preparing envelopes. A few are described on page 106.

(Continued on next page)

¶ As you can see in table 1, there could be a total of 24 truck-loads ~~of bricks~~ used for Allieds facility in Ray town. (I've) drafted a proposal for your review and have attached it to this letter. We need to discus*s* the details *during our meeting next* of this project, ~~on~~ Monday.

¶ If ~~it appears that~~ we ~~will~~ submit a bid for this project, we need to notify the Kansas City office so that they can *manufacture* ~~produce~~ sufficient bricks for this ~~substantial~~ order. The allied facility would provide a real sales boost for the Kansas City office, which has been lagging behind *the* other divisions the past two quarters. /

[*Your initials*] / Attachment

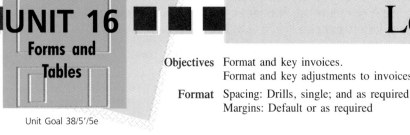

UNIT 16
Forms and Tables

Unit Goal 38/5'/5e

Lesson 109

Objectives Format and key invoices.
Format and key adjustments to invoices.

Format Spacing: Drills, single; and as required
Margins: Default or as required

A. Keyboard Skills

Key lines 1–4 once. Then, concentrate on your space bar technique in line 5. Repeat lines 1–4, or take a series of 1-minute timings.

Speed	1 They both want to take their time as they drive their auto.	12
Accuracy	2 Five experts judged my new black quarter horse on its size.	12
Numbers	3 On page 47 I saw that 29 times 38 was much less than 1,560.	12
Symbols	4 Please order 670# of #8 grade @ $15.34 before September 29.	12
Technique	5 a b c d e f g h i j k l m n o p q r s t u v w x y z a b c d	

| 1 | 2 | 3 | 4 | 5 | 6 | 7 | 8 | 9 | 10 | 11 | 12

B. 12-Second Timings

Take three 12-second timings on each line, or key each line three times. Try to key with no more than 1 error on each timing.

6 How sure are you that the sun will be up by the time we go?
7 We drove the auto to the park where we could see the birds.
8 Add these numbers so that the total is shown on that paper.

| 5 | 10 | 15 | 20 | 25 | 30 | 35 | 40 | 45 | 50 | 55 | 60

Automatic Addressing		Many word processing programs have an automatic envelope-addressing feature, particularly if envelopes are being prepared from a database or "address book" (a computerized list of names, addresses, and telephone numbers).
Stored Formats		It may be possible to create and save an envelope format (margins and tabs) and to call up the envelope format as the final page of a letter instead of creating it each time.
Block Copy		After the envelope format is prepared as the final page of a letter, the inside address of the letter can be block copied to the envelope.
Case Conversion		This feature converts a block of copy keyed in caps and lowercase to all caps, or it converts a block keyed in all caps to lowercase. If the inside (mailing) address of a letter has been keyed in caps and lowercase, it can be converted to all caps after being copied to the envelope.

No. 6 3/4 envelope is 6 1/2 by 3 5/8 inches.

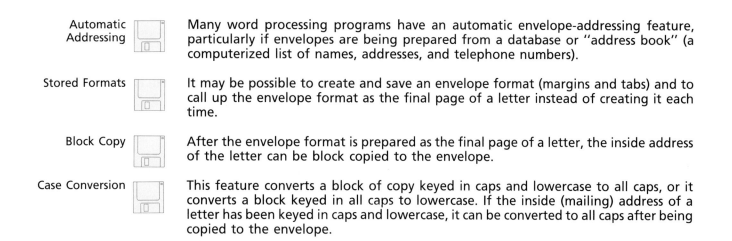

No. 10 envelope is 9 1/2 by 4 1/8 inches.

Note: The U.S. Postal Service recommends an OCR format—all caps, no punctuation—with a nine-digit ZIP Code. Either format illustrated is acceptable for first-class mail on an envelope of any size.

Envelopes E1–3.44

Address three envelopes. Create an envelope format for each size of envelope, and save the formats if your software has the stored formats feature.

1. Use the No. 6 3/4 (small) envelope format and the copy in the illustration of the small envelope above.

2. Use the No. 10 (large) envelope format and the copy in the illustration of the large envelope above.

3. Use the No. 10 envelope format. Copy the return address and mailing address from Envelope 1, and use case conversion to change both addresses to all caps. If you do not have case conversion, rekey the mailing address only in all caps.

special olympics
88 desert view road
crossroads nm 88114

yes i would like to donate to special olympics enclosed is my donation for
$_____

name	business

address	city	state	zip

Letter L69.108

Modified-block style. Use the address, salutation, and closing lines of Letter L65.106 (page 242) for this letter to Mr. Chaney. Send the letter by Express Mail. Date the letter July 10, 19--, and use a one-line second-page heading.

Here is the information you ~~asked for~~ *requested* on my recent *division* trip to

Kansas City. My Omaha Trip Report will be delivered to you next

week when I return to the office. ¶I had the opportunity to talk

to Malcolm Ketterling, Construction Supervisor for the project,

and he'll be accepting bids for materials on August 30th. The

building will be constructed *primarily* of brick, and ~~the~~ *a* description of the

specific materials required is estimated as follows:

¶It appears that the construction project planned for Allied Com-

puters, Inc., is going ahead as ~~planned~~ *scheduled*. It'll be located in the

Truman industrial park *on Maple Avenue* in Raytown. This 30,000-sq.-ft. facility

will be the largest outlet for Allied Computers in the U.S.

TABLE 1

Brick Requirements for Allied Computers
August 15, 19--

Face Brick (Red/Sand)	10 truckloads
Common Brick	8 truckloads
Tapestry Brick	4 truckloads
Enameled Brick (blue/azure)	2 truckloads
TOTAL	24

(Continued on next page)

Personal-Business Letter With Envelopes
L5.44

Block style. Mixed punctuation. Address a small and a large envelope for this letter as shown in the illustrations on page 106.

March 15, 19--/Bit and Byte, Inc./5583 Industrial Circle/ Garden Grove, CA 92641/ Ladies and Gentlemen:/Last week I purchased two boxes of Bit and Byte 3.5-inch double-sided, double-density disks from the Bullseye store in Colorado Springs, Colorado. Each time I tried to format one of the disks on my Writetech 7000 word processor, I received a disk-error message. ¶ When I took the disks back to the Bullseye store and explained the situation, the manager, Mr. Harold Thomason, said that he would have to ship the disks back to you in order to determine if the problem is with my hardware or with your software. ¶ The warranty on my word processor expires April 30. Would you please let me know as soon as possible whether or not the disks are faulty? The UPC number on the boxes is 51121 31206./Yours truly,/Ms. Lucinda Turner/2418 Norwood Avenue/Broadmoor, CO 80906

Lesson 45

Objectives Capitalize words correctly while keying sentences.
Reinforce skill on discrimination reaches.
Format enclosure and attachment notations.
Reinforce personal-business letters and envelopes.

Format Spacing: Drills, single; Timings, double; and as required
Margins: Default or as required

▲. LAB 3
Capitalization

Key lines 1–4 once, providing the missing capitals. Review your copy as your teacher reads the answers. Then key lines 1–4 again.

1 jim asked aunt marie--his aunt--to meet us in denver again.
2 the colonel, tom bork, told us the base was west of austin.
3 when we drove through the south, we visited uncle humphrey.
4 rod said reverend gilstrap had visited mr. and mrs. nelson.

B. Preview Practice   Key each line twice as a preview to the 5-minute timings below.

Accuracy   6   wage dozen exactly necessities entertainment transportation

Speed   7   when have your most know much make such food turn also some

C. 5-Minute Timings   Take two 5-minute timings on lines 8–24. Proofread, note your errors, and figure your speed.

8   Can you remember how easy it was when you were younger   12

9   and did not have to worry about money? In those years your   24

10   parents paid for what you needed or what you couldn't quite   36

11   do without; you didn't even have to give a thought to where   48

12   that money had originated. Now, though, you have dozens of   60

13   places where your limited amount of earnings must be spent.   72

14   Most of us know exactly how much money we can spend, and we   84

15   must make wise decisions and set realistic priorities about   96

16   spending.   98

17   Because you must make these wise, realistic judgments,   110

18   it is best to plan a budget. You, the wage earner, must be   122

19   careful enough to plan ahead. Items such as food, housing,   134

20   transportation, and any other necessities must be taken out   146

21   first. Only after all of these have been taken care of can   158

22   you afford to turn your attention to such items as clothing   170

23   and entertainment. Then you should also think about saving   182

24   some of the money you earned by working.   190

| 1 | 2 | 3 | 4 | 5 | 6 | 7 | 8 | 9 | 10 | 11 | 12 SI 1.45

Letter L68.108

Dictated coupon letter. Modified-block style.

march 10 19— dear merchants this spring will mark the tenth anniversary of the special olympics of crossroads each year hundreds of high school students across the country volunteer to help make this one day a year special for the young people who participate in the program *(paragraph)* the cost of the local special olympics is covered totally by donations from local businesses in crossroads all of the money that is donated is used directly for the operation of the events on the special olympics day *(paragraph)* if you would like to donate to this worthwhile activity please fill in the coupon below send the coupon along with your donation to the address shown on the coupon sincerely dan wilson executive director [*Your initials*]

- -

(Continued on next page)

Take a 1-minute timing on lines 5–7. Proofread, note your errors, and figure your speed.

```
5        Eight rafts were frozen in that ice, but the freighter      12
6   was able to slice through and pull the numb campers on deck      24
7   to safety.  One man suffered frostbite.                          32
    |   1   |   2   |   3   |   4   |   5   |   6   |   7   |   8   |   9   |  10  |  11  |  12
```

C. PRACTICE

SPEED: If you made 2 or fewer errors on the Pretest, key lines 8–13 twice each. Repeat if time permits.
ACCURACY: If you made more than 2 errors on the Pretest, key lines 8–10 as a group twice. Then key lines 11–13 as a group twice. Repeat if time permits.

Discrimination Reaches

```
8    kd kind skid dark docks decks drink desks drank dusky naked
9    sl slow loss lens skill slice lapse least stall slide nasal
10   ei cite dice tier sieve eight siege thief tried wield deify

11   de deed eddy edit deuce hides dress edict widen weedy media
12   fr fray raft free draft dwarf ferry fryer offer front graft
13   bn knob bank numb brown noble bacon bingo urban ebony bonus
```

D. POSTTEST

Take a 1-minute timing on lines 5–7. Proofread, note your errors, and figure your speed. Compare your performance with the Pretest.

E. Enclosure and Attachment Notations

When an item is sent with a letter, the word *Enclosure* is keyed at the left margin a double space below the writer's address. This reminds the sender to include the item, tells the receiver to look for the item, and serves as a record on the file copy. If the item is clipped or stapled to the letter, the word *Attachment* is used. For more than one item, key *2 Enclosures* or *3 Attachments,* etc.

```
Sincerely yours,  ↓4



Rob J. Stanley
54 Harbor Lane
Boston, MA 02140  ↓2

Enclosure
```

Personal-Business Letter With Envelopes L6.45
Block style. Mixed punctuation. Address a No. 6 3/4 envelope using capital and lowercase letters. Then address a No. 10 envelope in OCR format.

April 3, 19— / Mr. Don Trinh, Librarian / River Valley Library / 4545 West Paluxy / Jackson, MS 39202-4545 / Dear Mr. Trinh: / On March 12 I checked out Computers Today by Donald H. Sanders. It was to be returned by March 26. ¶ Two weeks ago I was involved in an accident that caused my car to overturn into a bayou. Everything in the car—including the book—was submerged in water. Fortunately, I was able to escape with only a few scratches; the book, however, was ruined. Would you please let me know what I need to do about payment for

(Continued on next page)

Letter L66.107
Key the coupon letter on page 244. Use modified-block style.

Letter L67.107
Modified-block style.

[*Today's date*] / Dr. Sadaharu Arakawa, President / Dalton Engineering / P.O. Box 303 / Dalton, MA 01226 / Dear Dr. Arakawa: / Our vice president, Dr. Kazuhiko Toshiba, has told me about your interest in our PRO Personal Computer and requested that I arrange an in-house demonstration for you and your managers. I am delighted to do this. ¶ To schedule a demonstration at your site, please fill in the tear-off section at the bottom of this letter and return it to me in the enclosed envelope. I will call you to finalize the date and time. ¶ Thank you for your interest in the PRO Personal Computer. / Sincerely, / Jerrald V. Zar / Sales Manager / [*Your initials*] / Enclosure

- -

Date_____

Mr. Jerrald V. Zar, Sales Manager
PRO Corporation
35 Wheeler Street
Cambridge, MA 02138

We would like a vendor demonstration of the PRO Personal Computer.

Company Name	Contact Person
Address	Telephone
City State ZIP	Preferred Dates (3)

Lesson 108

Objectives
Reinforce dictated letters.
Reinforce coupon letters.
Reinforce two-page letters.
Reinforce delivery notations in letters.
Key 38/5'/5e.

Format
Spacing: Drills, single; Timings, double; and as required
Margins: Default or as required

▲. Keyboard Skills

Key lines 1–4 once. In line 5 use the underline function on the underlined words. Repeat lines 1–4, or take a series of 1-minute timings.

Speed	1	I did not think it was my duty to pay the bill at the time.	12
Accuracy	2	Dave will make sixty quart jugs of blazing hot apple cider.	12
Numbers	3	The arena has 15,789 seats; only 12,346 of them were taken.	12
Symbols	4	Use the percent (%), an ampersand (&), and an asterisk (*).	12
Technique	5	I do not see why we have to get so many more bills by dark.

| 1 | 2 | 3 | 4 | 5 | 6 | 7 | 8 | 9 | 10 | 11 | 12

the book? The book's title page, which is still legible, is enclosed. My library card number is 05692. / Very truly yours, / Stewart Brewster / No. 5 Briargrove / Jackson, MS 39204-5916 / Enclosure

Personal-Business Letter With Envelope L7.45
Block style. Mixed punctuation. Address a No. 10 envelope using capital and lower-case letters.

August 29, 19-- / Dr. Paula Knutson / 901 blue ridge parkway / Louisville, KY 40223 / Dear dr. Knutson: / Today I recieved your bill for cementing my lose crown, and I noticed an error in the amount due. According to your statement, the fee was $45, and my insurance paid $37 on on the claim. This leave should a balance of $8. Your record however, shows a balance of $81. I have attached the statement and my check for $8. If the error is in the amount of the fee or the insurance payment, please let me know so that I can settle my account. / Yours truly, / Ms. Sarah Heyman / Apartment 34 / 36 South League / Louisville, KY 40272 / Attachments 2

Lesson 46

Objectives	Format and key a business letter.
	Reinforce addressing envelopes.
	Reinforce enclosure notations.
Format	Spacing: Drills, single; and as required
	Margins: Default or as required

▲. Keyboard Skills

Key lines 1–4 once. Then do what line 5 tells you to do. Repeat lines 1–4, or take a series of 1-minute timings.

Speed	1 The firm sent the forms over an hour after she called them.	12
Accuracy	2 Max quickly adjusted one fuzzy TV before the two pro games.	12
Numbers	3 Team scores were red, 59; blue, 37; gold, 12; and green, 4.	12
Symbols	4 Is this accurate: $35.78 + $9.65 + $4.01 + $8.94 = $58.38?	12
Technique	5 Repeat line 3, but key the colors in all caps.	

| 1 | 2 | 3 | 4 | 5 | 6 | 7 | 8 | 9 | 10 | 11 | 12 |

NAM National Association of Mayors

P.O. Box 2173　Washington, D.C.　20013　202-555-4739

October 10, 19--
↓6

No inside address; subject/ salutation covers all addressees.

To All NAM Members
Who Plan to Attend the
Chicago Convention:

This letter is to remind you that paid-up Association members only will be admitted to the convention sessions we will hold in November at the Drake Hotel in Chicago. Membership dues can, of course, be paid at the registration desk upon your arrival at the convention, but the charge there will be $25 more per individual than dues paid in advance. So we urge you to remit your dues in advance.

Use the coupon below. Just tear it off, fill it in, attach your check for $75, and mail in the enclosed envelope to our offices in Washington. Your membership card will be sent immediately.

Informal complimentary closing.

See you at the convention!

Initials may be on same line as writer's identification to allow room for coupon.

ts
Enclosure

Beverly T. Prescott
Executive Director
↓1

- -
↓2

Date_____
↓2

National Association of Mayors
P.O. Box 2173
Washington, DC 20013

Enclosed is my check for $75 in payment of my Association dues.
↓2

_____
Name

_____
Mayor of
↓2

_____
Address

City　　　　State　　　ZIP

B. 30-Second Timings

Take two 30-second timings on lines 6–7. Then take two 30-second timings on lines 8–9. Try to key with no more than 2 errors on each timing.

```
6  Since the rain began last week, all of the dirt that we had      12
7  hauled in and put on the yard has washed down the driveway.      24

8  When you drive the car, you must think to fill the gas tank      12
9  before you come home so that I can go to work the next day.      24
     |  1  |  2  |  3  |  4  |  5  |  6  |  7  |  8  |  9  |  10  |  11  |  12
```

C. Business Letters

A business letter represents a company, not an individual, and is therefore prepared on official company stationery called *letterhead.* The company's name, address, and telephone number are printed on the letterhead. A business letter and a personal-business letter have only a few differences. (Refer to the illustration on page 111.)

1. Since the writer's company name and address appear in the letterhead, they are not placed in the closing of the letter.

2. The writer's business title is usually keyed under the name, as in the illustration. (It may also be placed on the same line as the name, separated by a comma.) The name and title are called the *writer's identification.*

3. The initials of the person who keys the letter are placed a double space below the writer's identification. These initials are called *reference initials.*

4. The enclosure or attachment notation is keyed a *single space* below the reference initials. (As there is a blank line between the writer's identification and the initials, it is not necessary to have a blank line before the enclosure notation.)

Business Letter L8.46
Key the letter on page 111. Block style. Use your own initials for the reference initials. Address a No. 10 envelope.

Business Letter L9.46
Block style. No. 10 envelope.

October 3, 19— / Mrs. Dianne Finzer / 2112 Mountain View Lane / Hot Springs, AR 71913 / Dear Mrs. Finzer: / In September you visited our booth at the Arkansas State Fair and filled out a questionnaire about your home. You indicated that you would be interested in having one of our representatives give you a free estimate on the installation of our vinyl siding. ¶ Mr. Nicholas Jiminez, our manager for the Hot Springs area, will be available to visit your home and provide you with an estimate from October 15 to October 30. Indicate the date you would prefer on the enclosed postage-paid card, and drop it in the mail. Mr. Jiminez will call to arrange an appointment. ¶ Pyramid vinyl siding is the best material to make the exterior of your home beautiful and trouble-free for many years to come. We are confident that you will be pleased with the quality of our product and our work. / Cordially yours, / Mario Gionetti / General Sales Manager / [*Your initials*] / Enclosure

Objectives   Correct errors in subject-verb agreement while keying sentences.
Format and key coupon letters.
Reinforce memos.

Format   Spacing: Drills, single; and as required
Margins: Default or as required

▲. LAB 18
Subject-Verb Agreement

Key lines 1–4 once, correcting any errors in subject-verb agreement rules. Review your copy as your teacher reads the answers. Then key lines 1–4 again.

1 The managers at our Bismarck plant is all at a conference.
2 One of the programmers have written the software for Carmen.
3 The books on the floor is to be placed on the brown table.
4 One of the diskettes we ordered on June 2 have a bad sector.

◗. 30-Second Timings

Take two 30-second timings on lines 5 and 6. Then take two 30-second timings on lines 7 and 8. Try to key with no more than 2 errors on each timing.

5 We can't save the file until we have keyed all of the data;   12
6 then we will be able to start putting together this report.   24

7 We might be able to finish this task by next Thursday; then   12
8 we're going to have to make an additional request for help.   24

   | 1 | 2 | 3 | 4 | 5 | 6 | 7 | 8 | 9 | 10 | 11 | 12

Memo M8.107
Standard format.

MEMO TO: Dean Stinson / FROM: Marilyn Hargrove / DATE: February 9, 19__ / SUBJECT: School Visitation Day / As you know, Dean, Tuesday is School Visitation Day, and a number of students from area high schools will be visiting our company between 1 and 3:30 p.m. Please make sure that our computer presentation is ready and we have an ample supply of company logos for our visitors. We expect from 150 to 200 students on Tuesday. / [Your initials]

◖. Coupon Letters

Sometimes business letters are formatted so that there is a tear-off coupon at the bottom. This coupon is for the convenience of the person receiving the letter and is used to respond to some request. Study the illustration on page 244. To format a coupon letter:

1. Use default margins.

2. Separate the coupon from the letter with a line of spaced underscores. Single-space before the line; double-space after it.

3. Reference initials and an enclosure notation, if used, may be raised to align with the last line of the writer's identification.

4. Double-space between lines of underscores to allow room for the insertions.

Note: Coupon letters are form letters, so they often contain a "subject/salutation" instead of an inside address and salutation.

SOFTWARE CONNECTION

1551 Riverwalk Pensacola, FL 32507 (904) 555-4422

Letterhead

Date Line   ↓13
January 19, 19--
                ↓6

Inside   Mrs. Edith Neal
Address   Pensacola High School
              719 Vista Boulevard
              Pensacola, FL 32501
                          ↓2
Salutation   Dear Mrs. Neal:↓2

Body   Are you and your business students in a midyear slump? Do your
              classes need energizing? Software Connection has the solution to
              your problems.↓2

              On Friday, February 2, Software Connection is sponsoring a Soft-
              A-Wareness seminar for local schools. Students will have an
              opportunity for hands-on experience with the latest business
              software. Professional programmers will be available to answer
              technical and career questions. Drawings for free software will
              be held every hour--and a free lunch will be served to all
              seminar guests.↓2

              Make plans now to attend. Simply indicate on the enclosed
              postage-free card how many students you will be bringing, and
              mail it by January 25. We will do the rest!↓2

Complimen-   Sincerely yours,
tary Closing   ↓4

Signature   *Erin Higgins*

Writer's   Erin Higgins
Identification President↓2
(name and
title)   sls
Reference   Enclosure
Initials
Enclosure
Notation

BUSINESS LETTER
BLOCK STYLE

E. Delivery Notations

If a letter is to be delivered in any manner other than by standard first-class mail, an appropriate notation should be made on the letter. Key a delivery notation at the left margin, a single space below the reference initials or enclosure notation. Precede the delivery service with the word *By.* Other notations follow the delivery notation.

```
bno              gmm
By fax           By registered mail

rah              cgs
Enclosure        By Federal Express
By messenger     c:  Pearl Dunham
```

Letter L65.106

Modified-block style. Use a multiple-line second-page heading.

July 2, 19-- / Mr. Alex Chaney, President / Chaney Industries, Inc. / 2345 Takoma Avenue / Silver Springs, MD 20912 / Dear Mr. Chaney: / As you requested, I am faxing to you this letter on my recent trip to the central Division offices in Denver, Kansas City, and Omaha. Because of the urgency of the Denver situation, this fax will address that problem; only reports on the other division locations will follow by letter. I was able to obtain a considerable amount of information from the division managers during my trip. ¶ Pat Rivers was aware of the the problem that we (had/have) in the Denver area and has already taken steps to alleviate any similar problems in the future. Apparently, the building materials inventories were being depleted because of a number of major shopping mall construction projects in Pueblo, Aurora, Colorado Springs, and Greeley. Here is a summary of the truckloads of building bricks we needed for each of these projects:

Aurora	Tapestry	10
Colorado Springs	Face	8
Greeley	Face	13
Pueblo	Common	12

Because of these unusually high brick demands, we have increased our inventories of Tapestry, Face, and Common bricks by 30 truckloads per month. This increase, when combined with our current inventories, will accommodate any new "building booms" similar to the ones that we experienced this past quarter. Ms. Rivers Pat will be sending me weekly reports on the brick inventories during the entire quarter. / Sincerely, / Katherine Lee / National Sales Manager / [*Your initials*]

Lesson 47

Objectives Recognize how words are capitalized while keying sentences.
Apply proofreaders' marks while keying from rough-draft copy.
Edit documents using the search and replace function.
Key 32/3'/5e.

Format Spacing: Drills, single; Timings, double; and as required
Margins: Default or as required

▲. LAB 4
Capitalization

Key lines 1–4 once. Then repeat lines 1–4, or take a series of 1-minute timings.

1 Gail lost her shoes Tuesday on Flight 391; they are size 7. 12
2 Our favorite winter month is February with Valentine's Day. 12
3 An ice storm in April is a cruel trick Spring played on us. 12
4 Look at Diagram 16 in Appendix B, and read notes 3A and 7B. 12

| 1 | 2 | 3 | 4 | 5 | 6 | 7 | 8 | 9 | 10 | 11 | 12

7. Capitalize a noun that is followed by a number or a letter. **Note:** Do *not* capitalize the nouns *line, note, page, paragraph, size,* and *verse.*

Turn to page 73, and write the answers to Exercise 4 in Column 1.

8. Capitalize the names of days, months, holidays, and religious days, but do not capitalize the names of seasons unless they are personified (used as a person).

This spring we will celebrate Mother's Day and Father's Day.
When will you stop scorching the land, Summer?

⬛. PRETEST

Take a 3-minute timing on lines 5–12. Proofread, note your errors, and figure your speed.

5   Have you been wanting to know what kind of job is best 12
6   for you? You can analyze some things about your life which 24
7   will give you some good clues. First, which classes do you 36
8   enjoy? Do you like using office equipment? What do you do 48
9   with your extra time? Next, what do you value in life? Do 60
10 you like a challenge, or do you need prestige? Do you need 72
11 to feel secure in your job? Last, figure out what kinds of 84
12 things you learn best and how your skills can be developed. 96

| 1 | 2 | 3 | 4 | 5 | 6 | 7 | 8 | 9 | 10 | 11 | 12 SI 1.20

Take a 5-minute timing on lines 5–21. Proofread, note your errors, and figure your speed.

```
 5          Staying in shape is appropriate for us all, regardless    12
 6      of age.  Dozens of studies have shown that regular exercise    24
 7      will help us live longer lives.  Not only will our lives be    36
 8      longer, they will also be more enjoyable.  If we are out of    48
 9      shape, we find ourselves tiring rapidly when we are engaged    60
10      in activities that require physical strength or that may be    72
11      quite strenuous.                                              75
12          If you want to ensure that you remain in good physical    87
13      shape, here are some suggestions to help you along the way.    99
14      First of all, try to exercise three or four times each week   111
15      for at least 20 minutes a day.  Exercise can take the shape   123
16      of a lot of different actions, from a brisk walk to a short   135
17      swim.  Regardless of the type of activity you pursue, it is   147
18      important that you also find suitable foods for nourishment   159
19      and always try to eat well-balanced meals.  Experts caution   171
20      us also to limit fats and calories.  The above ideas may be   183
21      very helpful to you for many years.                          190
      |  1  |  2  |  3  |  4  |  5  |  6  |  7  |  8  |  9  |  10  |  11  |  12  SI 1.43
```

In the chart below find the number of errors you made on the Pretest. Then key each of the following designated drill lines three times.

Pretest errors	0–1	2–3	4–5	6+
Drill lines	25–29	24–28	23–27	22–26

Accuracy

```
22  for caution require physical exercise different appropriate
23  have helpful engaged strength activity strenuous regardless
24  shape shown staying balanced suitable enjoyable nourishment
25  that lives experts calories important ourselves suggestions
```

Speed

```
26  minutes dozens remain quite limit lives only want good year
27  studies ensure pursue times meals helps will when here type
28  regular tiring always about foods ideas also find some fats
29  rapidly longer years brisk short above three that four come
```

Take another 5-minute timing on lines 5–21. Proofread, note your errors, and figure your speed. Compare your performance with the Pretest.

In the chart below find the number of errors you made on the Pretest (page 112). Then key each of the following designated drill lines two times.

Pretest errors	0–1	2–3	4–5	6+
Drill lines	16–20	15–19	14–18	13–17

Accuracy

13 jobs need what know things office secure prestige developed
14 give last your kind extra valued enjoyed figuring equipment
15 out like next best with life using skills wanting challenge
16 how can feel good will which first learns classes analyzing

Speed

17 class kinds clues some been want have how can out for do in
18 learn skill which life some best your off hat ear all be or
19 about enjoy times feel give know next job kin ill wit is of
20 using equip liked will last best what and now ant our to an

D. POSTTEST

Take another 3-minute timing on lines 5–12 (page 112). Proofread, note your errors, and figure your speed. Compare your performance with the Pretest.

E. Proofreaders' Marks

Study the proofreaders' marks below; then apply them as you key Letter L10.47 (page 114), a rough-draft business letter.

Proofreaders' Mark	Draft	Final Copy	Proofreaders' Mark	Draft	Final Copy
ss Single-space	first line / second line	first line / second line	◯ Spell out	keep ① copy	keep one copy
			╱ Use lowercase letter	then go West	then go west
ds Double-space	first line / second line	first line / second line	new/old Replace	filed next week/year	filed next week

Search and Replace

The **search and replace** function allows the user to look for a word or phrase used throughout a document and replace it with another word or phrase. The replace function can be *automatic* (each use of the word or phrase will be changed as soon as it is found) or *manual* (the user must indicate whether or not to make the change each time the word or phrase appears).

Practice: Key the paragraph below. Then use the search and replace function to make the changes on page 114.

Edward Lawson, district representative, gave a report on changes proposed at the district level. Yearly dues are being increased from $20 to $30, but the higher fee will include a subscription to the new district business education magazine, which will be published quarterly. The district association will begin a membership drive in May, and each district has been asked to submit an outline of its plan by March 1.

(Continued on next page)

F

Flush Right

Some word processing programs have a feature called **flush right** or **right alignment** that will position copy at the right margin. If your software does not have a flush right function but does have a right tab feature, you can set a right tab at the right margin rather than backspacing for the date.

Production Practice. Set your margins for a 6 1/2-inch line. Set a center tab. Single spacing. Clean sheet of paper. Use Memo M7.105 below.

Single-Line Heading. Space down to line 7, and key the name of the addressee at the left margin. Tab to the center and key the number *2*. Use a flush right or right alignment command (or a right tab) to place the date at the right margin. Return twice, and then key the last paragraph in the memo. Check your work.

Multiple-Line Heading. Space down to line 7. Key the name of the addressee at the left margin. Return to the left margin. Key the word *Page* and the number *2*. Return. Key the date. Return twice, and key the last paragraph in the memo. Check your work. Which style was easier and faster to use?

Memo M7.105
Use a single-line heading for the second page.

MEMO TO: Katherine Lee / FROM: Alex Chaney / DATE: February 14, 19— / SUBJECT: Central Division Meetings / As you know, on June 10 you leave for a three-week trip to visit our Central Region offices. Like your trip in 1988, this year's trip will include stops in Denver, Kansas City, and Omaha. I have scheduled your Denver and Kansas City visitations first, because the division managers in those two cities will also be traveling during the final two weeks of your trip. Patricia Rivers in Denver will be out the second week of your trip, and Brad Douglas in Kansas City will be traveling the third week of your trip. ¶ I would like you to gather information on the following items from each of the division headquarters. More specifically, I need you to do some research on each of the following items.

1. <u>Denver Office</u>. I have had several letters from our field representatives throughout the Denver division concerning the unusual number of back orders for customers whose initial orders have come through the Denver warehouse. In one respect, this is a favorable sign—it means that we have experienced an unusually high number of sales in this division if our inventories are being depleted. However, we do not want to inconvenience our customers by having them wait two, three, or four weeks for their orders that ordinarily should have been processed immediately. If the problem is merely one of increasing our inventory for the items that have been placed on back order, the Denver office should be able to take care of the matter. If there is a different problem, however, we need to investigate the reasons for it.

2. <u>Kansas City Office</u>. The Chamber of Commerce in Kansas City has informed me that a major computer firm has purchased a large tract of land just beyond the city limits of Raytown. See if you can gather some additional information on their

(Continued on next page)

Lesson 48

Objectives Identify how words are capitalized while keying sentences.
Reinforce personal-business letters.
Reinforce business letters and envelopes.

Format Spacing: Drills, single; and as required
Margins: Default or as required

A. LAB 4
Capitalization

Key lines 1–4 once. Then repeat lines 1–4, or take a series of 1-minute timings.

1 Vera said to read paragraph 3 on page 94 by next Wednesday. 12
2 Marilyn's birthday is March 17, which is St. Patrick's Day. 12
3 During September we celebrated Yom Kippur and Rosh Hashana. 12
4 Our fall project involved reproducing Table 22 and Chart 5. 12

| 1 | 2 | 3 | 4 | 5 | 6 | 7 | 8 | 9 | 10 | 11 | 12

B. "OK" Timings

Take two 30-second "OK" (errorless) timings on lines 5–6. Then take two 30-second "OK" timings on lines 7–8. Goal: No errors.

5 You must spend quite a lot of time on drill work if you are 12
6 to become an expert on the keyboard. Give zip to your job. 24

7 Exercise can give your body the zip it needs to adjust to a 12
8 pace required to maintain good health. Walking is favored. 24

| 1 | 2 | 3 | 4 | 5 | 6 | 7 | 8 | 9 | 10 | 11 | 12

Personal-Business Letter L11.48
Block style. No. 6 3/4 envelope.

July 5, 19--/Dr. John H. Dutton /Wichita State University /1700 Regency Drive/ Wichita, KS 67208-1595 /Dear Dr. Dutton:/ On June 12 in Warren, Ohio, you received a standing ovation from over 7,000 business teachers for your speech "The American Work Ethic: Dead or Alive?" at the Phi Delta Lambda National Conference. I was one of those teachers. ¶ Your book, America Is Our Business, was for sale at a 30 percent discount during the conference, but the supply had run out by the time I visited the booth. I was given an order form to purchase the book by mail, but it has been misplaced. ¶ Would you please let me know how I can order the book at the reduced rate? I am eager to use it in my Personal Business Management Class this fall. / Very truly yours, / Benjamin Kalil / 46 Horseshoe Run /Huntington, WV 25703

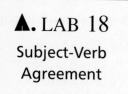

Lesson 105

Objectives Recognize correct subject-verb agreement while keying sentences.
Format and key two-page letters and memos.
Reinforce the flush right/right alignment command.

Format Spacing: Drills, single; and as required
Margins: Default or as required

▲. LAB 18

Subject-Verb
Agreement

Key lines 1–4 once. Then repeat lines 1–4, or take a series of 1-minute timings. (Subjects and verbs are underlined.)

```
1  One of the reasons for his success is his positive outlook.   12
2  The prices for milk, butter, and eggs have fallen in March.   12
3  One of you is to be commended for taking on this hard task.   12
4  His experience as counselor has prepared him for this work.   12
   |  1  |  2  |  3  |  4  |  5  |  6  |  7  |  8  |  9  | 10 | 11 | 12
```

2. Phrases and clauses between a subject and verb do not affect the number of the verb. If the subject is singular, use a singular verb; if the subject is plural, use a plural verb.

> The lost *box* of new letterheads *has been found.*
> The *container* of wrenches and washers *was opened.*

3. Use a singular verb after a phrase beginning with *one of* or *one of the.*

> Exception: Use a plural verb after the phrases *one of those who* and *one of the [items] that* because the verb refers to *those* or *[items].*

> *One of* her ankles *was* sprained. [Singular verb agrees with the subject *one.*]
> *One of the* new **desks** that **were** damaged *was* mine. [Singular verb agrees with *one*; plural verb agrees with *desks.*]

◗. Two-Page Letters and Memos

Long business letters and memos are often continued on a second page. The second page should be a plain sheet of paper of the same quality as the letterhead or memo form used for the first page. To format:

1. Use default margins; follow guide words for memos.

2. Carry over at least two lines of the body to the second page. A three-line paragraph cannot be divided. Use the widow/orphan feature if available.

3. Begin page 2 with a heading that includes the name of the addressee, the page number, and the date. **Style A:** Spread the heading on line 7. Key the name of the addressee at the left margin, key the page number at the center, and backspace the date from the right margin. **Style B:** Block the heading at the left margin. Key the name of the addressee on line 7; the word *Page* and page number on line 8; the date on line 9.

4. Double-space from the heading to the body.

Note: You may be able to use the header feature of your software for the second-page heading.

```
↓7
Ms. Tina Lewis              2              August 9, 19--  ↓2

If you need any further information, Ms. Lewis, please feel free
to write or call me at the number listed at the bottom of page 1
of this letter.  I look forward to seeing your article.

Very truly yours,
```

Style A: Single-Line Heading

```
↓7
Ms. Tina Lewis
Page 2
August 9, 19--  ↓2

If you need any further information, Ms. Lewis, please feel free
to write or call me at the number listed at the bottom of page 1
of this letter.  I look forward to seeing your article.

Very truly yours,
```

Style B: Multiple-Line Heading

Business Letter L12.48
Block style. No. 10 envelope.

~~June~~ *July* 10, 19-- / Mr. Benjamin Kalil / 46 Horse Shoe Run / Huntington, WV 25703 / Dear Mr. Kalil: / Thank you for your letter requesting instructions for ordering my book, <u>America is our Business</u>. ¶ Sales at the Phil Lambda Delta National ~~convention~~ *Conference* far exceeded our projections, and the first books were sold out by the end of the day. Therefore, we took postage-paid mail orders at the ~~discounted~~ rate. ¶ We will be happy to send you a copy of the book at the ~~lower price~~ *reduced rate*. Just fill out the enclosed order form and return it--~~Be sure to include your payment~~--*along with your check or money order* in the envelope provided. ¶ I hope that ~~my~~ <u>America Is Our Business</u> will prove beneficial to your *students* and will assist you in having a successful year school. / Yours truly, / John H. Dutton, Professor / Business administration / [*Your initials*] / 2 enclosures

Business Letter L13.48
Block style. No. 10 envelope in OCR format.

Block copy the body and closing of Letter L12.48 into a new document. Change the opening to Ms. Suzanne Karney / Apartment 161 / 3020 Pineridge Road / Gunnison, UT 84634 / Dear Ms. Karney:

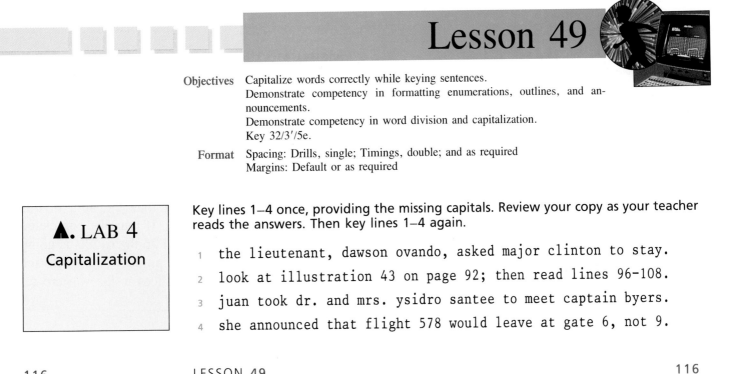

Lesson 49

Objectives Capitalize words correctly while keying sentences.
Demonstrate competency in formatting enumerations, outlines, and announcements.
Demonstrate competency in word division and capitalization.
Key 32/3'/5e.

Format Spacing: Drills, single; Timings, double; and as required
Margins: Default or as required

▲. LAB 4
Capitalization

Key lines 1–4 once, providing the missing capitals. Review your copy as your teacher reads the answers. Then key lines 1–4 again.

1 the lieutenant, dawson ovando, asked major clinton to stay.
2 look at illustration 43 on page 92; then read lines 96-108.
3 juan took dr. and mrs. ysidro santee to meet captain byers.
4 she announced that flight 578 would leave at gate 6, not 9.

▙. Boilerplates

A **boilerplate** is a file that can be created and then saved on a disk to be used repeatedly from one application to another. Boilerplate material is often used to prepare form letters, real estate papers, and legal briefs because of all the repetitive information that appears in each of these documents.

A boilerplate can also be created for the repetitive information appearing in forms such as memos. The guide words (*MEMO TO:, FROM:, DATE:, SUBJECT:*) that appear at the top of a memo (as well as the margins and tab stops) can be saved in a file and then retrieved and "filled in" whenever a memo must be prepared. Using such a technique is a timesaving step. When filling in a boilerplate form, you *must* be in typeover mode. If you use insert mode, you will alter the form.

To create a boilerplate memo form, follow these steps:

1. Open a document file.
2. Use standard default margins.
3. Clear all tab stops; then set a tab 10 spaces from the left margin.
4. On line 13 (2 inches from the top of the page) key the words *MEMO TO:*.
5. Double-space; at the left margin, key the word *FROM:*.
6. Double-space; at the left margin, key the word *DATE:*.
7. Double-space; at the left margin, key the word *SUBJECT:*.
8. Save the document as MEMO.

Note: You can use bold or different fonts (such as italic) for the guide words to make the guide words look different from the rest of the memo.

You may be able to create a memo form with the macro feature, if available.

Memo M4.104

Following the steps outlined above, create a boilerplate memo form. Use bold to highlight the guide words. (You must turn off bold after each colon or the words you fill in will also be in bold.)

Memo M5.104

Use boilerplate form.

[*MEMO TO:*] Shelly Norman / [*FROM:*] Mark Andrews / [*DATE:*] March 23, 19— / [*SUBJECT:*] Company Newsletter / I have just finished reading the first issue of the <u>Concorde Chronicle</u>, and I want to extend to you a "hearty congratulations" for a job well done. This was your first effort at the newsletter using our new desktop publishing software, and you did a superb job! ¶ I like your Company Capsule on page 4, in which you did an excellent job of sharing with our employees the major projects we have completed this quarter. Make sure to include this section in the next issue. ¶ Keep up the excellent work, Shelly. / [*Your initials*]

Memo M6.104

Dictated memo. Supply capitalization, punctuation, paragraphing, and correct subject-verb agreement. Use boilerplate form.

[*MEMO TO:*] jeffrey s johnson [*FROM:*] paula m daniels [*DATE:*] *today's date* [*SUBJECT:*] marketing questionnaire one of the questionnaires that were sent to your office at the beginning of the month must be completed no later than the 30th of this month as a reminder section II must be completed for questions 7 13 17 23 and 26 the results is going to be used to compare our product sales with the sales of the other district offices in the western region [*your initials*]

B. Preview Practice

Key each line twice as a preview to the 3-minute timings below.

Accuracy
Speed

5 worth quoted expected charming attitude realized difference
6 then work with met for did man and not it of is an or to he

C. 3-Minute Timings

Take two 3-minute timings on lines 7–14. Proofread, note your errors, and figure your speed.

```
              1              2              3            4
7       Will Rogers was quoted as saying he never met a man he   12
          5        6             7              8
8  did not like.  This does not mean that Will Rogers met only  24
         9           10            11             12
9  charming people; it means that he expected to like all whom  36
            13          14            15            16
10 he met.  It was his outlook that made the difference, since  48
           17        18           19            20
11 he realized the value and worth of each person.  This is an  60
        21          22               23           24
12 outlook that could help all of us at school or at work.  If  72
          25               26             27          28
13 we decide to like those with whom we work, then all will be  84
        29           30                31           32
14 richer for it; try it for just one week and see the change.  96
   |  1  |  2  |  3  |  4  |  5  |  6  |  7  |  8  |  9  |  10  |  11  |  12 SI 1.21
```

D. Word Division and Capitalization Practice

Refer to pages 86 and 87 for word division rules.

Refer to pages 80, 91, 102, and 112 for capitalization rules.

Key lines 15–24. When you reach the italicized word or phrase in each sentence, decide whether it may be divided. If it may be divided, do so at the best division point; return, and complete the sentence. If it should not be divided, key it; return, and complete the sentence. Provide missing capitals. Double-space between sentences.

15 the major, ben guthrie, offered *congratulations* to the winner.
16 oleg works in chicago, but he *commutes* from arlington heights.
17 cole was sent to the wrong *department* for an interview monday.
18 joyce was referred to *dr. marshall* with those fainting spells.
19 dominique's brother moved to *1909 holland drive* last november.
20 josey tried to find her *father-in-law* a size 17 shirt tuesday.
21 he saw 8,000 elk on the open range as he *toured* the northwest.
22 mr. and mrs. w. a. turner will leave *january 17* on flight 632.
23 at la guardia we heard *mrs. cayla guinland* paged from gate 31.
24 pressure was on their *quarterback* to lead his team to victory.

Refer to page 64 for horizontal centering and page 69 for vertical centering.

Centering C16.49 Announcement

Center vertically and horizontally in one column. Double-space. Use print enhancements.

```
The Precision Drill Team of      7:30 p.m.
SELFRIDGE HIGH SCHOOL            Matinee Performance
Proudly Presents                Sunday, April 28
A DECADE OF DANCE IN REVIEW      2:30 p.m.
Evening Performances            $3 for Adults
Friday and Saturday, April 26–27 $2 for Students
```

Take a 5-minute timing on lines 5–21. Proofread, note your errors, and figure your speed.

```
 5          Regardless of the type of job you have or the work you    12
                    3                      4
 6   do, it is quite important that you manage your time so that       24
          5                        6
 7   you can get more work accomplished.  It is not possible for       36
                          8                      9
 8   us to reuse time; therefore, we should organize our work so       48
                10                11                    12
 9   that the maximum is accomplished.  We have to remember that       60
                        13                    14
10   time can't be stolen, nor can we borrow it from others.  We       72
                15                        16
11   have to recognize that once it is gone, we can never get it       84
          17
12   back.                                                             85
                          18                        19
13          Two suggestions that may be employed for improving our     97
                    20                        21
14   use of time are not that difficult to put to good use.  For      109
      22                          23                      24
15   example, we can write down those jobs we wish to accomplish      121
                          25                26
16   that particular day.  This activity will take just a moment      133
                27                              28                29
17   or two, and we should use the beginning of each day for it.      145
                                  30                      31
18   The above suggestion can be a very powerful tool for saving      157
                        32                      33
19   time.  Another suggestion is to prioritize the list so that      169
          34                        35                      36
20   the most essential items are placed at the top.  Therefore,      181
                        37                          38
21   the critical jobs will be accomplished first.                    190
   |  1  |  2  |  3  |  4  |  5  |  6  |  7  |  8  |  9  |  10  |  11  |  12  SI 1.38
```

In the chart below find the number of errors you made on the Pretest. Then key each of the following designated drill lines three times.

Pretest errors	0–1	2–3	4–5	6+
Drill lines	25–29	24–28	23–27	22–26

Accuracy

```
22  possible organize important beginning accomplish regardless
23  remember employed recognize improving particular prioritize
24  activity powerful therefore essential difficult suggestions
25  quite borrows maximum example another critical accomplished
```

Speed

```
26  manage should reuse can't type have work that the you of or
27  stolen others never first your time more from can not do it
28  moment saving write items once gone back good for may so us
29  placed employ those above down jobs wish this top use to we
```

Take another 5-minute timing on lines 5–21. Proofread, note your errors, and figure your speed. Compare your performance with the Pretest.

Refer to page 81 for hanging-indented enumerations.

Refer to pages 92, 103, and 113 for proofreaders' marks.

Report R16.49 Enumeration

Hanging-indented style. Format: 1-inch side margins, 2-inch top margin, 4-space indent.

ZEBULON CORPORATION EMPLOYEE POLICIES _center_

1. All employees are ~~expected~~ to dress profesionally. Bluejeans are not appropriate atire.

SS
2. One 15-minute break may be taken in the morning and one in the afternoon. The employee may decide ~~exactly when~~ _what time_ to take these breaks.

3. Employees who have been with the company from ① to ⑤ years receive two weeks' paid vacation. Those who have been with the company over five years receive ③ weeks paid vacation.

4. Each employee receives ⑤ paid sickdays per year. These days can be accumulated and used at the discretion of the employee. Unused ~~sick~~ days may be "cashed in" upon retirement.

5. An exercise room, ~~is~~ _and an indoor jogging track are_ available to all employees. Hours and ~~schedules~~ are posted outside.

DS
6. All employees may use the Company Cafeteria, which is open from 7:00 a.m. to 7:00 p.m. monday through friday.

Report R17.49 Outline

Refer to page 84 for formatting outlines.

Format: 1-inch side margins, 2-inch top margin. Set appropriate tab stops. Remember to bold appropriate lines.

HOW TO MAKE DECISIONS ON THE JOB
I. DETERMINE WHAT CHOICES YOU HAVE.
A. Make use of all available reference materials.
1. Check company policy manuals.
2. Go to the company library or files.
B. Ask your co-workers and your supervisors questions.
C. Be observant and pay close attention in meetings.
II. DO NOT MAKE DECISIONS HASTILY.
A. If there is doubt about which decision to make, it is usually better to postpone making the decision.
B. Decisions based on emotions are usually not the best ones.
1. If you are angry, allow enough time to consider things calmly.
2. You will risk losing others' respect if you act impulsively.

(Continued on next page)

Memo M2.103
Standard format.

MEMO TO: Cary Stephens, department head /

FROM: Ben Grifith, Dean / DATE: (Apr.) 15,

19-- / SUBJECT: Executive Meeting / Our

next Executive Meeting will be held on

April
~~March~~ 22, and (I'd) like *you* to present your re-

port from the Computer (Committee Selection)

at that time. Please bring ~~a minimum of~~

20 copies of your report to the meeting,

as I have invited other selected Depart-

ment Heads to attend the meeting. ¶ I

ap*p*reciates all the hard work (you've) put

into this project; I look forward to hear-

next week
ing your report ~~on the 22d.~~ / [*Your*

initials]

Memo M3.103
Standard format.

MEMO TO: Rachael Quam / FROM:
Cary Stephens / DATE: April 17, 19__ /
SUBJECT: April 22 Executive Meeting /
As you know, Dean Griffith sched-
uled me to report to the Executive
Committee the findings of our
Computer Selection Committee.
Would you please make available
an overhead projector and screen
for my presentation because I have
a number of transparencies to show.
/ [Your initials]

Lesson 104

Objectives   Correct errors in subject-verb agreement while keying sentences.
Format and use boilerplate forms for memos.
Reinforce transcribing from dictation.
Key 38/5'/5e.

Format   Spacing: Drills, single; Timings, double; and as required
Margins: Default or as required

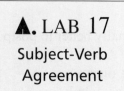

▲. LAB 17
Subject-Verb Agreement

Key lines 1–4 once, correcting any errors in subject-verb agreement rules. Review your copy as your teacher reads the answers. Then key lines 1–4 again from your edited copy.

1 Kimberley want to go to New Hampshire after she graduates.
2 They needs to sign the receipts before the check is written.
3 Sheryl always finishes her work no later than the deadline.
4 The managers needs to meet with their employees on April 24.

III. EVALUATE YOUR DECISIONS OBJECTIVELY.

A. Keep an open mind when you are considering the consequences of your decisions.

B. Learn from past decisions you have made.

1. Evaluate the results of each decision you make.

2. If something good can be learned from having made a poor decision, that experience has value.

Lesson 50

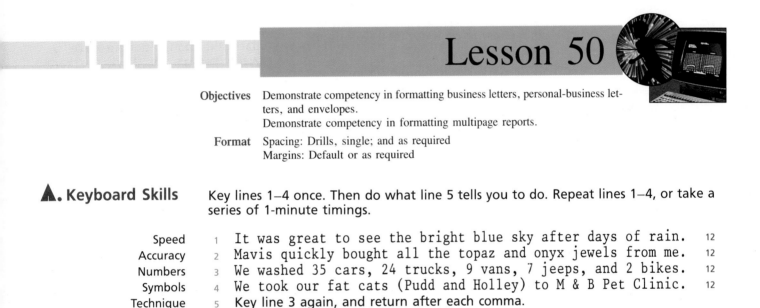

Objectives Demonstrate competency in formatting business letters, personal-business letters, and envelopes.
Demonstrate competency in formatting multipage reports.

Format Spacing: Drills, single; and as required
Margins: Default or as required

▲. Keyboard Skills

Key lines 1–4 once. Then do what line 5 tells you to do. Repeat lines 1–4, or take a series of 1-minute timings.

Speed	1	It was great to see the bright blue sky after days of rain.	12
Accuracy	2	Mavis quickly bought all the topaz and onyx jewels from me.	12
Numbers	3	We washed 35 cars, 24 trucks, 9 vans, 7 jeeps, and 2 bikes.	12
Symbols	4	We took our fat cats (Pudd and Holley) to M & B Pet Clinic.	12
Technique	5	Key line 3 again, and return after each comma.

| 1 | 2 | 3 | 4 | 5 | 6 | 7 | 8 | 9 | 10 | 11 | 12

Refer to pages 110 and 111 for formatting business letters.

Business Letter L14.50
Block style. No. 10 envelope.

June 14, 19— / Ms. Mary Jo Schattel / 808 Minette Road / Bon Secour, AL 36511 / Dear Ms. Schattel: / Miss Heather Collins, a former office education student of yours, has applied for a job as a word processing operator with us and has listed you as a reference. ¶ The position is for a person with at least six months of word processing experience. It will require use of all text-editing functions of a word processor to produce quality documents. Good language arts and proofreading skills are imperative. ¶ Would you please fill out the enclosed form and return it in the postage-paid envelope? In the last section of the form, please comment on Miss Collins' ability to take initiative and accept responsibility in her work. / Yours very truly, / Mrs. Latitia Wilson / Personnel Director / [*Your initials*] / 2 Enclosures

B. 12-Second Timings

Take three 12-second timings on each line, or key each line three times. Try to key with no more than 1 error on each timing.

5   Rick is sure the sun will shine all day long for our party.
6   I need to run to the store to pick up some fruit and chips.
7   We should get that dust off the printers as soon as we can.

```
       5    10   15   20   25   30   35   40   45   50   55   60
```

C. Memos

Memos are letters written to people in the same organization or business. Less formal than letters, memos do not have salutations or closing lines. Memos have a special heading that includes the guide words *MEMO TO:*, *FROM:*, *DATE:*, and *SUBJECT:*. When keyed on a computer, memos are usually prepared on plain paper or on letterhead. To format a memo:

1. Use default side margins (1 inch).

2. Begin the heading of the memo on line 13 (2 inches from the top edge).

3. Key the guide words at the left margin, double-spaced and in all caps.

4. Key the information following the guide words 10 spaces from the margin (2 spaces after *MEMO TO:*). Set a tab.

5. Triple-space between the heading and the body of the memo. Single-space the body; double-space between paragraphs. Block the paragraphs.

6. Key any notations a double space below the body, beginning at the left margin.

↓13

GUIDE WORDS
In all caps; tab 10 for copy that follows.

```
MEMO TO:   Chris Johnson, Department Head

FROM:      Rebecca Miller, Personnel Manager

DATE:      March 15, 19--

SUBJECT:   Interview Dates ↓3
```

BODY
Single-spaced; paragraphs blocked.

```
The interviews for the candidates who have applied for the sales
position in our Bowling Green office have been scheduled for
March 27, 28, and 29.

Please let me know if you have any conflicts with these dates by
completing and returning the enclosed form. ↓2
```

NOTATIONS
At left margin.

```
[Your initials]
Enclosure
```

Memo M1.103
Key the memo illustrated above.

Refer to pages 99 and 100 for formatting personal-business letters.

Personal-Business Letter L15.50
Block style. No. 10 envelope.

June 18, 19— / Mrs. Latitia Wilson / Personnel Director / Manchester Manufacturing / 5515 Westdale Drive / Mobile, AL 36693 / Dear Mrs. Wilson: / It is a pleasure to recommend Heather Collins for the position of word processing operator with your firm. Heather was in the office education laboratory her junior year and in the office education cooperative program her senior year; she was an outstanding student. ¶ As a participant in the cooperative program, Heather attended morning classes and worked as a word processing trainee for Foley Modular Home Manufacturing Company in the afternoons. Her employer was exceptionally pleased with Heather's work. ¶ The attached form shows that Heather's office skills are well above average. I know that she would do an excellent job as a word processing operator. / Sincerely yours, / Ms. Mary Jo Schattel / 808 Minette Road / Bon Secour, AL 36511 / Attachment

Refer to page 95 for formatting multipage academic reports.

Academic Report R18.50
Standard format.

Last Name 1 / Student / Teacher / Class / Date / Time Management / People today seem to be so busy that they do not have adequate time to do all the things that cry out for them to do. By managing your time properly, though, you will find that you can get more accomplished as well as relieve the stress of not meeting your deadlines. ¶ Begin by listing the things that need to be done for one day and estimating the time each task will take. When you feel comfortable planning for one day, you may want to expand to weekly or monthly master plans and break these down into daily lists. As each task is finished, be sure to cross it off your list. This not only serves as documentation of what is left to do but also is a source of encouragement, showing what you have accomplished. ¶ Group the jobs by some common factor—perhaps by urgency, difficulty, or length. Plan to do the most strenuous or stressful jobs during the time of day when you are most productive. For example, if you are a "lark" (a morning person), tackle the hard jobs before the middle of the afternoon. If you are an "owl" (a night person), start with the easier jobs and save the difficult ones for later in the day. ¶ Make your schedule flexible. When you least expect—or need—them, interruptions will nearly always occur. If you will break big projects down into smaller tasks and begin working on them early enough, you will be able to handle the unexpected hindrances when they arise and still get your job finished on time. ¶ Using these techniques to manage your time will increase your efficiency and make your days go better. Just looking over your list of accomplishments at the end of the day will energize you and give you a better outlook on life.

Letter L62.102

Modified-block style. Use the address of Letter L61.102, but send this letter to the attention of Sales Manager. Key the attention line as part of the inside address.

[Today's date] Ladies and Gentlemen: / Subject: Close-Out Sale / You will be pleased to hear that we have decided to close out our line of Star tennis shoes. Therefore, we are sending you this final shipment at a 30 percent discount. This is a substantial savings of $700 on your order of 20 pairs of shoes.

Thank you for doing business with us. If we can assist you in any other way, please do not hesitate to call. / (Same closing as in Letter L61.102.)

Letter L63.102

Modified-block style, with attention line keyed as a separate line. Correct any errors in punctuation and subject-verb agreement.

February 10, 19— / Parnelli Department Store / 604 Main Street / Wayne, NE 68787 / Attention: Computer Sales Department / Ladies and Gentlemen: / Subject: Purchase Order 2516 / The computer ribbons you ordered on February 5 (No. R246 and No. R250) are not in stock at this time. If you would like we will order substitute ribbons of the same quality and price. ¶ On page 73 of the enclosed catalog is a complete description of the substitute ribbons. After reviewing the description please let me know if this substitution is satisfactory to you. ¶ Let me remind you of our spring sale that will be held from March 10 through March 17. We are giving our preferred customers this opportunity to get in on some terrific bargains. We hopes to see you at that time. / Sincerely yours, / Darlene Stone, Manager / Order Department / [*Your initials*] / Enclosure

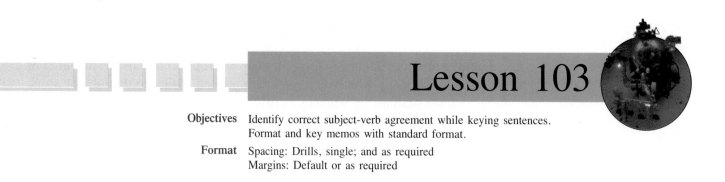

Lesson 103

Objectives   Identify correct subject-verb agreement while keying sentences.
Format and key memos with standard format.

Format   Spacing: Drills, single; and as required
Margins: Default or as required

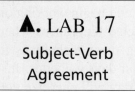

▲. LAB 17
Subject-Verb Agreement

Key lines 1–4 once. Then repeat lines 1–4, or take a series of 1-minute timings.

[P] 1   Six runners from our high school <u>race</u> in the March 7 event.   12
[S] 2   One runner from our high school <u>races</u> in the March 7 event.   12
[S] 3   Ashley <u>orders</u> all her supplies from the Maple Street store.   12
[P] 4   They <u>order</u> all their supplies from the Garner Street store.   12

| 1 | 2 | 3 | 4 | 5 | 6 | 7 | 8 | 9 | 10 | 11 | 12

Level 3

The use of the computer in the aerospace industry is growing every day. In addition to space exploration, the computer is used in the following areas: aircraft design, flight simulation, and noise analysis. Computation acoustics predict where noise comes from (inside the aircraft), and noise footprints deal with how noise affects surrounding areas (outside the aircraft).

Goals

1. Demonstrate keyboarding speed and accuracy on straight copy with a goal of 35 words a minute for 3 minutes with 5 or fewer errors.
2. Correctly proofread copy for errors and edit copy for revision.
3. Demonstrate basic formatting skills on reports, correspondence, and tables for personal use from a variety of input modes—arranged, unarranged, rough draft, and handwritten.
4. Apply rules for correct use of numbers and commas in written communication.

B. PRETEST

Take a 1-minute timing on lines 5–8. Proofread, note your errors, and figure your speed.

```
5        You should join many who have learned how to use their    12
6   keying skills on the job.  These skills can be used in many    24
7   walks of life, and they are just what you will need to help    36
8   you succeed.                                                   38
    |  1  |  2  |  3  |  4  |  5  |  6  |  7  |  8  |  9  |  10  |  11  |  12
```

C. PRACTICE

SPEED: If you made 2 or fewer errors on the Pretest, key lines 9–14 twice each. Repeat if time permits.
ACCURACY: If you made more than 2 errors on the Pretest, key lines 9–11 as a group twice. Then key lines 12–14 as a group twice. Repeat if time permits.

Left-hand Reaches

```
9    cdc cod clad cord cedar crowd cloud cadet child crude cider
10   wew wet week weed weave swear where worse weigh wheat wheel
11   ded den dear deaf dread greed horde stead adept defer dried
```

Right-hand Reaches

```
12   klk klk folk walk ankle silky balky milky links polka stalk
13   jhj just huge join harm joist hunch jumpy house judge heart
14   uyu your duly yule duty lucky young youth dusty yucca murky
```

D. POSTTEST

Take a 1-minute timing on lines 5–8. Proofread, note your errors, and figure your speed. Compare your performance with the Pretest.

E. Subject Lines

A subject line briefly identifies the main topic of a letter.

To format a subject line:

1. Key the subject line in initial caps at the left margin between the salutation and the body. Double-space before and after the subject line.

2. Follow the word *Subject* with a colon and 2 spaces.

```
Dear Ms. King:

Subject:  Battlefield Charity Dance

I am pleased that you thought of our firm in
tion with your charity dance.  We have found
```

Letter L61.102
Block style.

[*Today's date*] / Mr. ~~Stephen~~ *Steve* McDuffie / The Pro Shop Store / 1435 Farington St. / Honolulu, HI 96822 / Dear Mr. McDuffie: / Subject: New-idea Shoes / Since my visit to your store last month, we've aquired a new line of tennis shoes, the "New-idea" shoes. These shoes should sell especially well to ~~the young~~ tennis play-ers, because we can offer them in sizes from 5 to 13. Please call me at 808-555-8675 if you would like me to send you some samples for display. / Sincerely, / Karen Cobb / Sales Representative / [*Your initials*]

Lesson 51

Objectives   Reinforce tab skills.
Format two-column tables with titles.

Format   Spacing: Drills, single; and as required
Margins: Default or as required

A. Keyboard Skills

Key lines 1–4 once. Then do what line 5 tells you to do. Repeat lines 1–4, or take a series of 1-minute timings.

Speed	1	Jim would like to work for a bank while he goes to college.	12
Accuracy	2	Buzz quickly designed five new projects for the wax museum.	12
Numbers	3	We had 546 eagles here in 1973; but by 1990 there were 823.	12
Symbols	4	That Roland & Davidson report (#14) showed a 25% increase.*	12
Technique	5	Center the words in line 2 under each other. Single-space.	

| 1 | 2 | 3 | 4 | 5 | 6 | 7 | 8 | 9 | 10 | 11 | 12

B. 30-Second Timings

Take two 30-second timings on lines 6 and 7. Then take two 30-second timings on lines 8 and 9. Try to key with no more than 2 errors on each timing.

6   When the batter heard that sound of breaking glass, he knew   12
7   without even looking that the home run had truly gone home.   24

8   Race to finish these lines before the teacher says to stop.   12
9   Make those fingers glide over the keys like little skaters.   24

| 1 | 2 | 3 | 4 | 5 | 6 | 7 | 8 | 9 | 10 | 11 | 12

C. Tab Key

A technique drill.

Clear all tab stops; then set three tab stops, one every 10 spaces. Key lines 10–14; single-space. Repeat if time permits.

10	choose	chose	chosen	choosing
11	see	saw	seen	seeing
12	do	did	done	doing
13	lay	laid	laid	laying
14	lie	lay	lain	lying

D. Tables

Some information that might be included in a report is easier to understand if it is arranged in columns rather than in sentences. These columnar reports are called *tabulations* or *tables*. The basic parts of a table are discussed in the illustration on page 123.

your first and second preferences for a particular space at the conference we look forward to receiving your booth preferences thank you for deciding to join the many exhibitors who have chosen to participate in our conference sincerely yours karen springfield conference chairperson [*Your initials*] enclosure

Letter L60.101

Retrieve Letter L59.101 and make the changes below. Key the attention line as part of the inside address.

1. *Change the format to modified-block style with indented paragraphs.*
2. *Change the address to* Attention: Mr. James Doran / Estes Software House / 10532 Steele Street / Butte, MT 59702.
3. *Change the price range of the exhibit booths to* $75 to $125.
4. *Delete the final paragraph, and replace it with the following:* Please return your preference sheet by June 1 to guarantee your reservation for one of the booths.

Lesson 102

Objectives   Recognize correct subject-verb agreement while keying sentences.
Reinforce skill on left-hand and right-hand reaches.
Format and key letters with subject lines.
Reinforce letters with attention lines.

Format   Spacing: Drills, single; Timings, double; and as required
Margins: Default or as required

▲. LAB 17

Subject-Verb Agreement

Key lines 1–4 once. Then repeat lines 1–4, or take a series of 1-minute timings.

[S] 1   We believe Connie McElroy <u>knows</u> the answer to the problems.   12
[P] 2   The employees <u>want</u> all <u>managers</u> to take part in the events.   12
[S] 3   Blake Lanier <u>begins</u> his conditioning session on February 1.   12
[P] 4   Many of the <u>students</u> <u>talk</u> with their principal after class.   12

  | 1 | 2 | 3 | 4 | 5 | 6 | 7 | 8 | 9 | 10 | 11 | 12

1. A verb must agree with its subject in number and person. The letter *s* is usually added to a verb to indicate the third person singular.

	Singular	Plural
First person	I run.	We run.
Second person	You run.	You run.
Third person	He, She, or It *runs*.	They run.
	A child *runs*.	Children run.

A plural verb is always required after *you,* even when *you* is singular.

Correct: You [meaning "one"] run fast. *Wrong:* You runs fast.

BASIC PARTS OF A TABLE

TITLE. Identifies contents of table. Center and key in all-capital letters.

BODY. Consists of columns in the table. Center horizontally, usually with 6 spaces between columns. Single- or double-space.

COLUMNS. Listings of information. Align columns of words at the left.

CLASS SCHEDULE

↓3

First Period   Accounting

Second Period   English IV

Third Period   Information Processing

Fourth Period   World History

Fifth Period   Economics

Sixth Period   Computer Science

Seventh Period   Choir

Reminder: If you cannot set variable spacing within a document, use a double space after the title.

To format a table:

① **Prepare for Formatting.** Clear all tabs; use default margins.

② **Select the Guide Line.** The guide line consists of the longest item in each column plus 6 blank spaces for each open area between columns.

③ **Set Tab Stops.** Key the guide line; then use the automatic centering function to center the line. Set tab stops for each column. Use a left tab for word columns, which align on the left. When all tabs are set, delete the guide line.

Make sure you do not delete the codes for the tabs when you delete the guide line.

④ **Compute the Top Margin.** Center the table vertically (subtract the number of lines in the table from the number of lines on the page and divide by 2 to determine the top margin), or use the center page (top-to-bottom) command.

⑤ **Key the Table.** Center the title in all caps and bold. Leave 2 blank lines between the title and the body.

Practice. Center the table below. Use double spacing.

KEYING TABLES

Always   key
the   body
of   a
table   line
by   line.

	Tab	Tab
	↓	↓
GUIDE LINE:	Always	line.
	123456	

Letter L58.101
Modified-block style. Key the attention line as part of the inside address.

[*Today's date*] / Attention: Personnel Director / Western Personnel Services / 3486 Thomas Drive / Boulder, CO 80330 / Ladies and Gentlemen: / I am writing to you for your assistance in finding a candidate for our Education and Training Director position that has now been vacant for 6 months. The position announcement enclosed and the paragraph that follows will give you some detail as to the type of person we are seeking. ¶ The individual who will fill this position must have a bachelor's degree in a related area such as education or psychology. We require a minimum of 5 years' experience in a computer-related position, since our major thrust in the next 5 years will be for that person to direct our education program for computer literacy throughout our 5 districts. This person should be enthusiastic and present himself or herself well in front of groups. Please call me immediately at 303-555-8902 when you have found a suitable candidate. / Sincerely yours, / Candace Mallory / Vice president / [*Your initials*] / Enclosure

D. Transcribing From Dictated Copy

Much of the material in this program might normally be transcribed from shorthand notes or a machine transcriber, but it will be presented here in typeset unarranged copy and will be labeled "Dictated letter," "Dictated report," and so on. You will have to supply capitalization, punctuation, and paragraphing. You will also have to check spelling; many words sound alike but are spelled differently.

Letter L59.101
Dictated letter. Block style. Key the attention line as a separate line.

[*Today's date*] procom computer store 4217 ridgeview drive lincoln nebraska 68506 attention marketing director ladies and gentlemen we were delighted to receive your reservation for exhibitor space for the 10th annual national business education conference to be held in rochester new york at the carlton in exhibitors can choose one of three different exhibit booths ranging in price from $100 to $300 just check the appropriate square on the enclosed form to indicate your preference at the bottom of the form is a floor layout of all booth spaces and you can indicate

(Continued on next page)

Table T1.51
Double spacing.

BEST-SELLING PAPERBACKS

Animal Farm	Orwell
Baby and Child Care	Spock
Love Story	Segal
The Pearl	Steinbeck
The Thorn Birds	McCullough

	↓Tab	↓Tab
GUIDE LINE:	Baby and Child Care	McCullough
	123456	

Table T2.51
Single spacing.

STATE NICKNAMES

Arizona	Grand Canyon State
Arkansas	Land of Opportunity
Georgia	Peach State
Hawaii	The Aloha State
Maine	Pine Tree State
Missouri	Show Me State
New York	The Empire State
Rhode Island	Ocean State
Tennessee	Volunteer State
Washington	Evergreen State

Table T3.51
Double spacing.

OFFICE TECHNOLOGY OFFICERS

Kathy Birlew	President
LaRhonda March	Vice President
Angel Roach	Secretary
Marcus Wilson	Treasurer
Vivian Ray	Reporter
Holly McEvoy	Historian
Benny Payne	Parliamentarian

UNIT 15

Correspondence

Unit Goal 38/5'/5e

Lesson 101

Objectives Format letters and envelopes with attention lines.
Transcribe from "dictated" copy.

Format Drills, single; and as required
Margins: Default or as required

A. Keyboard Skills

Key lines 1–4 once. In line 5 use the caps lock key for each word in all-capital letters. Repeat lines 1–4, or take a series of 1-minute timings.

Speed 1 Go to the bay and try your luck at fishing by the new dock. 12
Accuracy 2 A frozen bird squawked vigorously as Joseph coaxed him out. 12
Numbers 3 We paid our bills for $10, $29, $138, $247, $356, and $478. 12
Symbols 4 At last! We will own over 1/2 of the stock (51%) @ $23.75. 12
Technique 5 Drive to ALAMO, not to BUTTE or BEULAH or COLFAX or CROSBY.

| 1 | 2 | 3 | 4 | 5 | 6 | 7 | 8 | 9 | 10 | 11 | 12

B. "OK" Timings

Take two 30-second "OK" (errorless) timings on lines 6–7. Then take two 30-second "OK" timings on lines 8–9. Goal: No errors.

6 They amazed six judges by quietly giving back four pages so 12
7 that all the right changes would be made in the next draft. 24

8 The exits were quickly filled by dozens of villagers who we 12
9 knew were trying to jump over the barricades to the booths. 24

| 1 | 2 | 3 | 4 | 5 | 6 | 7 | 8 | 9 | 10 | 11 | 12

C. Attention Lines

When a letter is addressed directly to a company, an attention line may be used to route it to a particular person or department. One of two formats may be used for an attention line in a letter:

(1) **As a separate line.** Key the attention line in initial caps at the left margin; double-space before and after it. Use a colon after the word *Attention*.

(2) **As part of the inside address.** Key the attention line on the first line of the inside address. Use a colon after the word *Attention*.

With an attention line, use an organizational salutation such as *Ladies and Gentlemen:, Gentlemen:,* or *Ladies:.*
On an envelope, key the attention line on the first line of the mailing address.

Note: The use of an attention line is decreasing. If the name of the person to whom the letter is directed is known, many companies prefer to have the letter addressed directly to that person.

```
Hammonds Industries
7832 Lilac Lane
Green Bay, WI 54302

Attention:   Sales Manager

Ladies and Gentlemen:
```

```
Attention:   Sales Manager
Hammonds Industries
7832 Lilac Lane
Green Bay, WI 54302

Ladies and Gentlemen:
```

Lesson 52

Objectives Recognize how numbers are expressed in sentences.
Reinforce adjacent and jump reaches.
Format tables with subtitles.

Format Spacing: Drills, single; Timings, double; and as required
Margins: Default or as required

A. LAB 5
Number Style

Key lines 1–4 once. Then repeat lines 1–4, or take a series of 1-minute timings.

```
1   Jan's order was for six legal pads and seven dozen pencils.   12
2   There are 539 students and 68 faculty members at this camp.   12
3   Seventeen members of the committee voted to adopt the book.   12
4   That passageway is exactly 9.5 feet long and 4.8 feet wide.   12
    |  1  |  2  |  3  |  4  |  5  |  6  |  7  |  8  |  9  | 10  | 11  | 12
```

1. Spell out numbers from *1* through *10*; use figures for numbers above *10*. (**Exception:** Spell out any number that begins a sentence.)

Only *three* walls have been painted.
Send *20* brochures and *65* order forms to Modlin.
Nineteen applications were processed today.

2. In technical copy and for emphasis, use figures for numbers: *2 liters, 7.5 miles, 6 spaces, 4 lines, page 5, $8.*

B. PRETEST

Take a 1-minute timing on lines 5–7. Proofread, note your errors, and figure your speed.

```
5       We have three memos for Miles Porter, Esq., but he was   12
6   seen only once since the middle of last fall; at that time,   24
7   he had completed a cruise across Hudson Bay.                  33
    |  1  |  2  |  3  |  4  |  5  |  6  |  7  |  8  |  9  | 10  | 11  | 12
```

C. PRACTICE

SPEED: If you made 2 or fewer errors on the Pretest, key lines 8–13 twice each. Repeat if time permits.
ACCURACY: If you made more than 2 errors on the Pretest, key lines 8–10 as a group twice. Then key lines 11–13 as a group twice. Repeat if time permits.

Adjacent Reaches

```
8   l; pal; ail; oil; fall; toil; will; poll; veil; pull; mall;
9   rt fort sort port warts carts darts dirty hurts marts parts
10  ., jr., sr., pp., Mrs., Wed., Oct., Fri., Dec., Esq., Inc.,
```

Jump Reaches

```
11  cr crew crib crop cries craze craft crawl crown crisp crash
12  mi mile mist mill might mince mirth mixed smile limit admit
13  ce pace once lace cease niece place juice brace since voice
```

D. POSTTEST

Take a 1-minute timing on lines 5–7. Proofread, note your errors, and figure your speed. Compare your performance with the Pretest.

Level 5

Underwater fault lines are monitored and underwater earthquakes are recorded by computers used for oceanographic seismology. Computers in oceanography also are used to calculate both the direction and speed of ocean currents. Oceanographers also work closely with weather forecasters.

Goals

1. Demonstrate keyboarding speed and accuracy on straight copy with a goal of 39 words a minute for 5 minutes with 5 or fewer errors.
2. Correctly proofread copy for errors and edit copy for revision.
3. Apply more advanced production skills in keyboarding and formatting copy for business documents from a variety of input modes, including simulated dictation.
4. Apply rules for subject/verb agreement, pronoun/antecedent agreement, and spelling in written communications.

E. Subtitles in Tables

Subtitles in tables are formatted the same way as subtitles in other documents: (1) Center the subtitles. (2) Double-space before and triple-space after subtitles. (3) Use initial caps. Single-space a subtitle if it takes more than one line.

Table T4.52
Double spacing.

SOME ENDANGERED ANIMALS

Worldwide Species ↓3

↓2

Bactrian camel	China
Black rhinoceros	Africa
Bobcat	Central Mexico
Cheetah	India
Giant panda	China
Gorilla	West Africa
Howler monkey	South America
Mountain zebra	South Africa
Tiger	Asia

Table T5.52
Double spacing.

COMPUTER ACRONYMS

Terms Used Frequently
by Computer Operators

bps	Bits per second
cps	Characters per second
CPU	Central processing unit
CRT	Cathode ray tube
EDP	Electronic data processing
I/O	Input/output
K	Kilobyte (1,024 bytes)
LAN	Local area network
OCR	Optical character reader
RAM	Random-access memory
ROM	Read-only memory
VDT	Video display terminal

Table T6.52
Single spacing; leave 1 blank line after every three entries.

HOME TEAMS IN VARIOUS STATES
Arranged Alphabetically by City

Atlanta	Falcons	Georgia
Buffalo	Bills	New York
Chicago	Bears	Illinois
Cincinnati	Bengals	Ohio
Houston	Oilers	Texas
Miami	Dolphins	Florida
Pittsburgh	Steelers	Pennsylvania
San Francisco	49ers	California
Seattle	Seahawks	Washington

Table T48.100
Ruled format; double spacing. Center column headings.

REFRIGERATOR SALE
SHANNON MALL

MODEL NUMBER	STORE PRICE	SALE DISCOUNT	SALE PRICE
R255F746	$1,649.99	10%	$1,484.99
R255F801	1,210.49	8%	1,113.65
R254G639	985.25	11%	876.87
R254G273	735.99	10%	662.39
R253T701	449.99	12%	395.99

Report R46.100
Business format.

SOFTWARE UNLIMITED

Business Plan

Introduction

This business plan will present the steps necessary to open a new software store in Douglasville, at the corner of Chapel Hill Road and Creekwood Drive. Also included in this discussion will be a projected time frame for completing the preliminary steps.

Preliminary Steps

Preliminary steps necessary to open the new software store are listed in the following paragraphs. The time frame for completing each of these steps is identified at the conclusion of each of the paragraphs.

Securing a Loan. It has been estimated that $50,000 will be required to cover the initial expenses for opening the store. This loan will be used to cover renovation charges on the building that has been purchased, to stock our inventory, and to cover necessary administrative start-up costs. The loan will be obtained from Trust Company Bank. It is estimated that two weeks will be required for processing the loan.

Obtaining a License. A business license must be obtained from the city of Douglasville. Since the City Council will be meeting on the 15th, it is estimated that this step can be concluded within one week.

Operational Steps

These steps will be taken after the loan has been secured and the license has been granted. After they have been completed, Software Unlimited will be ready for our Grand Opening sale.

Purchasing Inventory. Software products will be obtained from the Soft Warehouse in Atlanta, a wholesaler for both business and entertainment software. Additional items will be purchased from the Software Catalog out of Indianapolis, Indiana.

Interviewing/Hiring. Interviews for all sales staff positions will be conducted during the weeks of June 10 and June 17. It is anticipated that the hiring of all employees will be completed by July 1 so that our Grand Opening sale can be held on July 4, 5, and 6.

Advertising. We will advertise our Grand Opening sale on KDFW radio in Douglasville and on KATL in Atlanta. We will also run several ads in the local newspapers and prepare several fliers to be distributed at the local shopping malls.

Lesson 53

Objectives Identify how numbers are expressed in sentences.
Format tables with subtitles and numbers.

Format Spacing: Drills, single; and as required
Margins: Default or as required

▲. LAB 5
Number Style

Key lines 1–4 once. Then repeat lines 1–4, or take a series of 1-minute timings.

1 Ninety-eight students will tour Europe for four long weeks. 12
2 Try to mix 11.5 liters of liquid with 17.5 grams of powder. 12
3 We purchased 15 pairs of socks, 11 jackets, and 23 scarves. 12
4 Yes, 47 of the 198 national scholars are from this college. 12
   | 1 | 2 | 3 | 4 | 5 | 6 | 7 | 8 | 9 | 10 | 11 | 12

B. "OK" Timings

Take two 30-second "OK" (errorless) timings on lines 5–6. Then take two 30-second "OK" timings on lines 7–8. Goal: No errors.

5 People make decisions every day; most are just routine, but 12
6 a few require exact thinking and logical analyzing ability. 24

7 The ability to analyze a problem and make complex decisions 12
8 is a major skill that we develop through frequent practice. 24
   | 1 | 2 | 3 | 4 | 5 | 6 | 7 | 8 | 9 | 10 | 11 | 12

C. Numbers in Columns

Tab Stops. You learned in Lesson 51 that words in columns align on the left. When aligning numbers, whole numbers in columns align on the right, decimal numbers align on the decimal point.

a. Use a **left tab** for word columns.

b. Use a **right tab** for columns consisting of whole numbers.

c. Use a **decimal tab** for number columns that contain decimal numbers.

Note: If your word processor does not have right and decimal tabs, set a left tab for the beginning of each column. Space in for shorter numbers. In the illustration at the right, the tab for the first column would be set for the beginning of the number 1,031. In the third column, the tab would be set for the $.

DUGAN'S DEPARTMENT STORE		
President's Sale ↓3 ↓2		
119	Blouses	$ 61.50
7	Leather coats	799.19
1,031	Scarves	8.89
57	Shirts	53.99
248	Sweaters	39.57
↑ Right Tab	↑ Left Tab	↑ Decimal Tab

Right Tab A right tab causes text to move to the left as it is keyed. For example, as the number 119 is keyed, it will automatically move 3 spaces to the left of the tab. Therefore, a right tab must be set 1 space to the right of where the column is to end. Using a right tab is ideal for any column that must align at the right.

Practice: Set appropriate tab stops at 40 and 50 (or 10 spaces apart) for keying columns 1 and 3 in the table illustrated above. Double-space. After keying the columns, check to see if the numbers align at the right.

Letter L56.100
Modified-block style.

September 9, 19-- / Ms. Thomas Claire / 498 Grant Road / Pueblo, CO 81006 / Dear Ms. Thomas:

Thank you for your subscription to creative ideas for the home. We have a special section in this coming issue devoted to the holidays season; the following themes are presented: 1. Lawn Ornaments for the Halloween Season; 2. Thanksgiving Decorations for Your Home; and 3. Making Christmas Tree Ornaments, A Treat for All of Your Family Members. Also in next month's issue we will have an interview with Dana Andrews, the noted home decorating consultant whose articles have appeared in the leading Home Magazines throughout the country.

We hope you'll experience many hours of enjoyable reading in Creative Ideas for the Home. Please call us or write us if for some reason you do not receive your first issue next month. / Sincerely, / Juanita Sanchez / Publisher / [Your initials] / c: Mary Carson

Block this enumeration

Letter L57.100
Use your own return address and today's date; modified-block style. Correct any errors in punctuation.

[Today's date] / Mr. Mark Haynes, Editor / Brown Publishing Company / 2189 Nelson Street / Richmond, VA 23228 / Dear Mr. Haynes:

Would you please send me a copy of your catalog Creative Ideas for the Home that was advertised in the June issue of Women's World. I have enclosed a check for $23.75 for a one-year subscription. ¶ I am sure Creative Ideas will give me many wonderful ideas for decorating my home. / Sincerely, / [Your name] / Enclosure

---

Table T47.100
Blocked headings. Standard format; double spacing.

SELECTED WORLD GRAIN PRODUCERS

(In Thousands of Metric Tons)

Country	Corn	Rice	Wheat
China	89.0	177.0	65.6
India	46.9	90.0	8.0
Pakistan	13.9	5.2	1.1
U.S.A.	56.8	6.1	209.6
Russia	92.3	2.6	12.5
Total	298.9	280.9	296.8

Table T7.53
Double spacing.

OFFICE ELECTRONICS
Equipment Inventory
July 1, 19—

Atlas color computers, 20-meg hard drive	2,706
Atlas electronic typewriters, Model 2060	394
Atlas laser printers	513
Banner copiers, Model 3800	8
REM dot matrix printers, NLQ	96
REM monochrome computers, dual disk drives	1,029
Swift electronic calculators, desk model	84
Tech electronic typewriters, Model 7040	257

Table T8.53
Double spacing.

PRICE DEPARTMENT STORE
Special Sale Prices

Bell sheet sets, king	$ 34.49
Flex exercise set	1,049.99
Jogman stereo	63.24
Lane television, 19-inch	198.93
Silver cookware, 8-piece	55.48

Table T9.53
Double spacing.

Key the table illustrated on page 127.

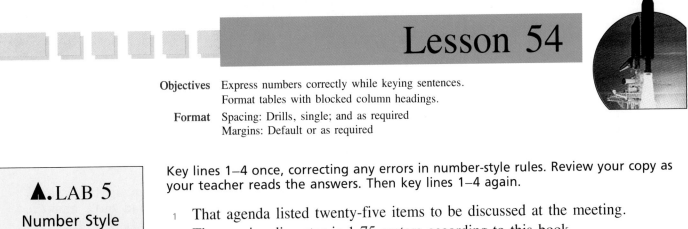

Lesson 54

Objectives Express numbers correctly while keying sentences.
Format tables with blocked column headings.

Format Spacing: Drills, single; and as required
Margins: Default or as required

▲.LAB 5
Number Style

Key lines 1–4 once, correcting any errors in number-style rules. Review your copy as your teacher reads the answers. Then key lines 1–4 again.

1 That agenda listed twenty-five items to be discussed at the meeting.
2 The precise diameter is 1.75 meters according to this book.
3 This order was for 10 computers, but they sent only 8.
4 537 teachers attended the convention.

Table T46.99
Standard format; single spacing.

CITY HIGH SCHOOLS

Enrollment Figures

Name of School	9th	10th	11th	12th
Central	237	215	220	246
Decatur	198	193	187	186
Winder	205	241	230	209
Winslow	247	253	261	238
Average	222	226	225	220

Report R45.99
Prepare the report in the column at the right. Use the following title and subtitle:

Title: **STATUS OF ENROLLMENT**

Subtitle: City High Schools

Enrollment for the city high schools stabilized this year, with the greatest number of students, 902, enrolled in the 10th grade. Total enrollment in all four schools was 3,566. This number represented an increase of 3 percent over enrollment in the previous school year.

Total enrollment by grade level for each of the city high schools is shown in Table 1 below.

[Retrieve Table T46.99 from your word processing or spreadsheet diskette, and place it in this area. Revise the final line of the table so that it reveals "Total" rather than "Average." Calculate the totals.]

Enrollment counts for each of the schools indicate that Winslow has the greatest number of students (999). Other school counts are as follows: Central, 918; Decatur, 764; and Winder, 885. Although Decatur has the lowest number of students enrolled, it has the greatest space problem. Decatur is the oldest of all the schools, and it has the least classroom space. Square footage per student at Decatur is 6 square feet below the average square footage per student for all other city high schools.

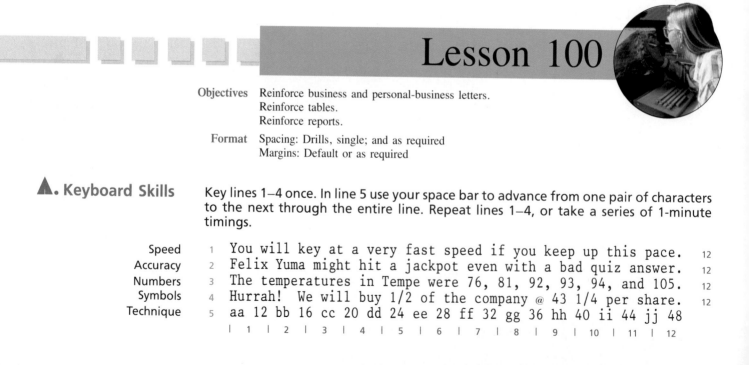

Lesson 100

Objectives   Reinforce business and personal-business letters.
Reinforce tables.
Reinforce reports.

Format   Spacing: Drills, single; and as required
Margins: Default or as required

▲. Keyboard Skills

Key lines 1–4 once. In line 5 use your space bar to advance from one pair of characters to the next through the entire line. Repeat lines 1–4, or take a series of 1-minute timings.

Speed   1   You will key at a very fast speed if you keep up this pace.   12
Accuracy   2   Felix Yuma might hit a jackpot even with a bad quiz answer.   12
Numbers   3   The temperatures in Tempe were 76, 81, 92, 93, 94, and 105.   12
Symbols   4   Hurrah! We will buy 1/2 of the company @ 43 1/4 per share.   12
Technique 5   aa 12 bb 16 cc 20 dd 24 ee 28 ff 32 gg 36 hh 40 ii 44 jj 48
            | 1 | 2 | 3 | 4 | 5 | 6 | 7 | 8 | 9 | 10 | 11 | 12

B. 12-Second Timings

Take three 12-second timings on each line, or key each line three times. Try to key with no more than 1 error on each timing.

```
 5  Tim had not studied for the college test he took last year.
 6  This time he has spent nine hours working on the math part.
 7  He hopes to get a much higher score than he made last time.
        5    10    15    20    25    30    35    40    45    50    55    60
```

C. Tables With Blocked Column Headings

Column headings help identify the data in each column of a table. Blocked headings are easy to format because the headings are keyed at the tab stops set for the columns. Blocked headings over a column of numbers block at the right—just like the numbers.

If the column heading is the longest item in the column (as shown in Table T10.54 below), it is selected for the guide line.

Key a column heading in initial caps and underscore it. Triple-space before and double-space after a column heading.

Note: If a column contains decimal numbers, use a right tab instead of a decimal tab. If a decimal tab is used, the column heading will align on the decimal.

Table T10.54
Double spacing.

MILEAGE CHART

U.S. and Canadian Cities ↓3

U.S. City	Canadian City	Miles ↓2
Anchorage	Vancouver	2,237
Chicago	Quebec	1,010
New York City	Montreal	382
Niagara Falls	Toronto	78
San Francisco	Winnipeg	1,951

Table T11.54
Double spacing.

LITTLE DUSTY HIGH SCHOOL

Faculty Room Assignments
September 1, 19—

Teacher	Course	Room
Baker, M.	Home Management	9
Cowling, D.	U.S. Government	57
Gorman, M.	Accounting	110
Jones, P.	Spanish II	1010
Pace, S.	English IV	307
Poole, P.	Nutrition	11
Samuels, R.	Music Appreciation	297
Winniford, J.	Biology	1016

Table T12.54
Double spacing.

ds [**ANTARCTICA EXPLORATIONS**
Expeditions to the South Pole

Year	Name	Mode of Travel
1772	Cook	ship
1908	Shackleton	Pony sledge
1911	Amundsen	Dog sled
1912	Scott Byrd	Dogsled
1928	Wilkins	Airplane
1929	Byrd	Airplane
1935	Ellsworth	Airplanes
1946	Rone	Airplane
1958	Thiel	Tractor
1989	Murden & Metz	Skis

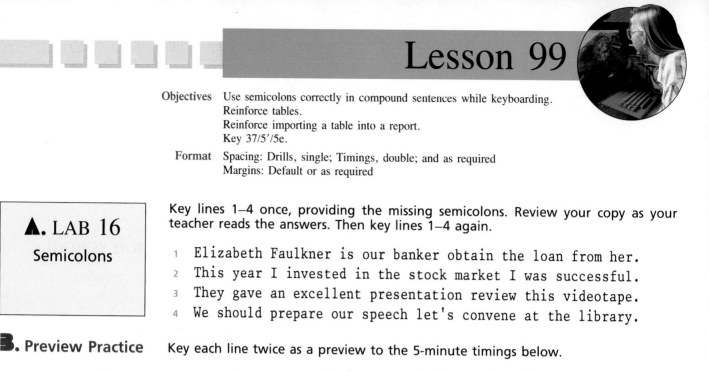

Objectives Use semicolons correctly in compound sentences while keyboarding.
Reinforce tables.
Reinforce importing a table into a report.
Key 37/5'/5e.

Format Spacing: Drills, single; Timings, double; and as required
Margins: Default or as required

A. LAB 16
Semicolons

Key lines 1–4 once, providing the missing semicolons. Review your copy as your teacher reads the answers. Then key lines 1–4 again.

1 Elizabeth Faulkner is our banker obtain the loan from her.
2 This year I invested in the stock market I was successful.
3 They gave an excellent presentation review this videotape.
4 We should prepare our speech let's convene at the library.

B. Preview Practice

Key each line twice as a preview to the 5-minute timings below.

Accuracy 5 expects accurate decisions excellent objectives categorized
Speed 6 with many that will year come they help make give been long

C. 5-Minute Timings

Take two 5-minute timings on lines 7–22. Proofread, note your errors, and figure your speed.

```
7      A report is an excellent way to share information with    12
8  many people.  Businesses use reports every day; it is quite   24
9  possible that their importance will not lessen in the years   36
10 to come.  Reports are factual and objective.  They can help   48
11 people make decisions and give an accurate picture of where   60
12 the company has been, where it is now, and where it expects   72
13 to be in the years to come.                                   77
14      Reports can be categorized in many ways.  One way they   89
15 can be grouped is by format; they may look like a letter, a  101
16 memo, or a short report.  Letter and memo reports look much  113
17 like the letters and memos we have keyed; they have some of  125
18 the same parts and can be about the same length.  The short  137
19 report is often no more than five or six pages long.  It is  149
20 written many times in the direct method; all of those items  161
21 which are the most crucial appear first in the pages of the  173
22 report.  Such a format saves the busy person a lot of time.  185
```
| 1 | 2 | 3 | 4 | 5 | 6 | 7 | 8 | 9 | 10 | 11 | 12 SI 1.35

Lesson 55

Objectives Recognize how numbers are expressed in sentences.
Reinforce table formatting.
Key 33/3'/5e.

Format Spacing: Drills, single; Timings, double; and as required
Margins: Default or as required

▲. LAB 6
Number Style

Key lines 1–4 once. Then repeat lines 1–4, or take a series of 1-minute timings.

```
1   The next interview is scheduled for August 15 at 10:45 a.m.   12
2   The bus to Glorieta leaves at 12 noon and arrives at 9 p.m.   12
3   The state game will be broadcast at 7:30 p.m. on October 9.   12
4   That new movie begins at 8:30 p.m. and ends at 12 midnight.   12
    |  1  |  2  |  3  |  4  |  5  |  6  |  7  |  8  |  9  |  10 |  11 |  12
```

3. In business writing, use figures for dates: *May 14, 1999.*

4. In business writing, use figures to express most periods of time: *45 minutes, 30 days, 8:30 p.m.* If there are no minutes, omit the colon and zeros: *5 p.m., 7 o'clock.* (Use small letters and no spaces for *a.m.* and *p.m.*; use *noon* or *midnight* with 12.)

The flight scheduled to leave at 10:15 a.m. actually left at 12 noon.

B. PRETEST

Take a 3-minute timing on lines 5–13. Proofread, note your errors, and figure your speed.

```
 5      One job that must be done in an office every day is to   12
 6   handle the mail.  Follow these steps.  First, sort the mail   24
 7   by the names of those who get it.  Then rank it by class of   36
 8   mail.  Next, open the letters.  Do not open private mail if   48
 9   you are not authorized to do so.  Items are frequently sent   60
10   with letters, so be sure to check the contents and clip all   72
11   enclosures to the letters.  Stamp the date and time on each   84
12   piece of mail.  As you read a letter, make notes so replies   96
13   can be written.                                              99
     |  1  |  2  |  3  |  4  |  5  |  6  |  7  |  8  |  9  |  10 |  11 |  12 SI 1.22
```

C. Retrieving a File Into a Document

Reminder: A by-line is not always used in reports.

Retrieving a file into a document is similar to retrieving a document, but some software packages require additional steps to accomplish the action.

With all software packages, however, be certain your cursor is in the exact position where you want the beginning of the imported file to be placed. Then follow these steps to retrieve a file into your document [*at the cursor location on the screen*]:

1. For WordPerfect and WordStar, retrieve the file with the appropriate function keys and control keys by calling up the file name to be imported.
2. For AppleWorks, escape to the Main Menu so that you can retrieve a file to the "desktop" by copying it. After the file has been copied to the desktop, return to your document and move the desktop file to your document [*at the cursor location on the screen*].

Report R44.98
Standard format. Correct any errors in language arts.

SALES REPORT

October 2, 19--

This report summarizes the 3d quarter sales figures for the Northeast districts. It was apparent during the 3d quarter, as was evident in the 1st and 2d quarters, that the Philadelphia district is once again leading all other districts in total sales. It was also apparent that the New York district will be merged with the Philadelphia office if sales do not show a dramatic turn around during the 4th quarter. Sales figures for all districts are summarized in Table 1, as follows:

[Retrieve Table T44.98 from your diskette (as either a word processing file or a spreadsheet file), and place it in this area. Don't forget to leave 3 blank lines above and below the table when you place it in the report. Add the table number.]

Analysis. The leader in sales revenues for the 3d quarter was Philadelphia with $67,386 Boston was second with $56,300. The lowest sales figures came from the Hartford district ($12,538) however, the largest decrease in sales from last years report come a from the New York office, where a decrease of $6,789 was reported.

Recommendation. It is the recommendation of this group that since the New York office's sales have dropped during the last three quarters, so dramatically this district be merged with the Philadelphia office at the beginning of the fiscal year. This recommendation will be revised if the New York district's sales show a significantly increase during the 4th quarter.

In the chart below find the number of errors you made on the Pretest (page 130). Then key each of the following designated drill lines two times.

Pretest errors	0–1	2–3	4–5	6+
Drill lines	17–21	16–20	15–19	14–18

Accuracy

14 day then must sent steps those which piece private contents
15 date each clip open check mailed letters replies authorized
16 read time next make notes stamps handles classes frequently
17 jobs done mail sort follow office ranked written enclosures

Speed

18 these names opens sure mail each with not are you can to so
19 first class which must date read sent get one who let on it
20 reply write sorts make note rank time job the and low by is
21 items steps piece done sure then open ice off ran pen of be

D. POSTTEST

Take another 3-minute timing on lines 5–13 (page 130). Proofread, note your errors, and figure your speed. Compare your performance with the Pretest.

Table T13.55
Single spacing.

BIRTHSTONES FOR EACH MONTH

Month	Birthstone
January	Garnet
February	Amethyst
March	Aquamarine
April	Diamond
May	Emerald
June	Pearl
July	Ruby
August	Peridot
September	Sapphire
October	Opal
November	Topaz
December	Turquoise

Table T14.55
Double spacing.

Spring Manufacturing

Employee Payroll Chart

Number	Employee Name	Hours
1001	Avey, Sheilla	42.5
1020	Baird, Jennifer	38.0
1003	Jana Boyd	9.5
1004	Fox, Steven	44.0
105	Gage, Jodi	40.0
1006	Gray, shannan	7.0
ds 1007	Harris, Ginger	40.5
1008	Kovacs, Anthony	48.0

Objectives Identify how semicolons are used in compound sentences while keyboarding.
Reinforce tables.
Import a table into a report.

Format Spacing: Drills, single; and as required
Margins: Default or as required

▲. LAB 16
Semicolons

Key lines 1–4 once. Then repeat lines 1–4, or take a series of 1-minute timings.

```
1  Carmen may be able to key your paper; Zachery can proof it.   12
2  Yes, Elizabeth took first place; Matthew took second place.   12
3  Jose prefers the new software version; Maria likes the old.   12
4  Robert works in our New York office; Paula works there too.   12
   | 1 | 2 | 3 | 4 | 5 | 6 | 7 | 8 | 9 | 10 | 11 | 12
```

B. 30-Second Timings

Take two 30-second timings on lines 5 and 6. Then take two 30-second timings on lines 7 and 8. Try to key with no more than 2 errors on each timing.

```
5  The man who won the race ran and ran and ran; when the race   12
6  was over, he was at least one mile ahead of all the others.   24

7  She is the best singer in the entire group; when she sings,   12
8  her clear voice can be heard above the others in the group.   24
   | 1 | 2 | 3 | 4 | 5 | 6 | 7 | 8 | 9 | 10 | 11 | 12
```

Table T44.98

Standard format; double spacing. Verify the increases and decreases in column 4. If you have access to spreadsheet software, enter a formula to verify the accuracy of the column 4 amounts.

TERRITORIAL SALES
Northeast Districts

District Office	This Year's Sales	Last Year's Sales	Increase/ Decrease
Albany	$24,485	$26,284	−$ 1,799
Boston	56,300	51,780	+ 4,520
Hartford	12,538	10,209	+ 2,329
New York	43,912	50,701	− 6,789
Philadelphia	67,386	53,825	+ 13,561

Table T45.98

Retrieve Table T44.98 and enter the following changes for "This Year's Sales": Albany, $25,289; Boston, no change; Hartford, $13,803; New York, $47,055; Philadelphia, $64,320. Add an "AVERAGE" line at the bottom for "This Year's Sales" and "Last Year's Sales." Use a ruled format for the table. Calculate (1) the increase/decrease for each city and (2) the averages for this year's and last year's sales.

If you have spreadsheet software, write formulas to do the calculations.

Table T15.55
Double spacing.

HISTORIC VOLCANIC ERUPTIONS

Date	Volcano	Country	Fatalities
1883	Krakatau	Indonesia	35,000
1902	Mt. Pelee	Martinique	30,000
1985	Nevado del Ruiz	Colombia	23,000
1669	Mt. Etna	Italy	20,000
1815	Tambora	Indonesia	12,000
1902	Santa Maria	Guatemala	1,000
1991	Mt. Pinatubo	Philippines	156
1980	Mt. St. Helens	United States	60

Lesson 56

Objectives Identify how numbers are expressed in sentences.
Format ruled tables.

Format Spacing: Drills, single; and as required
Margins: Default or as required

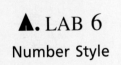

▲. LAB 6
Number Style

Key lines 1–4 once. Then repeat lines 1–4, or take a series of 1-minute timings.

1 Cheerleader practice is from 6:45 a.m. to 12 noon Saturday. 12
2 Lunch will be served at 11 a.m.; try to get there by 10:15. 12
3 He wants to take the test at 2:45 p.m. instead of 9:30 a.m. 12
4 If we leave at 12 midnight, we will get there by 11:20 a.m. 12
   | 1 | 2 | 3 | 4 | 5 | 6 | 7 | 8 | 9 | 10 | 11 | 12

B. 30-Second Timings

Take two 30-second timings on lines 5 and 6. Then take two 30-second timings on lines 7 and 8. Try to key with no more than 2 errors on each timing.

5 The days are getting longer, and soon winter will be behind 12
6 us; the earth will be painted again with fresh green grass. 24

7 The birds will build nests and then have to work so hard to 12
8 fill the gaping mouths of their babies that never get full. 24
   | 1 | 2 | 3 | 4 | 5 | 6 | 7 | 8 | 9 | 10 | 11 | 12

In the chart below find the number of errors you made on the Pretest (page 220). Then key each of the designated drill lines three times.

Pretest errors	0–1	2–3	4–5	6+
Drill lines	24–28	23–27	22–26	21–25

Accuracy

21 exact you're dozens consists multiply wonderful spreadsheet
22 kind values labeled required subtract worksheet accountants
23 placed copied numbers columns yourself commonly calculation
24 effort actual pattern perform software formulas information

Speed

25 divide hours these know will save meet into from you how to
26 office which users like rows upon what cell many use add if
27 needed words carry area your grid hold word time and all of
28 places times knows just that used have they want the one is

D. POSTTEST

Take another 5-minute timing on lines 5–20 (page 220). Proofread, note your errors, and figure your speed. Compare your performance with the Pretest.

Table T42.97

Standard format; double spacing. Calculate the gross pay for each of the five employees. Also compute an "AVERAGE" line for the requested information.

CHANDLER MANUFACTURING
Statement of Earnings

Employee Name	Hours Worked	Hourly Rate	Gross Pay
Margaret Collins	43	$12.50	
Warren Mazzio	41	10.25	
Steve Scully	40	10.55	
Frank Tippins	45	9.85	
Dennis Warfield	39	11.45	
AVERAGE			

Table T43.97

Retrieve Table T42.97 above, and recalculate gross pay with the following hours worked: Collins, 39; Mazzio, 43; Scully, 47; Tippins, 40; Warfield, 41. Recompute the "AVERAGE"-line information for the hours worked and gross pay.

C. Ruled Tables

In a ruled table, the parts of the table are separated by ruled lines. Column headings are not underlined separately. All horizontal rules extend to the edges of the table and are the exact length of the guide line.

To format ruled tables:

1. Center horizontally and vertically.

2. Set tabs as usual, but after setting the final tab, continue to space across the last column so you will know how long to make the ruled lines.

3. Use the underscore to make the ruled lines. Single-space before and double-space after each ruled line.

4. End the table with a ruled line.

Practice: Key the table in the next column. Use double spacing. The table is 16 lines in length (including the rules).

```
 1           COMPANY ACCOUNTANTS ↓2
 2
 3             Southwest Region ↓1
 4    ─────────────────────────────────
 5                                    ↓2
 6    Name                    City ↓1
 7    ─────────────────────────────────
 8                                    ↓2
 9    Matt Camp               El Paso
10
11    Boyd Glosup             San Antonio
12
13    Kevin Puckett           Oklahoma City
14
15    Shelley Stanley         Little Rock ↓1
16    ─────────────────────────────────
      Shelley Stanley         Oklahoma City
                       123456
```

Repeat Value

Some word processing programs have a feature that enables you to repeat a character through a single keystroke. The number of times the character is to be repeated is set, and the character is pressed once. **Example:** For each ruled line in ruled tables, you would press the underscore key only once.

Table T16.56
Double spacing.

UNITED STATES NATIONAL MONUMENTS

Name	State	Acreage
Agate Fossil Beds	Nebraska	3,000
Booker T. Washington	Virginia	200
Death Valley	California/Nevada	2,068,000
Great Sand Dunes	Colorado	39,000
Jewel Cave	South Dakota	1,300
Natural Bridges	Utah	7,800
Ocmulgee	Georgia	700
Statue of Liberty	New York/New Jersey	60

Objectives Recognize how semicolons are used in compound sentences while keyboarding.
Reinforce tables.
Reinforce the use of spreadsheet software.
Key 37/5'/5e.

Format Spacing: Drills, single; Timings, double; and as required
Margins: Default or as required

▲ LAB 16
Semicolons

Key lines 1–4 once. Then repeat lines 1–4, or take a series of 1-minute timings.

```
1  Mr. Dave Wainwright is ill today; he will be back tomorrow.   12
2  We must fill the tank immediately; the race may start soon.   12
3  June's speech will be given next week; it is now completed.   12
4  Kathryn is our treasurer; give her all of today's receipts.   12
   |  1  |  2  |  3  |  4  |  5  |  6  |  7  |  8  |  9  |  10  |  11  |  12
```

1. In LAB 11 (page 181), you learned to use a comma before *and, but, or,* and *nor* in compound sentences. When no conjunction is used, place a semicolon between the two independent clauses.

Rita paid in cash; Rick paid by check.
We have property in Atlanta; we also have property in Nashville.

B. PRETEST

Take a 5-minute timing on lines 5–20. Proofread, note your errors, and figure your speed.

```
 5       A spreadsheet is a wonderful kind of software.  If you   12
 6  know how to use a spreadsheet, you will save yourself hours   24
 7  of effort if you're required to add, subtract, multiply, or   36
 8  divide.  A spreadsheet is like a worksheet that accountants   48
 9  use; it consists of rows upon rows and columns upon columns   60
10  of area in which to perform many of your calculations.  All   72
11  of these rows and columns are placed in a grid pattern just   84
12  like on an actual worksheet that is used in the office.  In   96
13  the exact place at which one row and one column meet, users  108
14  can place information into what is commonly labeled a cell.  120
15       A cell can hold words, which are called labels; it can  132
16  carry numbers, which are called values.  Lastly, a cell can  144
17  have formulas, which are used for dozens of calculations as  156
18  they are needed.  Formulas can be copied from row to row or  168
19  from column to column.  They can be copied as many times as  180
20  you may want to copy them.                                   185
    |  1  |  2  |  3  |  4  |  5  |  6  |  7  |  8  |  9  |  10  |  11  |  12  SI 1.37
```

Table T17.56
Double spacing, ruled format.

TEN NATURAL WONDERS OF THE WORLD
Listed by World Travelers and Explorers

Name	Location
Carlsbad Caverns	New Mexico (U.S.)
Caves and Prehistoric Paintings	France and Spain
Giant Sequoia Trees	California (U.S.)
Grand Canyon	Colorado River (U.S.)
Great Barrier Reef	Australia
Harbor	Rio de Janeiro
Mount Everest	Nepal and Tibet
Paricutin (young volcano)	Mexico
Rainbow Bridge	Utah (U.S.)
Victoria Falls	Zimbabwe

Lesson 57

Objectives   Express numbers correctly while keying sentences.
Format tables with columns of mixed words and numbers.
Reinforce ruled tables.
Key 33/3'/5e.

Format   Spacing: Drills, single; Timings, double; and as required
Margins: Default or as required

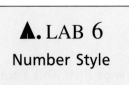

▲. LAB 6

Number Style

Key lines 1–4 once, correcting any errors in number-style rules. Review your copy as your teacher reads the answers. Then key lines 1–4 again.

1   The water will be turned off from 7:00 p.m. to 9:00 p.m. Tuesday.
2   We will have lunch at 12:00; the show starts at 1:15 p.m.
3   The tardy bell rang at 8:12 A. M., but Cory arrived at 8:15.
4   Our flight to Rome lands at six o'clock on Monday, October five.

Take three 12-second timings on each line, or key each line three times. Try to key with no more than 1 error on each timing.

```
6   The day was bright, and the sunbeams shone on the blue sea.
7   Just as the sun sets, all of us should take a long hayride.
8   As you may know, the line has many short, easy words in it.
```

5	10	15	20	25	30	35	40	45	50	55	60

Table T39.96
Standard format; single spacing.

SALES REPORT

(Monthly Sales & Commissions)

Name	Monthly Sales	Comission	Total Earnings
Robert Hammond	$3,325	7%	$3,557.75
Peggy Fletcher	5,850	5%	6,142.50
Charise Mulholand	4,709	6%	5,077.40
Manuel Ortega	6,565	4%	6,827.60
Rachael Sosebee	7,357	3%	7,596.25

Table T40.96
Standard format; double spacing.

CONVERSION OF FRACTIONS

(Decimal and Metric Equivalents)

Note: Mixed numbers align on the final digit of the whole number; thus "2," "5," and "0" in column 1 are aligned. Use a left tab and space in for the shorter numbers.

Mixed Number	Decimal	Centimeter Equivalent
2/3	0.6667	1.693
2 3/4	2.75	6.985
5 7/8	5.875	14.9225
10 9/16	10.5625	26.82875

Table T41.96
Retrieve Table T39.96. Give a 4 percent commission to all the salespeople, and recalculate the total earnings. Arrange the items in descending order, with the largest total earnings first. Add a total line to the table, using the data from the monthly sales and total earnings to calculate your totals.

Take a 3-minute timing on lines 5–13. Proofread, note your errors, and figure your speed.

```
5      Have you ever had to search for a job?  There are some   12
6   guides which will make this task less puzzling.  First, you   24
7   must find the jobs.  Some of the ways to start are with the   36
8   school counselor or placement office, ads in the paper, and   48
9   friends and relatives who work.  Also, there are firms that   60
10  do nothing but acquire jobs for people, but you have to pay   72
11  for this service.  Before you get in touch with a business,   84
12  you should prepare a data sheet which lists your experience   96
13  and top skills.                                              99
```

| 1 | 2 | 3 | 4 | 5 | 6 | 7 | 8 | 9 | 10 | 11 | 12 SI 1.24 |

In the chart below find the number of errors you made on the Pretest. Then key each of the following designated drill lines two times.

Pretest errors	0–1	2–3	4–5	6+
Drill lines	17–21	16–20	15–19	14–18

Accuracy

```
14  must ways some have people before should business relatives
15  your paper school guides nothing examine agencies placement
16  there start sheet office service friends puzzling qualities
17  which first touch skills search however strongest counselor
```

Speed

```
18  lists tasks works that jobs find ever key top are ads in to
19  sheet skill paper talk this less will but pay you and or in
20  place there which must make some with for get are the of it
21  first guide touch data your that ways had who job not do as
```

Take another 3-minute timing on lines 5–13. Proofread, note your errors, and figure your speed. Compare your performance with the Pretest.

E. Word and Number Columns

You have learned previously that words align on the left and numbers align on the right. Sometimes columns contain a mixture of both words *and* numbers.

To format a column of mixed words and numbers, align all entries at the left, as if they were all words.

In a business office, information such as that which is presented in Table T37.95 is often placed in a spreadsheet. A **spreadsheet software** package is used on computers to enable the operator to create tables of numbers on a screen. If the numbers need to be changed—such as the percentages in Table T37.95—then the answers are recalculated automatically.

Table T37.95
Standard format; double spacing.
Note: If you are using spreadsheet software, enter this table into the spreadsheet.

REVENUE DISTRIBUTION
(In Millions of Dollars)

Item	Dollar Amount	Percent
Wages/Salaries	$252.7	41.7
Operating Costs	118.4	19.5
Dividends	103.8	17.1
Taxes	82.9	13.7
Interest	48.2	8.0
Total	$606.0	100.0

Table T38.95
Retrieve Table T37.95 (either from your word processing file or from your spreadsheet file) and make the following changes: (1) arrange the items alphabetically, with Dividends as your first entry; (2) prepare the table in a ruled format.

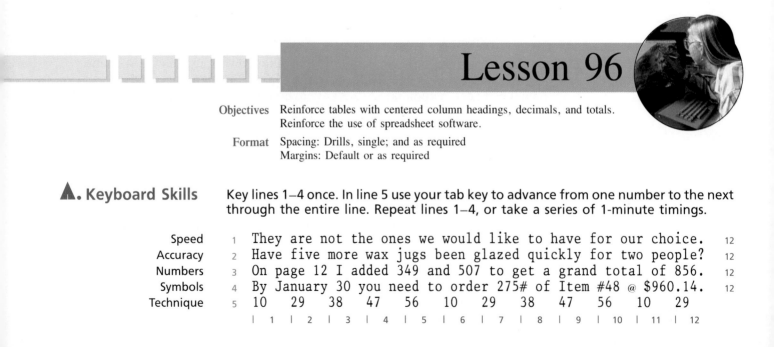

Lesson 96

Objectives	Reinforce tables with centered column headings, decimals, and totals. Reinforce the use of spreadsheet software.
Format	Spacing: Drills, single; and as required Margins: Default or as required

A. Keyboard Skills

Key lines 1–4 once. In line 5 use your tab key to advance from one number to the next through the entire line. Repeat lines 1–4, or take a series of 1-minute timings.

Speed	1	They are not the ones we would like to have for our choice.	12
Accuracy	2	Have five more wax jugs been glazed quickly for two people?	12
Numbers	3	On page 12 I added 349 and 507 to get a grand total of 856.	12
Symbols	4	By January 30 you need to order 275# of Item #48 @ $960.14.	12
Technique	5	10 29 38 47 56 10 29 38 47 56 10 29	

| 1 | 2 | 3 | 4 | 5 | 6 | 7 | 8 | 9 | 10 | 11 | 12 |

Table T18.57
Double spacing.

INFORMATION PROCESSING POSITIONS

Position	Experience	Education
Data Entry Clerk	None	High School
Word Processing Trainee	None	High School
Word Processing Specialist	2 Years	High School
Word Processing Manager	5 Years	College
Administrative Secretary	3 Years	College
Administrative Supervisor	5 Years	College
Programmer	2 Years	College
Systems Analyst	5 Years	College

Table T19.57
Double spacing.

THE FIRST TEN U.S. PRESIDENTS

Dates and Lengths of Terms

Name	Dates Served	Length of Term
George Washington	1789–1797	8 years
John Adams	1797–1801	4 years
Thomas Jefferson	1801–1809	8 years
James Madison	1809–1817	8 years
James Monroe	1817–1825	8 years
John Quincy Adams	1825–1829	4 years
Andrew Jackson	1829–1837	8 years
Martin Van Buren	1837–1841	4 years
William Henry Harrison	1841	31 days
John Tyler	1841–1845	4 years

Take a 5-minute timing on lines 5–20. Proofread, note your errors, and figure your speed.

```
 5        When you seek that first job, you will find that those      12
 6   skills you acquire during high school play a very essential      24
 7   role in your success.  Just as important are the traits you      36
 8   now possess that may help you keep that job and progress in      48
 9   it.  One of the most important traits you can possess is to      60
10   always be on time.  Punctuality is extremely important to a      72
11   business employer, and it is a valuable trait that can help      84
12   you succeed in any job.                                          89
13        Being on time is more than simply making it to work on     101
14   time every day, although that is important too.  People who     113
15   are punctual finish their work on time, seldom come late to     125
16   meetings, and finish their tasks as scheduled.  They can be     137
17   counted on; they're recognized as good team members and are     149
18   asked to join with other work groups because of their sound     161
19   work ethic.  If you want to be successful at your work, the     173
20   trait of being punctual is by far one of the most critical.    185
      |  1  |  2  |  3  |  4  |  5  |  6  |  7  |  8  |  9  | 10  | 11  | 12 SI 1.33
```

In the chart below find the number of errors you made on the Pretest. Then key each of the following designated drill lines three times.

Pretest errors	0–1	2–3	4–5	6+
Drill lines	24–28	23–27	22–26	21–25

Accuracy
```
21  simply skills possess success business progress punctuality
22  making during they're acquires employer extremely important
23  first school counted meetings valuable scheduled successful
24  those traits succeed punctual although essential recognized
```

Speed
```
25  always group asked when seek that keep more they you job in
26  people being other will find help most than good are the as
27  finish every sound high play very time work join may and it
28  seldom tasks ethic role your just come late task one can is
```

Take another 5-minute timing on lines 5–20. Proofread, note your errors, and figure your speed. Compare your performance with the Pretest.

Table T20.57
Double spacing; change default margins

SEVEN WONDERS OF THE ANCIENT WORLD

(Most Commonly Listed)

ds WONDER	Location	[Description
Colossus	Rhodes	Bronze statue on Aegean Sea
Hanging Gardens	~~Babylon~~	Irrigated flowers and ~~trees~~
Light House	Alexandria	(Important first) lighthouse
~~The~~ Mausoleum	Halicarnassus	tomb for Persian official
Pyramids	Egypt	Tombs for egyptian kings
~~The~~ Statue of Zeus	~~Babylon~~ Olympia	Statue of gold and ivory
Temple of Artemis	Ephesus	Temple for greek goddess

Lesson 58

Objectives Reinforce open and ruled tables.
Key 33/3'/5e.

Format Spacing: Drills, single; Timings, double; and as required
Margins: Default or as required

▲. Keyboard Skills

Key lines 1–4 once. Then key line 5 once using the caps lock key for the all-cap words. Repeat lines 1–4, or take a series of 1-minute timings.

Speed	1 We may visit a good friend today on our way home from town.	12
Accuracy	2 Have Jeb or Peggy Swartz quickly fix the fax machine today.	12
Numbers	3 Juanita left for the office at 29 Sixth Avenue at 7:15 a.m.	12
Symbols	4 You can get 25% more cards for only $3 more (plus tax)--$3!	12
Technique	5 Take JONES for the course--not ADAMS or FOX or ASH or VENN.	

| 1 | 2 | 3 | 4 | 5 | 6 | 7 | 8 | 9 | 10 | 11 | 12

Table T36.94
Standard format; double spacing.

WIND VELOCITY IN U.S. CITIES

Miles-per-Hour Rates

City	State	Average Wind Speed	Highest Wind Speed
Mt. Washington	New Hampshire	35	231
Cape Hatteras	North Carolina	11	110
Omaha	Nebraska	10	109
Galveston	Texas	11	100
Average	---------------	17	137

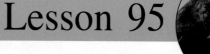

Lesson 95

Objectives   Use commas correctly with appositives while keying sentences.
Reinforce tables with centered column headings, decimals, and totals.
Use spreadsheet software, if available.
Key 37/5'/5e.

Format   Spacing: Drills, single; Timings, double; and as required
Margins: Default or as required

▲. LAB 15

Commas

Key lines 1–4 once, providing the missing commas. Review your copy as your teacher reads the answers. Then key lines 1–4 again.

1   My favorite book A Perfect Spy has been read by millions.
2   If you need more information, ask our teacher Mr. Santos.
3   Our principal Ms. Syzmanski scheduled the board meetings.
4   Will you need me on Monday March 25 to work at the booth?

B. Preview Practice

Key each line twice as a preview to the 3-minute timings below.

Accuracy 6 you quit tacks pencils another resource contained effective
Speed 7 sharp work pens will most have down with that are and if to

C. 3-Minute Timings

Take two 3-minute timings on lines 8–16. Proofread, note your errors, and figure your speed.

```
8      You will be able to work better if the place where you      12
9   spend most of your time is well organized.  Check to see if   24
10  you have all the work that you must do in one stack and all    36
11  the tasks that you have done in another.  Are your pens and    48
12  pencils stored together with the sharp points down?  Do you    60
13  have paper clips, tacks, and other small items contained in    72
14  one place?  Resource books should be easy to find and reach    84
15  without leaving the desk.  Do not quit planning to expedite    96
16  effective work.                                                99
    |  1  |  2  |  3  |  4  |  5  |  6  |  7  |  8  |  9  |  10  |  11  |  12  SI 1.24
```

Table T21.58
Double spacing.

LOIS B. HAYES HIGH SCHOOL HONOR GRADUATES

Bynum, Brandee	311 North Rutherford
Click, Jennifer	One 58th Avenue
Dornbusch, Samuel	2009 Lilac Lane
Greenville, Christy	4866 King Boulevard
Heyman, Isaac	55 Seventh Street
Mendosa, Charlotte	644 31st Street
Putman, Susan	720 West Drive, Apartment 31
Wolders, Neil	95 Larchmont Circle

Table T22.58
Double spacing.

Copy Table T21.58 and insert the subtitle Top 1 Percent of Senior Class. *Add the column headings* Name *and* Address. *Recenter vertically.*

Table T34.94
Standard format; double spacing.

CHEMICAL ELEMENTS
(Alkaline-Earth Metals)

Name	Chemical Symbol	Atomic Weight	Atomic Number
Barium	Ba	137.34	56
Beryllium	Be	9.0122	4
Calcium	Ca	40.08	20
Magnesium	Mg	24.312	12
Radium	Ra	226.	88
Strontium	Sr	87.62	38

D. Total Lines in Tables

A total (or average) line may appear in a table to total (or average) one or more columns.

To format a total line in unruled and ruled tables:

Tables Without Ruled Lines. (1) Place an underline under the last amount, on the same line. (2) Make the underline the same width as the longest entry in the column. (3) Activate the underlining function and space in the appropriate number of spaces if the last amount is not the longest entry in the column. (4) Double-space before keying the total.

Tables With Ruled Lines. Precede and follow the total with a ruled line that extends the full width of the table. Single-space before the ruled lines, and double-space after them.

Note: The word *total* or *average* may be keyed in initial capitals or in all-capital letters beginning at the left of the first column.

When no total (or average) is applicable to a column, key hyphens to the full width of the column. It is preferable to use the ruled format when some columns are not totaled. (See Table T36.94 on page 216.)

Table T35.94
Standard format; double spacing.

DISTRICT OFFICES COMPUTER INVENTORY
December 19--

District Office Location	Units	Unit Price	Total Unit Price
Pocatello	28	$2,755	$ 77,140
Hartford	23	3,120	71,760
Louisville	31	2,895	89,745
San Diego	42	2,950	123,900
Total	124		$362,545

Table T23.58
Double spacing. Key the body by arranging the lengths from shortest to longest.

MAJOR U.S. RIVERS

(Approximate Lengths in Miles)

River	Length	Origin
Arkansas	1,460	Colorado
Columbia	1,240	British Columbia
Colorado	1,450	Colorado
Mississippi	2,350	Minnesota
Missouri	2,320	Montana
Ohio	1,310	Pennsylvania
Red	1,270	New Mexico
Rio Grande	1,890	Colorado
Snake	1,040	Wyoming
Tennessee	900	North Carolina
Yukon	1,900	British Columbia

Table T24.58
Double spacing.

PULITZER PRIZE WINNERS

American Authors of Fiction

Author	Title	Date
Willa Cather	ONE OF OURS	1923
Edna Ferber	SO BIG	1925
Sinclair Lewis	ARROWSMITH	1926
Thornton Wilder	BRIDGE OF SAN LUIS REY	1928
Pearl S. Buck	THE GOOD EARTH	1932
Margaret Mitchell	GONE WITH THE WIND	1937
John Steinbeck	THE GRAPES OF WRATH	1940
Herman Wouk	THE CAINE MUTINY	1952
Ernest Hemingway	THE OLD MAN AND THE SEA	1953
Harper Lee	TO KILL A MOCKINGBIRD	1961
Alice Walker	THE COLOR PURPLE	1983

Table T32.93
Standard format; double spacing.

AIR DISTANCE BETWEEN CITIES
U.S. Departures

Point of Departure	Destination	Miles
Los Angeles	Cape Town	9,969
New York	Hong Kong	8,060
Washington	Tokyo	6,791
Chicago	Cairo	6,141
Los Angeles	Berlin	5,782

Table T33.93
Standard format; double spacing.

⊐LEADING SALES OFFICES⊏
Current ~~Quarter 3~~

District Office	This Year	Last Year
Albuqerque (u)	$70,285	$68,431
Trenton, NJ	69,034	65,937
Philadelphia	77,550	70,235
Baton Rouge	65,039	52,834
Sacramento (a)	46,961	63,375

Lesson 94

Objectives	Identify how commas are used with appositives while keying sentences.
	Format tables with two-line column headings.
	Format tables with total lines.
	Reinforce short and long centered headings in tables.
Format	Spacing: Drills, single; and as required
	Margins: Default or as required

▲. LAB 15
Commas

Key lines 1–4 once. Then repeat lines 1–4, or take a series of 1-minute timings.

1 The book I ordered, <u>Computer Marvels</u>, arrived early Monday. 12
2 My cousin, Alex Simons, played professional golf last year. 12
3 Their next vacation will start on Independence Day, July 4. 12
4 Tom Adair, our new insurance agent, is a very rapid typist. 12
   | 1 | 2 | 3 | 4 | 5 | 6 | 7 | 8 | 9 | 10 | 11 | 12

▌. "OK" Timings

Take two 30-second "OK" (errorless) timings on lines 5–6. Then take two 30-second "OK" timings on lines 7–8. Goal: No errors.

5 Have my six dozen quails joined two big flocks of sparrows, 12
6 or did they all return to the fields to feast on the grain? 24

7 Zachery joked about a group of wax squid from the carnival, 12
8 and he also laughed after seeing the clown perform his act. 24
   | 1 | 2 | 3 | 4 | 5 | 6 | 7 | 8 | 9 | 10 | 11 | 12

◖. Two-Line Column Headings

When a column heading is much longer than any item in the column, the column heading may be keyed on two (or more) lines.
   To format two-line column headings:
1. Center each line over the column.

2. Underline the words in each line of the heading in open tables; do not underline in ruled tables.

3. If the table contains both one- and two-line headings (such as in Table T34.94 on page 215), align the one-line heading with the bottom line of the two-line heading.

Lesson 59

Objectives Reinforce block style business letters.
Format modified-block style business letters.

Format Spacing: Drills, single; and as required
Margins: Default or as required

A. Keyboard Skills

Key lines 1–4 once. As you key line 5, practice smooth shift-key control. Then repeat lines 1–4, or take a series of 1-minute timings.

Speed	1	It will be nice to see the sun after days and days of rain. 12
Accuracy	2	Your six big checks equal the five major prizes Donald won. 12
Numbers	3	Our 9 cakes, 45 pies, 60 doughnuts, and 72 cookies arrived. 12
Symbols	4	Just look at Mitt & Mask, Fouls & Flies, and Hits & Misses. 12
Technique	5	Jack Dora Paul Rick Hank Cara Iris Wade Mort Vida York Earl

| 1 | 2 | 3 | 4 | 5 | 6 | 7 | 8 | 9 | 10 | 11 | 12

B. 30-Second Timings

Take two 30-second timings on lines 6 and 7. Then take two 30-second timings on lines 8 and 9. Try to key with no more than 2 errors on each timing.

6 When I tried to play my trumpet at home, the dogs howled so 12
7 loudly that I had to stop; I guess it made their ears hurt. 24

8 That cat loves to seek places where it is hard to find her; 12
9 right now she is sleeping in an empty box in a dark corner. 24

| 1 | 2 | 3 | 4 | 5 | 6 | 7 | 8 | 9 | 10 | 11 | 12

Review pages 101, 105, 108, and 110 or the Reference Section of this text for business letter formatting and block style if necessary.

Letter L16.59
Block style. No. 10 envelope.

[*Today's date*] / Miss Laura Cobb / One North 79 Avenue / Chicago, IL 60635 / Dear Miss Cobb: / Since you will be completing your undergraduate work and receiving your degree soon, you will be needing a full-service bank. We want to be that bank! ¶ Here are just a few of the many reasons why you should choose One Bank for your financial needs. There is no service charge on accounts that maintain a minimum balance of $300. We have convenient drive-through facilities in 35 locations throughout the city that are open until 7 p.m. on Friday evenings and from 9 a.m. to noon on Saturdays. Also, we offer starter loans to recent college graduates at the lowest interest rates in this area. The enclosed brochure explains all the benefits of our bank in detail. ¶ Why not stop by and get acquainted with the friendly people at One Bank. We know you will be pleased with the warm reception that awaits you. / Sincerely, / Mrs. Martha McGill / Vice President / [*Your initials*] / Enclosure

Take a 1-minute timing on lines 5–8. Proofread, note your errors, and figure your speed.

```
5        If you think you might enjoy a vacation by the sea for   12
6    relaxing or catching some fish, a trip to your local travel   24
7    agent may provide you with all kinds of information to help   36
8    you.                                                          37
     |  1  |  2  |  3  |  4  |  5  |  6  |  7  |  8  |  9  |  10  |  11  |  12
```

C. PRACTICE

SPEED: If you made 2 or fewer errors on the Pretest, key lines 9–14 as a group twice. Repeat if time permits.
ACCURACY: If you made more than 2 errors on the Pretest, key lines 9–11 as a group twice. Then key lines 12–14 as a group twice. Repeat if time permits.

Up Reaches

```
9    dark each felt gate harm idea abide barns clock depth earns
10   jobs kits lawn mark nail ours filed guest hotel judge lapse
11   pile rank self take used wage maple named often pairs range
```

Down Reaches

```
12   able bake camp film know lack about baked canal drink enjoy
13   nova only pack rank sink tank knack labor scout thank valid
14   vain acre have knew save wave acute blank candy habit known
```

D. POSTTEST

Take a 1-minute timing on lines 5–8. Proofread, note your errors, and figure your speed. Compare your performance with the Pretest.

E. Long, Centered Column Headings

When a column heading is longer than any item in the column, the column is centered under the heading. Follow these formatting instructions:

1. Subtract the number of spaces in the longest line in the column from the number of spaces in the heading.

2. Divide that answer by 2 (drop any fraction), and indent the column that number of spaces. In the example, 13 − 9 = 4 and 4 ÷ 2 = 2. Indent the column 2 spaces.

3. After keying the column heading, reset the tab stop.

Note: When the column heading is longer than the column, regard the heading as part of the guide line.

Table T31.93
Standard format; double spacing.

```
                Name of State  ←——— 13 SPACES

                    Arizona
                    Georgia
                    Tennessee ←——— 9 SPACES
                    Wyoming
```

U.S. HOME SALES

(Top Four State Markets)

Name of State	Percentage Increase
California	15.7
Alaska	13.4
Illinois	12.6
Arizona	11.8

C. Letters in Modified-Block Style

In the modified-block style, the date begins at the center on line 13 (2-inch top margin); the closing lines—complimentary closing, writer's name and title—also begin at the center. Any notations (reference initials, enclosures) begin at the left margin a double space below the closing.

The center point in 10 pitch is 42 (3.2 inches from the left margin). Clear any default tabs, and set a *left tab* at the center point.

Letter L17.59
Modified-block style, mixed punctuation. Center tab. No. 10 envelope.

[*Today's date*] ↓6

Mr. Stanley Preston Laughton
Laughton & Laughton, Inc.
4509 Warren Avenue
Detroit, MI 48207-9602

Dear Mr. Laughton:

Mrs. Yasmin Forrester, who was employed by your firm as a senior administrative secretary for the past eight years, has applied for a line of credit with our bank. Since Mrs. Forrester has recently moved to Chicago and has no acquaintances in this area, we need a data sheet to be completed by her most recent employer.

Would you please fill out and return the enclosed form so that we may process Mrs. Forrester's application. You will note that she has signed the release statement permitting you to disclose the information requested.

If you should have any questions concerning this matter, please call me at 312-555-9276, Ext. 40, between 9 a.m. and 3 p.m., CST. A postage-paid envelope is also enclosed for your convenience.

                    Cordially yours,
                              ↓4
                    Mrs. Martha McGill
                    Vice President

ts
2 Enclosures

Letter L18.59
Edit Letter L16.59. Change the format to modified-block style. Change the inside address and salutation as follows:

Mr. Reggie M. Nance / 6201 East Grand Avenue / Chicago, IL 60611 / Dear Mr. Nance:

Table T29.92
Standard format; double spacing.

Largest States
(Square Miles and Capitals)

State	Area	Capital
Alaska	586,412	Juneau
Texas	267,338	Austin
California	158,693	Sacramento
Montana	147,138	Helena
New Mexico	121,666	Santa Fe

Table T30.92
Standard format; double spacing.

PROMOTION STATISTICS
January 1, 19--

Name	Title	Salary
Atkinson, Brandon	Sales Clerk	$15,570
Cleary, Pamela	Accountant	30,845
Harvey, Kay	Accountant	32,125
Humphries, Jane	Secretary	17,430
McDaniels, Bill	Sales Clerk	16,750

Lesson 93

Objectives Recognize how commas are used with appositives while keying sentences.
Reinforce skill on up reaches and down reaches.
Format tables with long, centered column headings.

Format Spacing: Drills, single; Timings, double; and as required
Margins: Default or as required

▲. LAB 15

Commas

Key lines 1–4 once. Then repeat lines 1–4, or take a series of 1-minute timings.

```
1  Our teacher, Ms. Rodriguez, won the award for best teacher.   12
2  Mr. Long, the band instructor, posted our recital practice.   12
3  We will drive to our neighboring state, Missouri, tomorrow.   12
4  We believe our representative, Ms. Cantrell, should attend.   12
   |  1  |  2  |  3  |  4  |  5  |  6  |  7  |  8  |  9  |  10  |  11  |  12
```

7. An appositive is a word or a phrase that further describes or identifies a person or a thing. Use two commas to separate an appositive within a sentence. Use one comma if the appositive ends the sentence.

Mr. Edmondson, our state representative, voted for the bill.
(The words *our state representative* further identify Mr. Edmondson.)
The case was handled by Ms. Kirwolski, *our attorney.*
Class is canceled for Tuesday, *March 9.*

Lesson 60

Objectives Recognize how numbers are expressed in sentences.
Reinforce double and alternate reaches.
Format modified-block style letters with indented paragraphs.

Format Spacing: Drills, single; Timings, double; and as required
Margins: Default or as required

A. LAB 7
Number Style

Key lines 1–4 once. Then repeat lines 1–4, or take a series of 1-minute timings.

```
1  That hotel bill was for $358.50, but there was a $19 error.    12
2  In the late eighties, his salary rose to about $300 a week.    12
3  The first invoice was $23.15, and the second one was $9.88.    12
4  The heart surgery will cost Marie several thousand dollars.    12
   |  1  |  2  |  3  |  4  |  5  |  6  |  7  |  8  |  9  | 10  | 11  | 12
```

5. Use figures for exact or approximate amounts of money.

   $10, about $100

6. Spell out indefinite numbers and amounts.

   thousands of people, millions of dollars, in the sixties

B. PRETEST

Take a 1-minute timing on lines 5–7. Proofread, note your errors, and figure your speed.

```
5       The blazing paint gave off toxic odors that gagged the    12
6  nearby runners and joggers.  Soon the sunny sky grew dimmer    24
7  as it filled with acrid smoke, and everyone ran.              34
   |  1  |  2  |  3  |  4  |  5  |  6  |  7  |  8  |  9  | 10  | 11  | 12
```

C. PRACTICE

SPEED: If you made 2 or fewer errors on the Pretest, key lines 8–13 twice each. Repeat if time permits.
ACCURACY: If you made more than 2 errors on the Pretest, key lines 8–10 as a group twice. Then key lines 11–13 as a group twice. Repeat if time permits.

Double Reaches
```
8   mm comma gamma gummy mummy dummy yummy jimmy tummy hammy mm
9   gg baggy leggy foggy soggy doggy muggy piggy buggy jaggy gg
10  nn inner annoy sunny funny bunny bonny gunny nanny runny nn
```

Alternate Reaches
```
11  toxic blame paint their towns bland panda theme tucks blend
12  panel throb turns flame pause throw tusks bogus proxy title
13  tutor boric prism tithe ticks bowls prowl tight bugle psych
```

D. POSTTEST

Take a 1-minute timing on lines 5–7. Proofread, note your errors, and figure your speed. Compare your performance with the Pretest.

B. 30-Second Timings

Take two 30-second timings on lines 6 and 7. Then take two 30-second timings on lines 8 and 9. Try to key with no more than 2 errors on each timing.

```
 6   The rug firm is to pay us for the work if the work is good,    12
 7   but they will not have to pay us if we do not do good work.    24

 8   That game was won by the best team at the match, and all of    12
 9   your players went home very happy with how they had played.    24
     |  1  |  2  |  3  |  4  |  5  |  6  |  7  |  8  |  9  |  10 |  11 |  12
```

C. Short, Centered Column Headings

Lesson 54 introduced the formatting of blocked column headings in tables. However, column headings may also be centered over columns.

When a column heading is shorter than the longest line in the column, the heading should be centered over the column. Follow these directions:

1. Subtract the number of spaces in the heading from the number of spaces in the longest line in the column.
2. Divide the answer by 2 (drop any fraction), and indent the column heading that many spaces.

In the illustration below, the heading is 4 spaces long; the longest line is 12. Thus 12 − 4 = 8 and 8 ÷ 2 = 4. Indent the heading 4 spaces from the start of the column.

```
        ↓ 3
        Date  ←——— 4 SPACES
          ↓ 2
        September 12
        September 30  ←—12 SPACES
        October 10
```

Center Tabs

Some word processing software has a **center tab** feature as well as left, right, and decimal tabs. A center tab acts just like the center feature. To center a short column heading over a column, set a center tab at the midpoint of the column. When the copy is keyed, it will automatically center over the column.

Note: In some word processing programs you can use the center feature instead of the center tab feature when left tabs are used. Tab to the start of the column, space to the center of the column and activate the center feature. When the copy is keyed, it will center over the column.

Table T27.92
Standard format (6 spaces between columns); double spacing.

NEW EMPLOYEES
Southern District Offices

Name	Office	City
Randall Evans	Marketing	Tulsa
Trezzie Pressley	Personnel	Atlanta
Ruth Ann Riley	Accounting	Dallas
Diane Van Vliet	Marketing	Jackson
Jan Walker	Personnel	Mobile

Table T28.92
Standard format; double spacing.

COLLEGE CRITERIA ADMISSION
Ranked by Degree of Importance

Criteria	Rank	Category
Class rank	Second	Numeric
Test Scores	Third	Numeric
Grades	First	Numeric
Recomendations	Fourth	Written
Essay	Fifth	Written
Interview	Sixth	~~Numeric~~ Written

E. Letters With Indented Paragraphs

A variation of the modified-block style letter is to indent the first line of each paragraph. The usual indention is 5 spaces.

You will need two tab stops—one for the paragraph indention and one at the center point.

Letter L19.60
Modified-block style, indented paragraphs. No. 6 3/4 envelope.

[*Today's date*] / Mr. and Mrs. Michael Hitt / Star Route, Box 318 / Elk City, OK 73644 / Dear Mr. and Mrs. Hitt: / Congratulations on your recent purchase of the Model 3090 Jubilee combine! The Jubilee name on your combine assures you of quality unequaled in any other line of farm equipment. ¶ For the past 75 years, Jubilee has been working to help you—America's farmers—produce better crops faster and more efficiently. That is why every piece of Jubilee equipment is backed by a ten-year guarantee. Should your combine need servicing during that time, simply call one of our dealers in your area, and our service technicians will respond within 24 hours. ¶ We welcome you to the Jubilee family of satisfied customers. Please let us know whenever we can be of assistance to you. / Cordially yours, / Clayton Williamson / President / [*Your initials*]

Letter L20.60
Modified-block style, indented paragraphs. No. 10 envelope.

[*Today's date*] / Mr. Bruce Blackmon / The Place Farm / 450 Osage Road / Emporia, KS 66801 / Dear Mr. Blackmon: / After our telephone conversation this morning concerning the late delivery of three model

890 tractors to your dealership, I found that the tractors were originally shipped to Emporia, IN. ¶ Last month our corporate headquarters installed a new System Computer, which required many hours of reentering our shipping invoices. Apparently, the error in your order occurred at that time. All of our records of your business have now been corrected. ¶ Because of the inconvenience this has caused, we are allowing you 30 days free of interest charges on the tractors. The new contract reflecting this change is enclosed. You have been a valued customer for more than 20 years, and we shall look forward to serving you for many more years to come. / Sincerely Yours, / Marlin Anadarko / production manager / [*Your initials*] / 2 Enclosures

printing speeds of these printers.

TABLE 1 *← 2 double spaces before and after table*

☐ Printer	☐ Speed
Daisy wheel	40-100 characters/sec
Dot matrix	200-300+ characters/sec
Band; chain	3,000 lines/min

Use 6 spaces between columns

Nonimpact Printers

⑤ Non impact printers differ from impact printers in that a ribbon is ∧*not* used to print the characters on a page. Instead, the non impact printers use a feature such as heat or a laƶer to produce printed characters on paper. A brief sumary *m*∧ of each of the popular nonimpact printers appears in the following paragraphs.

⑤ 1. A thermal printer "burns" the characters *onto* ~~to~~ the page by using a (paper/ specially designed) that is heat-sensitive.

⑤ 2. An ink-jet printer uses tiny noz*z*les to spray the ink onto the paper in the form of images (characters). Actually, small dots *of ink* ∧ are sprayed onto the paper; but because so many dots are used to make up each letter, it appears that ~~solid~~ characters are printed ~~at all times~~.

⑤ 3. A laser printer uses tiny beams of (light/ laser) to form the characters on a page. Th*is* printer is the fastest but also the most expensive to purchase. Laser printers are used for jobs that require high-quality out put.

UNIT 14

Tables

Unit Goal 37/5'/5e

Lesson 92

Objective Format tables with short, centered column headings.
Format Spacing: Drills, single; and as required
Margins: Default or as required

▲. Keyboard Skills

Key lines 1–4 once. In line 5 use your tab key to advance from one word to the next through the entire line. Repeat lines 1–4, or take a series of 1-minute timings.

Speed	1	Key short words like but, for, nor, the, cot, tot, and map.	12
Accuracy	2	Calm Rex Whit quit many jobs before driving for a park zoo.	12
Numbers	3	Page 479 showed that 2 times 6 times 3 times 5 equaled 180.	12
Symbols	4	On 10/14/90 we placed an order for 17# of #6 stock @ $9.82.	12
Technique	5	am an as at be by do go ha he hi ho	

| 1 | 2 | 3 | 4 | 5 | 6 | 7 | 8 | 9 | 10 | 11 | 12

Lesson 61

Objectives Identify how numbers are expressed in sentences.
Increase skill in shifting and concentration.
Reinforce modified-block style letters.

Format Spacing: Drills, single; and as required
Margins: Default or as required

A. LAB 7
Number Style

Key lines 1–4 once. Then repeat lines 1–4, or take a series of 1-minute timings.

```
1  My savings account has nearly a thousand dollars in it now.   12
2  Lou was sent a check for $62, and Hal received one for $39.    12
3  The TV concert on June 7 was seen by over a million people.    12
4  The diamond watch costs $1,299, but the sale price is $899.    12
   |  1  |  2  |  3  |  4  |  5  |  6  |  7  |  8  |  9  |  10 |  11 |  12
```

B. "OK" Timings

Take two 30-second "OK" (errorless) timings on lines 5–6. Then take two 30-second "OK" timings on lines 7–8. Goal: No errors.

```
5  Bev majored in zoology after she qualified for an excellent    12
6  research grant.  She must speak with Dr. Haver, her mentor.    24

7  I am anxious because we must run a dozen errands and cannot    12
8  be late for class.  Have Paula adjourn the meeting quickly.    24
   |  1  |  2  |  3  |  4  |  5  |  6  |  7  |  8  |  9  |  10 |  11 |  12
```

C. Technique Drills

Key each line twice.

Shifting
```
9   Connie and Doug asked if I could go to Los Angeles in July.
10  Flight 1024 left New York for Sao Paulo, Brazil, on Monday.
```

Concentration
```
11  A proficient secretary manipulates microcomputers expertly.
12  Authorized institutions substitute experimental techniques.
```

Letter L21.61
Modified-block style (block paragraphs). No. 10 envelope.

November 26, 19— / Ms. Joan Schattel / 3521 West Lenox Street / Charlotte, TN 37036 / Dear Ms. Schattel: / Thank you for your letter of November 19 asking about the warranty on the Melody piano that you purchased from us last June. All of our pianos have a one-year warranty that entitles you to free tunings, repairs, and replacement of faulty strings and hammers. After the first year, you may receive these services for the cost of mileage to and from your home plus the cost of any replacement parts. ¶ You may call our toll-free number (1-800-555-9090) between 8 a.m. and 5 p.m. Monday through Friday for an appointment to have your piano tuned or repaired. ¶ Our service team has a combined total of more than 125 years of experience working with fine-quality musical instruments. Please do not hesitate to call on them if you have a question about your piano. We want satisfied customers! / Yours truly, / Miss Jane Bartlett / Customer Relations / [*Your initials*]

Take two 5-minute timings on lines 8–23. Proofread, note your errors, and figure your speed.

8	Much of the data that we work with in the office today	12
9	has been processed through a series of phases so that it is	24
10	arranged in a form that might help us use the data quickly.	36
11	For most offices, this process is known as input; and it is	48
12	the first step in what we call the processing cycle. Input	60
13	requires a number of separate steps relating to how complex	72
14	the data is with which we might be working.	81
15	When we input the data, we may have to key it into the	93
16	computer so that it can be used later. When it is entered,	105
17	it may have to be coded to make it easier to retrieve. The	117
18	names and phone numbers of clients are coded. Because many	129
19	people have the same last name, the absence of a code would	141
20	make it hard for the computer to recognize that each person	153
21	must have a separate file. Therefore, to retrieve a record	165
22	would be a very costly, tedious job and one that would take	177
23	too much time.	180

| 1 | 2 | 3 | 4 | 5 | 6 | 7 | 8 | 9 | 10 | 11 | 12 SI 1.33

Report R43.91
Paragraph enumeration format.

THE WORLD OF PRINTERS
By [*Your Name*]

Introduction ← *triple space*

A hard copy has always been a mainstay in the business office. Although much now is being stored via computers and microforms, the hard copy is still quite prominent. The print that appears in all of our letters, memos, reports, and tables has been embedded on those pages by a variety of impact *and nonimpact* printers. This report will review the basic features of the popular printers used in businesses today.

Impact Printers

We are probably more familiar with these printers, because they *are* were very much like the typewriters we have used in our schools and businesses ever since the first typewriter was manufactured in the 1800s. They place print on the paper when a character strikes metal an ink *ed* ribbon. Table 1 shows the printers that fall into the category of impact printers. It also reveals the approximate

(Continued on next page)

Letter L22.61

Modified-block style, indented paragraphs. No 6 3/4 envelope.

[*Today's date*] / Mr. Scott L. Ulene / 2600 Lyle Street / Brockton, MA 02402 / Dear Scott: / Standing room only is the description of a typical meeting of the Compucats computer club. Every month we draw large crowds with our dynamic programs and demonstrations. At each meeting there are as many as 10 machines up and running for trying software out. ¶ This group meets at our store near the Reed Air Base, which makes it possible for us to attract members from many parts of the World and always leads to an interesting exchange of ideas. ¶ Why not become a member of this group? Just return the enclosed card, or come to the next meeting at 2 p.m. this Saturday. / Yours very truly, / Jean Forrest, Manager / [*Your initials*] / Enclosure

Letter L23.61

Modified-block style, indented paragraphs. No. 10 envelope.

March 25, 19-- / Mr. and Mrs. Jason Brunswick / 61 Claiborne Court / Lebanon, TN 37087 / Dear Mr. and Mrs. Brunswick: / The Soft Pedal is having an April Fools' Day Sale, but this is no joke! Beginning at 7 a.m. on April 1, a different selection of pianos will be reduced from 25 to 40 percent each hour. If the piano you want is not on sale when you arrive, just check back an hour later to see if it has been drastically reduced.

We are having this special sale to show our appreciation for our valued customers as we celebrate our twenty-fifth anniversary. While you shop for the right piano, we will be serving cake, punch, and coffee.

Make a note now to join us for the celebration of the decade. We will be looking for you on April 1. / Cordially yours, / Mrs. Marie Noland / Sales Manager / [Your initials]

of all the oceans, reaching a depth of 36,000 feet. It is also the largest of the oceans, covering nearly 64 million square miles of the earth's surface. The area of each of the oceans (expressed to the nearest million square miles) is as follows:

TABLE 1

Name of Ocean	Area
Pacific Ocean	64,000,000
Atlantic Ocean	32,000,000
Indian Ocean	28,000,000
Arctic Ocean	5,000,000

The Ocean as a Climate Control

Because of the great area covered by the oceans, our climate is influenced by these bodies of water. The average surface temperature of the oceans ranges from about 25 degrees near the poles to 85 degrees near the equator. This great mass of water has a cooling effect on the land temperature. It also provides land masses with rainfall from the extensive evaporation that constantly takes place over each ocean's surface. Without these climatic controls, life on earth would not be possible because of the severe cold that would occur during the nights and the extreme heat that would build up during the days.

Report R42.90

Retrieve Report R41.90 (page 207) and make the following changes: (1) add the depth of each of the oceans to Table 1 in the report; use <u>Depth</u> as the heading for the third column and the following depth information for each of the oceans, respectively: *36,000; 27,000; 25,000;* and *18,000.* (2) In the last sentence before the table, insert the words *and the depth of each (expressed to the nearest thousand feet)* after *miles)* and change *is as follows:* to *are as follows:*.

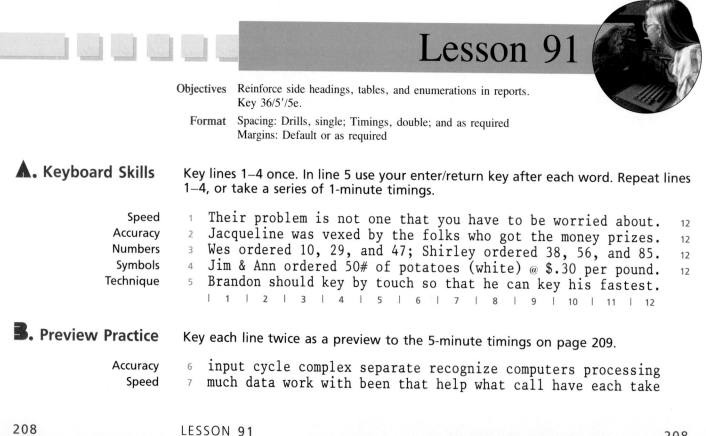

Lesson 91

Objectives Reinforce side headings, tables, and enumerations in reports. Key 36/5'/5e.

Format Spacing: Drills, single; Timings, double; and as required
Margins: Default or as required

A. Keyboard Skills

Key lines 1–4 once. In line 5 use your enter/return key after each word. Repeat lines 1–4, or take a series of 1-minute timings.

Speed	1	Their problem is not one that you have to be worried about.	12
Accuracy	2	Jacqueline was vexed by the folks who got the money prizes.	12
Numbers	3	Wes ordered 10, 29, and 47; Shirley ordered 38, 56, and 85.	12
Symbols	4	Jim & Ann ordered 50# of potatoes (white) @ $.30 per pound.	12
Technique	5	Brandon should key by touch so that he can key his fastest.	

| 1 | 2 | 3 | 4 | 5 | 6 | 7 | 8 | 9 | 10 | 11 | 12

B. Preview Practice

Key each line twice as a preview to the 5-minute timings on page 209.

Accuracy	6	input cycle complex separate recognize computers processing
Speed	7	much data work with been that help what call have each take

Lesson 62

Objectives Express numbers correctly while keying sentences.
Format copy notations.
Reinforce modified-block style letters.
Key 34/3'/5e.

Format Spacing: Drills, single; Timings, double; and as required
Margins: Default or as required

▲. LAB 7
Number Style

Key lines 1–4 once, correcting any errors in number-style rules. Review your copy as your teacher reads the answers. Then key lines 1–4 again.

1 Yue Huo was hired at four-forty an hour but is now making $5.25.
2 This auction raised 1000 of dollars for storm victims.
3 The high temperatures in November were in the mid-80s.
4 Their monthly parking fees were raised from $95.00 to $115.25.

B. PRETEST

Take a 3-minute timing on lines 5–13. Proofread, note your errors, and figure your speed.

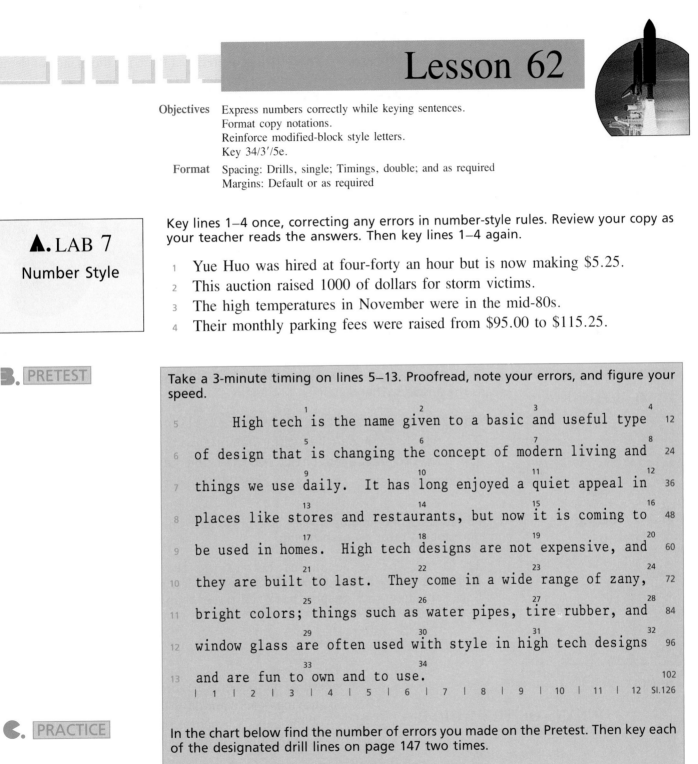

```
5       High tech is the name given to a basic and useful type    12
6   of design that is changing the concept of modern living and    24
7   things we use daily.  It has long enjoyed a quiet appeal in    36
8   places like stores and restaurants, but now it is coming to    48
9   be used in homes.  High tech designs are not expensive, and    60
10  they are built to last.  They come in a wide range of zany,    72
11  bright colors; things such as water pipes, tire rubber, and    84
12  window glass are often used with style in high tech designs    96
13  and are fun to own and to use.                              102
    |  1  |  2  |  3  |  4  |  5  |  6  |  7  |  8  |  9  |  10  |  11  |  12  SI.126
```

C. PRACTICE

In the chart below find the number of errors you made on the Pretest. Then key each of the designated drill lines on page 147 two times.

Pretest errors	0–1	2–3	4–5	6+
Drill lines	17–21	16–20	15–19	14–18

would weigh approximately 375 pounds on Jupiter because of the strong gravitational force on the largest planet. All of the large planets have atmospheres consisting primarily of hydrogen and helium and methane gas is also prominent in the atmospheres of two of the planets.

Notable Features

The most interesting feature of Jupiter is its Great Red Spot, which is more than three times the diameter of Earth. Saturn is noted for its rings and we have recently discovered that there are thousands of them. Because of the tilt of its axis Uranus has no day and night—it simply tilts its southern and northern halves toward the sun. Of the four largest planets, Neptune is located the farthest distance from the sun.

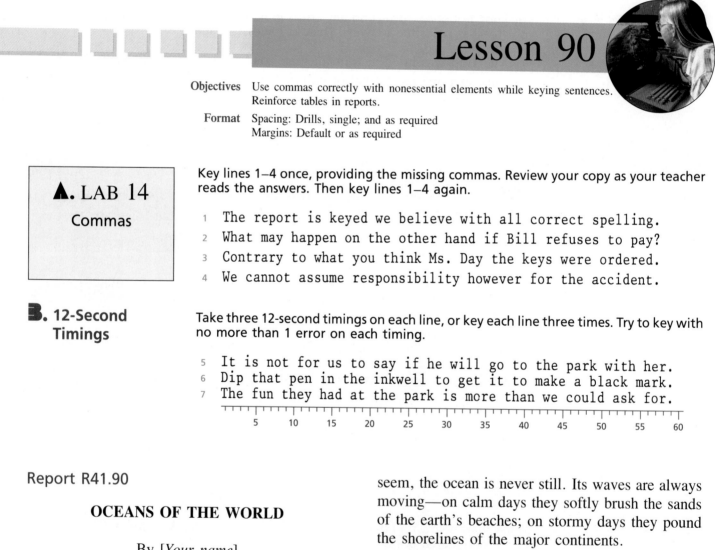

Lesson 90

Objectives   Use commas correctly with nonessential elements while keying sentences. Reinforce tables in reports.

Format   Spacing: Drills, single; and as required
Margins: Default or as required

▲. LAB 14

Commas

Key lines 1–4 once, providing the missing commas. Review your copy as your teacher reads the answers. Then key lines 1–4 again.

1   The report is keyed we believe with all correct spelling.
2   What may happen on the other hand if Bill refuses to pay?
3   Contrary to what you think Ms. Day the keys were ordered.
4   We cannot assume responsibility however for the accident.

B. 12-Second Timings

Take three 12-second timings on each line, or key each line three times. Try to key with no more than 1 error on each timing.

5   It is not for us to say if he will go to the park with her.
6   Dip that pen in the inkwell to get it to make a black mark.
7   The fun they had at the park is more than we could ask for.

5	10	15	20	25	30	35	40	45	50	55	60

Report R41.90

OCEANS OF THE WORLD

By [*Your name*]

Introduction

The major oceans of the world cover more than 70 percent of the earth's surface. Unusual as it may seem, the ocean is never still. Its waves are always moving—on calm days they softly brush the sands of the earth's beaches; on stormy days they pound the shorelines of the major continents.

The Four Great Oceans

The four oceans of the world are the Pacific, Atlantic, Indian, and Arctic. The Pacific is the deepest

```
14  own basic quiet stores design concept expensive restaurants
15  built style pipes range bright rubber window appeal designs
16  use and are zany tech living modern useful designs changing
17  now but used come water things colors coming places enjoyed
```

```
18  glass daily wide sign such tire come like home with has not
19  homes given high tech name type long used they last now are
20  appeal living useful given basic things daily long type use
21  colors bright stores water pipes style glass range wind are
```

D. POSTTEST

Take another 3-minute timing on lines 5–13 on page 146. Proofread, note your errors, and figure your speed. Compare your performance with the Pretest.

E. Copy Notation

Businesses keep copies of their outgoing documents for their own records. Each copy may be on paper (called a **hard copy**) or on a computer disk or tape (called a **soft copy**).

Office workers make hard copies on photocopy machines, use computer printers to make multiple copies, or use carbonless paper, especially for business forms such as invoices, purchase orders, and so on.

When a copy of a letter is sent to someone in addition to the addressee, a copy notation is keyed on the original and all copies.

To format a copy notation:

1. One line below the reference initials (or the enclosure notation), key c:, two spaces, and the name of the person receiving the copy.

2. If more than one person is to receive a copy, key the additional names on separate lines, beginning under the first name. Do not repeat c: before each name.

3. Use a title before the name only if the first name or initial is unknown.

```
                              Sincerely yours,


                              Renee Wilson
                              Supervisor

rls
c:  Mrs. Harrison
```

```
                              Sincerely yours,


                              Renee Wilson
                              Supervisor

rls
Enclosure
c:  Marian Moseley
    Clarence Propes
```

Letter L24.62
Modified-block style, indented paragraphs. No. 10 envelope.

[*Today's date*] / Mr. Donald J. Hofner / Winooski Mills / 85 N. Third Avenue / Burlington, VT 95442-7661 / Dear Mr. Hofner: / We are searching for a supplier of colored burlap. During the past four months, we have sold thirty bolts of natural colored burlap,

(Continued on next page)

In the chart below find the number of errors you made on the Pretest. Then key each of the following designated drill lines three times.

Pretest errors	0–1	2–3	4–5	6+
Drill lines	24–28	23–27	22–26	21–25

Accuracy

21 impact people always changed percent pleasing questionnaire
22 should mailed example current project consumers information
23 error because helpful improved referred accepted hopefully,
24 items return getting business follow-up questions organized

Speed

25 offend about many used item that easy read this lot the out
26 second third they want will bias rate only good any all and
27 mailing tool need find when have sent more mail eye you may
28 increase from free kind must once make time for the out lot

D. POSTTEST

Take another 5-minute timing on lines 5–20 (page 205). Proofread, note your errors, and figure your speed. Compare your performance with the Pretest.

E. Displays and Tables in Reports

To format a display or table in the body of a report, follow these steps:

1. Center the display or table horizontally between the set margins. Do not go beyond the set margins; reduce the space between columns if necessary.

2. Separate the display or table from the text with a double space. However, if the display or table contains a title and/or column headings, separate the display or table by a quadruple space (2 double spaces).

3. Single-space the body of the display or table unless told to do otherwise.

4. Use standard formatting directions for titles, column headings, and space between columns. (See pages 123 and 129.)

5. Try to place the display or table (a) immediately after the point in the text where it is referred to, (b) at the end of the paragraph in which it is referred to, or (c) at the bottom of the page.

6. If the display or table will not fit on the page where the reference occurs, place it at the top of the next page and insert a reference in the text indicating where the display or table is located, such as *the table on page 4.*

Report R40.89
Correct any errors in punctuation. **Note:** Review Section 81E, page 190, before keying this report.

THE SOLAR SYSTEM'S LARGE PLANETS

By Kenneth Kosobud

The Planets

The nine planets in the solar system range in size from Jupiter (the largest) to Pluto (the smallest). The four largest planets and their diameters are listed in Table 1.

TABLE 1

Planet	Diameter
Jupiter	89,000
Saturn	75,000
Uranus	32,000
Neptune	31,000

Three of the largest planets have at least 15 moons but Neptune has only 2. The longest year on any of these planets is on Neptune and is equal to 165 Earth years. A person weighing 150 pounds on Earth

(Continued on next page)

but our customers want really a variety of colors. ¶ Teachers in both private and public schools use burlap as a background cover for their bulletin boards and special displays, and students use it in various school projects. the demand for colors stems from a desire to coordinate the displays with school colors and with seasonal and holiday colors. ¶ We are unable to fill our customers' orders because the mills that usually supply our fabric produce burlap in one or two colors only. If you have burlap in several bright colors-- especially red, green, blue, and yellow--please let me know immediately so that I may place an order. / Very truly Yours, / Ms. Anette Teague / General Manager / [*Your initials*] / c: Madge Sorenson / Lillian Wood

Letter L25.62
Modified-block style (blocked paragraphs). No. 10 envelope.

[Today's date] / Ms. Anette Teague / General Manager / Sew What? / 4290 Waterbury Plaza / Waterbury, CT 06704-9543 / Dear Ms. Teague: / Yes! We have burlap in a variety of colors, and it can be shipped the same day that we receive your order. ¶ Simply choose the colors you want from the enclosed sample card; then call 1-800-555-1357 to place your order. If you prefer, you can mail your order using the handy form on the back of the sample card. Payment for wholesale orders is due in 30 days. ¶ We know that you will be pleased with the high quality and wide variety of our fabrics, and we look forward to hearing from you soon. / Sincerely, / Donald J. Hofner / Sales Manager / [Your initials] / Enclosure / c: Joseph Hendrix

Lesson 89

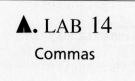

Objectives Identify how commas are used with nonessential elements while keying sentences.
Format displays and tables in reports.
Key 36/5'/5e.

Format Spacing: Drills, single; Timings, double; and as required
Margins: Default or as required

▲. LAB 14
Commas

Key lines 1–4 once. Then repeat lines 1–4, or take a series of 1-minute timings.

1 As you know, at least 50 nations participated in the games.   12
2 I will not miss the seminar, Mr. North, as I first thought.   12
3 Jean will have, I believe, enough support for the election.   12
4 It is not my belief, however, that we should turn back now.   12

| 1 | 2 | 3 | 4 | 5 | 6 | 7 | 8 | 9 | 10 | 11 | 12

B. PRETEST

Take a 5-minute timing on lines 5–20. Proofread, note your errors, and figure your speed.

5   A questionnaire is a helpful tool for getting a lot of   12
6 good information from many people. For example, it is used   24
7 by many people in business to project if the item they want   36
8 to make will be accepted by consumers. It may also be used   48
9 to find out if any of their current items should be changed   60
10 or improved.   62

11   When a questionnaire is to be mailed out, it should be   74
12 free of errors of all kinds and should be organized so that   86
13 it is pleasing to the eye and easy to read. Your questions   98
14 always must be free of all bias and must not offend anyone.   110
15 Because the return rate is only about 20 to 30 percent, the   122
16 questionnaire may have to be sent out more than once. When   134
17 it is sent out a second or third time, it is often referred   146
18 to as a follow-up. Hopefully, this second or third mailing   158
19 will increase the return rate to 40 percent, a rate that is   170
20 a fairly good return for a mail questionnaire.   179

| 1 | 2 | 3 | 4 | 5 | 6 | 7 | 8 | 9 | 10 | 11 | 12 SI 1.36

Objectives   Recognize how numbers are expressed in sentences.
Reinforce personal-business letters and business letters.
Reinforce letters with copy notations.

Format   Spacing: Drills, single; and as required
Margins: Default or as required

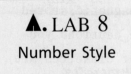

A. LAB 8
Number Style

Key lines 1–4 once. Then repeat lines 1–4, or take a series of 1-minute timings.

```
1  The clinic is on Fourth Street; the hospital is on Seventh.   12
2  We have 25 minutes to walk from 57th Avenue to 69th Avenue.   12
3  The address was changed from One Eighth Street to 141 48th.   12
4  They celebrated their forty-fifth anniversary on October 2.  12
   |  1  |  2  |  3  |  4  |  5  |  6  |  7  |  8  |  9  |  10  |  11  |  12
```

7. Generally spell out all ordinal numbers that can be expressed in one or two words. A hyphenated number counts as one word.

first, nineteenth, two hundredth, seventy-fifth

8. Spell out street names from *first* through *tenth;* use figures for street names above *tenth.* Also use figures for all house numbers except *one.*

One Third Avenue, 7 Fifth Avenue, 12 West 22d Street, 89 45th Street

Note: Use the ordinal signs (*st, d, th*) with figures except in dates when the day follows the month.

B. 12-Second Timings

Take three 12-second timings on each line, or key each line three times. Try to key with no more than 1 error on each timing.

```
5  I told Pam how pretty she looks, but she does not think so.
6  Some people just cannot accept nice things said about them.
7  Why do people feel ill at ease when a nice comment is made?
   5    10    15    20    25    30    35    40    45    50    55    60
```

Refer to pages 99 and 101 for formatting instructions if necessary. From now on, block paragraphs unless indenting is indicated.

Letter L26.63
Modified-block style. No. 6 3/4 envelope.

June 21, 19— / Manager of Housekeeping / City Plaza Hotel / 5107 Tenth Avenue / Washington, DC 20007 / Dear Sir or Madam: / I was one of the members of the Texas All-State Youth Choir who stayed in your hotel June 12–15. After returning home from our tour two days ago, I discovered that my leather jacket was missing. I believe that I may have left it hanging in the closet in Room 2783. ¶ The jacket, a size 8, is forest green suede leather, and the brand name is Paris Mist. If it has been found, I will be happy to pay the charges for having it shipped to me. ¶ The jacket was a special graduation gift, and I am eager to find it. You may telephone me at 903-555-4970 after 3:30 p.m., CST. / Yours truly, / Makala Duhon / 4207 Judson Road / Longview, TX 75605

CHOOSING A COLLEGE
By Robert Loth

Choosing the right college is a very important decision for you to make. You want to make sure that your choice is the best one and that you are happy with that choice.

Start Early

You need to investigate the many colleges available to you at least during your junior year in high school. Write to those in which you are especially interested, and obtain as much information as possible. Using this approach, you will be able to choose from a large list of schools.

Obtain Pertinent Information

Try to get the same information from all the schools you contact so that you can make valid comparisons when you receive all the information. Here are some questions that you should consider:

1. What is the tuition cost per year?
2. What does room and board cost per year?
3. What are the entrance requirements (SAT, ACT, G.P.A., class standing, and so on)?
4. What is the school's reputation for offering a quality education?
5. What is the school's reputation for offering a quality program in the major field you wish to study?

Visit the Campus

You can learn a lot about a college if you visit the campus, and it is strongly recommended that you do. By visiting the campus, you will find out how far you will have to walk to your classes, where you will park, where your dormitory is located, how pleasant the surroundings are, and how well groomed the campus grounds are.

CARING FOR YOUR DISKETTES
By Andrew Hashakawa

Diskettes are a major source of input for computers, and it is extremely important that we take good care of them. If they are not properly cared for, you may lose some or all of the data that has been magnetically stored on them. Some basic precautions you should take in caring for diskettes are discussed in the following enumerated paragraphs.

1. Do not touch the exposed area of the diskette with your fingers. Doing so may leave oil on the diskette surface, making it difficult for the computer read mechanism to capture the data.

2. Do not bend, scratch, or fold the diskette. If the diskette is damaged in any of these ways, it won't be possible for the computer to read the data that is stored on it.

3. Do not let the diskette be exposed to high temperatures from direct sunlight or other high-temperature heat sources.

If implemented, the above suggestions for caring for your diskettes will minimize data loss that occurs for many people. Other concerns associated with diskette care are storing the diskette near a magnetic source such as a magnet, spilling liquids on the diskette surface, and storing the diskette in an area where it is not protected from dust and other elements.

Report R39.88
Retrieve Report R37.88 and reformat all the side headings as paragraph headings.

Letter L27.63
Modified-block style. No. 6 3/4 envelope.

March 11, 19— / Mrs. Kathy Patterson / General Manager / Vacations Unlimited / One Kings Way / Vicksburg, MS 39181 / Dear Mrs. Patterson: / My wife and I will be celebrating our twenty-fifth anniversary in June, and I would like to surprise her with a vacation cruise to some of the islands. ¶ Would you please send me information about cruises to the Bahamas, the Virgin Islands, Jamaica, and Bermuda. I would also be interested in any special vacation packages available for these areas. Since my traveling experience is somewhat limited, I will need an expert travel agent to help me plan the perfect anniversary vacation. ¶ My work schedule makes it impossible for me to come in and discuss arrangements with you before next month. However, I will read any information you can send and will try to have some choices in mind. / Sincerely yours, / Blaine Johnson / 707 Crystal Lane / Utica, MS 39175

Letter L28.63
Modified-block style. No. 10 envelope.

March 15, 19-- / Mr. Blaine Johnson / 707 Crystal Lane / Utica, MS 39175 / Dear Mr.

Johnson: / We at Vacations Unlimited are truly excited about the surprise anniversary vacation for your wife. One of our agents, Barbara Hoffmire, specializes in Caribbean vacations and will gladly help you plan your dream trip. ¶ Several leaflets and brochures featuring both cruises and airfare / hotel packages are enclosed. Take some time to read over them. Then you and Barbara can work out all of the details to your satisfaction when you come in next month. ¶ Since this is a surprise for Mrs. Johnson, we will not telephone you. If you have any questions or need additional information, please let us know. We look forward to seeing you in April. / Cordially yours, / Kathy Patterson / General Manager / [Your initials] / 5 Enclosures / c: Barbara Hoffmire

Lesson 64

Objectives
Identify how numbers are expressed in sentences.
Format postscript notations in letters.
Reinforce modified-block style letters.
Key 34/3'/5e.

Format
Spacing: Drills, single; Timings, double; and as required
Margins: Default or as required

▲. LAB 8
Number Style

Key lines 1–4 once. Then repeat lines 1–4, or take a series of 1-minute timings.

1　The bus stops at 349 11th Avenue and 1091 West 47th Street.　12
2　Liz stayed at 38 West Third Street from April 5 to June 30.　12
3　Lois will be at 132d Street and Eighth Avenue at 1 o'clock.　12
4　My seventeenth birthday is a week before your twenty-first.　12
　　| 1 | 2 | 3 | 4 | 5 | 6 | 7 | 8 | 9 | 10 | 11 | 12

structure, and content. Our final draft must be our *very* best effort.
If necessary, we should have another person proofread our work so
that all of ~~these~~ *our* errors are corrected before ~~our~~ *the* final report is
submitted.

Report R36.87
Retrieve Report R35.87 (page 202) and make the following changes: (1) reformat the enumeration in hanging-indented style; (2) delete enumeration item 3 and renumber. Use the paragraph tab for the numbers, set a left tab for the indent (4 spaces after the first tab).

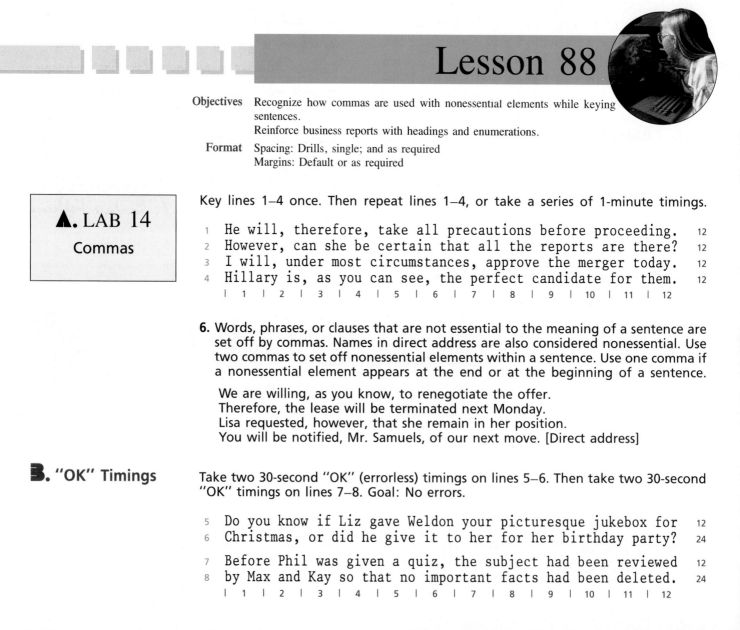

Lesson 88

Objectives Recognize how commas are used with nonessential elements while keying sentences.
Reinforce business reports with headings and enumerations.

Format Spacing: Drills, single; and as required
Margins: Default or as required

▲. LAB 14
Commas

Key lines 1–4 once. Then repeat lines 1–4, or take a series of 1-minute timings.

1 He will, therefore, take all precautions before proceeding.   12
2 However, can she be certain that all the reports are there?   12
3 I will, under most circumstances, approve the merger today.   12
4 Hillary is, as you can see, the perfect candidate for them.   12
   | 1 | 2 | 3 | 4 | 5 | 6 | 7 | 8 | 9 | 10 | 11 | 12

6. Words, phrases, or clauses that are not essential to the meaning of a sentence are set off by commas. Names in direct address are also considered nonessential. Use two commas to set off nonessential elements within a sentence. Use one comma if a nonessential element appears at the end or at the beginning of a sentence.

We are willing, as you know, to renegotiate the offer.
Therefore, the lease will be terminated next Monday.
Lisa requested, however, that she remain in her position.
You will be notified, Mr. Samuels, of our next move. [Direct address]

B. "OK" Timings

Take two 30-second "OK" (errorless) timings on lines 5–6. Then take two 30-second "OK" timings on lines 7–8. Goal: No errors.

5 Do you know if Liz gave Weldon your picturesque jukebox for   12
6 Christmas, or did he give it to her for her birthday party?   24

7 Before Phil was given a quiz, the subject had been reviewed   12
8 by Max and Kay so that no important facts had been deleted.   24
   | 1 | 2 | 3 | 4 | 5 | 6 | 7 | 8 | 9 | 10 | 11 | 12

B. PRETEST

Take a 3-minute timing on lines 5–13. Proofread, note your errors, and figure your speed.

```
                1                    2                    3                    4
5        When you go for a job interview, there are some things        12
           5                    6                    7              8
6    you should and should not do.  First, you want to be neatly      24
           9                    10                   11             12
7    groomed and suitably dressed; this will give you a positive      36
               13                   14                   15        16
8    feeling about yourself.  Second, wait for the person who is      48
           17                   18                   19         20
9    interviewing you to shake your hand.  Have a firm handshake      60
           21                   22                   23         24
10   but not one that squeezes.  Try to relax and smile and keep      72
           25                   26                   27         28
11   good eye contact.  Come prepared to ask questions about the      84
               29                   30              31           32
12   position to determine if this is the job for you and if you      96
           33              34
13   are the right one for the job.                                  102
     |  1  |  2  |  3  |  4  |  5  |  6  |  7  |  8  |  9  |  10  |  11  |  12  SI 1.27
```

C. PRACTICE

In the chart below find the number of errors you made on the Pretest. Then key each of the following designated drill lines two times.

Pretest errors	0–1	2–3	4–5	6+
Drill lines	17–21	16–20	15–19	14–18

Accuracy

```
14   about deter first person smiling groomed position interview
15   quest smile views second relaxed feeling positive determine
16   comes dress gives neatly viewing contact suitably handshake
17   relax thing groom should dressed squeeze prepared questions
```

Speed

```
18   feels keeps shake good some when mine one but are ask if to
19   thing given waits hand your suit will sit and you who be go
20   firms right there neat that mile this not eye for the do is
21   pared hands comes self wing want have try vie job our in or
```

D. POSTTEST

Take another 3-minute timing on lines 5–13. Proofread, note your errors, and figure your speed. Compare your performance with the Pretest.

In the chart below find the number of errors you made on the Pretest. Then key each of the designated drill lines three times.

Pretest errors	0–1	2–3	4–5	6+
Drill lines	24–28	23–27	22–26	21–25

Accuracy

21 just period future faster players invaded business addition
22 past coming chance larger become common software technology
23 now have popular simpler storage horizon machines computers
24 six quite likely compact smaller converse powerful possible

Speed

25 these their being will same this work all now are the it in
26 years times seven more were that used our not did any is to
27 disks store makes find hard data they lot are and use be or
28 finds music today much come five just now run may ago on of

D. POSTTEST

Take another 5-minute timing on lines 5–20 (page 201). Proofread, note your errors, and figure your speed. Compare your performance with the Pretest.

Report R35.87
Paragraph enumeration format.

WHY WE NEED REPORTS

By Jeanette McArthur

Why do we need reports? Every business needs reports. *for a variety of reasons* Some would argue that reports waste a lot of time and cost a lot *of money*, but a report is an excellent means for sharing information with ~~all of~~ your subordinates, ~~your peers,~~ and your superiors. Basically, we need reports for the following reasons:

1. We need reports to give us *some* indication of where we have been and how far we have come.

2. We need reports to inform the public of who we are and what we do.

ds 2.³ We need reports to keep records of how successful *(or unsuccessful)* we have been. In addition, many laws require that we keep excellent records of all our business transactions and that we report our operations to Governmental and Regulatory agencies.

5⅓.⁴ We need reports to help us make decisions that are important for the day-to-day operations of our business. ¶When writing reports, we need to be sure that we draw all of our conclusions from the facts that have been revealed in our ~~research.~~ We need (also) to be sure that we proofread our work very carefully to catch errors ~~such as~~ *in* spelling, punctuation, grammar, sentence

(Continued on next page)

E. Postscript (PS:)

A postscript (*PS:*) is an additional message in paragraph form at the end of a letter. To format a postscript:

1. Double-space after the last item in the letter.
2. Begin the postscript at the left margin if paragraphs are blocked; indent 5 spaces if paragraphs are indented.
3. Key *PS:* and space two times. Key the message.

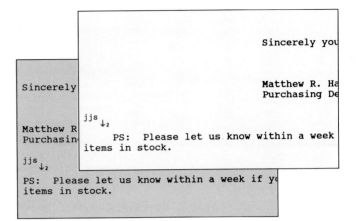

Letter L29.64
Modified-block style, indented paragraphs. No. 10 envelope.

March 20, 19— / Mr. Chris Bedard / 8764 Greeneway / Juneau, AK 99801 / Dear Chris: / Make plans now to attend our annual roundup for high school seniors on April 7–8. You will arrive on campus Friday afternoon and will be our guest in Rawlings Hall. After a complimentary dinner in our cafeteria, a brief orientation meeting will be held in the auditorium. Tours of the campus will be conducted by university students until 8 p.m.; then individual dorms will host games and movies until midnight. ¶ Breakfast will be served from 6:30 to 7:30 Saturday morning, and you may test and interview for departmental scholarships between 8 a.m. and 12 noon. A picnic lunch will be served on the student-center lawn, and entertainment will be provided by different university choirs and dance groups. ¶ We are looking forward to having you join us on April 7–8. Just fill out the enclosed card and drop it in the mail so that we can reserve a dorm room for you. We think you will agree that Seattle Pacific University is where you want to be! / Sincerely yours, / Gary W. Hunter / Admissions Director / [*Your initials*] / Enclosure / PS: If you wish to audition for a music scholarship, please call 903-555-2790 by March 31 to make an appointment.

Letter L30.64
Modified-block style. No. 10 envelope.

[*Today's date*] / Ms. Alice Featherstone / 2516 North 18th Street, Apt. 243 / Denver, Colorado 80205 / Dear ~~Miss~~ *Ms.* Featherstone: / Thank you for ~~agreeing~~ *accepting* to speak at our fall meeting on the topic of the office of the ~~future.~~ *nineties* We have had ~~a lot~~ *hundreds* of requests for such a speech, and I know your ~~ideas~~ *thoughts* are going to be very *much* welcomed by our group.

Please send me the title of your speech as soon as you can so that I can place ⎡in⎦⎡it⎦ our program. ¶ If you've *any* questions, please call *me* at 555-3298. / Yours sincerely, / Sue Anne Clardy / Program Director / [*Your initials*] / PS: We would like you ⎡send⎦⎡to⎦ us a copy of the handouts for your presentation *ta* so that we can duplicate enough copies for all who attend your session.

Objectives Use commas correctly after introductory words and phrases while keying sentences.
Reinforce business reports with enumerations.
Key 36/5'/5e.

Format Spacing: Drills, single; Timings, double; and as required
Margins: Default or as required

▲. LAB 13
Commas

Key lines 1–4 once, providing the missing commas. Review your copy as your teacher reads the answers. Then key lines 1–4 again.

1 In other words you must key this entire document for Jane.
2 Well I can always wait until the rain has stopped falling.
3 For example have you ever copied the line to another file?
4 Yes Bryant can attend the meeting if he makes up his work.

B. PRETEST

Take a 5-minute timing on lines 5–20. Proofread, note your errors, and figure your speed.

```
5        In the past decade, computers invaded just about every    12
6   facet of the business office.  In addition, they are now so    24
7   popular that it would be hard to find any business that did    36
8   not use such machines to do the work.  In this same period,    48
9   they have become smaller and faster.  It is quite common to    60
10  find computers being used today that are six or seven times    72
11  faster than they were just five years ago.                     81
12       In the coming years, computers will likely become much    93
13  more powerful.  They will have larger storage, they will be   105
14  able to run more software, and they will be much simpler to   117
15  use.  What makes all of this possible is the new technology   129
16  that is just now on the horizon.  In the future, we will be   141
17  able to store a lot of our data on compact disks, much like   153
18  the disks that are used today in many of our music players.   165
19  There is also, I think, a chance that we will converse with   177
20  most computers.                                               180
    |  1  |  2  |  3  |  4  |  5  |  6  |  7  |  8  |  9  |  10  |  11  |  12  SI 1.36
```

Objectives Express numbers correctly while keying sentences.
Reinforce postscripts and copy notations.
Reinforce personal-business and business letters in modified-block style.

Format Spacing: Drills, single; and as required
Margins: Default or as required

A. LAB 8
Number Style

Key lines 1–4 once, correcting any errors in number-style rules. Review your copy as your teacher reads the answers. Then key lines 1–4 again.

1 The parade began at 4th Avenue and Fifty-seventh Street at 10:30.
2 His latest address was 21 Thirty-eighth Street, not eleven 3d Street.
3 The 200th anniversary is known as the bicentennial.
4 He will celebrate his 23d birthday on November 23d.

B. 30-Second Timings

Take two 30-second timings on lines 5 and 6. Then take two 30-second timings on lines 7 and 8. Try to key with no more than 2 errors on each timing.

5 That big pine tree in front of our house had to be cut down 12
6 when Dad said it could infect all of the trees on our farm. 24

7 We are going to plant a new tree; of course, it will take a 12
8 long time to grow. Someday my children may play around it. 24
   | 1 | 2 | 3 | 4 | 5 | 6 | 7 | 8 | 9 | 10 | 11 | 12

C. Punctuation Spacing

Key each line twice.

9 Pam bought apples, peaches, corn, and tomatoes at the farm.
10 I can run fast. You have a dog. Can we go? Yes, you can.
11 My sister-in-law took a true-false test--and she failed it.
12 He said, "I can't sleep; maybe I should be counting sheep."

Letter L31.65
Modified-block style. No. 6 3/4 envelope.

August 4, 19— / Mr. George T. Arnold / Vice President / Swift Runners, Inc. / 4488 Washoe Avenue / Carson City, NV 89701 / Dear Mr. Arnold: / On July 7 I purchased a pair of Swift Runners, Model 53, from Athletic Shoes in the Fresno Mall. After breaking them in with several two-mile runs, I wore them in the Monterey Marathon on July 24. After the tenth mile, I sensed that something was wrong with my right foot. When I looked down, I saw that the sole was ripping away from the sides of the shoe. Naturally, I had to drop out of the race.¶When I took the shoes back to the store, the manager examined them and said it appeared that the seams had been intentionally cut. He refused to refund my money or to exchange the damaged shoes for another pair.¶I am extremely unhappy about this situation, and I expect you to take some corrective action immediately. / Yours very truly, / Samuel M. Long / 45 East Seventh Street / Fresno, CA 93765 / PS: I will mail the shoes to you if you will agree to pay for the shipping costs.

USING QUESTIONNAIRES

By [*Your name*]

A questionnaire is one of the basic tools for gathering information for a report. If you work for a company, you will likely be involved with other people in preparing a questionnaire. Here are some basic rules to follow when preparing a questionnaire:

General Information

A series of questions for obtaining general information should be placed at the beginning of your questionnaire. Answers to these questions will help you make comparisons between and among different groups that you survey.

Specific Information

This information will pertain to the questions you need to ask that relate to the specific nature of your study. If your study focused on the use of computers in your company, then these questions would relate specifically to that topic.

Writing and Format Guidelines

Whether you include general or specific questions, you should follow certain writing guidelines when preparing your questionnaire. Here are a few of the guidelines you should follow:

1. Write your questions clearly so that they will not be misinterpreted by the respondents.

2. Since the questionnaire should be fairly short, include only essential questions that pertain to the precise nature of your study.

3. Define any terms with which the respondent may not be familiar.

It is also important that you prepare your questionnaire so that it will be easy to code once the respondents have returned it. A good suggestion to follow is to make certain that most of your answers are listed at the left margin of your paper. You should also try to minimize the number of "opinion" questions you include, because they are difficult to tabulate.

Report R34.86
Retrieve Report R33.86 and make these changes:

(1) *Replace the enumerated items with the following items:* 1. Do not prepare questions that lead the respondent to an answer. 2. Arrange your questions in a logical order. 3. If your survey includes questions that are argumentative, write them so that they are unbiased and fair to all the respondents. (2) *Replace the final paragraph with the following:* Following these guidelines will help you prepare a better questionnaire for obtaining information from other people.

Letter L32.65
Modified-block style. No. 6 3/4 envelope.

August 17, 19-- / Mr. Samuel M. Long / 45 E. Seventh Street / Fresno, CA 93765 / Dear Mr. Long: / We are sorry [apologize] for the problems you had with your Swift runners, model 53, which forced you to drop out of the Monterrey Marathon. In addition, Mr. Tally, our dealer in Fresno, was in error when he did nothing to rectify this matter. You are justified in being angry.

We discovered last week that the equipment used to sew the Model 35 shoes is faulty. As the seams were stitched, a sharp edge that is out of alignment was cutting the material.

That is why Mr. Tally thought that the shoes had been intentionally cut. All of our dealers now have been informed of this situation, and the Model 53 shoes have been removed from stock. Mr. Tally has been instructed to refund your money in full and also to give you for free a pair of shoes from his inventory. We hope that this will restore your faith in swift runners and that you will enjoy many more miles of running with our shoes. PS: Please give the damaged shoes to Mr. Tally when you go to the store so that he can ship them to us. / Sincerely yours, / George T. Arnold / Vice President / [*Your initials*] / c: Paul Tally

---

Lesson 66

Objectives   Reinforce letters.
Key 34/3'/5e.

Format   Spacing: Drills, single; Timings, double; and as required
Margins: Default or as required

▲. Keyboard Skills

Key lines 1–4 once. Then follow the instructions in line 5. Repeat lines 1–4, or take a series of 1-minute timings.

Speed	1	Short words seem easier when you are trying to build speed.	12
Accuracy	2	Jacqueline was glad her family took five or six big prizes.	12
Numbers	3	If I need 56 points, then 47, 29, 38, or 10 would not help.	12
Symbols	4	She decided that 1/2 of $28 = $14 and that 20% of $30 = $6.	12
Technique	5	Key line 3 again and boldface the numbers.	

| 1 | 2 | 3 | 4 | 5 | 6 | 7 | 8 | 9 | 10 | 11 | 12

Objectives Identify how commas are used after introductory words and phrases while keying sentences.
Reinforce skill on the tab key.
Format business reports with enumerations.

Format Spacing: Drills, single; and as required
Margins: Default or as required

▲. LAB 13
Commas

Key lines 1–4 once. Then repeat lines 1–4, or take a series of 1-minute timings.

1 During our next class, we might review all of the chapters. 12
2 In my judgment, there is not enough evidence for the trial. 12
3 No, you may not take the books out of the library tomorrow. 12
4 For the third time, we ordered the chairs over a month ago. 12

   | 1 | 2 | 3 | 4 | 5 | 6 | 7 | 8 | 9 | 10 | 11 | 12

▶. 30-Second Timings

Take two 30-second timings on lines 5 and 6. Then take two 30-second timings on lines 7 and 8. Try to key with no more than 2 errors on each timing.

5 We sit and throw rocks in the big lake as the sun sets, but 12
6 we cannot see if they are going to skip over the big waves. 24

7 The lane that goes down to the lake turns and goes to town, 12
8 but we do not know if you can use it all the way right now. 24

   | 1 | 2 | 3 | 4 | 5 | 6 | 7 | 8 | 9 | 10 | 11 | 12

◀. Tab Key

Set five tabs, 10 spaces apart—the first tab is a left tab, the next two are decimal tabs, the last two right tabs. If you do not have decimal or right tabs, set all left tabs. Key each line once.

		L	D	D	R	R
9	depth	king	10.29	338.47	561	29,738
10	light	safe	7.56	9.10	47	56
11	favor	jump	.83	92.65	9	470
12	grows	home	74.01	384.72	492	6,501

◼. Enumerations in Business Reports

Enumerations (pages 79 and 81) are often contained in the body of a report. The format you use will depend on the type and the length of the items.

Hanging-Indented Format. If the enumerated items are short (one or two lines), use the hanging-indented format:

1. Display the enumeration by indenting it 5 spaces from the left margin.
2. Single-space the items; double-space between items; hang-indent turnover lines.
3. Leave 1 blank line above and below the enumeration.

Paragraph Format. If the enumerated items are long (three or more lines) or are paragraphs that have been numbered for clarity, use the paragraph format:

1. Use the same margins used in the report. If paragraphs are indented in the report, indent the first line of each enumerated item as well.
2. If the report is double-spaced, double-space the enumeration. Do not leave any extra blank lines.
3. If the report is single-spaced, single-space the enumeration. Leave 1 blank line above and below the enumeration and between items.

Note: If report paragraphs are blocked, use the hanging-indented format, but do not indent from the left margin.

B. Preview Practice

Key each line twice as a preview to the 3-minute timings below.

Accuracy   6   screen excess fatigue quality computer employees ergonomics
Speed   7   angle each work like seem help must tilt from eye day be or

C. 3-Minute Timings

Take two 3-minute timings on lines 8–16. Proofread, note your errors, and figure your speed.

8   Ergonomics refers to setting up a workplace that suits   12
9   the workers and helps relieve a lot of the stress each day.   24
10   The design of chairs, the height of desks, and the angle or   36
11   tilt of a computer screen can cause fatigue if they are not   48
12   just right. Those employees who may seem to be lazy may be   60
13   workers who suffer eyestrain from poor light or stress from   72
14   excess noise each day at work. These things can have major   84
15   effects on the quality of work that is produced. An office   96
16   today must be planned to help.   102

| 1 | 2 | 3 | 4 | 5 | 6 | 7 | 8 | 9 | 10 | 11 | 12 SI 1.28

Letter L33.66
Modified-block style. No. 6 3/4 envelope.

May 14, 19-- / Dr. Hans Rosenburg / Allergy and Asthma Clinic / 2005 Eighth Avenue / Milwaukee, WI 53203 / Dear Dr. Rosenburg: / My doctor has suggested that I may need to be tested for allergies since I have been suffering from chronic colds and upper respiratory infections for the past year. ¶ Before I make an appointment to have the test done, there are some questions I need answered. How long does a complete allergy test take? Is the cost covered by major medical insurance? Is the test done in a hospital or in your clinic? ¶ Any additional information that you can give me about the testing process would be greatly appreciated. / Yours truly, / Rosa Ortega / 39 McFarland Road / Madison, WI 53714 / PS: If the testing takes longer than one day, are overnight accommodations available nearby?

E. Paragraph Headings in Business Reports

Paragraph headings further subdivide a report. To format paragraph headings:

1. Key paragraph headings at the beginning of a paragraph.

2. Capitalize important words; underline the entire heading.

3. Follow a paragraph heading with a period and 2 spaces.

Report R31.85

Standard business format. Remember to bold all side headings.

Tennis

By Michael S. Johnson

History

Tennis was first played in ancient Greece, but it wasn't until the 1400s that it was revised by the French into the game that we know today. In the beginning, there was no net. Instead, the ball was hit over small embankments on the ground. The game of tennis was first played in the United States in 1874, and the first Wimbledon tournament was played four years later.

Organized Tennis

Tennis in the United States is organized into several divisions, thereby permitting players with varying talents to compete with other players of their own caliber.

Amateur Tennis. Players who participate in amateur tennis cannot receive money for playing the game. However, they do compete in several matches and tournaments. Amateur players can even compete in international tournaments, because the amateur division includes teams from more than 85 countries.

Professional Tennis. Players at this level generally earn their living by competing in matches sanctioned by groups such as World Championship Tennis. Professional tennis players also earn money by representing firms that make tennis equipment.

Open Tennis. In this category, players from either group can compete with each other.

The Tennis Court

A tennis court is rectangular in shape, 27 feet (for singles) or 36 feet (for doubles) wide by 18 feet long. The net is 3 feet high at the center and 3½ feet high at the sides. The court is divided into sections designating service areas and playing areas.

Report R32.85

Retrieve Report R31.85 and make the following changes: (1) Place the side heading *The Tennis Court* (and narrative) after the narrative for *History*. (2) Change the order of the paragraphs under *Organized Tennis* so that *Professional Tennis* is first, *Amateur Tennis* is second, and *Open Tennis* is last. (3) Add the following sentence as the final sentence for *The Tennis Court* paragraph:

A court may have one of several surfaces: asphalt, clay, concrete, or grass.

Letter L34.66
Block style. No. 10 envelope.

May 17, 19— / Ms. Rosa Ortega / 39 McFarland Road / Madison, WI 53714 / Dear Ms. Ortega: / We are pleased to answer your questions about allergy testing. The complete test takes two days. This includes food allergy tests as well as the usual tests for plants, animals, mold spores, and so on. The cost is $250, and most major medical insurance plans pay 80 percent of this fee, minus the deductible. All the testing is done here at our clinic. ¶Since we have many patients who need overnight accommodations, the Colonial Inn, which is two blocks from our clinic, offers reduced rates to our clients if we make the reservations. ¶Enclosed is a brochure that explains the testing process and follow-up treatments. / Cordially yours, / Hans Rosenburg, M.D. / [*Your initials*] / Enclosure / PS: Our toll-free telephone number for making appointments is 1-800-555-9691.

Letter L35.66
Block style. No. 6 3/4 envelope.

December 13, 19-- / Miss Victoria Guthrie / Assistant manager / Sophisticated Petite / 5420 Town Center Mall / Mesquite, TX 75150-4418 / Dear Miss Guthrie: / I was in your store last Saturday and tried on a *gold satin* sleeveless blouse, size Petite. ~~Even though~~ *although* I liked the blouse very much, I didn't purchase it, and now I wish that I had. It would be ~~just right~~ *perfect* for the upcoming holiday festivities. ¶Because I live 2 hours ~~away~~ *from Mesquite*, it is not possible *for me* to return to your store within the next 2 weeks. If you still have ~~it~~ *the blouse* in my size, could you ship it to me and ~~charge~~ it on my main line card? ¶You may telephone me at 903-555-2525 after 4 p.m. / Sincerely, / Carole Stanislovsky / Route 4, Box 913 / Hallsville, TX 75650

Lesson 85

Objectives Recognize how commas are used after introductory words and phrases while keying sentences.
Reinforce skill on left-hand and right-hand reaches.
Format business reports with side and paragraph headings.

Format Spacing: Drills, single; Timings, double; and as required
Margins: Default or as required

▲. LAB 13
Commas

Key lines 1–4 once. Then repeat lines 1–4, or take a series of 1-minute timings.

```
1  In other words, you can now see the program of your choice.   12
2  During the session, the first person used very good charts.   12
3  In my opinion, I can't proceed until we have all the facts.   12
4  For example, the charts in the next two chapters are keyed.   12
   |  1  |  2  |  3  |  4  |  5  |  6  |  7  |  8  |  9  |  10 |  11 |  12
```

5. Place a comma after introductory words and phrases such as *first, in my opinion, for example,* and so on.

Yes, the conference will be held next week. [Word]
In my opinion, we must continue our research. [Phrase]
In response to your letter, we sent the package. [Phrase]

B. PRETEST

Take a 1-minute timing on lines 5–7. Proofread, note your errors, and figure your speed.

```
5        You will key a draft of your tasks at a very fast rate   12
6  if you use a word processor.  Your copy will look very good   24
7  when you are done because you'll have made all corrections.   36
   |  1  |  2  |  3  |  4  |  5  |  6  |  7  |  8  |  9  |  10 |  11 |  12
```

C. PRACTICE

SPEED: If you made 2 or fewer errors on the Pretest, key lines 8–13 twice each. Repeat if time permits.
ACCURACY: If you made more than 2 errors on the Pretest, key lines 8–10 as a group twice. Then key lines 11–13 as a group twice. Repeat if time permits.

Left-Hand Reaches
```
8   act bad car ear far east fast based draft eager great rates
9   gas rag sad tab wet face wave saved stage taxes verbs waste
10  age bet cat eat fed crew dear after beard cares fever serve
```

Right-Hand Reaches
```
11  mill hood plum pool pour pins mills hoods plums pools pours
12  hill hook join jump kill link hills hooks joins jumps kills
13  lion look loon loop lump milk lions looks loons loops lumps
```

D. POSTTEST

Take a 1-minute timing on lines 5–7. Proofread, note your errors, and figure your speed. Compare your performance with the Pretest.

Lesson 67

Objectives   Format academic reports with parenthetical references and long quotes.
Use macro feature of word processing software.

Format   Spacing: Drills, single; and as required
Margins: Default or as required

A. Keyboard Skills

Key lines 1–4 once. Then key line 5 once using the caps lock key for the all-cap words. Repeat lines 1–4, or take a series of 1-minute timings.

Speed	1 Please take good care of those disks as you use them today.	12
Accuracy	2 Wilma quit buying dozens of disks except for the five jobs.	12
Numbers	3 Most of the grades were 93, 95, and 97, but there was a 62.	12
Symbols	4 With our 6% increase, we bought 15# of #103 and #89 for $3.	12
Technique	5 After the show, TONY could not find KYLE or MARIA or PAULA.	

| 1 | 2 | 3 | 4 | 5 | 6 | 7 | 8 | 9 | 10 | 11 | 12

B. 12-Second Timings

Take three 12-second timings on each line, or key each line three times. Try to key with no more than 1 error on each timing.

6 If you rush a job and make errors, you have to do it again.
7 It would be better to take your time and get it done right.
8 You save time in the long run if you take time as you work.

| 5   10   15   20   25   30   35   40   45   50   55   60

C. Parenthetical References and Quotes

When you are writing a report in which you refer to or quote an idea, fact, or statement of someone else, you should give your readers the source of this information. In this way, you give credit to the original author. You also aid your readers, who may want to find additional information on the subject about which you are writing. In this lesson you will key a report with quotes followed by the sources. These are called *parenthetical references*.

Follow these guidelines to format quoted material and parenthetical references:

Parenthetical References

1. If the source or author's name is given before the quote, enclose in parentheses the page or pages where the quote was taken.

   Example: (157–58)

2. If the author's name is not given before the quote, enclose in parentheses the author's last name followed by the page number(s).

   Example: (Adams 157–58)

3. If there are two or three authors of the book or article, format the parenthetical reference like this:

   (Jones, Cass, and Noel 199).

4. If there are four or more authors, use the following format:

   (Martin et al. 215–17).

5. If there is no author, enclose in parentheses a shortened version of the title followed by the page or pages where the quote was taken.

   Example: (Critical Essays 59)

(Continued on next page)

LESSON 67

Report R29.84
Format: Double spacing, default margins, 5-space and center tabs.

COMMUNICATION BREAKDOWNS

By Joseph Corsi

It is essential that we watch very carefully the words we speak in daily conversation. Being careless with our words can cost us time, money, and wasted effort. If someone does not understand what we are saying, there is likely to be a communication breakdown. This breakdown can be caused by speaking too softly, by pronouncing words incorrectly, or by using the wrong words to express our ideas.

Word Choice Is Important

It is important that we give careful consideration to what we are going to say before we say it. Many people put little thought into what they are going to say before they attempt to communicate with someone. Others assume that the ''big words'' will be impressive and that they should be used to best express ideas. In reality, the shorter, less complicated words may be the most appropriate.

Evaluate the Listener

Your communication efforts will be improved if you speak to the vocabulary level of your audience. Select the words to use on the basis of the likelihood that your audience will comprehend what you are saying. Obviously, speaking to a group of high school students will require different words than a similar message addressed to a group of elementary-grade students. A suitable vocabulary will contribute substantially to your success as a speaker.

Putting It All Together

The words you use to communicate are very important, but equally important is the way in which you put those words together. Misplaced modifiers can make your message sound awkward or confusing. Likewise, a plural verb used with a singular subject is just as inappropriate. Generally speaking, the easiest people to understand are those who use simple sentences.

Report R30.84
Retrieve Report R29.84 and make the following changes:

1. Use your name as the author of the report.
2. Replace the side headings (in the same order) as follows: *Use Correct Words, Speak to Your Audience, Organize Your Words.*

Short Quotes (under 4 lines)

1. Enclose a direct quote in quotation marks. Do not enclose an indirect or paraphrased quote in quotation marks.

2. Place the parenthetical reference 1 space after the closing quotation mark or after the last word of an indirect quote. Place the ending punctuation mark after the reference. **Examples:**

```
"pace your work" (Barton 96).
at that time (Ceccione 194).
```

Long Quotes (four or more lines)

1. Do not use quotation marks.

2. Begin a double space below the line preceding the quote. Continue double spacing.

3. Indent the left margin 10 spaces for all lines of the quote. (Use the temporary left margin or automatic indent feature.)

4. Place the reference at the end of the quote 2 spaces after the ending punctuation mark. **Example:**

```
by tomorrow.  (Johnson 41)
```

Practice: Key the illustration below. Double spacing; 5-space tab. Use the temporary left margin or automatic indent 10 spaces from the left margin for the long quote. Check your work.

```
     Experts in communications have studied the effects of non-
verbal communications on personal relationships.  We give others
a nonverbal message by the clothes we wear; this communication
has been called an "object language" because it refers to our
use of objects such as clothing to communicate with those around
us#(Morrison 49).  We should remember this as we dress for work.
→ 10     Your appearance tells a great deal about you.  Empha-
         size your best features by dressing appropriately.  You
         will find when you work in an office that there are
         varying opinions about what clothing is appropriate.
         You may be given some suggestions for appropriate dress
         or may simply be expected to use your judgment.  A good
         way to decide what to wear is to observe other workers
         in the office.##(Stewart et al. 32)
     Clothes do say something about us as individuals.  If we are
to convey a positive message at work, we must put some thought
into the clothes that we wear.
```

Lesson 84

Objective Format business reports with side headings.

Format Spacing: Drills, single; Timings, double; and as required
Margins: Default or as required

A. Keyboard Skills

Key lines 1–4 once. In line 5 use the shift key to capitalize each word. Repeat lines 1–4, or take a series of 1-minute timings.

Speed	1	The lane to the lake may make the auto turn and go to town. 12
Accuracy	2	Jeff quietly moved his dozen boxes with Angy's power truck. 12
Numbers	3	Di saw 10 cats, 29 dogs, 38 mice, 47 rabbits, and 56 geese. 12
Symbols	4	Ronald* and Roberta* paid $7.14 for 3 tablets @ $2.38 each. 12
Technique	5	January February March April May June July August September

| 1 | 2 | 3 | 4 | 5 | 6 | 7 | 8 | 9 | 10 | 11 | 12

B. 12-Second Timings

Take three 12-second timings on each line, or key each line three times. Try to key with no more than 1 error on each timing.

6 You should key these lines fast and press for a high speed.
7 An ant is a tiny bug, but it can lift more than its weight.
8 We had a cake for lunch, and it was a very good one to eat.

5   10   15   20   25   30   35   40   45   50   55   60

C. Business Reports

Basic Format:
Default side margins,
5-space and center tabs,
double spacing

The format for keying academic reports was presented in Unit 7 (page 89) and in Unit 11 (page 157 ff). The format for keying business reports differs slightly from the school report format, and the information below presents each of the variations.

① Report Title. The report title is centered and keyed in all-capital letters and bold on line 13 (2 inches from the top).

② Subtitle or Byline. A subtitle (which further explains the title) or a byline (the name of the author of the report) is keyed a double space below the title. Use initial caps; that is, capitalize the first letter of each important word. Triple-space after keying the subtitle or byline. (Some reports include both a subtitle and byline.)

Note: Do not turn on double spacing until you have pressed Enter/Return three times after the subtitle or byline.

③ Side Headings. Side headings in a business report are keyed in initial capital letters and bold, flush with the left margin. They are preceded and followed by a double space.

④ Pagination (page numbering). Key the page number (the word *Page* is unnecessary) on line 7 at the right margin. Begin the text of the report a double space below the page number. (Use page numbering feature—not header.)

Note: If your software places automatic page numbering in the top margin area, you will have to change your top margin to 1 1/2 inches (9 blank lines). The page number may appear on line 6 instead of line 7.

D. Macros

Some software programs have a macro feature. A **macro** is a single instruction that takes the place of several words or functions. When preparing documents with common features, you can use a macro to save keystrokes. In this unit you will be using the same heading for all the reports. Prepare and save a macro for this heading information if your software offers this feature.

Refer to pages 89 and 95 for formatting instructions if necessary.

Academic Report R19.67
Standard format.

Last Name #
Student
Teacher
Class
Date

Classroom Absenteeism

Thomas Haynes Bayly once said that "absence makes the heart grow fonder" (2). This quote most certainly applies to the absence of a loved one, but it definitely does not pertain to the classroom environment. The high level of absenteeism at Northern State University creates problems for administrators, faculty, and students; and its presence warrants an in-depth look at the reasons why students are absent from classes.

According to the Northern State University <u>Academic Procedures Manual</u>, "Students are expected to be present for all class meetings in courses for which they are enrolled" (17). The current policy is to allow students who miss classes because of an excused absence every opportunity to make up the work that was missed during the absence. Excusable absences are as follows:

(a) Student participation in an authorized university activity, (b) confinement of the student due to illness with verification by a physician, (c) death in the student's immediate family, (d) any legal obligation that re-

quires the student to participate in legal proceedings. (Edwards 42)

A student who has an excessive number of absences may be dropped from a class. Excessive absences are those which occur four times in a class that meets three times a week, three times in a class that meets two times a week, and two times in a class that meets once a week (<u>Academic</u> 19).

One hundred students (25 each from the freshman, sophomore, junior, and senior classes) were asked to complete a questionnaire on student absenteeism. The students were chosen randomly in several locations at Northern State University. Of the 100 questionnaires that were completed, 88 could be used for this study. The findings of the study are based on 88 percent of the total number of students sampled.

Reasons students gave for missing classes were quite varied. Thirty-four percent of the students felt that the class's being uninteresting was their main reason for missing a class. The second most common reason for missing classes was illness. Five other reasons cited by students were inclement weather, oversleeping, attendance not taken, grades more important in other classes, and taking off early to run errands.

On the basis of the findings of this study, it is recommended that (a) instructors strive to add interest and enthusiasm to class lectures, (b) the absentee policy at Northern State University be strictly enforced, and (c) absentee records be included on the grade sheets.

Letter L53.83
Block style.

[*Today's date*] / Mr. David Hovey, Manager / ATC Appliances / 2589 Fulbright Avenue North / Springfield, MO 65803 / Dear Mr. Hovey:

Last March I purchased a spacious, new 21.8-cubic-foot refrigerator from ATC Appliances, and I need to know if the following problems I have been experiencing will be covered under the separate warranty contract, a copy of which is enclosed with this letter.

1. The ice maker does not produce enough ice to keep a daily supply on hand.
2. Excessive moisture is appearing on the outside of the freezer compartment.
3. The rubber seal around the freezer compartment is torn.

Please write to me at the address appearing below to respond to each of my concerns. / Sincerely, / Christopher Lee / R.R. 2, Box 224 / Marshfield, MO 65706 / Enclosure

Letter L54.83
Modified-block style, with indented paragraphs and display.

[*Today's date*] / Mr. Christopher Lee / R.R. 2 / Box 224 / Marshfield, Mo 65706 / Dear Mr. Lee: / Thanks *you* for your letter in which you expressed some concern about the warranty on your refrigerator. *You will be pleased to learn that* Your warranty covers all 3 problems you have been experiencing. ¶ We have 3 centers that can respond to your needs:

 *arrange as a 2-column display*

East end Appliances 555-3905 Glover Appliances 555-3814
Kendall Hardware 555-3726 ¶ We appreciate your business, Mr. Lee, and hope that we can include you as one of our select, preferred customers in the years to come. / Sincerely, / David Hovey, manager / [*Your initials*] / c: Gayle Settles / Bob Robinson

Letter L55.83
You select format. Compose a response to Letter L54.83, thanking Mr. Hovey for the names and telephone numbers of the service centers. Ask that he send you a new spring catalog so that you can continue shopping at ATC Appliances. Close with goodwill, using something similar to what you used in Letter L52.82.

Lesson 68

Objectives Recognize how commas are used in series while keying sentences.
Reinforce left-hand and right-hand reaches.
Format a list of works cited with hanging indents.
Reinforce parenthetical references in reports.

Format Spacing: Drills, single; Timings, double; and as required
Margins: Default or as required

A. LAB 9
Commas

Key lines 1–4 once. Then repeat lines 1–4, or take a series of 1-minute timings.

```
1  The ball, bat, and glove were in the garage beside the car.    12
2  Darby tried on two coats, five hats, and one pair of shoes.    12
3  Raymond went to the game, to the store, and to the factory.    12
4  Ava is president, Reta is secretary, and Cole is treasurer.    12
   |  1  |  2  |  3  |  4  |  5  |  6  |  7  |  8  |  9  |  10  |  11  |  12
```

1. In a series of three or more numbers, words, phrases, or clauses, use a comma after each item in the series except the last.

Numbers: This model costs $11, $13, or $15.
Words: The bakery has cookies, cakes, and pies.
Phrases: We went to the restaurant, to the movie, and to the mall.
Clauses: Chin grilled the steak, Juan made the salad, and Kim baked a cake.

B. PRETEST

Take a 1-minute timing on lines 5–7. Proofread, note your errors, and figure your speed.

```
5        Carter needs to develop clear photos of the long wagon    12
6  caravan going to Joplin next month.  Kim counted the number    24
7  of wagons that have joined.  They cannot travel fast.    35
   |  1  |  2  |  3  |  4  |  5  |  6  |  7  |  8  |  9  |  10  |  11  |  12
```

C. PRACTICE

SPEED: If you made 2 or fewer errors on the Pretest, key lines 8–13 twice each. Repeat if time permits.
ACCURACY: If you made more than 2 errors on the Pretest, key lines 8–10 as a group twice. Then key lines 11–13 as a group twice. Repeat if time permits.

Left-hand Reaches

```
8   apart basic caves exams baths reach fable ledge carry heard
9   carts exert facet needs raves share tasks teach offer meter
10  beads cease ideas farms waved ready sways taxed newer jewel
```

Right-hand Reaches

```
11  chimp knife pinch imply phone holly thump enjoy sloop lunch
12  rhino chill limit mount loops honor punch young plump moldy
13  month pound dimly plink gloom joins lingo photo quill roomy
```

D. POSTTEST

Take a 1-minute timing on lines 5–7. Proofread, note your errors, and figure your speed. Compare your performance with the Pretest.

Objectives Use commas correctly between adjectives while keying sentences.
Reinforce letters.
Key 35/5'/5e.

Format Spacing: Drills, single; Timings, double; and as required
Margins: Default

▲. LAB 12
Commas

Key lines 1–4 once, providing the missing commas. Review your copy as your teacher reads the answers. Then key lines 1–4 again.

1 You should always proceed slowly on the rough narrow road.
2 Ed listened to the soft relaxing music on their car radio.
3 I watched as the steam rose rapidly in the cold crisp air.
4 It will be very difficult to jog in the hot humid weather.

▋. Preview Practice

Key each line twice as a preview to the 5-minute timings below.

Accuracy   5 result positive revealed together exception accomplishments
Speed   6 that most each team what does then well work does must time

◖. 5-Minute Timings

Take two 5-minute timings on lines 7–21. Proofread, note your errors, and figure your speed.

7   Study after study has revealed that team effort can go   12

8 a long way in producing a lasting, positive result. A team   24

9 in the business world is no exception, and it is made up of   36

10 members who support one another. If a team succeeds in its   48

11 efforts, then all its members succeed just as well. A team   60

12 is made up of members who equally support its efforts; they   72

13 are organized to work as a single unit.   80

14   Teams follow certain rules, and the members must abide   92

15 by those rules. A team in the business world is similar to   104

16 a team in the sports world in that a certain game plan must   116

17 be followed to give the very best results. If members play   128

18 by all the rules and work as a team, then they can be proud   140

19 of the accomplishments that are made. These rules apply to   152

20 people who are involved in only one team or, as is often so   164

21 in the business work world, are members of many teams.   175

| 1 | 2 | 3 | 4 | 5 | 6 | 7 | 8 | 9 | 10 | 11 | 12 SI 1.33

E. Works Cited

Works Cited is an alphabetic listing of all the books and articles used in writing a report, including all parenthetical references cited in the report. To format a Works Cited page:

1. Begin on line 4 of a new page. Use the same format for numbering pages as used in the report, and continue the page numbers from the report. If you used a header in the report, also use the header for the Works Cited page.
2. Center the title on line 7; double-space the rest of the text.
3. Begin each entry at the left margin. Indent turnover lines 5 spaces.
4. List the entries in alphabetic order by the authors' last names. For an entry that has no author, alphabetize by the title of the book or article. Disregard words such as *The, A,* and *An* when alphabetizing titles.

5. If more than one book or article by the same author is cited, avoid repeating the author's name after the first listing by keying 3 hyphens, a period, and 2 spaces before the title. Alphabetize by titles. **Note:** The parenthetical reference must include a shortened version of the title after the author's name so the reader will know which publication was used.

6. Separate items within each entry with periods followed by 2 spaces.

7. If the entry is a magazine article or a part of a book, such as an essay or short story, list the page numbers of the entire selection at the end of the entry. (Do not list page numbers for complete books.)

Practice: Key the illustration below. Double spacing; 5-space tab.

Hanging Indents

You previously learned how to prepare enumerations in hanging-indented style. (You key the number at the margin before pressing indent.) When there is no number, the procedure is different. First press the *indent,* then use a **reverse tab** (shift tab) to return to the left margin. Continuation lines will automatically indent.

Jones 4
↓3

Works Cited

Brumley, Deborah, and Grace Brumley. "A Man of Peace." Digest

of History April 1990: 29-36.

"The History of the Olympic Games." History of Sports August

1991: 115-128.

Kokoris, Harold Mark. The Beginning of the Olympics. Los

Angeles: Dunne Publishing Company, 1992.

---. The Greeks. New York: Spartan Press, 1991.

Letter L50.82
Block style.

[*Today's date*] / Ms. Susan Duke / 2876 Dewey Avenue / Rochester, NY 14615 / Dear Ms. Duke:

Your request for banquet rooms at the hotel lakeside has been forwarded to me. We are pleased that you have selected the Lakeside for your ~~conference~~ *banquet*. We believe we have the most adequate, spacious banquet rooms of any of the area hotels. ¶So that I can accom*m*odate your request, please send me additional information on the following items:

1. The date of your ~~conference~~ *banquet*.

2. The number of people you expect at your ~~conference~~ *banquet*.

3. The price range you are considering for your banquet.

I know that our cap*a*ble, courteous staff will fulfill all of your needs during the banquet. / Sincerely yours, / Hillary Temple / convention manager / [*Your initials*]

information for our conference to be held November 11–13. We expect to register around 250 people for the conference, and all of them should be attending the banquet. Actually, we need the banquet room for our short, informal luncheons as well as for the closing banquet scheduled for November 13. Our banquet room needs, therefore, are as follows:

November 11	Luncheon --75 people
November 12	Luncheon --100 people
November 13	Banquet --250 people

We would like to keep the price range for the luncheons and the banquet within the $10–$15 range. I hope you can accommodate our wishes. /Sincerely, /Susan Duke /Program Chairperson / [Your initials]

Letter L51.82
Modified-block style. Remember to center table.

[Today's date]/Ms. Hillary Temple/ Convention Manager/Hotel Lakeside/ 1980 Ridge Road /Rochester, NY 14626/ Dear Ms. Temple:

Thank you for responding so quickly to my request for

Letter L52.82
You select format. Compose a response to Letter L51.82, that is, to Susan Duke (for Ms. Temple), indicating that you will be able to accommodate the number of people specified in her letter and that her price range is acceptable. Close with a "positive goodwill statement," something like the following: "We look forward to working with you during your conference in November."

Academic Report R20.68
Works cited.

Retrieve Report R19.67. Insert a hard page break at the end of the report. Set a 5-space indent for the turnover lines.

Last Name #

Works Cited

Academic Procedures Manual. Northern State University: University Press, 1992.

Bayly, Thomas H. Five Thousand Quotations for All Occasions. Garden City: Garden City Books, 1952.

Edwards, Michael J., ed. General Catalog. Northern State University: University Press, 1992.

Academic Report R21.68
Standard format. Use the standard heading (Last Name # / Student / Teacher / Class / Date).

Human Behavior And effective communication

What ever your career choice, it will be necessary for you to communicate with other people. How well you can do that may determine how quickly you advance. Research has revealed some things we need to understand about Human Behavior in order to communicate more effectively:

DS
It is necessary to understand the needs of others in order to communicate with them. People have 5 basic needs: physical (shelter, food, and clothing); safety and comfort; the need to be accepted as part of a group; the need to feel important; and the need to help others. (Clark, Zimmer, and Tinervia 12)

If you are ever to communicate success-

---

with others
fully, you must know their needs. "People in advertising are very skilled at determining the needs of their audience and thus communicating their messages effectively" (Wang 79). Whenever you can identify the needs of your listener, you can appeal to those needs in all of your communications. The key is to "put yourself in the place of the person to whom you are speaking or writing" (Sulpizio 125).

In order to determine the needs of others, you must always be observant; notice what motivates them, and be aware that a person's needs may change rapidly throughout the day. Listen to the tone of voice used, and pay special attention to all of the non-verbal communication expressed by others. Such things as "facial expressions, gestures, posture, body movements, attire, and grooming contribute greatly to what a person is truly saying" (Bellatoni 91). Remember that you communicate non-verbally to others, also. While you may be saying all the right things verbally, "your actions may be saying some very negative things" (Clark 104).

(Continued on next page)

Lesson 82

Objectives Identify how commas are used between adjectives while keying sentences.
Identify and practice the symbol keys on which more drill is needed.
Reinforce letters with enumerations and displays.

Format Spacing: Drills, single; Timings, double; and as required
Margins: Default

A. LAB 12
Commas

Key lines 1–4 once. Then repeat lines 1–4, or take a series of 1-minute timings.

```
1  Last week they went to a long, boring movie at the theater.   12
2  The attendant who served Jerry was a happy, helpful person.   12
3  He was always trying to be a helpful, courteous individual.   12
4  The space shuttle is transported on a long, sturdy vehicle.   12
   |  1  |  2  |  3  |  4  |  5  |  6  |  7  |  8  |  9  |  10  |  11  |  12
```

B. PRETEST

Take a 2-minute timing on lines 5–9 to find out which symbol keys are the most difficult for you. Force yourself to key rapidly—push yourself to your fastest rate. Note each symbol keyed incorrectly.

```
5  They sold 61 pints @ $5, 72 pints @ $7, and 83 pints @ $10.   12
6  Plant #985 makes 7% profit; #1204 makes 8%; #2575 makes 9%.   24
7  Clark & James and Porter & Wong predicted a $35 (11%) rise.   36
8  They used asterisks to multiply:  15 * 3 = 45; 12 * 4 = 48.   48
9  Key the following:  74 - 10 = 64; 86 + 7 = 93; 42 - 3 = 39.   60
   |  1  |  2  |  3  |  4  |  5  |  6  |  7  |  8  |  9  |  10  |  11  |  12
```

C. PRACTICE

Key lines 10–18 once. Then repeat any of the lines that stress the symbol errors you noted in the Pretest.

```
@   10  Frank sold 15 @ 11, 20 @ 22, 25 @ 33, 30 @ 44, and 35 @ 55.
*   11  Rome,* Venice,* Paris,* Berlin,* and Madrid* were selected.
#   12  We see that #9 weighs 56#, #7 weighs 34#, and #8 weighs 2#.
$   13  The seven girls saved $9, $10, $38, $47, $56, $72, and $89.
%   14  On those days the market rose 3%, 5%, 7%, 8%, 12%, and 18%.
&   15  The leaders are Kim & Dave, Robert & Mary, and Kay & Peter.
( )  16  We chose Marco (Florida), Daisy (Georgia), and Ulta (Utah).
-   17  The cartons were labeled as 29-92, 38-56, 47-10, and 59-28.
+ =  18  He said that 28 + 65 = 93, 47 + 15 = 62, and 10 + 99 = 109.
```

D. POSTTEST

Take another 2-minute timing on lines 5–9. Proofread, note your errors, and figure your speed. Compare your performance with the Pretest.

191   LESSON 82   191

¶ Studying human behavior is a fascinating

way to learn how to speak more effectively.

While you are learning about others, you

must may learn some very interesting

things about yourself.

Works Cited

Belatoni, Francis. Can You Hear What I'm

Not Saying? Los Angeles: Huffines &

Norton, 1989.

Clark, Lyn R., Kenneth Zimmer, and Joseph

Tinervia. Business English & Commu-

nication. 7th ed. Columbus:

Glencoe-Macmillan/McGraw, 1988.

Sulpizio, Danna. "Speak for Yourself."

Today's Office April 1990: 15–17.

Wang, Charlotte. "How to See What Others

Are Saying." The Communicator

February 1991: 54–57.

Lesson 69

Objectives Identify how commas are used in series while keying sentences.
Reinforce skill on numbers and symbols.
Format tables in reports.
Reinforce parenthetical references and works cited.

Format Spacing: Drills, single; and as required
Margins: Default or as required

▲. LAB 9
Commas

Key lines 1–4 once. Then repeat lines 1–4, or take a series of 1-minute timings.

1 I planted 5 pecan trees, 7 peach trees, and 12 apple trees. 12
2 Jake ran up the hill, around the curve, and over the river. 12
3 Marie read books, Tad cleaned house, and Jim went shopping. 12
4 Meg told about big cities, tall buildings, and busy people. 12
   | 1 | 2 | 3 | 4 | 5 | 6 | 7 | 8 | 9 | 10 | 11 | 12

B. 30-Second Timings

Take two 30-second timings on lines 5 and 6. Then take two 30-second timings on lines 7 and 8. Try to key with no more than 2 errors on each timing.

5 Most of those polled said they like the old movies in black 12
6 and white; only a few said they prefer to have color added. 24

7 Do you think some people in the future will try to take all 12
8 of the color from our movies and make them black and white? 24
   | 1 | 2 | 3 | 4 | 5 | 6 | 7 | 8 | 9 | 10 | 11 | 12

```
25  goals start about ahead life your that more time for not in
26  until often could right some does they what then are but is
27  their older basis task, well into high plan work the job an
28  years learn skill grows have good want both them you one of
```

D. POSTTEST

Take another 5-minute timing on lines 5–20 (page 189). Proofread, note your errors, and figure your speed. Compare your performance with the Pretest.

E. Displays and Tables in Letters

To format a display or a table in the body of a letter, follow these steps:

1. Horizontally center a display or table, following standard placement rules. If necessary, reduce the space between columns to keep the display within the margins of the letter.

2. Double-space before and after the display or table.

Note: Centering material on a microcomputer is often accomplished with a function key that is depressed before the material to be centered is entered on the keyboard. Material can also be centered after it is keyed by blocking the lines to be centered and then using a function key to center the work.

Letter L48.81
Modified-block style. Insert any missing commas.

[*Today's date*] / Mr. Linsy Atteberry / 6213 Palomas Drive, SE / Albuquerque, NM 87109 / Dear Mr. Atteberry:

Thank you for your request for information on our new acreage in the Sandia Mountain Hillcrest Addition. All three of our units are located within the city limits of Albuquerque. On one side are the serene peaceful Sandia Mountains; and toward the valley is the Rio Grande River.

To schedule an appointment, please call one of our three agents in your local Northeast office:

Ms. Mary Hallissey	555-2390
Mr. Richard Olson	555-4781
Ms. Reatha Price	555-5602

We look forward to having you visit our popular attractive subdivision. / Sincerely, / Coleen LaBarge / Manager, Northeast Realty / [*Your initials*] / c: Karen Broderick

Letter L49.81
Retrieve Letter L48.81 and make the following changes:

Format: Block
Addressee: Mr. and Mrs. Thomas Grove / 811 University Avenue / Grand Forks, ND 58201
Agents: Mr. Paul Baker (555-2910), Mr. Sigvald Karsten (555-5633), Ms. Anita Torkelson (555-3847)

C. Number and Symbol Review

Key each line twice.

9 They found 10 @ 56, 56 @ 47, 47 @ 38, 38 @ 29, and 29 @ 10.
10 Our new scale shows #10 at 29#, #38 at 47#, and #29 at 56#.
11 Gray,* Moletti,* Young,* Hernandez,* and Jones* won prizes.

12 Our show tickets should cost us $10, $29, $38, $47, or $56.
13 Your sales increased 10%, 29%, 38%, 47%, and 56% last year.
14 Lea & Madera, Yung & Poe, and Day & Cole are all attorneys.

15 Label the square cartons as 47-10, 56-38, 38-47, and 10-29.
16 We know that 38 + 47 = 85, 29 + 10 = 39, and 56 + 70 = 126.
17 Lund (Utah), Leon (Iowa), and Troy (Ohio) were represented.

D. Tables in Academic Reports

To format a table in an academic report:

1. Try to place the table (a) immediately after the point in the text where reference is made to it, or (b) at the end of the paragraph in which reference is made to it, or (c) at the bottom of the page.
2. Key the table at the left margin, and use the ruled format.
3. Double-space the table. Do not go beyond the margins. Reduce space between columns if necessary.
4. The first line of the table is the table number. Key the word *Table* and its number at the left margin, a double space below the last line of the text.
5. Key the title at the margin in initial caps, a double space below the table number.
6. Use hyphens instead of underscores for the rules.
7. A parenthetical reference, if any, is keyed a double space below the table.

Academic Report R22.69
Standard format; 4 spaces between columns. Use standard heading.

The Evolution of Computers

Computers seem to be everywhere today—in businesses, schools, hospitals, government offices, transportation centers, homes—and it is difficult to imagine a time when there were no computers. Of course, computers are a relatively "young" invention, but they have been in the minds of people for many centuries (Clark 290–300).

The table below shows the progression of calculating devices that ultimately led to the successful creation of the computer.

(Continued on next page)

Take a 5-minute timing on lines 5–20. Proofread, note your errors, and figure your speed.

```
 5        Setting goals in life is an extremely important aspect    12
 6   of planning for your future.  Some people believe that goal     24
 7   setting does not materialize until they are well into their     36
 8   careers, but the task of setting goals begins in the early,     48
 9   formative years.  You should start before you complete high     60
10   school so that you have a good vision of who you want to be      72
11   and what you want to do.                                         77
12        Goal setting is a continuous task, and it is often one     89
13   that requires that your goals be adjusted frequently as you     101
14   grow older and as you learn more about your career choices.     113
15   Setting realistic goals could pay big rewards as you decide     125
16   what you want to do in life on the basis of your skills and     137
17   your strengths.  You should decide on both short-term goals     149
18   and long-term goals; then work toward them all in the years     161
19   that lie ahead.  The time for you to start on your goals is     173
20   right now.                                                      175
```
| 1 | 2 | 3 | 4 | 5 | 6 | 7 | 8 | 9 | 10 | 11 | 12 SI 1.32

In the chart below find the number of errors you made on the Pretest. Then key each of the following designated drill lines three times.

Pretest errors	0–1	2–3	4–5	6+
Drill lines	24–28	23–27	22–26	21–25

Accuracy

```
21   vision early, aspect setting requires formative materialize
22   choice should people adjusted planning important continuous
23   decide before career believe long-term realistic frequently
24   starts school begins rewards short-term strengths extremely
```

(Continued on next page)

Table 1

Significant Advances in the History of Computers

Name	Invention	Date
Blaise Pascal	Mechanical adding machine	1642
Gottfried von Leibniz	Mechanical calculator	1671
Charles Babbage	Analytical engine	1850
Herman Hollerith	Punched-card machine	1887
Howard Aiken	Digital computer	1944

(Sanders 35–40)

Many of the early inventors had the concept of how a computer would work, but the technology was not available to build these machines in their lifetimes (Dublin 37). They were unable to see their ideas develop into reality. It is our generation who is benefiting from the concepts and labors of a great number of mathematicians and inventors forced to work only with theories.

Some people today think that our computers will be the stepping-stones to much greater achievements than we experience now. For example, computers may be used to enable those who are paralyzed to walk again and to help the blind to see (Bitter 254–57). The possibilities for the future of computers may be limited only by what our minds can conceive.

Works Cited

Bitter, Gary G. Computer Literacy: Awareness, Applications, and Programming. Menlo Park: Addison, 1986.

Clark, James F., and Judith J. Lambrecht. Information Processing. Cincinnati: South-Western, 1985.

Dublin, Peter, and Peter Kelman. Macmillan Computer Literacy. New York: Macmillan, 1986.

Sanders, Donald H. Computers Today. 3d ed. New York: McGraw, 1988.

Letter L46.80
Block style.

[*Today's date*] / Mr. Alan Meyer / 1953 Washington, Apt. 4 / Lincoln, NE 68502 / Dear Mr. Meyer: / We received your letter requesting information on the software we have available for producing overhead transparencies. To process your order, we need the following information:

1. The brand of computer you use (Apple, Commodore, IBM, IBM compatible, etc.).

2. The memory size of your computer (256K, 512K, 1 Mb, or larger).

3. The type of disk drive you use (3 1/2-inch or 5 1/4-inch).

As soon as we receive this information, we will send you the appropriate literature. Thank you for your interest in the ProCom Computer Store. / Sincerely, / Karen Vigen / Sales Manager / [*Your Initials*]

Letter L47.80
Modified-block style with indented paragraphs. Rekey Letter L46.80 above, but replace the second sentence in the first paragraph with the following:

There are many different programs available, and to determine which packages will better suit your needs, we need the following information:

Lesson 81

Objectives Recognize how commas are used between adjectives while keying sentences.
Format and key letters with displays and tables.
Key 35/5'/5e.

Format: Spacing: Drills, single; Timings, double; and as required
Margins: Default

▲. LAB 12

Commas

Key lines 1–4 once. Then repeat lines 1–4, or take a series of 1-minute timings.

```
1  The soft, furry kitten slept peacefully near the fireplace.   12
2  Roger purchased a noise shield for the loud, rapid printer.    12
3  Karen has what I would call dynamic, forceful presentation.    12
4  The sleek, colorful tractor won first prize at the contest.    12
   |  1  |  2  |  3  |  4  |  5  |  6  |  7  |  8  |  9  | 10  | 11  | 12
```

Adjectives describe or *modify* nouns. Note the adjectives in italics:

fast trains	*powerful* trains	*fast, powerful* trains
bright light	*intense* light	*bright, intense* light

4. When two or more consecutive adjectives describe the same noun, place a comma between the adjectives. In all other cases, use no comma. To determine whether the adjectives do describe the same noun, use the following test:

Chris gave a *short, emotional* speech. (Say "A speech that was short <u>and</u> emotional." Does it make sense? Yes, proving that each adjective describes *speech* and that the comma is needed.)

She mailed a *new spring* schedule. (Say "A schedule that is new <u>and</u> spring." Does it make sense? No, proving that each adjective does not describe the noun *schedule.* No comma is needed.)

Objectives   Use commas in series correctly while keying sentences.
Use the block-protect feature of word processing software.
Format tables in reports.
Reinforce parenthetical references and works cited.
Key 35/3'/5e.

Format   Spacing: Drills, single; Timings, double; and as required
Margins: Default or as required

▲. LAB 9

Commas

Key lines 1–4 once, providing missing commas. Review your copy as your teacher reads the answers. Then key lines 1–4 again.

1   Will you feed the fish walk the dog and put out the cats?
2   They need burgers buns chili mustard relish and chips.
3   Raul ran Faith walked Georgia swam and Carly took a nap.
4   They sent 11 computers 5 printers 25 disks and no paper.

B. PRETEST

Take a 3-minute timing on lines 5–13. Proofread, note your errors, and figure your speed.

```
              1              2              3              4
5        Can you name the five steps in the cycle of processing   12
              5          6                    7              8
6    information?  First is input.  This is all of the data that   24
              9              10              11              12
7    have to be altered in some way.  The next step, processing,   36
              13              14              15              16
8    sets up the words in a certain form or mode.  Output is the   48
              17              18              19              20
9    third step.  This is a job which has been done in the right   60
              21              22              23              24
10   format.  The fourth step is the distribution of the output,   72
              25              26              27              28
11   which may require the use of specialized mail.  Last is the   84
              29              30              31              32
12   storage and retrieval step, which involves saving the files   96
              33              34              35
13   on disk and getting them back for future use.               105
     |  1  |  2  |  3  |  4  |  5  |  6  |  7  |  8  |  9  |  10  |  11  |  12  SI 1.29
```

C. PRACTICE

In the chart below find the number of errors you made on the Pretest. Then key each of the designated drill lines on page 167 two times.

Pretest errors	0–1	2–3	4–5	6+
Drill lines	17–21	16–20	15–19	14–18

Key lines 9–18 once. Then repeat any of the lines that stress the digit errors you noted in the Pretest.

1	9	We saw 11 computers, 11 boards, 11 monitors, and 11 drives.
2	10	By 2:22 p.m. on the 22d they had 2.0 or 2.2 inches of rain.
3	11	The programs were found in Seats 3, 30, 31, 32, 33, and 34.
4	12	Set margins at 14 and 74; clear tabs at 24, 34, 44, and 54.
5	13	The student scores on the 15th were 51, 53, 55, 57, and 59.
6	14	The spreadsheet cell listed 16, 26, 36, 46, 56, 66, and 67.
7	15	January 7, March 7, April 7, May 17, and July 17 were open.
8	16	Can Jack add these: 1/8, 2/8, 3/8, 4/8, 5/8, 6/8, and 7/8?
9	17	They found $9.99, $9.19, $9.29, and $9.69 in the registers.
0	18	It isn't difficult to total 10, 20, 30, 40, 50, 60, and 70.

D. POSTTEST

Take another 2-minute timing on lines 6–8 (page 186). Proofread, note your errors, and figure your speed. Compare your performance with the Pretest.

E. Enumerations in Letters

Reminder: Set a left tab for the indent.

Enumerations are often included in the body of a letter; a hanging-indented style is used. Follow guidelines:

Letter with blocked paragraphs

1. Use the same margins as are used in the document.
2. Indent turnover lines 4 spaces from the left margin.
3. Single-space the items; double-space between items.
4. Leave 1 blank line above and below the enumeration.

Letter with indented paragraphs

1. Use the same margins as are used in the document.
2. Indent the first line of the enumeration 5 spaces from the left margin; indent turnover lines 9 spaces from the left margin.
3. Single-space the items; double-space between items.
4. Leave 1 blank line above and below the enumeration.

```
Office managers offer these suggestions to whose who are thinking
of purchasing word processing equipment:

1.  Consider the change fully.  Word processing is not just fast
    "typewriters"; it is a change in the way the office operates.

2.  Get expert help from the beginning, and test the equipment in
    your own office.

I hope this information will be helpful to you as you plan your
new office equipment purchases.
```

```
    Office managers offer these suggestions to those who are
thinking of purchasing word processing equipment:

    1.  Consider the change fully.  Word processing is not just
        fast "typewriters"; it is a change in the way the of-
        fice operates.

    2.  Get expert help from the beginning, and test the equip-
        ment in your own office.

    I hope this information will be helpful to you as you plan
your new office equipment purchases.
```

14	quire words future format mailed certain involves publicize
15	saves input phase public fourth output retrieval processing
16	modes backs third others lasted storage changed information
17	next steps named saving inform getting require distribution

Speed

18	files other words done this back last all the can use on be
19	store disks forms some them five mode and has job put up to
20	first cycle right name form have been rib you out for is in
21	names which third mail that four sets may mat his her of or

D. POSTTEST

Take another 3-minute timing on lines 5–13 (page 166). Proofread, note your errors, and figure your speed. Compare your performance with the Pretest.

E. Tables in Reports

If a table in a report will not fit on the page where the reference occurs, place it at the top of the next page, and insert a reference in the text indicating where the table is located, such as *Table 2 on page 3*.

Block Protect

Some software programs have a feature called **block protect** that enables you to keep a block of copy together, so that it will not break between pages. Use this feature whenever you have a table in a report.

Academic Report R23.70
Standard format.

Last Name / Student / Teacher / Class /

Date / Over coming Communication

apprehension / Before our lives end,

~~just about all~~ *most* of us will have to speak

~~in front of~~ *before* a group at least once. Some

of us believe that our ~~lines~~ *lives* will end at

the moment of that ocurrence. Speaking

before groups is some thing the majority

of us do *not* enjoy; and yet, more communi-

cation takes place through the (written)

word than through the (spoken) word (Clark,

Zimmer, and Jinervia

563). The fear of speaking in

(situations/public) is known as communi-

cation aprehension (Thomas and Bahniuk

57). While nearly every one suffers

from it to *some* extent chronic communication

apprehension can be a serious liability

in ~~today's~~ *the business* world (Wanmer 10). fortu-

nately, positive steps can be taken to

correct communication apprehension.

First, you should ~~understand~~ *realize* that your

fear *of speaking* is normal and is shared by nearly

everyone you know. In a recent study,

people were asked about the social

situations they feared most. the

(Continued on next page)

F. Composing a Letter

Up to this point, your composing activities have been restricted to a paragraph in length. Composing a letter is a similar task in that you are merely composing several paragraphs together in the body of the letter. To compose a letter, keep these points in mind:

① **Always start with a positive opening:** "Thank you for sending the information on the new condominiums."

② **Get to the point! If possible, respond to any information that was sent** to you previously, or let the reader know what action you plan to take: "I enjoyed the material you sent me describing the new units. I plan to visit the lake area next weekend."

③ **Close with a positive message of goodwill.** "Please let me know if you can join me as I tour the lake area on Friday and Saturday. It would be a pleasure to visit the lake sites with you at that time."

Letter L45.79

Compose a letter in which you respond (as Ms. Judy Glawe) to Letter L44.79, using the steps outlined above. Give a positive opening, indicating that you are interested in becoming an owner of a Vacation Property condominium. In your second paragraph, state that you would like a two-bedroom unit with a beachfront. Also state that you plan to drive up to the lake area next weekend to look at the properties. In your final paragraph, close with a statement of goodwill. State that you are returning the card that was sent to you and that you look forward to visiting with Mr. Van Vliet next weekend. Mr. Van Vliet's address is Treetop Investments, 1912 Manitowac Road, Green Bay, WI 54302.

Lesson 80

Objectives Identify and practice the number keys on which more drill is needed.
Format and key letters with enumerations.

Format Spacing: Drills, single; Timings, double; and as required
Margins: Default

▲. Keyboard Skills

Key lines 1–4 once. In line 5 use the caps lock key for each word in all-capital letters. Repeat lines 1–4, or take a series of 1-minute timings.

Speed	1	The eight chapels sit by the end of the lake and the field.	12
Accuracy	2	Jacqueline was glad her family took five or six big prizes.	12
Numbers	3	The bags were numbered as follows: 10, 29, 38, 47, and 56.	12
Symbols	4	Jane said that 9% is equal to $24.75 (or nearly that much).	12
Technique	5	The colors are RED and BLUE and WHITE and GREEN and PURPLE.	

| 1 | 2 | 3 | 4 | 5 | 6 | 7 | 8 | 9 | 10 | 11 | 12 |

B. PRETEST

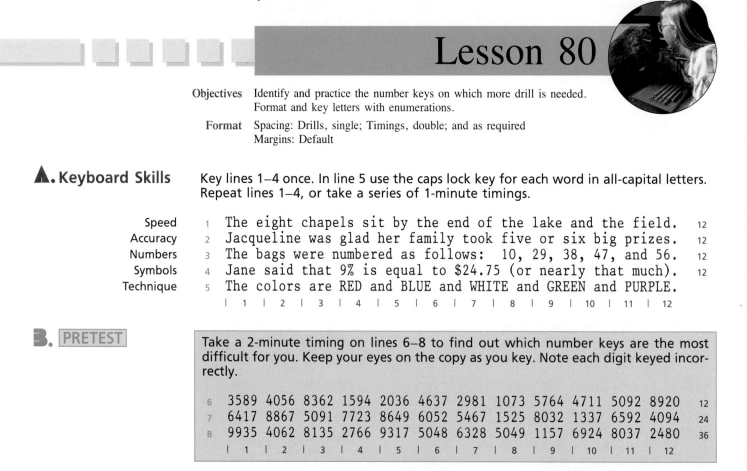

Take a 2-minute timing on lines 6–8 to find out which number keys are the most difficult for you. Keep your eyes on the copy as you key. Note each digit keyed incorrectly.

6	3589 4056 8362 1594 2036 4637 2981 1073 5764 4711 5092 8920	12
7	6417 8867 5091 7723 8649 6052 5467 1525 8032 1337 6592 4094	24
8	9935 4062 8135 2766 9317 5048 6328 5049 1157 6924 8037 2480	36

| 1 | 2 | 3 | 4 | 5 | 6 | 7 | 8 | 9 | 10 | 11 | 12 |

responses are shown in Table 1 on Page 2. Clearly, the vast majority of people fear public speaking; Accept this fact, and then determine to overcome it as have so many others.

Table 1
Most Feared Social Situations

Greatest Fear	Percent
A party with strangers	74
Giving a speech	70
Asked personal questions in public	65
Meeting a date's parents	59
First day on a new job	59
Victim of a practical joke	56
Talking with someone in authority	53
Job Interview	46
Formal dinner party	44
Blind date	24

(Thomas and Bahniuk 64)

Second, watch tapes or films of speakers, and visualize yourself being a successful speaker. Develop good role models, and study their techniques.

3d, learn relaxation techniques to do just before you speak. Yawn to relax the muscles in your throat (Wallace and Masters 190). Use controlled breathing exercises to induce relaxation. Try flexing and relaxing the muscles in your feet and legs slowly. These techniques will help reduce the tension and anxiety you experience while speaking.

Communication apprehension can be conquered with the proper motivation and practice techniques, most of us can and will become good public speakers and perhaps even learn to enjoy speaking before groups.

Works Cited

Clark, Lynn R., Kenneth Zimmer, and Joseph Tinervia. Business English and Communication. 7th ed. Columbus: Glencoe-Macmillan/McGraw, 1988.

Thomas, Edward G., and Margaret Hilton Bahniuk. "Minimizing Communication Apprehension." Facilitating Communication for Business. Reston: National Business Education Association, 1988: 57-68.

Wallace, Harold R., and L. Ann Masters. Personality Development for Work. Cincinnati: South-Western, 1998.

Waner, Karen. "Marketable Skills Provide Competitive Edge." Business Education Forum February 1990: 9-11.

Take a 3-minute timing on lines 9–17. Proofread, note your errors, and figure your speed.

```
                      1              2                3              4
9        Printers have gone through quite a few changes in just    12
        5            6                7                8
10   the past few years.  There was a time not long ago when the   24
        9              10                11              12
11   keys on the typewriter provided the only printers, and then   36
        13            14              15              16
12   only one print size could be used at a time.  The advent of   48
        17            18              19              20
13   the element machine gave us more than one size of print and   60
        21              22              23              24
14   more than one typeface.  The dot matrix printers enabled us   72
        25              26              27              28
15   to print pictures and graphic displays on our pages.  Today   84
        29            30              31              32
16   we have harnessed the power of laser beams to create a page   96
        33              34            35
17   filled with different typefaces and graphics.               105
     |  1  |  2  |  3  |  4  |  5  |  6  |  7  |  8  |  9  |  10  |  11  |  12  SI 1.33
```

D. PRACTICE

In the chart below find the number of errors you made on the Pretest. Then key each of the designated drill lines three times.

Pretest errors	0–1	2–3	4–5	6+
Drill lines	21–25	20–24	19–23	18–22

Accuracy

```
18   size only quite machine enabled changes printers typewriter
19   power today could create printers through element harnessed
20   pages laser beams filled advent provided pictures different
21   the gone gave past years matrix displays graphics typefaces
```

Speed

```
22   years there print have gone just past and the was not of in
23   could today power year time long when our few ago one on be
24   laser beams pages keys only then more the dot and our at us
25   graph fills types used with page than not and one the to by
```

E. POSTTEST

Take another 3-minute timing on lines 9–17. Proofread, note your errors, and figure your speed. Compare your performance with the Pretest.

Letter L44.79
Modified-block style with indented paragraphs.

[*Today's date*] / Ms. Judy Glawe / 508 Crestview Lane / DePere, WI 54115 / Dear Ms. Glawe:

Your name has been forwarded to me as someone who might be interested in making an important real estate investment. Your excellent credit rating places you in a very select group of people with whom we would like to do business. ¶ The enclosed information explains in more detail the development we have planned for 150 acres around the Chain of Lakes area, just 110 miles from your residence. Year-round activities will be available to you in fishing, swimming, waterskiing, skiing, and hunting. ¶ Please return the enclosed card if you are interested in becoming an owner of a Vacation Property condominium. / Sincerely, / Andrew Van Vliet / Public Relations Manager / [*Your initials*] / 2 Enclosures

Lesson 71

Objectives   Reinforce skill on the alphabet.
Reinforce enumerations.
Reinforce outlines.

Format   Spacing: Drills, single; and as required
Margins: Default or as required

A. Keyboard Skills

Key lines 1–4 once. Then follow the instructions in line 5. Repeat lines 1–4, or take a series of 1-minute timings.

Speed
Accuracy
Numbers
Symbols
Technique

1   The best time for me to study is when I get home every day.   12
2   My fine black ax just zipped through the wood quite evenly.   12
3   Our 16 girls and 24 boys ate 7 pies, 8 cakes, and 9 pizzas.   12
4   We purchased 13 dozen pens @ $1.05. (The sale ends today!)   12
5   Key line 3 again, and underline the words but not the numbers.

| 1 | 2 | 3 | 4 | 5 | 6 | 7 | 8 | 9 | 10 | 11 | 12

B. Alphabet Review

Key each line three times.

6   axle aide ache away bite brag brim bowl caps come crew chip
7   duet drag down dive east etch ends exit feud fame from flat
8   gale give glow grip hope have hill help ills into iced idea

9   joke jump jail jest knit kiln keep know line late lump lost
10 maze more mist melt norm nice nail numb odor over oath open
11 paid pour prod pest quad quip quiz quay ride reap rake room

12 sing stay sort shop team task thin tray ugly upon used unit
13 vote vast vine vest wage when wire worm axis oxen exit flax
14 yell yard year yolk yawl type zinc zeal zone zero zany buzz

Report R24.71 Enumeration

Hanging-indented style, 2-inch top margin, 1-inch side margins. (Review pages 81 and 82 if necessary.)

GETTING READY TO LOOK FOR A JOB

1. Determine what type of person you are—outgoing or shy—and whether you prefer to work with a small group of the same people or with a wide variety of different people.
2. Decide if you want to work in calm, quiet surroundings or if you enjoy excitement and pressure.
3. Consider whether your health and physical condition will permit you to do the work required.
4. List the educational training you have had. Emphasize courses and skills that qualify you for the specific job you want.
5. Take an inventory of the school activities in which you are involved. Include all positions of leadership such as club or class officer, newspaper or yearbook editor, band section leader, and so on.
6. List all of your work experience, even though it may not be related to the type of work you are seeking. Odd jobs such as baby-sitting and mowing lawns show responsibility and initiative. Also list any volunteer work you may do.
7. Write down your career goals. State both your short-term and long-term goals.

Letter L42.78
Modified-block style. Correct any punctuation errors in the body of the letter.

[*Today's date*] / Mr. David Hovey / Training Officer / PrintPower Company / 2476 Braddock Street / Tampa, FL 33607 / Dear Mr. Hovey: / Thank you for responding to our literature inviting you to participate in a computer literacy workshop during the week of May 20. As you know, our workshop is conducted at your facility in Tampa. We provide professional instructors and each participant will receive a notebook of computer literacy materials. ¶ As you requested I am enclosing a list of companies that have completed our computer literacy workshops during the past year. I'm sure you will find that they have been extremely satisfied with our performance. ¶ Complete registration materials will be sent to you next week. / Sincerely yours, / Alexa North / Marketing Director / [*Your initials*] / Enclosure

Letter L43.78
You select format. Retrieve Letter L42.78 and replace the last paragraph with the following:

Please complete the enclosed registration materials, and send them back to me in the preaddressed envelope that is also enclosed. *Change Enclosure to 3 Enclosures. Add a postscript:* PS: As a bonus, we are giving away a software package to the first ten participants who send us their applications.

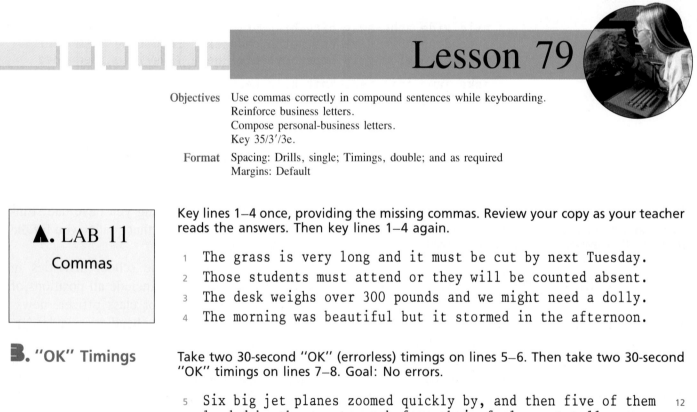

Lesson 79

Objectives Use commas correctly in compound sentences while keyboarding.
Reinforce business letters.
Compose personal-business letters.
Key 35/3'/3e.

Format Spacing: Drills, single; Timings, double; and as required
Margins: Default

▲. LAB 11
Commas

Key lines 1–4 once, providing the missing commas. Review your copy as your teacher reads the answers. Then key lines 1–4 again.

1 The grass is very long and it must be cut by next Tuesday.
2 Those students must attend or they will be counted absent.
3 The desk weighs over 300 pounds and we might need a dolly.
4 The morning was beautiful but it stormed in the afternoon.

▣. "OK" Timings

Take two 30-second "OK" (errorless) timings on lines 5–6. Then take two 30-second "OK" timings on lines 7–8. Goal: No errors.

5 Six big jet planes zoomed quickly by, and then five of them   12
6 landed by the new tower before their fuel was totally gone.   24

7 Jeff amazed the audience by giving a dazzling presentation,   12
8 and later he quickly summarized two reports in six minutes.   24
    | 1 | 2 | 3 | 4 | 5 | 6 | 7 | 8 | 9 | 10 | 11 | 12

Report R25.71 Outline
Use a 2-inch top margin on page 1; all others 1-inch.
Set appropriate tabs. (Review page 84 if necessary.)

FINDING AND GETTING THE RIGHT JOB

I. LOCATE JOB OPENINGS
A. School placement services
B. Friends, relatives, teachers, and school counselors
C. Advertisements in newspapers and magazines
D. Personnel departments of companies
E. Employment agencies
1. Public
2. Private
F. Additional sources
II. PREPARE A RESUME
A. List information about yourself
1. Name, address, telephone number
2. Position for which you are applying
3. Work experience
a. Chronological order, most recent job first
b. Brief description of duties
4. Educational background
B. Provide names and addresses of references
III. PREPARE LETTER OF APPLICATION

A. Tailor to fit each job for which you apply
B. Create favorable impression
1. Mention position in which you are interested
2. Stress major points of educational preparation
3. Point out what you can do for the company
4. Request an interview
IV. FILL OUT APPLICATION FORM
A. Be neat, accurate, complete
B. Ask for clarification of questions you do not understand
V. INTERVIEW WITH PROSPECTIVE EMPLOYER
A. Pay attention to your appearance
1. Plan what to wear ahead of time
2. Dress conservatively
3. Be well groomed, neat, and clean
B. Go alone and be early
C. Anticipate questions
1. Be ready to answer interviewer's questions
2. Be prepared to ask your own questions
D. Follow up
1. Thank interviewer at end of interview
2. Write follow-up letter next day

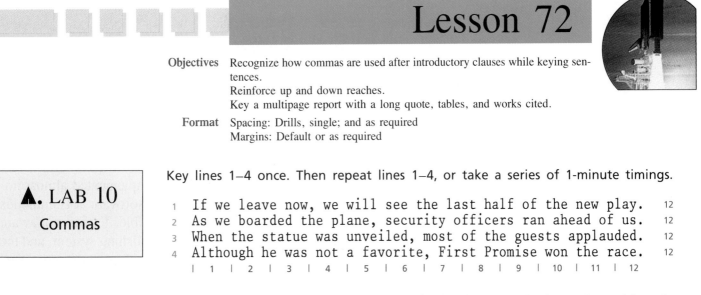

Lesson 72

Objectives Recognize how commas are used after introductory clauses while keying sentences.
Reinforce up and down reaches.
Key a multipage report with a long quote, tables, and works cited.

Format Spacing: Drills, single; and as required
Margins: Default or as required

▲. LAB 10

Commas

Key lines 1–4 once. Then repeat lines 1–4, or take a series of 1-minute timings.

```
1   If we leave now, we will see the last half of the new play.    12
2   As we boarded the plane, security officers ran ahead of us.     12
3   When the statue was unveiled, most of the guests applauded.     12
4   Although he was not a favorite, First Promise won the race.     12
    |  1  |  2  |  3  |  4  |  5  |  6  |  7  |  8  |  9  |  10  |  11  |  12
```

2. Use a comma after an introductory clause that begins with *if, as, when, although, since, because,* or a similar conjunction. Note the examples in lines 1–4.

B. Technique Drills

Key each line twice.

Shifting

5 Alice Larry Wayne Pearl Grace Henry Clyde Margo Isaac Velma
6 Iowa Utah Texas Maine Alaska Hawaii Georgia Arizona Vermont

Caps Lock

7 We went to HARBOR & DELANEY, INC., to see CARLOS and LINDA.
8 We MUST take that TRUE/FALSE test. I yelled, "HELP, FIRE!"

C. PRETEST

Take a 1-minute timing on lines 9–11. Proofread, note your errors, and figure your speed.

9   Driving from the city to the farms in an auto can be a   12
10 real winner. The key is to keep a good map so you will see   24
11 all the scenic lakes, small creeks, and rolling fields.   35
   | 1 | 2 | 3 | 4 | 5 | 6 | 7 | 8 | 9 | 10 | 11 | 12

D. PRACTICE

SPEED: If you made 2 or fewer errors on the Pretest, key lines 12–17 twice each. Repeat if time permits.
ACCURACY: If you made more than 2 errors on the Pretest, key lines 12–14 as a group twice. Then key lines 15–17 as a group twice. Repeat if time permits.

Double Reaches

12 ll bell call fall drill jelly pulls shall small tells wills
13 ss boss kiss miss bless cross dress fussy gloss guess issue
14 ee been deem weed creep fleet bleed meets needy sheet green

Alternate Reaches

15 also body city dial fuel half amend blame chair dials eight
16 halt idle kept lake maps name fight giant handy ivory laugh
17 owns paid rich sign than with panel right spend throw visit

E. POSTTEST

Take a 1-minute timing on lines 9–11. Proofread, note your errors, and figure your speed. Compare your performance with the Pretest.

Letter L41.78
Block style.

[*Today's date*] / Ms. Cheryl Hagen / Information Consultant / 1050 Newton Avenue North / Minneapolis, MN 55411 / Dear Ms. Hagen:

Your visit to Hammonds Industries was very timely, because the recommendations you made to improve our communications will be implemented almost immediately. The acquisition of our new desktop publishing software at Hammonds will provide us with printing capabilities never before possible. ¶ I was not aware of the savings we could realize by purchasing a desktop publishing system, and the software will also improve our image because of the quality of our correspondence and reports. ¶ Thank you for the suggestions; I look forward to receiving your complete, written report in the next week or so. / Sincerely, / Wesley T. Argue / President / [*Your initials*]

Take a 1-minute timing on lines 5–7. Proofread, note your errors, and figure your speed.

```
5        Do you recall when Cathy was walking by the stream and   12
6   she fell?  She seemed in a daze and rambled when she spoke.    24
7   We called her physician; he was amazed by her reaction.        35
    |  1  |  2  |  3  |  4  |  5  |  6  |  7  |  8  |  9  | 10  | 11  | 12
```

SPEED: If you made 2 or fewer errors on the Pretest, key lines 8–13 twice each. Repeat if time permits.
ACCURACY: If you made more than 2 errors on the Pretest, key lines 8–10 as a group twice. Then key lines 11–13 as a group twice. Repeat if time permits.

Up Reaches

```
8   ra raid rake rams raise rains raced rabid racks rabbi radar
9   ki kilt kind kick kings kiosk skied skiff skimp skirt skill
10  ok book look took crook brook yoked pokes stoke evoke spoke
```

Down Reaches

```
11  ca call cats care camps cameo canny cargo cases catch cater
12  az lazy hazy raze dazed crazy amaze graze razor blaze jazzy
13  1? all? owl? oil? coil? cell? fall? dill? mail? evil? nail?
```

Take a 1-minute timing on lines 5–7. Proofread, note your errors, and figure your speed. Compare your performance with the Pretest.

Academic Report R26.72

Standard format. Use the standard heading. Begin the report, and continue in Lessons 73 and 74

Finding and Getting the Right Job

The job market is becoming more competitive each day. While some employers actively seek applicants to fill positions, most businesses have the advantage of receiving more applications than they have positions to fill. Employers are looking for top-quality employees. If you are looking for a job, there are some specific guidelines that can help you find and get the job that is right for you.

Where do you search for a job? Many large high schools and almost all colleges, universities, and private business schools have a placement service that can provide you with a list of job openings. Often recruiters from large companies visit schools to interview prospective employees. Friends, relatives, teachers, and school counselors can also lead you to job openings (Luke and Steigler 590). These

people can let you know when a position becomes available. They can give you accurate information about the skills and previous experience required. They can also provide you with the names of people who can be contacted for information about specific positions (Luke and Steigler 590–91).

Want ads in newspapers and magazines are another important source of information (Brown and Clow 356). Many newspapers publish special ''Help Wanted'' sections each week. Help wanted ads usually include the position available, the qualifications needed, and a telephone number you can call or an address where you can write to inquire about the position (Luke and Steigler 591).

The personnel departments of companies where you would like to work are also excellent places to look for jobs. Often they have positions available within the company posted on bulletin boards or in the reception area. You may want to have a copy of your resume with you in case you are asked to fill out an application form while you are there.

(Continued on next page)

Letter L38.77
Modified-block style.

[*Today's date*] / Ms. Regina Land / Customer Relations Department / United Automotive Corporation / Detroit, MI 48232 / Dear Ms. Land: / Recently I purchased a new Grand Aero from Metro Motors in Douglasville, Georgia. As a former sales representative for an auto dealer in Birmingham, Alabama, I know how seldom you receive letters that express "a job well done." Therefore, I want to take a few minutes of your time to share with you how pleased I have been with the purchase of my Grand Aero and how much I appreciate quality performance. ¶ This is the first car I have owned that I have never had to take back to the dealer for even the slightest problem. ¶ So, congratulations to your Quality Control people—they did an excellent job on this automobile! / Sincerely, / David Benedict / 2356 West 17 Street / Atlanta, GA 43901 / c: Metro Motors

Letter L39.77
Modified-block style. Correct any punctuation errors in the body of the letter.

[*Today's date*] / Dr. Noel Powell / Department of Business Education / Fort Gordon College / Woonsocket, RI 02895 / Dear Dr. Powell: / Thank you so very much for agreeing to come to our annual Career Day at Carrollton High School. I know that all the students will be looking forward to your presentation "The Business World in Your Future." Many of our seniors go on to attend Fort Gordon College and they recently attended the early registration session on your campus. ¶ Your presentation is scheduled at 1:30 p.m. in the auditorium. Please allow about 30 minutes for your talk and another 5 or 10 minutes at the end for student questions. I look forward to seeing you on the 9th. / Yours truly, / Frances Jackson / 821 Davis Road / New London, CT 06320

Letter L40.77
Modified-block style.

Retrieve Letter L39.77 and replace the last paragraph with the following:

We have you scheduled for two presentations at 1:30 p.m. and 2:30 p.m. in Lecture Hall 204. Please allow around 40 minutes for your talk so that students can ask a few questions at the conclusion of each presentation. Your sessions should be well attended; over 100 students have signed up for your presentation.

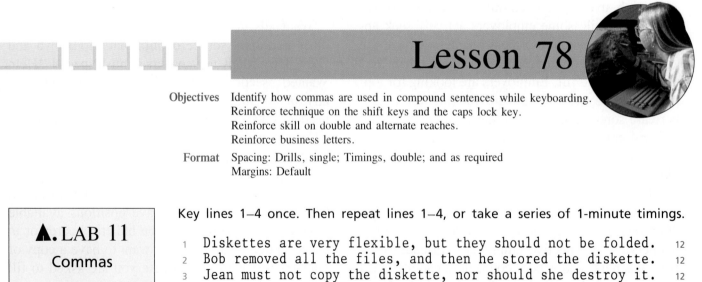

Lesson 78

Objectives   Identify how commas are used in compound sentences while keyboarding.
Reinforce technique on the shift keys and the caps lock key.
Reinforce skill on double and alternate reaches.
Reinforce business letters.

Format   Spacing: Drills, single; Timings, double; and as required
Margins: Default

▲. LAB 11

Commas

Key lines 1–4 once. Then repeat lines 1–4, or take a series of 1-minute timings.

1 Diskettes are very flexible, but they should not be folded. 12
2 Bob removed all the files, and then he stored the diskette. 12
3 Jean must not copy the diskette, nor should she destroy it. 12
4 Complete the label, and then put it firmly on the diskette. 12
   | 1 | 2 | 3 | 4 | 5 | 6 | 7 | 8 | 9 | 10 | 11 | 12

Another possibility for locating a job is through an employment agency. Public and private employment agencies are solely in the business of matching job openings with prospective employees. Public employment agencies do not charge for their services; private agencies do. Sometimes an employer will pay the agency's fee. If the employer does not pay the agency fee, you will be required to pay the fee when you accept a job that you obtained through the agency.

Additional sources of job openings include the civil service, professional associations, trade unions, and temporary employment services. The more sources you use and the more places you apply, the better your chances of getting the job you want.

The next step in securing a job is to prepare a resume, which is sometimes called a personal data sheet. A resume is simply a well-organized list of information about yourself that can be sent with a letter of application, presented to an interviewer, and used as a source of reference when you are filling out application forms (Clark, Zimmer, and Tinervia 606). The resume should be limited to one page and must be free of errors.

The principal items that should be included in a resume are your name, address, and telephone number; your work experience—in chronological order, with the most recent job listed first; your educational background; and references—names and addresses of people who can provide information about you. Many people also include the position for which they are applying. Always obtain permission from people you want to use as references before listing them on your resume.

(Continues in Lesson 73)

Lesson 73

Objectives Identify how commas are used after introductory clauses while keying sentences.
Continue keying a multipage report with a long quote, tables, and works cited.

Format Spacing: Drills, single; and as required
Margins: Default or as required

A. LAB 10
Commas

Key lines 1–4 once. Then repeat lines 1–4, or take a series of 1-minute timings.

```
1  Since we are ahead of all other teams, our coach is calmer.   12
2  Because we stopped to eat, we got home well after midnight.    12
3  When Cal saw the flashing lights, he slowed down instantly.    12
4  As we were talking, four men walked up and asked for money.    12
   |  1  |  2  |  3  |  4  |  5  |  6  |  7  |  8  |  9  |  10  |  11  |  12
```

B. "OK" Timings

Take two 30-second "OK" (errorless) timings on lines 5–6. Then take two 30-second "OK" timings on lines 7–8. Goal: No errors.

```
5  I quickly explained that few big jobs involve many hazards,   12
6  but the directors felt that we needed more safety measures.   24

7  Peter reviewed the subject before giving Kay and Max a quiz   12
8  on the computer; they like using the machine to take tests.   24
   |  1  |  2  |  3  |  4  |  5  |  6  |  7  |  8  |  9  |  10  |  11  |  12
```

Lesson 77

Objectives Recognize how commas are used in compound sentences while keyboarding.
Reinforce skill on adjacent and jump reaches.
Reinforce personal-business letters.

Format Spacing: Drills, single; Timings, double; and as required
Margins: Default

▲ A. LAB 11
Commas

Key lines 1–4 once. Then repeat lines 1–4, or take a series of 1-minute timings.

1   You should always tell the truth, and you should be honest.   12
2   Michelle did an honest day's work, and Michael was pleased.   12
3   Chapter 9 is on ethics, and Chapter 10 is on office morale.   12
4   She defined ethics, and then we practiced ethical behavior.   12
   | 1 | 2 | 3 | 4 | 5 | 6 | 7 | 8 | 9 | 10 | 11 | 12

An *independent* clause is one that can stand alone as a sentence. Here are two examples of independent clauses:

Philip used a spreadsheet. Paige used a database.

3. When two independent clauses are joined by the conjunction *and, but, or,* or *nor* into one compound sentence, place a comma before the conjunction.

Philip used a spreadsheet, but Paige used a database.
They have one integrated package, and soon they will add another.

B. PRETEST

Take a 1-minute timing on lines 5–7. Proofread, note your errors, and figure your speed.

5   A computer may very well be the best source from which   12

6   we obtain any data. We can obtain whatever we want in just   24

7   a few seconds, and it very seldom contains any errors.   35
   | 1 | 2 | 3 | 4 | 5 | 6 | 7 | 8 | 9 | 10 | 11 | 12

C. PRACTICE

SPEED: If you made 2 or fewer errors on the Pretest, key lines 8–13 twice each. Repeat if time permits.
ACCURACY: If you made more than 2 errors on the Pretest, key lines 8–10 as a group twice. Then key lines 11–13 as a group twice. Repeat if time permits.

Adjacent Reaches

8   er here mere were defer enter fewer merge paper stern terms
9   op copy drop open adopt hoped ropes scope shops stops topic
10   as asks base sash chase erase grasp haste lease taste waste

Jump Reaches

11   be belt beam bend beast bench berth beach beard below begin
12   ec echo deck neck check fleck piece leech niece speck wreck
13   mi milk mint mist might mince mirth mixed minor minus miser

D. POSTTEST

Take a 1-minute timing on lines 5–7. Proofread, note your errors, and figure your speed. Compare your performance with the Pretest.

Academic Report R27.73 (Continued)

The following table shows how 152 companies ranked information that they felt needed to be included on a resume as well as information they felt was not needed.

Table 1
Needed and Unneeded Resume Items

Needed Items	Unneeded Items
Name	Religion
Address	Race
Telephone number	Gender
Degree	Photograph
Name of college	Marital status
Major	Birthplace
Jobs held	Transcript of grades
Employers	Height/weight
Dates of employment	Church involvement

(Harcourt, Krizan, and Gordon 35–36)

This table reflects an emphasis on a person's job-related abilities, skills, and experience rather than on personal information. Employers are primarily interested in how you can benefit the company.

Once you have several job leads and have completed your resume, you must prepare a brief letter of application for any position that requires you to apply in writing. The application letter will give a prospective employer a first impression of you. This may be the beginning—or the end—of your employment prospects with that company. Because employers sometimes receive hundreds of applications for a single job, it is impossible for them to interview everyone who applies. Therefore, application letters and resumes are used to determine who will be selected for an interview. As Kushner states:

> Remember that the letter of application is really a sales letter. It is a letter in which you capitalize on your academic and personal preparation by tailoring the information you give to fit the job that you are seeking. You must demonstrate to the employer that you possess the particular personal qualities, abilities, and skills required

in that business. (27)

The main purpose of an application letter is to obtain an interview. To do this, the letter must create a favorable impression of you. In the letter you should mention the specific position you are interested in, stress at least one major point of educational preparation, point out what you can do for the company, and close by asking for an interview (Luke and Steigler 593). Check your letter carefully to be sure it is neat and accurate. Remember, your letter reflects you and the quality of work you can produce.

Most companies require prospective employees to fill out an application form. Be sure your application is neat, accurate, and complete. Have a copy of your resume, a small dictionary, and several pens with you when you go to fill out an application. This eliminates the need for you to ask for things and helps you appear organized. Before you begin filling out the application, read through the entire form. Follow all directions carefully. If some questions do not apply to you, write *NA* (not applicable) or a dash in the space beside the question to show that you have not skipped the item. If you leave any questions unanswered, it may appear that you were careless in filling out the form.

Be sure to ask for clarification of any questions that you do not understand. If possible, save all your questions to ask at one time. Your care in filling out the application form neatly, completely, and accurately could result in an interview with the company (Luke and Steigler 595).

The interview allows the company to gather information about you that does not appear on your resume or the application form. This information includes such things as your career plans, appearance, personality, poise, and attitudes (Luke and Steigler 598). There are several things you should keep in mind when you go for an interview. Plan what you will wear ahead of time. If you are unsure of what to wear, dress conservatively. Be sure your clothing is neat, clean, and comfortable. Pay attention to such details as well-groomed nails, clean hair, appropriate accessories, and well-cared-for shoes.

(Continues in Lesson 74)

Key lines 21–33 once. Then repeat any of the lines that stress the errors you made in Pretest 1.

AB	21	A ale and ant aunt aide aisle B bid bay bud belt bulk balmy
CD	22	C cut cat cod cove cube clerk D did dry dim dorm debt doubt
EF	23	E ear elm end ease etch edges F fir few fly foil four front
GH	24	G gun gag gap gaze goal grant H hit hot hue have half hitch
IJ	25	I ice imp ire into idea infer J jam jar jet jury just joker
KL	26	K key keg kid keen kind kayak L law lad let land lamb laugh
MN	27	M may mix mad make mind month N new nor now note next noise
OP	28	O own old oil oath ouch ought P peg par pay prod plea purge
QR	29	Q que qui quo quip quit quest R rod rig rug raft ream right
ST	30	S ski six sod salt sent scale T tag tin toy tend toil toast
UV	31	U ups urn use undo unit using V vow van vie volt vile virus
WX	32	W why won wet wipe wrap waver X axe fox mix lynx text waxen
YZ	33	Y yam yes yaw yoke year yards Z zig zip zoo zinc zing zesty

F. POSTTEST 1

Take another 2-minute timing on lines 17–20 (page 179). Proofread, note your errors, and figure your speed. Compare your performance with the Pretest.

G. PRETEST 2

Take a 1-minute timing on lines 34–36. Proofread, note your errors, and figure your speed.

Discrimination Practice

34   To merge many addresses with one letter is truly quite   12

35 a job for certain people. However, for a person who voices   24

36 this opinion, this tedious task is as easy as can be.   35

| 1 | 2 | 3 | 4 | 5 | 6 | 7 | 8 | 9 | 10 | 11 | 12

H. PRACTICE 2

SPEED: If you made 2 or fewer errors on the Pretest, key lines 37–42 twice each. Repeat if time permits.
ACCURACY: If you made more than 2 errors on the Pretest, key lines 37–39 as a group twice. Then key lines 40–42 as a group twice. Repeat if time permits.

Left-hand Reaches

37 rer red crew here dread cheer bread chore cream clerk dream
38 asa ash base sane flash saint haste sauce spasm salty toast
39 rtr art dirt tray ports heart tract shirt trade spurt trail

Right-hand Reaches

40 pop pods chop post stop spool sport adopt depot topic polar
41 oio toil coil riot boil joins lions hoist avoid going onion
42 iui suit quit unit ruin build quilt quiet quick guilt fluid

I. POSTTEST 2

Take another 1-minute timing on lines 34–36. Proofread, note your errors, and figure your speed. Compare your performance with the Pretest.

Lesson 74

Objectives Use commas correctly after introductory clauses while keying sentences.
Continue keying a multipage report with a long quote and tables.
Key 35/3'/5e.

Format Spacing: Drills, single; Timings, double; and as required
Margins: Default or as required

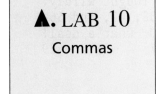
A. LAB 10
Commas

Key lines 1–4 once, providing missing commas. Review your copy as your teacher reads the answers. Then key lines 1–4 again.

1 As he gazed at the sky last night Leon saw a falling star.
2 Although our bill had been paid they kept sending notices.
3 If you are certain about the price I will buy those boots.
4 When you leave this evening please turn off the computers.

B. Preview Practice

Key each line twice as a preview to the 3-minute timings below.

Accuracy
5 puzzle concise acquire examine familiar sentences courteous

Speed
6 guide both five give work will good each jobs any one as if

C. 3-Minute Timings

Take two 3-minute timings on lines 7–15. Proofread, note your errors, and figure your speed.

7 If you work in an office, one of your jobs could be to   12
8 write letters. There are five words that help guide you as   24
9 you compose a letter: clear, complete, concise, courteous,   36
10 and correct. If you use these rules, all your letters will   48
11 acquire a crisp, clean tone and not puzzle your readers. A   60
12 good letter should have both short sentences and words that   72
13 are familiar to the reader. It must give all of the needed   84
14 facts with the fewest words and still have a friendly tone.   96
15 Examine each letter closely for any mistakes.   105

| 1 | 2 | 3 | 4 | 5 | 6 | 7 | 8 | 9 | 10 | 11 | 12 SI 1.30

Correspondence

Unit Goal 35/5'/5e

Lesson 76

Objectives   Reinforce technique on the tab and the space bar.
Identify and practice the alphabet keys on which more drill is needed.
Reinforce skill on left-hand and right-hand reaches.

Format   Spacing: Drills, single; tabs every 7 spaces; Timings, double, 5-space tab
Margins: Default

A. Keyboard Skills

Key lines 1–4 once. In line 5 use your tab key to advance from one number to the next through the entire line. Repeat lines 1–4, or take a series of 1-minute timings.

Speed	1	The cat wants to lie down in that same place when it rests.	12
Accuracy	2	Judy gave a quick jump as the zebra and lynx fought wildly.	12
Numbers	3	If we have 10 days, our count should be 29, 38, 47, and 56.	12
Symbols	4	At $5.37 we can make 16% more profit from #20--what a deal!	12
Technique	5	561 382 473 294 105 156 247 338 429	

| 1 | 2 | 3 | 4 | 5 | 6 | 7 | 8 | 9 | 10 | 11 | 12

B. Technique Review

Key lines 6–9 and 10–13 once each to determine which of the two groups gave you the most difficulty. Then repeat the difficult group once.

Tabulator Review

6	at	be	do	go	hi	in	me	no	pi
7	so	to	up	we	an	ho	it	my	pa
8	ant	bed	cot	den	elf	fry	get	hop	ink
9	jog	kid	lie	mop	nor	ode	pan	que	rid

Space Bar Review

10   If it is to be, you are not the ones to say that it is not.
11   You are the one to be at the home when all of us have gone.
12   It is a good idea to have me save all of my pay that I can.
13   Use the key all the time to move from one line to the next.

C. 12-Second Timings

Take three 12-second timings on each line, or key each line three times. Try to key with no more than 1 error on each timing.

14   If they did not take that course, they may not play sports.
15   The order is a big one, and we might make a very nice sale.
16   I know that the job may take about an hour or two or three.

| 5   10   15   20   25   30   35   40   45   50   55   60

D. PRETEST 1

Take a 2-minute timing on lines 17–20 to find out which alphabet keys are the most difficult for you. Force yourself to key rapidly—push yourself to your fastest rate. Note each letter keyed incorrectly.

17   Park my huge, bronze jet and quickly wax it for five hours.   12
18   Jack would pay for fixing my novels if Elizabeth requested.   24
19   The expert quickly noted five bad zircons among the jewels.   36
20   Mack played the jukebox while Fritz sang a very quick song.   48

| 1 | 2 | 3 | 4 | 5 | 6 | 7 | 8 | 9 | 10 | 11 | 12

Academic Report R28.74 (Continued)

Always go alone to an interview, and arrive slightly early. Stand as you greet the interviewer. Shake hands with a firm grasp. During the interview, maintain good posture both while standing and while sitting. Take your cues from the interviewer; for example, do not sit down until you are asked. Never chew gum, smoke, or touch things on the interviewer's desk. Look directly at the interviewer as you listen to and answer questions. Try to appear confident. How you look, walk, sit, and carry yourself reflect the type of person you are. Table 2 shows the top seven verbal and nonverbal interview skills that company recruiters look for when interviewing prospective employees. Interviewers rate not only what you say but also how you say it.

Table 2
Important Interview Skills

Verbal	Nonverbal
Honesty	Attitude
Grammar	Maturity
Articulation	Attentiveness
Organization	Enthusiasm
Directness	Personal hygiene
Vocabulary	Listening
Tone of voice	Promptness

(English and Walker 13–14)

Anticipate questions that an interviewer may ask you, and be ready to answer them. Before going to the interview, learn as much as you can about the company and about the position for which you are applying. Also, be prepared to ask your own questions. An interview should provide you with an opportunity to determine whether the job is right for you.

Before leaving the interview, ask when the interviewer expects to make a decision and when you should expect to hear about the job (Chiri et al. 186). Then thank the interviewer for taking the time to meet with you, and express a positive interest in the job.

After an interview, it is appropriate to send a follow-up letter. The letter serves to remind the employer of your name and your interest in the job. Composing and sending a follow-up letter takes only a few minutes, yet those few minutes may be your last chance to convince the interviewer that you are the person for the job (Luke and Steigler 605).

Works Cited

Brown, Betty J., and John E. Clow. Our Business and Economic World. Columbus: Glencoe-Macmillan/McGraw, 1992.

Chiri, Judith A., Jacqueline P. Kutsko, Patricia Seraydarian, and Ted D. Stoddard. Houghton Mifflin Information Processing: Keyboarding, Formatting, and Applications Mastery. 2d ed. Columbus: Glencoe-Macmillan/McGraw, 1989.

Clark, Lyn R., Kenneth Zimmer, and Joseph Tinervia. Business English and Communication. 7th ed. Columbus: Glencoe-Macmillan/McGraw, 1988.

English, Donald E., and Janet I. Walker. "On-Campus Recruiters' Attitudes Toward the Importance of Selected Nonverbal Skills, Verbal Skills, and Characteristics and Background Factors of Students During On-Campus Interviews." TBEA Journal 1987: 12–15.

Harcourt, Jules, A. C. Krizan, and Glenn Gordon. "Resume Content Preferences of Fortune 500 Companies." Business Education Forum February 1989: 34–36.

Kushner, John A. How to Find and Apply for a Job. 5th ed. Cincinnati: South-Western, 1989.

Luke, Cheryl M., and C. B. Steigler. Office Systems and Procedures. 2d ed. Columbus: Glencoe-Macmillan/McGraw, 1987.

Level 4

Computer models are used in weather analysis to determine the velocity and direction of storms. Satellite imagery is used to track storms. In television weather reporting, computers are used to project maps and to overlay graphics on those maps in order to indicate storm fronts, temperature bands, amounts of precipitation, and so on. Computers also are used to create the graphics for 3- to 5-day forecasts.

4 DAY FORECAST

FRIDAY	SATURDAY	SUNDAY	MONDAY
78	83	85	76
61	57	59	61

FRIDAY

Goals

1. Demonstrate keyboarding speed and accuracy on straight copy with a goal of 37 words a minute for 5 minutes with 5 or fewer errors.
2. Correctly proofread copy for errors and edit copy for revision.
3. Apply basic production skills in keyboarding and formatting copy for correspondence, reports, and tables from a variety of input modes—arranged, unarranged; rough draft; handwritten; unedited, incomplete, and/or composed.
4. Apply rules for correct use of the comma and semicolon in written communications.

Lesson 75

Objectives   Reinforce personal-business and business letters.
Reinforce open and ruled tables.

Format   Spacing: Drills, single; and as required
Margins: Default or as required

A. Keyboard Skills

Key lines 1–4 once. Then key line 5 once using the caps lock key for the all-cap words. Repeat lines 1–4, or take a series of 1-minute timings.

Speed
Accuracy
Numbers
Symbols
Technique

1   A nice way to escape your daily cares is to read for a bit.   12
2   Vita Drew and Jack Lopez quietly bought six new farm tools.   12
3   On May 29 that doctor saw 13 boys, 24 girls, and 18 adults.   12
4   Pen & Ink and Nate & Fox paid for 674# of #95 glue @ $1.82.   12
5   PLEASE take a TRAIN or a BUS or a PLANE or a SHIP or a CAR.
    | 1 | 2 | 3 | 4 | 5 | 6 | 7 | 8 | 9 | 10 | 11 | 12

B. 30-Second Timings

Take two 30-second timings on lines 6 and 7. Then take two 30-second timings on lines 8 and 9. Try to key with no more than 2 errors on each timing.

6   Do you prefer a class where your teacher lectures while you   12
7   take notes or one where you learn by doing supervised jobs?   24

8   Each person has a learning style that may be different from   12
9   another. Find how you learn best, and make the most of it.   24
    | 1 | 2 | 3 | 4 | 5 | 6 | 7 | 8 | 9 | 10 | 11 | 12

Letter L36.75
Block style. No. 6 3/4 envelope.

[*Today's date*] / Ms. Marla S. Pemberton / Personnel Director / Windsor Software, Incorporated / 77 Norwood Industrial Park / Des Moines, IA 50317-6891 / Dear Ms. Pemberton: / Ms. Troiana Prokosch, a word processing specialist with your firm, told me that you will have an opening for a word processing operator soon. I would appreciate an opportunity to discuss my qualifications for this position with you. ¶ As you can see on the enclosed resume, I have been working part-time as a word processing trainee while attending Des Moines City College. With a major in information processing systems and three years of work experience in that field, I believe that I can be an asset to your company. ¶ May I have an appointment to discuss this position with you? You can telephone me at 515-555-3886 from 1 to 5 p.m. Monday through Friday. / Yours truly, / Francisco Herrera / 468 Waukee Road / Des Moines, IA 50318 / Enclosure

Letter L37.75
Modified-block style, indented paragraphs. No. 10 envelope.

[*Today's date*] / Mr. Francisco Herrera / 486 Waukee Rd. / Des Moines, IA 50318 / Dear Mr. Herrera: / Thank you for your letter inquiring about employment with our company as a word processing operator. We do have an opening for this position. ¶ Your education and work experience are very impressive, and we would like to discuss the position with you an in interview. Please call my secretary, Paul, at 515-555-2047 to schedule a meeting at your convenience. ¶ Please complete the application form enclosed, and bring it with you to the interview. I look forward to talking with you next week. / Sincerely yours, / Marla S. Pemberton / Personnel director / [*Your initials*] / Enclosure

Table T25.75
Open format. Double spacing.

TEN MOST POPULAR NAMES

Girls' Names	Boys' Names
Sarah	Michael
Ann	Brian
Nicole	Steven
Elizabeth	Joseph
Brittany	Matthew
Lauren	Alan
Ashley	Christopher
Marie	David
Renee	Eric
Catherine	Robert

Table T26.75
Ruled format. Double spacing.

EARLY UNITED STATES EXPLORERS

Name	Area Explored	Date
Christopher Columbus	Bahamas	1492
John Cabot	Delaware coast	1497
Juan Ponce de Leon	Florida coast	1513
Francis Drake	California	1579
John Smith	Virginia	1607
Henry Hudson	New York	1609

Skillbuilding

Alphabetic Pretest/Practice/Posttest

PRETEST

Key as many 30-second "OK" (errorless) timings as possible out of three attempts on lines 1–3. Then repeat the effort on lines 4–6.

1 My folks proved his expert eloquence was just a big hazard.
2 Jack's man found exactly a quarter in the woven zipper bag.
3 Why did Max become eloquent over a zany gift like jodhpurs?

4 Six jumbo elephants quickly moved the wagon from the blaze.
5 Bo ran quickly from the zone when dogs jumped over an exit.
6 The six zebras very quickly jumped out of the winter glare.

PRACTICE

Key each line twice.

A 7 Ada and Anna had an allowance and always had adequate cash.
B 8 Barbara grabbed back the brown bag Bob bought at a bargain.
C 9 Charles can accept and cash any checks the church collects.
D 10 David drove down and deducted the dividends he had divided.
E 11 Everyone here exerted extra effort each week we were there.

F 12 Fred Ford offered to find fresh food for five fine fellows.
G 13 Guy suggested getting eight guys to bring George's luggage.
H 14 Hank hoped that she had withheld the cash they had to have.
I 15 Iris insists their idea is simply idiotic in this instance.

J 16 Jack and Jerry joined Joe just to enjoy a journey to Japan.
K 17 Kathy asked Ken to take a blank checkbook back to her bank.
L 18 Larry helped several little fellows learn to play baseball.
M 19 Mr. Ammon made many mistakes in estimating minimum markets.
N 20 Nan never knew when any businessman wanted an announcement.

O 21 One or two of those older tool orders ought to go out soon.
P 22 Please provide proper paper supplies for plenty of persons.
Q 23 Quenton quietly inquired what sequences required questions.
R 24 Run over for another order from the firm across the street.

S 25 She says she sold us some shiny steel scissors or snippers.
T 26 Try to get the truth when they talk about better attitudes.
U 27 Unless you pour out your mixture, you could hurt our stuff.
V 28 Vivian raved over violets and even saved several varieties.

W 29 William will work well whenever we know where we will work.
X 30 X rays exceed examinations except for external exploration.
Y 31 Yes, any day they say you may be ready, you may try to fly.
Z 32 Zenith Franz realizes that he idealized the zigzag friezes.

POSTTEST

Key as many 30-second "OK" (errorless) timings as possible out of three attempts on lines 1–3. Then repeat the effort on lines 4–6. Note your improvement.

46 wam

The results of a citizenship test taken by a selected group of high school students were shocking. The test was conducted to determine how much knowledge young people have of our system of government. It also questioned whether they know about how to split their ballot when they vote. Only one-third of the students participating in the program knew that a voter could split his or her party choice. The majority were ignorant of politics altogether.

48 wam

Veterinarians are doctors who are trained to treat and prevent diseases in animals. Although they go to different medical schools than doctors trained to treat people, their course of study and training is much alike. Vets can limit their practice to one kind of animal. If they choose to specialize in horses, they can be highly paid because the patients are often priceless race horses. Some vets, on another hand, work with or conduct special research on wild animals.

50 wam

The Inca Indians lived hundreds of years ago near what is now called Peru. They were a great nation recognized for their unique buildings. These buildings, in fact, are still visible in ruins of the jungle. The temples that remain can be scrutinized for clues about their religion, beliefs, culture, and way of life. Some knowledge already exists, for we have learned that they were a people of many skills. Perhaps in time we can uncover the answer to the secret of why the Incas vanished.

Drills

Alphabetic Words A
1 ache aged aide arch aunt able acid acre afar ajar alas apex
2 aisle abide about above abuse acorn actor acute adapt agent

B
3 baby bias body busy bare bark bike bell belt bend beak brag
4 batch beach birch black board boast braid burst brave bride

C
5 calm cent chap clam coat crew curb czar cane cede cord cuff
6 caulk cease chant clang coast crane curve catch chief cling

D
7 damp deal dine done drag dust deck dent disk down drip dime
8 dance depth ditch dodge draft drove doubt dread drawl drone

E
9 each earn ease east edge else etch easy echo ever evil emit
10 earth eaves eight elect erase evoke event excel every entry

F
11 fact feat file flaw folk from fuse fang fend film flip form
12 false fence first flare force frame frost fault field flour

G
13 gain germ gift glib goat grim gulf gait gear girl glad gown
14 gauge ghost gland glare gouge grand grind guest grain grape

H
15 hail hear hike hold hulk hark helm hide honk huge hire howl
16 harsh heist hoist hutch haste hence horse hunch hotel husky

I
17 inch itch idle into iron item idea imps ills irks ibex iris
18 icing ideal igloo image imply index inept inert infer inlet

J
19 jest jilt jinx join joke jump jugs just jury jade jail jabs
20 jaunt jeans joist judge juice jelly jewel joker jolly juror

K
21 keel knot keep kelp kemp kick kiss kite knew knee knit knob
22 knack knead knife knock kayak kitty knows kinks khaki karat

L
23 lace left lick loft lump lynx lack lash lend lens life loud
24 lapse large ledge leave lodge lymph lapel legal logic lower

M
25 made mast mesh melt mild mint mole mold mule must mask mere
26 month midst march match merge mound mouth movie music motor

N
27 name nail near news none nose numb next nice noun note neck
28 nerve niece night ninth noise north notch nurse nudge noble

O
29 once oath ouch oboe odor oily obey open only omit oval odds
30 ought ounce ocean offer often orbit olive order onion other

P
31 page pale pail perk peat pert pile pike pine plea plop plot
32 paint pants paste pearl peach peace place plate pound pride

38 wam

Have you ever been on a fairly long trip by car only to find yourself bored because you didn't have much to do? You, the passenger, can engross yourself in a good book. This answer to the boredom can make time seem to pass more rapidly. You could purchase several paperbacks at a local bookstore; and as you read, you can capture many hours of entertainment and enjoyment.

40 wam

Today, a quick way to get from one place to another is by plane. You can choose from among many airlines for your flight. In addition, airlines throughout the nation offer daily service to many cities here and abroad. Passengers on domestic and international flights should allow enough time before departure to secure seats on board the plane and to check in baggage at the airport terminal.

42 wam

Each year when winter approaches, you might look up at the sky and view hundreds and maybe even thousands of birds flying toward warmer weather. Quite simply, they migrate just to escape the severe days that come so soon. Many experts do hypothesize that birds migrate because they physically cannot last in the harsh winters of the cold north. Other experts think that birds migrate to find better food sources.

44 wam

Most successful newspapers are large businesses with a big staff and several readers. Now, though, there are a growing number of smaller papers. Their aim is to focus on a community or one subject. A small paper that is well produced will concentrate on and serve a local public. In addition, operating it is challenging and rewarding for those who are in the business. Besides, newspapers give everyone a vehicle for free speech.

Alphabetic Words (Continued)

Q
33   quid quit quack quake queen quest quill quote quiet quavers
34   quip quiz quail quart quell quick quilt quirt quash quintet

R
35   rage raid read rest rink ripe roam roar rule rung rate ream
36   ranch raise reign reach rough round rainy recap rigid royal

S
37   sail said scar scan seal serf shin show skim soft span star
38   saint sauce scare scold serve share since slang smart solve

T
39   tale tart test teak them thus tilt time tone toil trap turn
40   taste taunt tempt tease there theme torch touch trade twist

U
41   urge used ugly undo uses unless unload unkind unfair unfold
42   undue upset union urban unite usher uncle until using under

V
43   vane vase veal veer vice view volt vote vast verb vine vise
44   vague verse value valve voice vault vocal verge vouch vowel

W
45   wade walk west were when whip word work wrap wise weld wing
45   waist waved weigh wedge wheat while worst would wreck wrist

X
47   flex hoax jinx apex text exam axle taxi axis exit waxy foxy
48   fixed mixed sixth exact extra relax sixty exile latex toxic

Y
49   yarn yawn yard year yell yelp yoke yolk your yule yowl yoga
50   yeast yield young yours yacht yearn youth yummy yucca yards

Z
51   zig zest zeal zinc zing zone zoom zero zany zips zoos zebra
52   zigzag zinnia zipper zodiac zircon zoology zealous zucchini

Alphabetic Sentences

1   Quietly, six zebras jumped back over the eight brown rafts.
2   Park my gray, bronze jet and quickly wax it for five hours.
3   Five more wax jugs have been glazed quickly for two people.
4   Jo quoted two dozen passages from Val's chemistry textbook.
5   The disc jockey won six bronze plaques for helping Mr. Van.
6   Ben auctioned off the pink gems and my quartz jewelry next.

Speed Sentences

1   The book is new and will not be sold at the fair next year.
2   It is not the right time for us to talk about all the work.
3   The juice in that glass was cold, clear, and good to drink.
4   The light is dim, but it will give us all the light I need.
5   The bird flew way up in the sky to get away from the smoke.
6   We would like to know if you are going to the play at five.

28 wam   When shopping in this country, we generally accept the
price tag of merchandise as the final price the store will
consider. If we want the item, we pay the amount asked.
In other nations, prices might vary every moment, depending
on the ability of the purchaser to bargain.

30 wam   National parks are owned by the people of America, and
they are preserves for wildlife and timber. The government
cares for these parks to make certain they stay protected
and guarded resources. Rangers help prevent forest fires,
analyze weather conditions, and keep watch on the wild
animals.

32 wam   You simply do not go rafting down the quick river that
flows through the Grand Canyon without skills and plenty of
help. The hazards are just too severe. The lovely canyon
is rocky, thorny, and hot in summer. Sometimes it is even
so windy that sand sprays, hitting you in the face with a
brisk and stinging jolt.

34 wam   A batik is a dyed cloth that has hot wax painted on it
to form a design. The artist melts wax, tints it various
colors, paints a design, and then dyes the cloth. Some
artists prefer to paint the cloth with clear wax. Then the
batik is dyed again and again, using many colors. Only the
part not coated with that wax becomes colored.

36 wam   Working with plants could be an exciting and fun hobby
for you. If you have never waited with anticipation for a
small sprig to sprout into a plant, you have missed a joy.
In fact, plants make suitable pets for apartment dwellers.
They neither bark nor meow, and the neighbors don't grumble
about being kept awake or about being annoyed by a noisy
pet.

Right-Hand Words

1. mum pun lip yolk lion look loom lump oily holly jolly nippy
2. hip hop him join kink moll poll pink hook hilly lymph puppy
3. mom mop nip loll milk mill noon noun hull milky mummy poppy
4. kin joy oil honk holy hymn hook hunk loop lumpy union onion
5. pin you nun hoop link jump limp lily loin hooky nylon pupil
6. ink ill inn only pool pull pump upon pill knoll jumpy imply

Left-Hand Words

1. act bad car acre babe beat cage data ears gates safes taste
2. ads bag cat acts beet beds card date ease great seats taxed
3. are bar ear adds bags beef care draw east grade serve tests
4. ate bat eat ages bare bees cars dear edge grace staff texts
5. art bed far area bats best case debt eggs greet state tract
6. ade bet fed arts bear beer cast deed ever grate sweet trade

Alternate-Hand Sentences

1. The lane to the lake may make the auto turn and go to town.
2. The man and the dog did go to the lake to dig for the dock.
3. The duck, the fox, and the fish make problems for the girl.
4. They may wish to blame me for the fight to end the problem.
5. She is busy with the work but is to go to town for the pen.
6. I am to go to work for the audit firm by the eighth of May.

Double-Letter Words

1. burr ebbs eggs been less need fill look keep soon well tool
2. book will seem toss sees feel pool good pass mill miss ball
3. goods green skill added seeks proof small radii guess dizzy
4. fluff abbey sunny ditto apple gummy petty upper sleep shall
5. succeeds quitters withhold slowness grammar vacuums shopper
6. possible followed carriage occasion shipper accused cabbage

2-Letter Words

1. ad am an as at ax be by do el go ha he hi ho id if in is it
2. la ma me my no of oh or ow ox oz pa re so to up us we ye yo

3-Letter Words

1. aid air and ant apt bid big bit bow bud bus but cod cow cut
2. did die dig dog due dug dye end eye fir fit fix foe fur got
3. jam key lay man map may men oak own pay pep rid rob rod row
4. rub she sir sit six sod sue the tie tow via wit woe ago jet
5. bay can cad ink lab max van age boy fly had one par put sky
6. act add ads are art egg eve fee few sad sat saw see set sew

4-Letter Words

1. able acid also bake bale band cake came chat days dial diet
2. else eyes fair fame felt firm game gift girl hair half halt
3. idle jury kept keys lake lame land mail make maps nail name
4. owns paid pair push rich ride rise self send sick tame than
5. vote wait want ants arms auto bird bite boat cite clay coal
6. does down dust fish flat fuel glad goal grow hand help horn

Pacing

The Pacing routine builds speed and accuracy in short, easy steps, using individualized goals and immediate feedback.

This section contains a series of 2-minute timings for speeds ranging from 20 wam to 50 wam. The first time you use these timings, select a passage that is 2 wam higher than your current keyboarding speed. Use a two-stage practice pattern to achieve each speed goal—first concentrate on speed and then work on accuracy.

SPEED GOAL. Take three 2-minute timings on the same passage until you can complete it in 2 minutes (do not worry about the number of errors).

When you have achieved your speed goal, work on accuracy.

ACCURACY GOAL. To key accurately, you need to slow down—just a little bit. Thus, to reach your accuracy goal, drop back 2 wam to the previous passage. Take three 2-minute timings on this passage until you can complete it in 2 minutes with no more than 2 errors.

For example, if you achieved a speed goal of 30 wam, you should then work on an accuracy goal of 28 wam. When you have achieved the 28 wam goal for accuracy, you would then move up 4 wam (for example, to the 34 wam passage) and work for speed again.

If you are not using the correlated software, your teacher (or someone you select) will call out each 1/4-minute interval as you key. Strive to be at the appropriate point in the passage which is marked by a small superior number at each 1/4-minute interval.

20 wam

The old man who walks[1] in the park always has[2] a huge smile on his face.[3] He talks to the people[4] who cross his path.[5] He gives assistance in his quiet[6] way and is excited when[7] he makes a new friend.[8]

22 wam

There is no equal to the[1] flavor of ice cream on hot,[2] humid days. Choices of[3] all types are out to engage[4] the eye, and the snappy clerks[5] will fix just the mix and[6] size to suit you best.[7] A cup or a cone will be fine.[8]

24 wam

To see the artists pain[1] is a joy. The zeal with which[2] they work to have the exact tints[3] show up on the pad is fun[4] to watch. As they glide the[5] new brush quickly across the pad,[6] the radiant hues take form[7] and bring smiles to our faces.[8]

26 wam

When you work with people[1] every day, you get to know what[2] it is that they like best. You also[3] find out quickly what does make[4] them frown. A bit of extra[5] kind effort in a dozen small ways[6] will make your office a pleasant[7] place in which to do your duties.[8]

5-Letter Words

1 abide affix alarm bakes blade blend cakes charm civic dealt
2 desks dough eight ended equal fancy fifth flags gleam grant
3 guess happy heirs helps issue items ivory labor lapse lathe
4 magic maple mayor occur ought owned parks photo plane range
5 rocks royal sense shade shape taken thank title visit vital
6 voted waist wants whale yacht yield youth acute blank chest

Space Bar Drills

1 a b c d e f g h i j k l m n o p q r s t u v w x y z a b c d
2 aa bb cc dd ee ff gg hh ii jj kk ll mm nn oo pp qq rr ss tt
3 aaa bbb ccc ddd eee fff ggg hhh iii jjj kkk lll mmm nnn ooo
4 1 2 3 4 5 6 7 8 9 0 1 2 3 4 5 6 7 8 9 0 1 2 3 4 5 6 7 8 9 0
5 11 22 33 44 55 66 77 88 99 00 11 22 33 44 55 66 77 88 99 00
6 111 222 333 444 555 666 777 888 999 000 111 222 333 444 555

Tabulator Key Drills
Set tab every 8 spaces.

1 aid   air   and   ant   apt   bid   big   bit
2 bow   bud   bus   but   cod   cow   cut   did
3 dig   dog   due   dug   dye   end   eye   fir
4 fit   fix   foe   for   fur   jam   key   lay
5 man   map   may   oak   own   pay   rid   rob
6 rod   row   rub   she   sit   six   sod   the

Capitalization Drills

1 A Alex B Barb C Carl D Dawn E Earl F Faye G Glen H Hope Hal
2 I Inez J Jeff K Kate L Lory M Mike N Nell O Opel P Phil Pam
3 R Rona S Suzy T Troy A Alan B Beth C Chad D Drew E Eric Eva
4 A Alvin B Betty C Carol D David E Edwin F Frank G Garth Gus
5 H Helen J Joann K Kevin L Lloyd M Mavis N Nancy O Olive Ora
6 P Patsy R Randy S Sarah T Twila V Viola R Ronny S Steve Sam

Acceleration Sentences

1 She is busy with the work but is to go to town for the pen.
2 Jan got the forms for the firm and may also work with them.
3 He may wish to pay them if and when they go to work for us.
4 Both the men may go to town if he pays them for their work.
5 The name of the firm they own is to the right of the forms.
6 The coal firm also pays them when they load down rock jams.

Number Drills

1 101 191 181 171 161 151 141 131 121 202 292 282 272 262 252
2 242 232 212 303 393 383 373 363 353 343 323 313 404 494 484
3 474 464 454 434 424 414 505 595 585 575 565 545 535 525 515
4 606 696 686 676 656 646 636 626 616 707 797 787 767 757 747
5 737 727 717 808 898 878 868 858 848 838 828 818 909 989 979
6 969 959 949 939 929 919 090 080 070 060 050 040 030 020 010

Symbol Drills

1 a!a s@s d#d f$f f%f j&j k*k l(l ;); ;'; ;"; ;-; ;-; ;=; ;+;
2 aq!a sw@s de#d fr$f ft%f ju&j ki*k lo(l ;p); ;p-; ;p-; ;=+;
3 a!!a s@@s d##d f$$f f%%f j&&j k**k l((l ;)); ;--; ;--; ;++;
4 $56 $47 $38 $29 $10 56# 47# 38# 29# 10# 1/2 1/3 1/4 1/5 1/6
5 56% 47% 38% 29% 100% 1 & 2 & 3 & 4 & 5 & 6 & 7 & 8 & 9 & 10
6 (1)* (2)* (3)* (4)* (5)* 1-2 3-4 5-6 7-8 9-10 1 + 2 + 3 = 6

Timing 9

1   Whenever you have an opportunity to look for your very   12   4

2 first job, you will most likely participate in an interview   24   8

3 before securing the position. Although all interviews vary   36   12

4 significantly, almost all employers try to identify certain   48   16

5 aspects of your background and personality.   57   19

6   Communications skills are considered to be critical in   69   23

7 most interviews. Many job applicants will not perform well   81   27

8 while communicating because they do not know how to express   93   31

9 themselves when asking and answering questions, because the   105   35

10 vocabulary they use during the interviewing session doesn't   117   39

11 reveal a command of the English language, and because their   129   43

12 listening skills are not developed. Remember, there cannot   141   47

13 be any communication without listening.   149   50

14   Employers often may express an interest in a potential   161   54

15 employee's maturity level. This is especially important if   173   58

16 you're applying for a position in which you will be working   185   62

17 closely with other people. It is also important if you are   197   66

18 applying for a position in which you'll be required to make   209   70

19 critical decisions that involve using good judgment. Every   221   74

20 employer wants to hire the best person possible for the job   233   78

21 opening and may devote considerable time and effort to find   245   82

22 this very special person.   250   84

1' | 1 | 2 | 3 | 4 | 5 | 6 | 7 | 8 | 9 | 10 | 11 | 12
3' | 1 | | 2 | | 3 | | 4

Transposition Errors
(we for ew)

1. few hew new anew blew crew drew grew renews reviews viewing
2. owe wed weak weed week weld went west weary wedding western
3. Few in the weary crew knew that the weed grew in wet grass.
4. A crew grew weak and weary viewing wet weather in the west.

Transposition Errors
(er for re)

1. real rent reason regard regress relate relish remain remedy
2. ever leer alter fever lever lover sheet steer desert sorter
3. A store merchant had reasons for renting the camera to her.
4. He regretfully returned the sheer dress to the store clerk.

Transposition Errors
(rt for tr)

1. try trot true trade tribe trust truth travel truant trouble
2. art cart dart mart part tart alert heart shirt start cohert
3. The tattered tramps toiled to tow the trailer to the truck.
4. The new report revealed that the river had started to rise.

Transposition Errors
(po for op)

1. drop flop hoop hope loop opal open rope opera optic operate
2. poem poet pork port pose post porous porter portion posture
3. Those poems the poor poet composed were popular with Polly.
4. A job of the sponsor is to appoint the proper, polite poet.

Transposition Errors
(u for i; i for u)

1. fire hire inch milk mine pile size light limit waist finish
2. blue glue hulk much plug rust true lunch plump plush unhook
3. Jim Hunter had a delicious dinner with Muriel Mire at noon.
4. Hugh and Ivy Lute will visit their cousin in Biloxi in May.

Transposition Errors
(o for i; i for o)

1. light might quick nights simple identify quantity imaginary
2. hold home move once only crows occurs oppose people follows
3. A diary is a precise daily record of your personal actions.
4. A highlight at the spring fashion fair is an Oriental suit.

Transposition Errors
(a for s; s for a)

1. his lose loss lost miss mist pose rose snip snow stop knows
2. all ate way bake cake fake lake make rank take wait trained
3. Adam ate all the cake Barbara baked, but James had no cake.
4. Ms. Sarah Sands must stop at the Custer Museum some Sunday.

Transposition Errors
(e for d; d for e)

1. did lid duds duly duty card lard doubt drool ballad discard
2. elk east easy eves ebony empty emblem empire enchant energy
3. A dedicated editor decided to edit an address on education.
4. Ed Dodds read the report that Ted Edward prepared on weeds.

Transposition Errors
(m for n; n for m)

1. not now news note plan known night noble noise notch nickel
2. mad maid mail main male malt meal more maize magnet magnify
3. Ned nominated his nephew to navigate a nice, new steamship.
4. My magnificent machine managed to mangle the massive metal.

Transposition Errors
(l for o; o for l)

1. oak out coke cope home only open took cooked copper objects
2. lap let lip nil dell lace land lard lash large rifle ladder
3. I opened the cupboard doors and saw oranges and other food.
4. A large lumberjack loaded the last of the long, light logs.

Timing 8

1   Productivity measurement techniques are often employed   12 4

2 in word processing installations today in order to evaluate   24 8

3 the amount of output that is produced. This technique will   36 12

4 allow management to compare active work loads with inactive   48 16

5 work loads that will improve scheduling and work dispersal.   60 20

6   Productivity measurement also is able to aid a company   72 24

7 by recording, calculating, and tracking employee production   84 28

8 over a period of time. Supervisors are then able to create   96 32

9 performance standards designed just for their organization.   108 36

10 This method of measurement can be used to assist management   120 40

11 in making reliable decisions regarding salary increases and   132 44

12 promotion of word processing personnel.   140 47

13   A measure of production might also assist those people   152 51

14 who are more able in a variety of other ways. For example,   164 55

15 when compared to their peers, their abilities and successes   176 59

16 will be accented. Using this particular technique, all the   188 63

17 employees are evaluated on a parallel basis. Very talented   200 67

18 workers, therefore, are rewarded. Lastly, this measurement   212 71

19 technique can assist in removing subjectivity that is often   224 75

20 predominant in company measurement systems that are used in   236 79

21 employee evaluations.   240 80

1'	1	2	3	4	5	6	7	8	9	10	11	12
3'		1			2			3			4	

Timings

Scales are provided for 1- and 3-minute timings. Speed markers are provided for 5-minute timings.

	1′	3′

Timing 1

1   Raising dogs can be a combination of both fun and hard   12   4

2 work. Before you even start, you have to decide just which   24   8

3 breed can best adapt to your life-style. If you need a dog   36   12

4 to protect your house, a dachshund will not give you enough   48   16

5 protection. If you are in your own apartment, a collie may   60   20

6 be too large. When you have chosen the dog for you, expect   72   24

7 to have to train it. This can be done quickly with a zesty   84   28

8 puppy that is willing to learn.   90   30

1′ | 1 | 2 | 3 | 4 | 5 | 6 | 7 | 8 | 9 | 10 | 11 | 12
3′ | 1 | 2 | 3 | 4

	1′	3′

Timing 2

1   For students who can speak a foreign language, there's   12   4

2 an amazing job market today. Numbers of major companies in   24   8

3 other countries have been buying control of or investing in   36   12

4 American businesses. Their demand for workers with foreign   48   16

5 language skills can be seen in the increased number of help   60   20

6 wanted ads for experts with language skills.   69   23

7   The fact that so many Americans cannot speak, read, or   81   27

8 write another language is very tragic because the countries   93   31

9 of the world today are closely linked. International trade   105   35

10 is vital to business and government today, and young people   117   39

11 cannot afford to be unequipped to meet the challenge of the   129   43

12 future.   130   44

1′ | 1 | 2 | 3 | 4 | 5 | 6 | 7 | 8 | 9 | 10 | 11 | 12
3′ | 1 | 2 | 3 | 4

Timing 7

1   One of the many unique elements of a democracy is that   12   4

2   everyone of legal age has the right to vote. Voting should   24   8

3   be taken very seriously because it is a responsibility. It   36   12

4   is apparant that a government will not be representative if   48   16

5   people do not take an active part in choosing the people to   60   20

6   represent them. It is easy to criticize our leaders, but a   72   24

7   part of the blame rests with those citizens who do not care   84   28

8   enough about our country to vote.   91   30

9   Voting is done at many levels of government. Federal,   103   34

10   state, county, and city elections must be planned for every   115   38

11   year to choose officials whose terms have ended. Primaries   127   42

12   are held to narrow the number of persons running. The year   139   46

13   in which a president is chosen creates a lot of excitement,   151   50

14   but the citizens should be interested in and vote for their   163   54

15   choice at each election.   168   56

16   A good voter should pay careful attention to the major   180   60

17   issues and the candidates. Newspapers, public debates, and   192   64

18   interviews are good sources of information. Choose the one   204   68

19   who shares your views and is qualified to do the job.   215   72

1'	1	2	3	4	5	6	7	8	9	10	11	12
3'		1			2			3			4	

Timing 3

1   Businesses and individuals can write letters to people   12   4

2 in Washington. There are several persons to whom you might   24   8

3 send such a letter. You could write to the President, to a   36   12

4 senator, or to a representative. Each person who is chosen   48   16

5 to go to Washington takes along a staff who can answer most   60   20

6 of the mail their constituents send. Using the mail is one   72   24

7 way that legislators continually keep in touch with what is   84   28

8 going on in their individual congressional districts.   95   32

9   People send inquiries on many subjects. They may want   107   36

10 to express a positive feeling, or they may want to complain   119   40

11 about taxes, pollution, or foreign policy. Some letters do   131   44

12 influence how lawmakers make their decisions.   140   47

```
1'| 1 | 2 | 3 | 4 | 5 | 6 | 7 | 8 | 9 | 10 | 11 | 12
3'|     1     |     2     |     3     |     4
```

Timing 4

1   Autumn in the "northlands" is very exciting. You jump   12   4

2 up in the early morning; walk out under a clear, azure blue   24   8

3 sky; and feel the strong chill in the air. The leaves have   36   12

4 lost their brilliant green. It appears that they have been   48   16

5 tinted by someone passing by. The truth is that during the   60   20

6 night hours a frost has painted the green to hues of brown,   72   24

7 yellow, orange, and scarlet. It is a breathtaking panorama   84   28

8 in technicolor. The leaves seem not to move in the quietly   96   32

9 persistent breeze. Then, suddenly, a brisk puff lifts them   108   36

10 from the limbs and carries them gently like feathers to the   120   40

11 ground below. You watch as legions of leaves jump free and   132   44

12 float to the earth, covering it like a quilted blanket that   144   48

13 looks much like moss. When you walk on top of the blanket,   156   52

14 it cushions each step you take as though you are walking on   168   56

15 top of air.   170   57

```
1'| 1 | 2 | 3 | 4 | 5 | 6 | 7 | 8 | 9 | 10 | 11 | 12
3'|     1     |     2     |     3     |     4
```

Timing 5

1   Have you ever felt run down, tired, and fatigued? The   12   4
2 symptoms listed above are common to many of us today. They   24   8
3 affect our job performance, they limit the fun we have with   36   12
4 our family and friends, and they might even affect our good   48   16
5 health. Here are just some of the ways that we can quickly   60   20
6 minimize the problems and become more active persons in all   72   24
7 the things that we do daily.   78   26
8   It is essential that we get plenty of sleep so that we   90   30
9 are rested when we get up each morning. We must eat a good   102   34
10 breakfast so that we can build up energies for the day that   114   38
11 follows. Physical exercise is a necessity, and it might be   126   42
12 the one most important ingredient in building up our energy   138   46
13 reserves. We must participate in vigorous exercise so that   150   50
14 we make our hearts beat faster and cause our breathing rate   162   54
15 to appreciably increase. These are things that can help us   174   58
16 to increase our energy and to make us healthier people.   185   62

```
1'| 1 | 2 | 3 | 4 | 5 | 6 | 7 | 8 | 9 | 10 | 11 | 12
3'|     1     |     2     |     3     |     4
```

Timing 6

1   Many people have often wondered what might possibly be   12   4
2 the greatest structure on earth. The tallest buildings and   24   8
3 the longest bridges and the mightiest dams might be closely   36   12
4 examined in an attempt to find the answer to this difficult   48   16
5 question. In the minds of many people, perhaps, one of the   60   20
6 greatest structures ever built was the Great Wall of China.   72   24
7 It's well established that its features are so overwhelming   84   28
8 that astronauts can view the Wall from their spaceships.   96   32
9   The structure was built primarily by mixing just earth   107   36
10 and bricks. It is wide enough at the top to permit several   119   40
11 people to walk abreast on it. It winds for miles through a   131   44
12 large section of the country, over mountains and across the   143   48
13 valleys. It was constructed to keep out unwelcomed tribes.   155   52
14 It is believed that building the Wall required the labor of   168   56
15 many thousands of persons for dozens of decades. The first   179   60
16 sections of the Great Wall were built in the Age of Warring   191   64
17 States (403-221 BC).   195   68

```
1'| 1 | 2 | 3 | 4 | 5 | 6 | 7 | 8 | 9 | 10 | 11 | 12
3'|     1     |     2     |     3     |     4
```